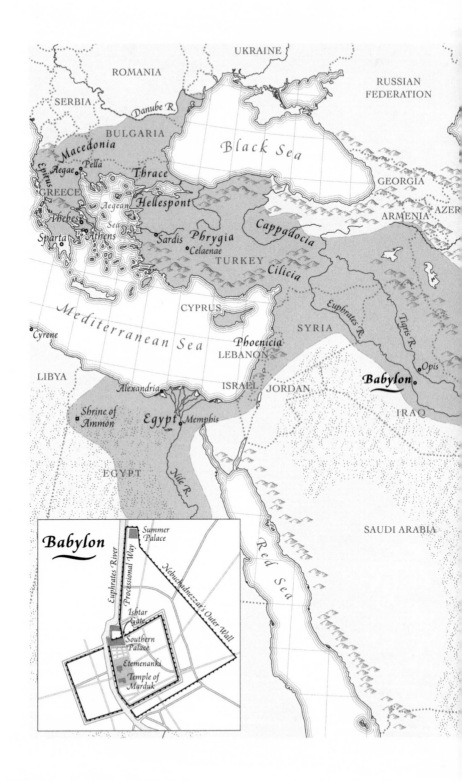

KAZAKHSTAN

KYRGYZSTAN

Caspian
Sea

UZBEKISTAN

CHINA

TAJIKISTAN

Sogdiana

TURKMENISTAN

Zariaspa○ Bactria

Hindu Kush

AFGHANISTAN

Indus R.

India

Hyphasis R.

IRAN

Indus R.

○Persepolis

PAKISTAN

INDIA

Gedrosia

Persian Gulf

QATAR

U.A.E.

Arabian Sea

OMAN

0 km   500 km

0 miles   500 miles

YEMEN

Alexander's Empire

at the time of his death, 323 B.C.

····· *International boundaries, 2011*

Ghost on the Throne

Eumenes the Greek with Alexander's widow and son

Ghost on the Throne

The Death of Alexander the Great
and the War for Crown and Empire

JAMES ROMM

ALFRED A. KNOPF
New York 2011

THIS IS A BORZOI BOOK
PUBLISHED BY ALFRED A. KNOPF

Published in the United States by Alfred A. Knopf,
a division of Random House, Inc., New York, and in Canada
by Random House of Canada Limited, Toronto.
www.aaknopf.com
Knopf, Borzoi Books, and the colophon
are registered trademarks of Random House, Inc.

Library of Congress Cataloging-in-Publication Data
Romm, James S.
Ghost on the throne: the death of Alexander the Great and
the war for crown and empire / by James Romm.
p. cm.
Includes bibliographical references and index.
ISBN 978-0-307-27164-8
1. Greece—History—Macedonian Hegemony, 323–281 B.C.
2. Macedonia—History—Diadochi, 323–276 B.C.
3. Alexander, the Great, 356–323 B.C.—Death and burial. I. Title.
DF235.4R66 2011
938'.08—dc22
2011008657

Front-of-jacket photograph by Tanya Marcuse | Back-of-jacket image:
Tetradrachm of Kingdom of Egypt with head of deified Alexander the Great,
struck under Ptolemy I, silver, 318–315/4 B.C. Museum of Fine Arts,
Boston. Henry Lillie Pierce Fund. 04.1181
Jacket design by Jason Booher

Manufactured in the United States of America
First Edition

For my mom and stepfather,
Sydney and Victor Reed

The death of Demosthenes on Calauria and of Hyperides near Cleonae made the Athenians feel almost a passion and a longing for the days of Alexander and Philip. Just so, when Antigonus had died, and those who followed in his place had begun to inflict outrages and pains on the people, a farmer was seen digging up the ground in Phrygia. Someone asked him what he was doing. With a groan, he replied: "I am looking for Antigonus."

—Plutarch *Phocion* 29.1

Contents

Illustrations

Preface

The Macedonian Empire was one of the world's largest but, without doubt, its most ephemeral. It attained its greatest extent in 325 B.C. with Alexander the Great's invasion of the Indus valley (today eastern Pakistan), at the end of a ten-year campaign of conquest in Europe, Asia, and North Africa. But it began to collapse in 323 following Alexander's sudden and unforeseen death. It existed in a full and relatively stable form for only two years.

The story of Alexander's conquests is known to many readers, but the dramatic and consequential sequel to that story is much less well-known. It is a tale of loss that begins with the greatest loss of all, the death of the king who gave the empire its center. "He died just when men most longed for him," writes Arrian, one of the ancient historians who dealt with this era, implying both that Alexander's talents were needed to keep the empire together and that the king had become an object of adoration, even worship, in the last years of his life. The era that followed came to be defined by the absence of one towering individual, just as the previous era had been defined by his presence. It was as though the sun had disappeared from the solar system; planets and moons began spinning crazily in new directions, often crashing into each other with terrifying force.

The brightest celestial bodies in this new, sunless cosmos were Alexander's top military officers, who were also in some cases his closest friends. Modern historians often refer to them as "the Successors" (or "Diadochs," a Greek word meaning virtually the same thing). But that term is anachronistic for the first seven years after

Alexander's death, when none of these men tried to succeed the king; they vied for his power but not his throne. During the entire span I cover in this book, there were living Argeads (members of the Macedonian royal family) who alone had the right to occupy that throne. Hence I refer to those often termed Successors simply as Alexander's generals; they were contestants for military rather than royal supremacy. Many of them would eventually occupy thrones, but only after 308 B.C., when it became clear that the Argead era was well and truly over.

The conflicts of these generals took place across a huge swath of Alexander's empire, often with clashes occurring simultaneously on two or even three continents. I have used snapshot-like frames, starting in the third chapter, to organize disparate but interconnected events, each headed by a rubric to remind readers of the place, time, and principal characters involved. It should be noted that the dates I have used in the rubrics are contested and may differ by a year from those found elsewhere. Historians are divided over two rival schemes, the so-called high and low chronologies; the dates I have given here belong to the high chronology, endorsed most recently by Brian Bosworth in his masterful study *The Legacy of Alexander.* It is Bosworth's authority that has decided this matter for me, since I think both schemes have sound arguments and valid evidence behind them, as does a recently proposed hybrid that blends elements of the two.

The ancient record of this era is frustratingly incomplete, even though two talented Greek historians wrote studies of it, and one of them was a witness to its major events. Hieronymus of Cardia was a Greek soldier of fortune who found himself at the center of the post-Alexander power struggle. His firsthand account, sometimes known by the title *History of the Successors,* was probably one of the great historical narratives written in antiquity, but it became extinct in the Darwinian process whereby widely copied school texts survived the end of the ancient world while other works did not. Before its disappearance, however, it was mined for information by Arrian of Nicomedia, an intelligent Greek writer of the second century A.D., as he prepared his own detailed chronicle of the years between 323 and 319. This work too has been lost, but one reader, Photius, the patriarch of Constantinople, took notes on its contents in the ninth century A.D. Photius' sparse outline of Arrian, made for personal use and without regard for the needs of posterity, survives today under the title *Events After Alexander*, in essence a dim reflection, at two removes, of Hieronymus' account.

There is, however, one Greek narrative of the post-Alexander period that brings us closer to the lost primary sources, and it survives intact. In the first century B.C., Diodorus Siculus compiled a universal Greek history usually known as the *Library*. Diodorus, who was a middling good writer but no historian, gave artistic shape to the material he found but muddled its chronology, reduced its detail, and omitted events that did not fit his plan. His shortcomings are many, but in treating the struggle for control of Alexander's empire, in books 18 through 20 of the *Library*, he produced his best work, largely because he relied heavily on Hieronymus.

Around the same time as Diodorus, a Roman writer, Pompeius Trogus, compiled a general survey of the Macedonian empire titled *Philippic History*, but this work has utterly perished. Like Arrian's *Events After Alexander*, it is known through a thin and reductive summary, compiled probably in the third century A.D. by another Roman, Justin.

The most colorful but least straightforward accounts of this period come from the *Lives* of Plutarch, the great Greek essayist and biographer of the late first and early second centuries A.D. Plutarch too mined the historical treatise of Hieronymus, along with other primary texts, but did so mostly in search of insights into character rather than a record of events; his interests were ethical more than historical. Nonetheless, I have cited him frequently in this book, along with other unconventional sources: Polyaenus, compiler of military stratagems; Athenaeus, collector of gossip and anecdotes; and the anonymous author of *The Lives of the Ten Orators*. These writers give insights, however unverifiable, into the personalities that dominate this age, and I have used them to convey those personalities, for I believe, as Plutarch did, that historical action cannot be understood outside the context of character.

But judgment of character is a subjective affair. One has only to read the modern biographies of the players in the power struggle—in English alone there are recent lives of Lysimachus, Ptolemy, Eumenes, Phocion, Olympias, Seleucus, and Antigonus—to see how many questions of intention and motivation are open to dispute. It is a *Rashomon*-like experience, a witnessing of one set of events through many pairs of eyes. The perspective varies not only with changes of historical focus but with changes of author, for some interpreters are inclined to see the worst impulses in the figures they deal with, others, the best.

One figure in this group has proved especially controversial. Surviving accounts of the Greek general Eumenes are strongly positive, but they are also clearly influenced by the favoritism of Hieronymus, who was Eumenes' friend and countryman, perhaps even his kinsman. Eumenes is shown not just as a brilliant tactician, full of tricks, inventions, and ruses, but as a man with a noble purpose—the protection of the Macedonian royal family, in particular Alexander's imperiled young son. Modern historians have rejected this gallant portrait and painted Eumenes as a mere opportunist. I have in what follows taken the view of the ancient sources more seriously. I believe that Eumenes *was* the last defender of the Argeads, if only because they were his own best hope for political survival.

Where ancient authors are in agreement about the events described in the narrative, or where there is no reason to doubt the testimony of Diodorus (the fullest source), I have not troubled to explain in the Notes how each historical fact has been recovered. Those who want to carefully trace the evidence can best consult Waldemar Heckel's *Who's Who in the Age of Alexander the Great,* a book that combines a biographical scheme of organization with a clear and comprehensive system of citation. I do, however, provide references in the Notes for information derived from more obscure sources and for statements about the private lives and inner thoughts of historical figures. Such statements cannot be vouched for as true to the same degree as public events, so I have tried to assure readers that they were not simply made up, or at least not by me.

The names of people and places mentioned in this book are spelled in a Latinate form and hence will often appear differently in texts that transliterate directly from Greek. Craterus here is elsewhere Krateros, Aegae is elsewhere Aigai. Where there is dispute over the form or spelling of a name, I have followed Heckel in *Who's Who,* for the convenience of those using that invaluable book as a reference. In cases where a person is known by more than one name, I have used the more distinctive one, to minimize confusion; Adea, who became Eurydice after her marriage, remains Adea here since there is another Eurydice in the story. In the case of Alexander's half brother Arrhidaeus, who as king became Philip, it was impossible to avoid overlap, and I have simply called him Arrhidaeus before his accession, Philip afterward.

The bibliography is divided into segments based on the primary focus of the works listed, and these foci have been roughly organized so as to follow the sequence of the narrative. It is my hope that this system will partly take the place of the annotations that would be found in a more scholarly treatment. Readers can see at a glance the secondary works on which I have most relied, without wading through a mass of notes. The subdivisions will be a help to those following up on specific interests, but an inconvenience to those looking for complete citations of works referred to in the notes; such readers might have to look in two or three sections in order to find a single item. I hope, however, that the rubrics of these sections will make the task easier.

Finally, I have taken the unusual step of providing Web addresses in the bibliography for translations of the ancient sources, rather than citing the more scholarly texts I have used myself. Many of these texts are hard to find outside university libraries, and a crucial one, Arrian's *Events After Alexander,* cannot be found in any book at all (except in Greek). Though the online translations are not all they could be, they are taken from reputable published books in the public domain. All translations from Greek and Latin that appear in this book are my own.

Note on Pronunciations

Readers should feel no fear in pronouncing proper names, since there are few ways they can go far wrong. The evolution of these names from Greek to Latin to English means that there is often more than one valid way to sound them out. The vowel combination *ae* is pronounced by some to rhyme with "buy," by others "bay," and still others "bee"; the first is more authentic but all are possible. Many classicists are eclectic, choosing whichever sounds right in a particular word. My own preference is for the "eye" sound in both syllables of *Aegae,* the ancient capital of the Macedonian state.

Some consonants also offer more than one possibility. *C* can be sounded soft, like *s,* or hard, like *k.* Most English speakers follow our own language and allow it to be soft before the vowel *i* (as in *Phocion*) and before some *e*'s. Likewise the letter *g* becomes soft (like *j*) before *e* but is hard elsewhere; this will help distinguish *Antigonus,* hard, from *Antigenes,* soft, two names that are otherwise maddeningly similar.

The syllable *-es* at the end of a name is always sounded "eez," so that *Eumenes* and *Demades* have three syllables (with the first one stressed). A final *e* is either "ee" or "ay" but is always voiced as a syllable. The Greek language had no silent vowels, and no silent consonants either: in *Ptolemy* the initial *P* is usually dropped by English speakers, but those courageous enough to sound it will be saying the name as the Greeks did.

The issue of syllabic stress sometimes causes stress for readers. A good rule to follow is that in four-syllable names—*Antigonus, Leosthenes, Hyperides*—the emphasis usually falls on the second syllable. *Alexander* of course breaks this rule, as he broke all the others.

Acknowledgments

My colleagues in the field of ancient history have generously shared their expertise in replies to my insistent questions. I would especially thank Edward Anson, Liz Baynham, Gene Borza, Brian Bosworth, Elizabeth Carney, Waldemar Heckel, Judson Herrman, and Ian Worthington. Others were equally generous in sharing photographs or artwork, especially Frank Holt, Andrew Stewart, and Stella Miller-Collett. All of these scholars made a relative newcomer like me feel welcome in their bailiwick, as did Robin Waterfield, who kindly steered me toward new or obscure publications in the field we were simultaneously working on. Robin also shared with me the typescript of his forthcoming book, though it did not arrive in time for me to consult it as I finished my own.

I am grateful for the generous support I received at various stages of this project from the Guggenheim Foundation and the National Endowment for the Humanities. My home institution, Bard College, allowed me to reserve a portion of my time for writing and research even in the midst of a hectic teaching schedule. This book could never have gotten started without the help of two good friends: Daniel Mendelsohn, who brainstormed with me over many an Indian dinner, and Dan Akst, who did likewise over Japanese lunches. Readers who encouraged it along the way also deserve my thanks: Jim Ottaway above all, whose sharp pencil improved every page, but also Ken Marcuse, Jake Nabel, Eve Romm, and Alex Zane. Paul Cartledge, a beacon of inspiration to me and many others, read the manuscript and saved it from errors, though I take responsibility for any that remain.

I am fortunate to have worked on this book with an editor, Vicky Wilson, who made me feel it deserved our best efforts. I have learned from Vicky, with whom I share a love of cycling, that good historical narrative should be like a good road bike: streamlined and stripped of all excess weight. I would also like to thank Vicky's gracious assistant, Carmen Johnson, for help organizing the manuscript and the illustrations. Other people to whom I owe thanks are: my agent, Glen Hartley; my cartographer, Kelly Sandefer of Beehive Mapping; Ingrid Magillis, who secured rights and permissions for the illustrations; copyeditor Ingrid Sterner; Laurie Nash, Evelyn Krueger, and Jane Hryshko of Bard College; Sara Roemer and Jessica Shapiro of the Institute for the Study of the Ancient World; and, for technological help and advice, my brother-in-law Victor Liu.

My wife, Tanya Marcuse, has contributed more than a mere acknowledgment could express. Sharing a life with this wise and loving woman has helped me see what is important in the study of the ancient world, and in all things.

The book is dedicated to my mother and stepfather, Sydney and Victor Reed, in hopes it will bring them even a fraction of the joy they bring to each other.

Ghost on the Throne

The Opening of the Tombs

Vergina (Northern Greece)

1977–79

"Be as calm as possible," Manolis Andronikos told his assistants as he slowly widened a hole leading down into darkness. It was the afternoon of November 8, 1977, outside the northern Greek village of Vergina, and he was about to make the most spectacular discovery of modern Aegean archaeology.

Andronikos had been digging for twenty-five years in the Great Tumulus at Vergina, a mound of sand, earth, and gravel more than forty feet high, and had moved thousands of tons of it to find what was beneath. He was convinced he was on the site of Aegae, the ancient capital of the Macedonian nation and the burial place of its kings. Now, after nearly giving up on another fruitless season, he had uncovered the walls of two structures beneath an unexplored portion of the mound. One had turned out to be a looted chamber tomb, its floor strewn with human remains scattered by ancient robbers, its walls adorned with magnificent paintings. Next to that first tomb, below twenty-three feet of earth, Andronikos had uncovered the top of a second building and was preparing to climb down a ladder into the chamber below.

As he disappeared through the opening, he made a stunning announcement to his assistants. "Everything is intact!" he exclaimed as his flashlight caught the glint of silver and the dull green of oxidized bronze. Dozens of precious objects, any one of which would have repaid a year's excavation, revealed themselves in the beam of Andronikos' light. Armor and weaponry, the indispensable gear of the Macedonian warrior, stood propped against walls and in corners; finely wrought drinking vessels lay in heaps. At the center of the room Andronikos found a hollow marble chamber covered with a lid; when this was later opened, the excavators were astonished to discover an exquisite gold box containing the cremated bones of an adult male. A similar gold box, this one holding the remains of a woman in her twenties, was found in a small antechamber adjoining the main room.

On the floor of the tomb, amid the decayed remains of the wooden couch they had once adorned, Andronikos found five delicately carved ivory heads (nine more were eventually recovered). These miniature masterworks portrayed a gallery of heroic male types, two of them bearded and grave, the others smooth cheeked, limpid, and youthful (a few have been seen as women). The sense of character emanating from the portraits was startling. Given that pottery finds dated the tomb between 350 and 315 B.C., Andronikos quickly identified one bearded portrait as Philip II, father of Alexander the Great, assassinated in 336. Another head, that of a slender, beardless youth with his neck bent at an odd angle, seemed an image of Alexander himself. Andronikos took these portraits to his quarters and spent a sleepless night of fervid excitement gazing into what seemed to be the faces of the two greatest Macedonian kings and their comrades.

Across the facade of the tomb (now known as Tomb 2), Andronikos' team found a remarkable painted frieze. When cleaned and stabilized, it revealed a hunting tableau, with ten powerful figures stabbing and spearing various kinds of game. Once again the faces seemed expressive and lifelike, perhaps individual portraits; Andronikos again thought he recognized Philip and Alexander, portrayed as a mature man of forty and a youth of twelve or thirteen. The other figures in the hunt scene, beardless youths slightly older than "Alexander," he identified as royal

Alexander's Companions
The ivory portraits recovered from Tomb 2 by Manolis Andronikos

pages, the sons of nobility who, as we know, grew up at Philip's court and later became Alexander's close friends.

The finds of 1977 posed enough riddles to last any scholar a lifetime, including the question—still unresolved after more than three decades—of the identity of the tomb's occupants. But Andronikos was not done exploring the Great Tumulus. Eighteen months later, digging elsewhere in the mound, he unearthed a third structure, Tomb 3, which he came to call the Prince's Tomb. Its contents too had remained intact, protected by the immense thickness of earth above. They were less sumptuous than those of the neighboring tomb but still, by any measure, spectacular. This tomb held the remains of a single occupant, housed in a large silver drinking vessel rather than a gold chest; analysis indicated a boy in his early teens. Given evidence that dated the tomb to the late fourth century, this could only be the son and successor of Alexander the Great, killed by his political enemies in 309 or 308 B.C.

It had become clear by this point that the Great Tumulus was, in effect, a time capsule of the tumultuous period following Alexander's death. Here was the boy-king whose lot it was to follow the most potent conqueror the world had known, thrust by his lineage into a maelstrom of dynastic turmoil. Here too were the portraits, in both paint and ivory, of the Companions of Alexander, the intimates who grew up with him, fought under him, and survived him to become his too-faithful followers,

The facade of Tomb 2, with the frieze of the royal hunt across the top

bloodying his empire again and again in their bids to control it. Here also, if one leading theory about the occupants of Tomb 2 is correct, were Alexander's half brother and niece, two royals who had been killed trying to lay sole claim to Alexander's throne. The bones of this couple seemed to bear witness to the troubled times in which they lived, for one expert judged they had undergone "dry" cremation, after the flesh upon them had already decayed. Had they been buried here, in this sumptuous tomb, only after first being left to rot elsewhere?

Those whose bones and images emerged from the Great Tumulus were Alexander's contemporaries, and their fame has largely been eclipsed by his. Yet their tales are among the most tempestuous and tragic in any of history's tomes. They were the ensemble cast in a great drama of downfall: they saw the rending of an empire, the collapse of a political order, and the death of a dynasty that had endured almost four centuries. Their faces can be seen today at Vergina, once Aegae, in the museum that houses Andronikos' finds. Their stories are told in the pages that follow.

Bodyguards and Companions

Babylon

MAY 31–JUNE 11, 323 B.C.

No one knew what was killing Alexander. Some thought he could not die; his conquests during his twelve-year reign had been more godlike than mortal. It was even whispered he was the son not of Philip, his predecessor on the throne of Macedonia, but of the Egyptian god Ammon. Now, as Alexander grew more sickly during the first week of June 323, it seemed that he *could* die, indeed, was dying. Those closest to Alexander, his seven Bodyguards, and the larger circle of intimates called his Companions watched his decline helplessly, and watched one another carefully. They were able commanders, leaders of the most successful military campaign ever fought, and were accustomed to managing crises. At this moment, to judge by later events, none knew what to do, what the others had in mind, or what would happen next.

Amid the gloom of the deathbed watch, their thoughts went back to the previous year and to an incident that had seemed unimportant at the time. Alexander's army was then on the march, returning from India (eastern Pakistan today), the farthest reach of its conquests. (Maps at the beginning and end of this book show all the major regions of Alexander's empire.) Accompanying the troops was an Eastern holy man named Calanus, an elderly sage who had become a kind of guru to some of the senior officers. But Calanus fell ill as the army reached Persis and, foreseeing a slow decline toward death, arranged to commit suicide by self-immolation. In a solemn ceremony he said farewell to each of his devotees, but when Alexander approached, he drew back, saying cryptically that he would embrace the king when he saw him in Babylon. Then he climbed atop a tall pyre before the entire Macedonian army, and all forty thousand watched as he burned to death, sitting calmly and still amid the flames.

Now they had come to the wealthy city of Babylon (in the south of modern Iraq), and Calanus' words had begun to make sense. Other recent incidents, too, suddenly took on ominous meaning. A few days before Alexander fell ill, an interloper never seen before dashed into the palace throne room, put on the diadem and royal robes—left by Alexander when he went to take exercise—and seated himself on the throne. Under interrogation he claimed to have followed the instructions of an Egyptian god called Serapis, or perhaps (according to a different account) merely to have acted on a whim. Alexander, however, suspected a

The ancient city of Babylon, digitally reconstructed, seen from the north (as Alexander would have seen it on his first approach)

plot and ordered the man's execution. Whatever its motives, the act seemed vaguely threatening, a portent of danger to the state.

The throne room in which the bizarre episode took place was famous for such portents. The great Babylonian king Nebuchadnezzar had built this room three centuries earlier as the grand central hall of his palace. It was here that Belshazzar, his descendant, held a vast banquet at which guests saw a disembodied finger write a mysterious sentence on the wall: *Mene mene tekel upharsin.* The message, decoded by a seer named Daniel (one of the Hebrew captives taken to Babylon from Jerusalem), was that Belshazzar had been weighed in the balance and found wanting; his empire would fall and be divided among the new powers contesting dominion in Asia, the Medes and the Persians. The prophecy came to pass that very night, according to the biblical version of the tale. Belshazzar was killed in a sudden invasion, and his throne was occupied by Persian kings—Cyrus the Great, Darius, Xerxes, and others—for more than two hundred years.

Now the Persians too had fallen, and the great throne room belonged to the new rulers of Asia, the Macedonians, and to their king, Alexander. And though the writing on the wall had long faded from view, this new omen, the stranger on the throne, seemed to hold a similarly troubling meaning. As all who witnessed the episode knew, there was no one in line to inherit that throne, no one to take command of an empire stretching from the shores of the Adriatic to the Indus River valley, three thousand miles in breadth. And there was no one fit to command the army that had won that empire, a terrifyingly destructive fighting force, other than Alexander himself. In the past two years even he had barely kept it controlled. What chaos might it unleash on a still-nascent world order without his leadership?

A legend found in several ancient sources tells that Alexander, on his deathbed, was asked to whom his power should pass. "To the strongest," he replied. In some versions the conqueror added that he foresaw an immense contest over his tomb, referring with grim double meaning to the Greek custom of holding athletic competitions at the burial of a hero. Perhaps these words are apocryphal, but they nonetheless hold an essential truth. Lacking an obvious heir or a plan for succession, Alexander would, with his death, ignite a struggle for power such as the world had never seen, with the world itself—dominion over Asia, Africa, and Europe—the prize of victory.

The funeral games of Alexander were indeed to become one of the most intense and complex contests in history. In the years following the king's death, half a dozen generals would box with one another in wars fought across three continents, while half a dozen members of the royal family would wrestle for the throne. Generals and monarchs would team up for mutual expediency, then switch sides and combat each other when *that* was more advantageous. The contest would become a generational relay race, with military leaders handing off their standards to sons, queens passing scepters to daughters. It would be nearly a decade before winners began to emerge, and these would be a wholly different set of contestants from those who stood at the starting line, in Babylon, at the side of the dying king.

Alexander's return to Babylon in the spring of 323, when Chaldaean priests warned him he would incur doom by entering the city, posed a sober contrast to his first visit there seven and a half years before. Alexander was then twenty-five, with superhuman energy and ambition. A few weeks before, he had defeated the Persians in the largest battle the world had yet seen, personally leading a cavalry charge aimed right at Darius, the Great King of Persis, and putting him to flight. Alexander, still wary of his new Asian subjects, approached Babylon with his army deployed for battle, but the Babylonians welcomed him as a liberator from Persian rule, not as a new conqueror. They thronged the road to welcome him, strewing flower petals in his path, singing hymns, and lighting silver incense burners all along the approach to the great Ishtar Gate. If one had to choose the Macedonian army's most triumphant day in the whole of its eleven-year march through Asia, the day in October 331 when it first entered Babylon would be a top contender.

A month of feasting and celebration gave Alexander's troops their first taste of the wonders of the East. The Macedonians had been a provincial people, shepherds and farmers for the most part; few had ever left their rocky land before Alexander brought them into Asia. They were astounded by the great palaces and towers that were Nebuchadnezzar's legacy; by the Hanging Gardens atop one palace's roof, watered by an elaborate system of buckets and pulleys; and by the massive triple walls ringing the city, adorned with reliefs of lions, bulls, and dragons. The commanders Alexander billeted in the great Southern Palace found themselves in a labyrinth of more than six hundred rooms, many facing onto vast, echoing courtyards. At the center of the maze was the great throne

Babylon's Ishtar Gate, rebuilt today in Berlin's Pergamon Museum

room of Nebuchadnezzar, its walls of glazed brick depicting palm trees and lions against a dark blue background. There they watched as Alexander first took his seat upon an Asian throne.

Alexander had done what he had set out to do. After becoming king of Macedonia at age twenty, he wasted no time picking up where his father, Philip, assassinated just as he prepared to lead an invasion of the Persian empire, had left off. Taking a force of forty-five thousand across the Hellespont (now known as the Dardanelles), Alexander fought the Persians three times over three years and won resounding victories each time. Amid these battles he made a six-month excursion into Egypt, where he was hailed as a liberator and claimed by the god Ammon as a son (according to some reports of his visit to the god's oracle in the North African desert). Perhaps he began to believe himself he had sprung from Ammon, for he had won power and wealth beyond mortal measures. His defeat of the Persians unleashed a cascade of gold and silver, tribute amassed for centuries and hoarded in the great palaces of Susa and Persepolis. His seeming invincibility attracted powerful allies, including many former Persian enemies, to his side.

Alexander might have stopped there, in Babylon, content with his already epochal achievements, but he was only halfway done. He led his army north and east, into Bactria and Sogdiana (what is now Afghanistan, Uzbekistan, and Tajikistan), pursuing the refugee king Darius and others who tried to claim the throne. He spent two years among the unruly nomads of these regions, suffering worse losses in ambushes and traps than in any of his open-field battles. Undaunted, in 327 he crossed the Hindu Kush into India (now eastern Pakistan), ascending the seven-thousand-foot passes in early spring, when the troops starved and horses floundered in chest-deep snow.

Another two years were spent in India, years that exhausted the stamina of his troops. Those who had savored the wonders of the East on their entry into Babylon had by now seen its terrors: zealous guerrilla fighters, duplicitous tribal leaders, intense desert heat, and, most fearsome of all, trained Indian war elephants, a devastating weapon they had never before encountered. Finally, at the easternmost of the Indus tributaries, the river Hyphasis (modern Beas), they reached their breaking point. Alexander ordered his troops to advance but was met, for the first time, with rebellion. His men wanted no more worlds to conquer and would not cross the river. Alexander grudgingly led them back toward the West. But, angered by the mutiny, he threw his troops into tough battles against entrenched Indian resisters, battles his men were barely willing to fight.

At one rebel town in India, Alexander spearheaded an assault himself, with catastrophic consequences. He scaled a siege ladder his men were reluctant to climb and, as if shaming them, stood atop the wall exposed to hostile fire. A brigade of infantry sprang up after him, but the ladder broke under their weight. Unfazed, Alexander leaped down off the walls and into the town, accompanied by only three comrades. In the ensuing melee, an Indian archer sent a three-foot-long arrow right through Alexander's armor and into his lung. His panic-stricken troops burst open the gates to the town and dragged his body out; an officer extracted the arrow, but fearsome spurts of blood and hissing air came with it, and the king passed out.

Panic seized the army as rumors spread that Alexander had been killed. When a letter from Alexander was circulated a short while later, the men denounced it as a forgery devised by the high command. Order began to break down, until Alexander recovered enough strength to show himself to his men. He was carried by ship down a nearby river and past the assembled army, feebly lifting an arm to show he was conscious. When his ship put in at the riverbank, he ordered attendants to bring his horse and prop him up on its back, causing a scene of mass ecstasy: as he dismounted, soldiers thronged him on all sides, throwing flowers and clutching at his hands, knees, and clothing.

Alexander's close call in India was a dress rehearsal for his death, and it did not go well. Alexander had trained a superb senior staff but had made no one his clear second; he had divided top assignments among many lieutenants, deliberately diffusing power. Without his centering presence, the rank and file had become despondent and mistrustful and had looked in vain for a clear-cut chain of command. Only the king's reappearance had prevented total collapse.

Alexander gradually recovered from his lung wound. In the summer of 325 he took his army out of India, sending some by land across the mountains and others by ship through what is now the Arabian Sea. He led his own contingent through the desert region called Gedrosia (today Baluchistan in southern Iran), exposing them to horrors of privation and heat as supply lines and support networks failed. A depleted and diminished column emerged from this grim wasteland and reentered the fertile lands at the center of the old Persian empire. Restored and reunited with their comrades, they followed Alexander back to the scene of their glorious celebration seven years earlier, the city of Nebuchadnezzar, the home of the Hanging Gardens, wealthy Babylon.

On the seventeenth of the Macedonian month Daisios, the first of June 323 B.C. by the modern calendar, the Macedonian troops at Babylon got their first sign that Alexander was ill. The king appeared outside Nebuchadnezzar's palace to lead that day's sacrifice to the gods, his duty as head of the Macedonian nation, but had to be carried on a bier. He had been drinking at a private party the night before with his senior staff, and after returning to his quarters, he had become feverish. By morning he was too ill to walk.

After this brief and disquieting appearance, Alexander withdrew into the palace and rested. In the evening his officers were summoned to his quarters to discuss a campaign against the Arabs that was scheduled to begin three days later. There was as yet no change in the plans for this campaign, no suggestion that Alexander's condition would be a hindrance.

The men who attended that meeting were Alexander's inner circle, above all, his seven *Somatophylakes,* or Bodyguards. Far more than a security detail, these were his closest friends, the sharers of his counsels, and, in battle, the holders of his top commands. Most were about his own age, and several had grown up with him. Not all were great generals or tacticians. They didn't have to be, since Alexander devised tactics for them. But all were distinguished by their rock-solid loyalty to Alexander and his

cause. They understood the king's goals and backed them unstint-
ingly; they supported him through every crisis, against all opposition. Alexander could trust them implicitly, even though they did
not always trust, or like, one another.

Ptolemy was there, a close comrade of Alexander's since boyhood, a man perhaps a few years older than the thirty-two-year-
old king. Ptolemy had been with the Asian campaign from the
start but for years had held no command post; his nature and
temperament were not obviously those of a warrior. Alexander
had made him a Bodyguard midway through the campaign based
purely on personal ties and thereafter began giving him combat
assignments as well. In India he assigned Ptolemy his first critical
missions, thrusting his old friend into ever-greater dangers. In one
Indian engagement, Ptolemy was struck by an arrow said to be
tipped with poison; legend later reported that Alexander himself
administered the antidote, after extracting juice from a plant he
had seen in a dream. Ptolemy was hardly the most skilled of
Alexander's officers, but perhaps the cleverest, as his subsequent
career would prove.

Perdiccas, by contrast, had been in the army's top ranks from
the start of the campaign and had by now accrued the most distinguished service record of those in Babylon. It was he who had
taken charge, probably on his own initiative, when Alexander's
lung wound was healing in India. Perdiccas was perhaps a few
years older than the king, one of the aristocratic youths who had
grown up at the palace as pages of Alexander's father, King Philip.
Indeed, his first act of prowess had come in his teens, when, as an
honorary attendant to Philip in his final public appearance, he
chased down and killed Philip's assassin. Perdiccas belonged to
one of the royal families that had once ruled independent kingdoms in the Macedonian highlands. These families had been
stripped of power as Philip's empire grew, but their offspring
retained a privileged place at Alexander's court so long as they
were loyal, and Perdiccas was certainly that.

Leonnatus was another of Philip's former pages, also sprung
from royal blood, and had helped Perdiccas dispatch the king's
escaping assassin. He had risen to top commands late in the Asian

campaign but in India had covered himself in glory at the siege where Alexander was shot. Leonnatus was one of the three men cut off with the king in the besieged town; he had incurred serious wounds while using his own body to shield the fallen Alexander, a signal display of heroism and devotion. Another soldier, Peucestas, had done likewise in that same action; Alexander had rewarded him with promotion to the Bodyguard, creating an unprecedented eighth slot.

Also present was Nearchus, a Greek, one of Alexander's oldest and closest friends, but not a member of the Bodyguard (Greeks were a kindred but foreign race in Macedonian eyes and not permitted into the charmed circle of seven). Alexander had summoned Nearchus from a rear-guard post and brought him to India, eventually assigning him to captain the huge fleet that sailed down the Indus and back to Persis. It was the hardest assignment any subordinate ever received. The voyage went awry from the start, and Nearchus' ships endured long stretches without food or water. When the fleet and the land army linked up once again, Alexander at first failed to recognize his wasted and weatherworn friend, then took his hand, shedding tears of relief.

There was another Greek at that meeting, Eumenes, thirty-seven years old with a boyish face and a slender build, who also had known Alexander from childhood but whose services to him had been of a different kind. Alexander's father had long before made Eumenes royal secretary, a new post created to handle the complex paperwork of a growing empire. According to one report, Philip had simply liked the look of the boy when he spotted him winning a *pancration,* a no-holds-barred wrestling match, and hired him on the spot. During the Asian campaign, other Companions smirked that Eumenes followed Alexander with pen and writing tablet rather than with sword and shield, and sometimes forcefully put him into what they saw as his place. In India, Eumenes received a painful slight when Hephaestion, Alexander's favorite, took away his designated quarters and reassigned them to a common flute player. Eumenes complained bitterly to Alexander, who at first took his scribe's part and scolded Hephaestion but later changed sides and railed at Eumenes for demanding

royal protection. No one knew quite where to rank a Greek foreigner, and a noncombatant, in a Macedonian hierarchy based on
military valor.

Ultimately, Alexander decided that Eumenes, too, might pos-
sess that valor, or might be allowed to earn it. In India Alexander
entrusted his scribe with a minor cavalry command, assigning
him to lead a troop of horsemen to two rebel towns and demand
their submission. As it turned out, the townspeople had fled
before Eumenes arrived, but the mission nonetheless allowed
Eumenes to lead men in hostile territory and demonstrated that
Macedonian cavalry, if ordered by Alexander, would accept a
Greek as their captain. Then, in the last year of his life, Alexander
made a much more dramatic move, appointing Eumenes commander of an elite cavalry unit formerly headed by lofty Perdiccas.
No Greek had held such a distinguished post in Alexander's army
before. Little Eumenes had risen high, indeed—and was destined
to rise still higher.

Most of the men in the room with Alexander had waded
through rivers of blood in the course of winning their commands.
The Indian campaign had been particularly harsh: Alexander had
slaughtered civilians, even prisoners of war, hoping that this distant province could be terrorized into subjection. His generals followed such orders because they believed a greater good justified
them. With the Persians subdued and tribes beyond the Caspian
Sea and the Hindu Kush cowed into nonaggression, Alexander
felt he was close to melding the whole known world into a single
state. Religious and cultural freedom, economic development,
and even (where possible) local autonomy would make the
empire's peoples willing sharers rather than grudging subjects.
Alexander himself, his image carefully crafted to project tolerance,
harmony, and progress, would be the banner under which the
nations would unite.

All that was needed to bring this brave new world into being
was the obliteration of those who threatened it, either by attack
from without or by rebellion from within. The generals who
helped conduct Alexander's massacres were not butchers but loyal
supporters of his driving vision. They had agreed to pursue his
multiethnic world-state, certain they would one day share in rule

over it. Indeed, Alexander had made clear how large a role they would have. In the royal pavilion he set up in Persis in his final year, a magnificent tent surrounded by thousands of elite troops in concentric rings, he stationed the Bodyguards on silver-footed couches directly around his own golden throne—the innermost orbit of the cosmos of which he formed the center.

Now these trusted generals were preparing to move against the Arabs, a people that had not directly threatened their empire. But after the army's return to Babylon, when many unconquered peoples sent embassies to Alexander offering submission, the Arabs sent none. Their silence was worrisome because of their geographic position, astride the waterways connecting the empire's Asian heartland to Africa and Europe. As foes, they could rob Alexander's cities of trade revenue or limit the range of his warships. Under Macedonian control, conversely, their coasts offered harbors and anchorages for the ships that would sail, in Alexander's plans, between the Mediterranean and the East.

The discussion that first night of Alexander's illness focused on strategy and logistics. The army was more than adequate for the job ahead. The infantry phalanx, a massive block of warriors wielding eighteen-foot-long spears called *sarissas,* would form the anchor of the expeditionary force. The elite Companion cavalry, the army's principal striking arm, would also be brought forward, and siege weaponry of all kinds—massive wheeled towers housing battering rams and drawbridges, catapults and artillery weapons newly designed by crack engineers—would be broken down into pieces and carried aboard ship. The fleet would also store provisions for the land army and materials for building the garrison towns that would dot the Persian Gulf coast, once the Arabs were subdued.

Alexander no doubt appointed the generals who would lead each unit. Perdiccas, as senior officer present, would have received command of the land army, since Alexander himself planned to travel with Nearchus' fleet. Eumenes would assume his crucial new position at the head of a troop of Companion cavalry. No one could be sure how well a Greek would fill this role, never mind a Greek with no real combat experience, but Alexander seemed determined to find out.

When the meeting concluded, Alexander was carried out of the palace, placed aboard a ship, and taken up the Euphrates River, probably to the little Summer Palace in Babylon's northern quadrant. Here there was what the Persians called a *paradeiza* (*paradeisos* to the Greeks, the root of "paradise"), a nature preserve and game park designed for the pleasure of Achaemenid kings, as well as cool breezes to temper the choking Mesopotamian heat. Alexander was seeking relief from the fever that had raged for a full day now, but also, in all likelihood, he wanted secrecy. After what had happened when he was near death in India, it was important that few people know how ill he was.

The senior staff who met with Alexander that first day convened again two days later, this time in the secluded quarters of the Summer Palace. The king's condition was somewhat improved. His fever had come and gone intermittently, and he had at times been able to eat and converse. The Arabian campaign, now only two days away, was going ahead as planned.

During these days the generals must have talked about what they would face should Alexander's condition worsen. They had reason to be anxious. The previous autumn a top officer, Hephaestion, then at the peak of health and strength, had succumbed in seven days to a fever much like Alexander's. Moreover, both men had fallen ill after a bout of drinking, which raised the question of poison. At some point the generals must have acknowledged, to one another or to themselves, the possibility that Alexander was the victim of an assassination plot.

There were many who would be glad to see Alexander dead. The conquered Persians bore him little love, though on the whole they seemed a passive lot, content with the share of rule—a rather large share—Alexander had allotted them. Alexander's Greek subjects, however, were feistier and less easily appeased. From their city-states in Europe they had mounted two rebellions already and were at that moment, as would soon be revealed, preparing to launch a third. Alexander had been taught by Greek tutors, including the philosopher Aristotle, and tried to show a commitment to Hellenic ideals, but his style was often that of an autocrat rather than a philosopher-king. Indeed, a Greek philosopher had stood against him when he proposed a plan that his courtiers should bow down to him in Persian style, and he had later found a pretext to have the man arrested or even (some sources say) executed. That man was Callisthenes, Alexander's court historian, who happened to have been a relative and protégé of Aristotle's. Was it possible that Aristotle, then living in Athens, had taken revenge by arranging the poisoning of his former student?

Then too there were the conservatives among the king's Macedonian subjects, those opposed to his strange visions of shared empire and cultural fusion. Many such reactionaries had been purged, though one remained in power: old man Antipater, at this point past seventy, who had loyally guarded the Macedonian home front on Alexander's behalf for twelve years, with help from his son Cassander, a man just Alexander's age. But the king had resolved to unseat Antipater, either by retirement or a more extreme method. Alexander sent orders for him to surrender his post and report to Babylon, but for unknown reasons the senior general stayed put in Macedonia, sending his son in his stead. Cassander, who was known to dislike Alexander and to scorn the newly Asianized ways of the court, had arrived in Babylon only just before Alexander fell ill. Might he and his father, either out of hatred for what Alexander had become or out of fears for their own safety, have conspired to murder their king?

Many Greeks and Macedonians answered yes to these questions, in particular the latter. Rumors circulating at the time of Alexander's death claimed that a lethal drink, collected by Aristotle from a spring that supposedly gave rise to the river Styx, had been brought to Babylon by Cassander at the behest of his father. The numbingly cold toxin, according to these rumors, had been transported inside a mule's hoof, since it was said to eat through any other vessel, even solid iron, with its corrosive power. Then it had been slipped into Alexander's cup by Cassander's brother Iolaus, who, all too conveniently, was at that time the king's wine pourer. The theory made sense from the standpoint of motive, means, and opportunity. It was so widely believed that Alexander's mother, as will be seen, had Iolaus' buried remains dug up and scattered as punishment for his presumed part in the plot.

How much credence should be given to these rumors is

unclear. Those who stood by Alexander in his final days would go on to control his image and to vie for his power; they manipulated the published records of his death (and indeed of his entire reign) to suit their own purposes. They were even capable of circulating false accounts to implicate rivals. (The stories in the so-called *Liber de Morte* or *Book About the Death,* a lurid narrative purporting to reveal the poisoning conspiracy, seem to have arisen in this way.) In the years following 323, the question of who killed Alexander, or whether he died of natural causes, would be spun one way and another for political advantage, making the truth very hard to recover.

One document has particularly bedeviled modern interpreters. The *Ephemerides,* or *Royal Journals,* is now lost but was drawn on by both Plutarch and Arrian in their accounts of Alexander's last days. The *Journals* depicted Alexander as gradually succumbing to a long fever, not at all the quick, violent demise of a poisoning victim, and makes no mention of a suspicious detail reported by other sources, that Alexander cried out from a stabbing pain in his back after drinking a huge goblet of wine. The document is thought to have been composed by Eumenes, Alexander's Greek scribe, a witness to the events it records and therefore, in some eyes, a sound authority. But it also might have been forged, or Eumenes himself might have tampered with it to cover up a plot. Further complicating the question are the differences, some of them significant, between the summaries Arrian and Plutarch give of the *Journals.* Clearly one of the two writers was looking at an altered copy—or both were.

The disputes among Alexander's contemporaries over the cause of his death make it hard to accept *any* evidence on its face. This is a hall-of-mirrors world where the more convincing an account seems, the more it might be suspected to be the work of clever assassins concealing their crimes. But historical research has to begin somewhere; if nothing can be trusted, nothing can be known. The events described here are based on Arrian's summary of the *Royal Journals,* but with an awareness that none of our sources has an absolute claim on truth.

.   .   .

After the meeting on June 3, Alexander passed the night racked by fever but managed the next day to conduct the morning's sacrifice and meet with his senior staff. On June 4 his condition was worse, but the next day he met again with the high command and continued to plan for the Arabian expedition (apparently postponed from its original launch date). So far, Alexander refused to admit that his condition might endanger the enterprise. In the past he had regarded campaigning as a kind of restorative. After the death of his closest friend, Hephaestion, had sent him into a prolonged depression, Alexander finally roused his spirits by charging off into the mountains of Media (now northern Iran), through deep snowdrifts, to attack a stiff-necked people called the Cossaeans, "using warfare to console his grief, as though going off on a hunt—a hunt of men," as Plutarch says.

In the private quarters of the palace, meanwhile, at least one woman helped look after the ailing Alexander, if we can place any credence in the sources that mention her. Alexander's wife Rhoxane, or Rauxsnaka (Little Star) as she was known in her native tongue, was much younger than Alexander, perhaps in her late teens, and as far removed from him in culture as Pocahontas from Captain John Smith. She came from a place (probably modern Uzbekistan) in the rugged, mountainous region the Greeks called Bactria. Alexander's army had slogged through two tough years of guerrilla warfare there, and Rhoxane's father, Oxyartes, had been one of its most determined enemies. After securing his surrender, Alexander had made him an ally, cementing the tie by marrying his daughter.

Rhoxane had become pregnant within a year of her marriage to Alexander, but the child either was stillborn or died in infancy. In June 323 she was in the third trimester of her second pregnancy. What passed between her and her dying husband during his illness is almost totally unknown, except that the *Liber de Morte* and the *Alexander Romance,* two works that contain much unreliable material, do record a bizarre and moving story involving the couple. According to their account, no doubt fictionalized but perhaps based on some real incident, Rhoxane entered the king's sickroom one night to find his bed empty. Seeing a secret passageway standing open, she crept out of the palace in pursuit of her husband, catching up to him as he crawled feebly toward the Euphrates. There the two embraced, and Rhoxane, weeping, convinced her husband to give up what she realized was his plan to drown himself. "You have robbed me of immortality," Alexander lamented as he obediently returned to the palace. He had been trying to make his body disappear, so that his followers might suppose he had really been a god.

Two other women besides Rhoxane must have monitored Alexander's condition anxiously, for like Rhoxane they were totally reliant on him for their status, even their safety. These were Stateira and Parysatis, daughters of the last two Persian kings, who had become Alexander's second and third wives about a year earlier. It is not clear whether the princesses were with their husband in Babylon, or had remained at Susa, one of the Persian royal capitals, where Alexander had kept them since 331 and where he had wed them in 324. Even at Susa, though, they must have known of Alexander's illness within a day or two of its onset. News traveled quickly between the two cities, carried by the fleet Persian postal system and by fire signals.

Alexander's marriages to the two Persian princesses were part of his effort to fuse his army's leadership with the elites of Asia, to create a hybrid ruling class for his tricontinental empire. He had staged a mass wedding ceremony at Susa and had matched scores of his Companions with brides from the noble families of Persis and Bactria, carefully calibrating each bride with the favor he wished to bestow on the groom. He gave the greatest prize, the sister of his own bride Stateira, to Hephaestion, so that his children and Hephaestion's would be first cousins. He singled others out as well for the high honor of inclusion in his extended family. Nearchus, Eumenes, and Ptolemy were each married to a relative of Barsine, a former mistress of Alexander's and the mother of his only living child, a son named Heracles. Craterus, another of his top generals, was wed to a cousin of Stateira's, a girl named Amastris. Like the other royal women, she had been captured in 331 and maintained in state ever since, learning high classical Greek from the tutors Alexander had appointed.

But Craterus was not happy with his new bride. He was older than other members of the king's inner circle, in his late forties rather than his thirties, and his traditionalism put him at odds with Alexander's Euro-Asian fusion. Though Craterus revered his king and was fiercely loyal, he felt entitled to tell him, on several occasions, that he had gone too far in embracing Persian ways. Alexander resented such interventions, especially since they made Craterus a hero to the rank-and-file soldiers, former peasants and farmers who, like Craterus, still regarded the Persians as vanquished enemies, not partners in rule. But Alexander needed Craterus' talents too much to punish his dissent. By giving him highborn Amastris as bride, Alexander was perhaps making a last effort to enlist Craterus in a project he deeply mistrusted.

The mass wedding was held in the royal palace at Susa. A row of nearly a hundred richly wrought couches was laid out in a great hall, and the Companions reclined, holding cups of wine. A toast was drunk by all, and then, in a carefully choreographed movement, the Asian brides entered and each went to sit beside her groom. Alexander took his two brides by the hand and kissed them on the lips, the Persian custom for contracting a marriage; as though on cue, the rest of the Companions did likewise. A great feast was held, and each groom escorted his bride to a waiting bedchamber in the palace complex. How Alexander stage-managed his own double-wedding night has not been revealed by our sources.

Five days of festivities and pageantry followed, during which Alexander presented golden wreaths to those who had served with distinction in India. Leonnatus and Peucestas, the men who had saved him from enemy archers in the rebel town, received these glittering tokens of honor. Nearchus, the Greek admiral who had gotten the fleet safely through a terrible voyage, also got one, in just recognition of his sufferings. Ptolemy too was garlanded with gold, an acknowledgment that the king's old friend had in India proved himself as a combat officer. The stalwart Craterus, however, perhaps having objected too often to Alexander's fusion program, received no wreath at this ceremony. Neither did Eumenes, whose duties in India had still been largely those of a scribe, not a soldier.

.   .   .

By the end of the first week of June, in the bivouacs outside Babylon, the Macedonian army was growing uneasy. Alexander had
not been seen for many days after first appearing on a litter at
morning sacrifices. It was unusual for the king to be absent from
view for so long, especially when he was about to lead his men
into action. Nevertheless, they continued to prepare their
weapons and gear for the Arabian campaign.

Most of these troops fought with the long infantry lance
called the *sarissa,* as well as with short swords and shields. At the
outset of his reign, Philip, Alexander's father, had introduced the
sarissa, a strong wooden shaft perhaps eighteen feet long tipped
with a two-pound metal blade, and had recruited strong young
men to wield it, forging a new kind of phalanx that changed the
face of battle overnight. Now Philip's recruits were past fifty but
still fighting in the front lines, thrusting their *sarissas* with both
hands as they advanced toward an enemy, their shields slung
around their necks. The discipline gained through decades of
fighting, in every terrain and tactical situation, had made these

Macedonian infantrymen, as seen in a tomb painting roughly contemporary with Alexander

veterans unassailable to any enemy, except, as they would soon learn, one another.

Philip had also created an elite corps of infantry, the *Hypaspists,* or Shield Bearers, who carried lighter gear than the men of the phalanx and could move about more quickly. Selected for their strength, stamina, and loyalty to the king, the three thousand Shield Bearers were the first called in for difficult operations or when Alexander's safety was threatened. They traveled up to forty miles a day over rough terrain, scaled cliffs and assaulted walls while under fire, endured desert heat and unthawed mountain passes without loss of morale. Alexander cherished these men and kept them close both on and off the battlefield. In India, where the Shield Bearers endured their greatest perils yet, he honored them by having their armor coated with silver, thus giving rise to their new unit name, the Silver Shields.

Recently, though, the bonds between the king and his veterans had come under strain. Alexander had recruited Persians and Bactrians and trained them to fight in the Macedonian style, enrolling them in even his most elite units. This offended both the pride and the prejudices of his countrymen. They had accepted, grudgingly, his use of Persians as high officials, his adoption of Persian dress and court rituals, even the marriages of the king and his top staff to Asian women. But the integration of the armed forces was a more serious matter. When Alexander announced, at an army assembly in the Persian city of Opis, that he would send ten thousand of his Macedonian troops back home and install Persians in their place, the soldiers flatly refused.

Things quickly spiraled out of control during this mutinous assembly at Opis. The men became contemptuous, sneering that the king did not need *any* of them since his "father" would see him through—a mocking reference to the rumors tracing Alexander's descent from the god Ammon. Alexander, enraged, waded into their midst, guards at his side, and picked out his most vocal opponents for summary execution. Then he retreated to his quarters and refused to admit his countrymen, receiving Persian officers instead. He took steps to replace his *entire* army, even the hallowed Silver Shields, with units recruited from Asia. He allowed his new Persian courtiers to greet him by kissing him on the mouth, an intimacy permitted by Persian kings to their favorites. He was taking his Macedonian troops at their word; he would show that he did not need *any* of them.

A more serious breach had opened between king and soldiery than the earlier mutiny in India. Then, Alexander had had no choice but to yield, since there were no other armies he could draw on. But the heartland of the Persian empire now regarded Alexander as a legitimate ruler, and the Asian chiefs who had once fought for Darius were prepared to fight for him. He was no longer hostage to the army's will, and both he and they knew it. The troops held out for three days. When they could bear the separation no longer, they went en masse to Alexander's tent and threw down their weapons before its entrance, begging the king to take them back into favor. Like jilted lovers, they bemoaned the kisses Alexander had given his Persians, kisses no Macedonian had yet received.

This show of remorse was enough to satisfy Alexander. Coming out to greet his countrymen, he invited them to kiss him as the Persians had done. He would restore them to favor and be their leader once again. The men became ecstatic with relief and, after giving their kisses, went back to camp singing a joyous victory song. Alexander held a huge banquet to celebrate the reconciliation, and his triumph. Then he sent away the ten thousand veterans as he had planned, assigning Craterus (not coincidentally the senior officer most resistant to his policies) to lead them home. Among them were the Silver Shields, long cherished by Alexander for their prowess and loyalty, now regarded, after the mutinies at the Hyphasis River and at Opis, as troublemakers.

The men departing for Europe received a discharge bonus of a silver talent each—many years' pay, at standard rates—while those remaining behind, perhaps six thousand infantrymen, had their salary increased to several times starting levels. The raise was an attempt to forestall further mutinies, and to compensate the troops for the indignity of serving side by side with barbarians. It was also Alexander's way of acknowledging that his army's mission had changed. His troops had set out twelve years earlier to fight a war; now they were being asked to maintain an empire. They had become transformed, gradually and without consultation, into a permanent military class, the human infrastructure supporting Alexander's world-state. They could never return to sheepcotes and farms even if they wanted to, and after twelve years of conquests probably few of them did. Like mercenaries, they had sold their lives, and Alexander felt they deserved a high price.

The Macedonian infantrymen who remained at Babylon, and who now prepared for the march to Arabia, were thus a privileged lot. In addition to their high pay, and their leadership roles in the new mixed-race phalanx, they formed what their countrymen revered as the royal army, the troops serving directly under the king. Under long-standing Macedonian tradition, it was the royal army's privilege to assemble and to make certain decisions by a kind of voice vote, including their most weighty duty, the approval of a new successor to the throne. Some must have begun to wonder, as Alexander's disappearance stretched out to a week or longer, whether they would soon be called on to perform that solemn task.

Among the Bodyguards gathered at Babylon's Summer Palace, the pretense that Alexander would soon recover was by now hard to maintain. The king's condition had not improved, and he was still carried on a litter when he performed each morning's sacrifice. Yet he continued to hold councils of war to discuss the coming campaign.

After more than a week in seclusion, Alexander prepared to move back down the Euphrates to the Southern Palace, and he called for all battalion and unit commanders to stand ready there. Perhaps he was anticipating the start of the march against the Arabs. His condition was now very grave, and it seems beyond belief that he was prepared to board ship for barely known stretches of the Persian Gulf, but many of his feats of stamina surpass belief, such as his grueling march through the desert of Gedrosia only months after surviving a punctured lung. Alternatively, he might have realized he was near death and summoned his officer class to hear his directives for the coming transfer of power.

Whatever orders he meant to give were never given. By the next day Alexander had lost his power of speech. He was now in a constant high fever. A ship brought him down the Euphrates to central Babylon, and he was carried, by his Bodyguards, no doubt, back into the palace he had left a week earlier.

June 10 and 11 were dismal days for the Macedonians in Babylon. Alexander was unable to move or speak. Some of the Companions, desperate to help their king even by supernatural means, slept in the temple of a local deity after asking the god whether Alexander should be brought there. In dreams that night they received the reply: it would be better if he stayed where he was. Later, after Alexander died, this was interpreted to mean that in the eyes of the god, death was a "better" outcome than recovery.

Access to the king's person was strictly controlled by the Bodyguards, and the soldiers began to chafe. Rumors spread that the king was already dead and that the high command was concealing that fact. Old mistrusts that the troops had felt in India began to resurface; their mood grew dark and violent. A crowd gathered outside the palace and demanded admittance, threaten-

A Babylonian clay tablet recording the death of Alexander on a date corresponding to June 11, 323 B.C.

ing the Bodyguards with force or, according to one report, breaking through a wall to defy their blockade. At last the senior staff
bowed to necessity and let the troops enter the king's chambers.

A long line of soldiers and Companions filed past the wasted
figure on the deathbed, who summoned enough strength to shift
his eyes or move his head in greeting to each man. It was clear to
all that death was inevitable. This was their last farewell, unless, as
Calanus had hinted before his fiery suicide, they might embrace
again in some world beyond the grave.

The end came on June 11, toward evening. On this day a
nameless Babylonian scribe made a note in his astronomical diary,
a log used by seers to correlate political and celestial events. Pressing a wedge-shaped stylus into a clay tablet, fragments of which
are now in the British Museum, he created the most toneless and
indifferent, but in some ways the most powerful, of the records
that survive from the age of Alexander. In the entry for that date,
Aiaru 29 according to the Babylonian calendar, he wrote: "The
king died." Then, explaining his inability to make observations of
the night sky, he added, simply, "Clouds."

Some three and a half centuries earlier, a different Macedonian
king, Alexander's great-great-great-great-great-great-great-great-
great-grandfather, lay on a different deathbed, and gave instructions to his son regarding his burial. That son, named Argaeus,
about to become king in his own right, was told to found a royal
cemetery in the city where he then lived, Aegae. The kings of
Macedon must all be buried there, Argaeus was warned, for the
dynasty would end if any were entombed elsewhere.

Aegae was at that time the royal seat of the Macedonians. The
name of the town reveals much about the humble origins of
the people, for it closely resembles the Greek word meaning
"goats." Herdsmen for much of their history, the Macedonians
suddenly, almost miraculously, transformed themselves into warriors and conquerors under Philip and Alexander. A legend
recorded by the Roman historian Justin speaks of this transforma-
tion as something foreseen, if not decreed, by the gods. An ancient
oracle declared that goats would lead the Macedonians to a great
empire. One of their early kings, recalling this oracle, founded

Aegae where he saw a herd of wild goats and thereafter always led his warriors into battle with goats depicted on his standards. Thus the name of Aegae came to stand for the imperial destiny of this world-conquering people, rather than their goat-herding past.

The name of King Argaeus, too, carried mythic weight for the Macedonians, for it seemed to trace their monarchy to the Greek city of Argos. Argaeus' father had been an exile from Argos, according to legend, and had won control of Macedonia by force of arms, thus establishing a Greek royal house in a non-Greek region. No one in the Greek world knew whether to credit this myth (though it was accepted around 500 B.C. by a panel screening out non-Greeks from the Olympic Games), and modern scholars tend to regard it as propaganda. But the Macedonian kings took pride in the link to Argos that Argaeus' name seemed to imply, along with the name of an even more remote ancestor, Argeas, said to be a grandson of Zeus. The royal family came to call themselves by a collective name, the Argeads, that stressed their connection to this ancestor and to the Argive Greeks.

For three and a half centuries before Alexander, the Argeads formed the central pole of Macedonian political life. They were the sole legitimate government, for all appointments and offices were at the discretion of the king. In a land divided by geography into fractious cantons, the royal house defined national identity; one was Macedonian if one was ruled by an Argead. The monarchy became a hallowed institution in the eyes of its subjects, their principal way of understanding who they were. They arranged themselves into concentric rings around the reigning king; the highborn styled themselves his "friends" and "companions," drank with him at riotous banquets, joined him on boar hunts, and sent their young sons to the palace to serve as "the king's boys."

But the Argeads were not an easy lot to revere. Lacking a system for selecting heirs, they easily fell into fratricide or civil war to decide dynastic disputes. Their polygamy generated multiple family lines that competed, sometimes viciously, over succession. Winners of such contests often wiped out rivals; Alexander did this when he succeeded his father, Philip, leaving the royal house perilously short of heirs. In the end, the Argead who took the throne was the one who *could* take it, and the people hailed their new ruler by vocal acclamation, a rite performed by an assembly of armed soldiers.

For three and a half centuries this quarrelsome family had ruled the Macedonian nation and buried its dead at Aegae, as Argaeus had been taught. Even when the royal seat was moved to Pella, a more outward-looking locale with easier access to the sea, the ancient capital continued to house their tombs. It was as though the family believed the prophecy Argaeus heard from his father, that their dynasty would endure only so long as they kept the royal burial site. The Argeads had clung to the tradition, and they had endured.

But now Alexander had chosen to break the chain. In some of his last instructions, he asked that his body be buried in western Egypt, near the desert oracle of the god Ammon. He had visited this shrine eight years earlier and consulted it about his origins; some said he was told he was Ammon's son, not Philip's. Whatever he heard there, he chose to spend eternity in one of the most inaccessible places in the world, today known as the oasis of Siwa. His corpse would dwell in splendid isolation, surrounded by trackless and forbidding wastes, rather than in the bosom of his ancestors at Aegae. It was as though he wanted only a god as his kin.

The problem of whether to grant Alexander's bizarre request was one of many the Bodyguards faced on the night of June 11. They would not be able to address it for some time, since more pressing problems were soon to demand their attention. Two years hence, it was to be resolved in a way none of them, or Alexander himself, could have foreseen. Alexander's corpse, like his dynasty and his empire, was about to embark on a perilous and unprecedented journey.

The Testing of Perdiccas

Babylon

JUNE 11–LATE SUMMER 323 B.C.

In his last days of life, according to several ancient accounts, Alexander made his only attempt to deal with the power vacuum his illness had created. From his sickbed he passed to his senior Bodyguard, Perdiccas, the signet ring with which he sealed his executive orders. The significance of this gesture was clear. Alexander had given Perdiccas authority to oversee the army and the empire, until either Alexander recovered or a new king emerged.

Alexander's army had no clear hierarchy that made one individual second-in-command, but the post of chiliarch, the head of the first squadron of the elite Companion cavalry, stood highest in rank. Until the previous autumn, Hephaestion had occupied it, but his death from illness had left it vacant. Alexander, grieved at the loss of his closest friend, at first decreed that no one else should lead this top cavalry squadron, so that it would forever bear the name of Hephaestion. But eventually he appointed Perdiccas to take Hephaestion's place and put Eumenes, his own Greek secretary, into the cavalry command held by Perdiccas.

Perdiccas was a natural but not inevitable choice to succeed Hephaestion as top-ranking officer. Perdiccas had royal blood, from one of the now-obsolete dynasties that had ruled the mountainous regions outside central Macedon. His career of service was long and distinguished. He had become a Bodyguard some five years into the Asian campaign, a mark of his unstinting loyalty to the king. In India, Perdiccas led several critical operations, including the crucial task, shared with Hephaestion, of bridging the Indus River. One ancient source reports that it was Perdiccas who extracted the arrow from Alexander's chest in India, a task that most were too terrified to perform for fear of causing the king's death (others say it was a Greek doctor named Critodemus).

There were several Companions who must have been dismayed to see Perdiccas made chiliarch and not themselves. Of these, Craterus perhaps had the most grounds for envy. He was older than the rest, in his late forties, with an authority greatly revered by troops and officers alike. Alexander often relied on Craterus to bring up the phalanx, gear wagons, and elephant train while he dashed ahead with more mobile troops. But though Craterus had fulfilled every commission with distinction, he was known to oppose Alexander's program of Euro-Asian cultural fusion, and that made him an outsider at court. Ultimately, Alexander had sent him home at the head of the veterans returning to Macedonia, with orders to assume command of Europe— an honorable discharge from the royal army.

Ptolemy, too, might have hoped to be marked as Alexander's most favored. Ptolemy had risen to high rank only late in the Asian campaign but since then had progressed from strength to strength. He was among the king's oldest and most trusted friends, and trustworthiness, more than any other factor, determined promotion at Alexander's court. And what of Leonnatus, who had proved his trustworthiness by protecting Alexander's prostrate body with his own after the king was wounded in India? Leonnatus too had dreams of higher station. For some time now he had patterned his clothes after Alexander's and even his hair, flipping it back from his forehead on both sides in the king's signature style.

In the end it was Perdiccas who succeeded Hephaestion as chiliarch, and to whom Alexander, in his last days of life, passed the signet ring. But in taking that ring from the king's hand,

Perdiccas took it away from all the others, even from Craterus, then hundreds of miles away on the march toward Macedon. Each was worthy, in his own eyes at least, of the highest honor the king could bestow. During his campaign Alexander had kept them in a careful equipoise, distributing marks of favor evenly so as not to give any (except Hephaestion) too great a sense of entitlement. "They were so equal in his honor that you might have thought each one a king," writes Justin of Alexander's top officers, though he misses the point by attributing to a malign Fortune, rather than to state policy, the balance of their strengths.

Perdiccas had shown on many occasions his ability to manage a crisis, and never more than in the panicky moments after Alexander was wounded in the Indian town—if it was indeed Perdiccas who performed emergency surgery on the king. Alexander had been dragged out of harm's way with a three-foot arrow still protruding from his chest. The arrowhead was lodged in his breastbone, and no one dared saw off the shaft for fear the bone would splinter. Alexander, still conscious, tried to cut the shaft with his own dagger, but loss of blood had already sapped his strength. Some onlookers began to weep, and others drew back in terror, while Alexander rebuked them as cowards and traitors. To

A medallion struck by Alexander depicting
an Indian archer of the type who dealt him
his near-fatal chest wound

step forward at such a moment, as one source says that Perdiccas did—using his sword as a scalpel when there was no time to find proper instruments—took exceptional steeliness of nerve. Doctors, under the rough justice administered by angry Macedonians, could be killed for not saving the lives of their patients.

Now a new crisis was at hand, and Perdiccas needed all his steadiness of nerve. He would be blamed in this case not for Alexander's death but for not being Alexander. His every move would draw the jealousy and resentment of his rivals. The army in Babylon, perhaps six thousand Macedonian infantry, barely trusted him; only yesterday they had defied his orders and forced past him to see Alexander on his sickbed. Their behavior had become alarmingly headstrong in recent years, even toward Alexander. From whom would they take orders now that their only master was dead?

The steps taken by Perdiccas to deal with the crisis of 323 are known only imperfectly, since ancient accounts vary widely. Indeed the week following June 11 in Babylon was so violent and chaotic that no two witnesses could have recalled it in quite the same way. The divergent reports in three ancient chronicles— Arrian's *Events After Alexander,* Diodorus' *Library,* and Justin's summary of Pompeius Trogus—are like three strands from which a modern historian must weave a braid of likelihood. Complicating this task is a fourth source that, for these first days of the post-Alexander period, gives a highly detailed account of events but is often at variance with the other three. Quintus Curtius, a Roman statesman living under the early Caesars, continued his history of Alexander's life for several weeks past the king's death, fascinated, as a Roman of that era would be, by the perils of a power vacuum. But Curtius' readiness to see Roman patterns in Macedonian history, or even to superimpose them, calls his reliability into question.

It is certain that on June 12, a council of high officers met in the room where Alexander lay in state, the throne room of Nebuchadnezzar's palace. The seven Bodyguards were there, along with a handful of others, armed as if for battle to highlight the urgency of the moment. Perdiccas, according to Curtius, had prepared a startling backdrop for this meeting: Alexander's empty throne, now decked with the king's diadem, armor, and robes. It was as though he wanted Alexander's ghost to preside over the deliberations. Curtius reports that Perdiccas even placed Alexander's signet ring, his own great token of authority, among those relics—a remarkable gesture of humility, if true.

Perdiccas opened the proceedings by taking up the most pressing matter facing the generals, the selection of a successor to the throne. Alexander's wife Rhoxane, he pointed out, was in her final weeks of pregnancy. If her child was male and survived, the Macedonians would have a legitimate heir. The best thing now, Perdiccas said, was for the army to wait and hope for both those outcomes.

Nearchus, Alexander's top naval officer, spoke next. He was not among the Bodyguards, but Alexander had counted him a close friend. Nearchus now proposed that the child named Heracles, Alexander's son by a mistress named Barsine, be proclaimed the new king. After all, he argued, here was a living, breathing heir—perhaps four years old at this time—not just an even chance at one. Nearchus was, however, interrupted by a disapproving din from the other officers. Not only had he proposed a child who was illegitimate and therefore not eligible for the throne, but, as a Greek in an assembly of Macedonians, he was speaking very much out of turn. Perhaps too he was suspected of self-interest, for in the Susa mass marriage he had wed a daughter of Barsine, so that Heracles was now his half-brother-in-law.

An infantry captain named Meleager spoke next, bluntly raising the problem of Euro-Asian fusion that had deeply troubled the army. Both Heracles and Rhoxane's unborn child, he observed, had mothers who were at least part Asian (Barsine was half Greek) and who belonged to races conquered and ruled by the Macedonians. Perhaps Alexander had wanted such boundaries ignored, but not all could follow his lead, least of all Meleager and his infantry comrades. Why not an heir of purer blood, a son of Philip by a European wife, and one already grown to manhood: Alexander's half brother Arrhidaeus? The man was right there in Babylon, accompanying the army, ready to take power in an instant.

Now it was Ptolemy's turn to speak and to voice an awkward truth. Arrhidaeus was not mentally competent to rule. He could speak and function reasonably well, but his capacity was that of a child—in modern terms he was developmentally disabled—and like a child he would need a guardian or regent. Rather than hand power to such a surrogate, Ptolemy said, the Macedonians should appoint a board of top-ranking generals to govern instead of a king. These men could meet before Alexander's empty throne, as they now were meeting, and take decisions by majority vote. In this way, Ptolemy reasoned, the Macedonians would gain leaders of proven talent, men who had already succeeded at exercising command.

Many no doubt cast sidelong glances at Perdiccas while Ptolemy spoke. It was Perdiccas, as Alexander's chiliarch and the man who had received the ring, who, logically, would be guardian of an infant or a mental invalid. Ptolemy's proposal to decentralize authority, even to eliminate the monarchy, was, by any reading, a hit at Perdiccas. Ptolemy himself must have known what impact his words would have. He had thrown the first gauntlet in what was to be a fight to the death between these two leading Bodyguards.

There may have been more speeches at that fateful meeting (Curtius reports a proposal that Perdiccas be crowned, but this seems a Roman fantasy imported into the Macedonian setting). In the end, Perdiccas' plan was adopted. The army would wait for Rhoxane to give birth, and if she had a son, that boy would be king. The infant's guardians (who also would presumably rule if the child was a girl) would be a board of four: Bodyguards Perdiccas and Leonnatus, plus Craterus, now in western Asia slowly leading his column of veterans homeward, and Antipater, the grand old man of Macedonian politics, who for the past twelve years had been in charge of the European home front. Ptolemy, who ranked not far below three of these men and higher than Leonnatus, was somehow left out of the arrangement. Probably he was already regarded as a dangerous rival by Perdiccas.

A rough division of sovereignty was laid out for these four regents: Craterus and Antipater would hold command in Europe, Perdiccas and Leonnatus in Asia. Craterus was accorded some vague executive status, entitling him to act as the king's representative and therefore to draw on the royal treasuries. This was a sop

to the well-loved older general who, with ten thousand decommissioned veterans under his command, possessed the greatest
troop strength of any Macedonian leader. Craterus could easily
storm into Babylon and seize sole power, once he learned of
Alexander's death, as he would do in a day or two.

Those in the throne room swore an oath of loyalty to the
board of four, and then the entire cavalry, summoned to the
courtyard outside the palace, took a similar oath. The generals
hoped to get the cavalry in line behind the scheme and then present it to the infantry—by far the larger of the two branches of the
army—as a fait accompli. But they badly misjudged their ability
to win over the rank and file. For even while they were in session,
reports arrived that the infantry, meeting separately, had made a
different choice of monarch—Arrhidaeus, Alexander's mentally
impaired half brother. Perdiccas dispatched Meleager, the infantry
officer who had already spoken in favor of Arrhidaeus in the
council session, as emissary to the foot soldiers—the first error of
the many he would commit as head of the new regime.

It is unclear how far the infantry was from the palace or how
much the foot soldiers knew of the cavalry's decisions. Justin
implies the two groups had no contact, while Curtius puts the
infantrymen right outside the throne room, listening to the
speeches there and finally breaking in as a violent mob. Whatever
their physical distance, the two groups were miles apart in outlook. The gulf that had opened in India, when the foot soldiers
had nearly rioted against cavalry officers whom they thought were
concealing Alexander's death, had only grown wider in the intervening two years. Now the time for choosing Alexander's successor was at hand, a task that by custom required a broad army
assembly, but the army had not been convened. In the crisis
atmosphere, it was easy for the infantry to assume the worst about
their generals' intentions.

Mistrust of superiors came easily to these foot soldiers.
Alexander had routinely promoted those he cherished from
infantry to cavalry, leaving the former feeling passed over and
estranged from their higher-ups. The greatest estrangement had
resulted from the king's experiments in cultural fusion. Alexander

had taken to wearing the purples of Persian royalty, had accepted the toadying of Persian courtiers, had even married a Bactrian and then two Persian women. Then he had moved, in the last year of his life, to mix Asian recruits into the ranks of his *grande armée*. He had formed a new phalanx, in their eyes a grotesque hybrid, made up of only one Macedonian for every three barbarians. (The cavalry too had been internationalized, but to a lesser degree; Macedonians and Greeks were still in the majority there.)

The foot soldiers had thus seen huge changes during their decade or more of service, and *they* had changed as well. Hardened by constant warfare, emboldened by their successful mutiny in India, they had become headstrong and intractable, demanding of pay and perquisites. They still revered the Argead monarchy and the towering figure of Alexander, but their reverence was more grudging than before, like that paid by a half-wild dog to a master who can hit it on the snout. The commander they loved, by contrast, was Craterus, the soldier's soldier, who had given voice to their own feelings on several occasions when he had challenged Alexander's Asianizing policies. In their eyes Craterus stood for a culturally pure past, when their identity, and that of their foes, had been both clear and morally gratifying.

Meleager, the top officer leading the infantry, had also criticized Alexander's internationalism, and his plain speech had cost him dear. Years before, in India, Meleager had attended a banquet celebrating Alexander's new alliance with Ambhi, a local raja. Alexander had lavished gifts on his Indian host, including the huge sum of one thousand talents of silver. Drunk, and embittered at seeing such wealth bestowed on a barbarian, Meleager let his irritation show. "How nice for you," he sneered at the king in the hearing of all, "that finally in India you found a man worthy of one thousand talents." Thereafter, Meleager's career had languished. Of all those who started the Asian campaign as taxiarchs (captains of infantry brigades), only Meleager had stayed in that mid-level post, rather than moving up to the more distinguished cavalry.

It was no coincidence that Meleager, in the council session at the palace, had backed Arrhidaeus as successor at the same moment that his infantry battalions, meeting elsewhere, made the same choice. In both cases, the preference for Arrhidaeus over Rhoxane's unborn child sprang from a longing for the past. Arrhidaeus, as a son of the great Philip, evoked the days before Alexander when Asians had still been enemies and slaves, not comrades-in-arms. The foot soldiers who anointed him left no doubt about their hopes for his reign. They took the step, unprecedented in their history, of changing the new king's name, dubbing him Philip after his revered father.

Meleager knew why his infantry comrades had hailed Arrhidaeus as monarch and rejected Rhoxane's unborn child, whose mixed blood embodied the hated program of Euro-Asian fusion. He shared their feelings, yet he had been sent to their camp to persuade them to reverse course. Perdiccas was counting on him to reconcile his men to the choice made by the cavalry. He was the perfect go-between, since his stalled career gave him unmatched credibility among the infantry; he was the one officer who had stayed in their ranks. He had a fair chance of quelling their revolt if he spoke in support of the generals and their fetal king.

But he also had a fair chance of leading that revolt to victory if he followed his own inclinations. As he entered the infantry camp, where the foot soldiers were hailing the newly renamed Philip, Meleager took stock of the opportunity before him. Here was an incompetent king who needed a guardian to tend him; here was an army that already regarded *him* as its chief, troops far more numerous than those of Perdiccas. Leading this army, championing this king, Meleager could grasp supreme power as easily as Perdiccas, indeed more easily, since he would stand beside a flesh-and-blood monarch, not a mere in utero hope. He took the dare Fortune offered. He put on armor and stood beside the former Arrhidaeus, now Philip—a gesture that signaled his acclamation of the king.

The infantry went wild, clanging spears on shields to hail the new head of their mutiny. Meleager made a speech that fanned their anger into a demand for action. Armed and accompanied by a bewildered Philip, the rebellious mob marched on the palace. As they had done just two days before, they demanded admittance to the chamber where Alexander lay.

Forewarned, Perdiccas had assembled a few hundred picked

troops in the throne room and barred the doors. He was hoping to hold the room and thereby preserve his tenuous grasp on power. Alexander's corpse, and the empty throne decked with royal armor and insignia, were locked in with him, the talismans of authority. Whoever possessed these, it now seemed, controlled the empire.

The infantry forced the doors and spilled into the room, javelins at the ready. Meleager, at the head of the mob, confronted Perdiccas face to face. A full-scale battle loomed, but Perdiccas and his men saw they were outmatched. They made a tactical retreat and left the palace by a side door, then rode for the safety of the plains outside the city.

In one swift coup Meleager had gained control of the room, the throne, and the corpse. He and the infantry now set up their new government before Alexander's still-untended body. Philip, their half-wit king, was installed as head of that government and invested with the royal garb left on the empty throne, Alexander's robe and diadem.

Perdiccas and the other generals had vanished, all except one. Little Eumenes, Alexander's former secretary, only recently promoted to cavalry commander, remained in the palace in hopes of mediating the conflict. Eumenes made the case that as a Greek with no interest in Macedonian politics and nothing to gain or lose, he could be trusted by both sides. This reasoning was quite likely advanced by Eumenes in perfect sincerity and was accepted by Meleager's men—though events of years to come would make it seem laughably naive.

According to legend, Alexander predicted on his deathbed that a great funeral contest would be held over his tomb. But even he might not have believed that, within a day of his demise, the two main branches of the army would draw weapons on each other over his very corpse. The speed of the unraveling, the scale of the breakdown of trust and order, was breathtaking. The saving grace for the Macedonians was that events at Babylon were moving faster than the messengers reporting them to the world. Provinces that might have profited from the disorder, subject peoples that might have rebelled, did not yet even know that Alexander was dead.

Meleager's first move was to order the arrest of his displaced rival, Perdiccas. He must have sensed that his time in power would be short if Perdiccas still lived. Despite the mistrust between cavalry and infantry, the army's traditional leaders could still command the loyalty of many in the rank and file. Indeed Perdiccas seemed to be waiting to reclaim that loyalty, remaining inside Babylon while sending his fellow officers out. Meleager was determined to prevent him from doing so. It was a simple matter to obtain the requisite authority: Meleager explained to King Philip why Perdiccas posed a danger to the state, and the king's befuddled silence was taken for assent. A squad was dispatched to arrest Perdiccas, or to kill him if he resisted.

Perdiccas responded to the bold attack with superb sangfroid. He was at his quarters with an honor guard of sixteen page boys, too few to defend him, when Meleager's men approached. Showing no fear but only righteous anger, he appeared in his doorway in full armor and denounced his would-be captors as traitors and slaves of Meleager. The tactic worked. Shamed by the reproaches of their top general, the men slunk away without completing their mission. Perdiccas hastened to leave the city before other hit men could arrive.

Meleager's failed strike at Perdiccas sparked a contrary swing of emotion in the mutinous army. The next day saw recriminations against Meleager and even a judicial inquiry into his abuse of power. King Philip himself was questioned and admitted he had approved the move against Perdiccas. But, he argued— apparently able to speak and reason to a limited degree— Perdiccas was still alive, so why make so much trouble? Meleager survived, but his position was much weakened. The throne room began to feel like a hollow sham of a government seat: envoys came and went, state business went on as usual, but those in attendance glowered silently at one another, afraid to admit their fears and doubts.

After three days of sullen anticipation, word arrived that the cavalry counterstrike had begun. The horsemen stationed outside Babylon had cut off the city's food supply, threatening to starve the infantry into surrender. The mutineers became disturbed not only by their own plight but also by the restive movements of the city's population, deprived as it was of provisions. Some troops went to Meleager and demanded that he either fight Perdiccas or arrange a deal. Eumenes, the Greek who had thus far remained on the sidelines, began intervening at last, urging the mutineers to reconcile with their former leaders before more harm was done.

Reluctantly but resignedly, Meleager opened negotiations with Perdiccas. The cavalry initially announced harsh terms, insisting that the heads of the mutiny be handed over for summary punishment. Then Perdiccas himself appeared before the infantrymen to sound a conciliatory note. Fearlessly walking into their midst, he delivered an impassioned speech about the dangers that now loomed. The Macedonians would inflict on themselves the defeat they had never suffered at the hands of their enemies; all their labors would be for nothing; they would appease with their own blood the ghosts of their slaughtered foes. The voice of familiar authority stirred the rebellious soldiers. They made clear they were prepared, under suitable terms, to take back Perdiccas as their leader.

The path to a compromise now lay open, though it was a bizarre compact that was struck. Perdiccas and the cavalry recognized Philip, formerly Arrhidaeus, as monarch, while Meleager and the infantry agreed that Rhoxane's child, if a son, would become a second king. Philip would have first position in this dual monarchy under the fiction that he had the ability to rule, at least more ability than a newborn baby. Meleager was added to the board of guardians administering the empire in the kings' names, replacing Leonnatus, who was mysteriously removed. Meleager would be subordinate to Perdiccas in Asia, while Craterus and Antipater would remain joint custodians of Europe. His mutiny had bought him a sizable share of control of the empire, though he was not destined to enjoy it for long.

The crisis had been defused. By creating a joint kingship, a peculiar arrangement at odds with the very notion of *mon*archy, the two sides pulled back from the abyss of civil war. Infantry and cavalry were reunited into one army, though the breakdown of trust was not so easily healed. Both sides must have known,

despite the appearance of an amnesty, that there were still scores
to be settled, once the traditional leaders were back in power.

Several days had passed since the death of Alexander. The king's
body lay in state in the palace throne room, mute witness to the
struggle that had taken place in its awesome presence. Amid the
tumult, there had been no opportunity to take measures against
decomposition. But miraculously, according to Plutarch and
Quintus Curtius, the corpse remained uncorrupted, still radiating
the beauty, strength, and fragrant smell that distinguished the
king in life. Indeed the embalmers who were now at last summoned feared to treat a corpse that still seemed alive. Perhaps they
were right to be afraid: a panel of experts who analyzed Alexander's death in 1996, and who published their findings in *The New
England Journal of Medicine,* suggested that the king did not die
on June 11 but rather entered a paralytic state that closely resembled death.

The Macedonians did not customarily use embalming, an
Egyptian and Babylonian practice, to treat their dead. It must have
been Perdiccas who decided Alexander's body should be emptied
of organs and mummified, then placed in a golden casket filled
with aromatics, so that all could continue to gaze upon their king
without revulsion. He designated an officer named Arrhidaeus (a
different person from Alexander's half brother, now known by his
new royal name, Philip) to oversee the construction of a magnificent hearse and to take charge of the desiccated corpse until this
was built. Arrhidaeus was instructed to convey the corpse to its
final destination, which was still at this point, evidently, Alexander's chosen burial ground, the shrine of Ammon in Egypt.

For Perdiccas, the past week had been damaging but not
hopelessly so. Meleager's betrayal had caught him by surprise; he
had misjudged the infantry leader, had thought him reliable and
sound, indeed had sent him on the very mission that gave him
control of a hostile army. Perdiccas had been watching his cavalry
colleagues for disaffection, especially Ptolemy, and considering
ways to deal with his absent rivals Craterus and Antipater. The
rebellion of the infantry had blindsided him. But Perdiccas had
quickly regained his balance. He had made the troops listen to

him and accept his authority. And the other members of the high command had stuck by him; even his rival Ptolemy had remained loyal. The traditional hierarchy of the army had been restored.

The question now was how the mutineers, in particular Meleager, should be dealt with. The best model Perdiccas could look to for an answer was Alexander. Alexander too had been challenged, despite his godlike power. Men had refused to obey his orders, had stood up to him in front of others and even jeered at him. In every case, those men were now dead.

First had come Cleitus, the one they called Cleitus the Black, a nobleman and commander of high rank. He had saved Alexander's life in the first battle against the Persians, cutting off the arm of an enemy swordsman just as it was about to strike the king's head. Years later, when drunk at a banquet in Bactria (in what is now Uzbekistan), Cleitus had begun to grumble that Alexander owed not only his neck but also his conquests to the efforts of others; that he wore his borrowed glory too proudly, decking himself out like a Persian fop; that he was less of a man than his father, Philip. Alexander finally could take no more and reached for a weapon. The Bodyguards grabbed hold of the king and restrained him while Cleitus was hustled out of the banquet hall. But a few moments later, when the Bodyguards had relaxed their grip, Cleitus returned with more taunts on his lips. Alexander grabbed a *sarissa* and thrust its massive blade into Cleitus' chest, killing him on the spot. It was a rash and unpremeditated murder but perhaps one Alexander did not regret.

Callisthenes was next, the Greek literary light who accompanied the army as court chronicler. Aristotle's grandnephew, an esteemed intellectual, Callisthenes lent respectability to Alexander's campaign, especially since he was usually eager to exalt it. But suddenly, about a year after Cleitus' death, Callisthenes balked. In an impromptu speech he attacked an idea, floated by the king's agents, that courtiers should bow down before Alexander as the Persians did before their monarchs. This was confusing man with god, Callisthenes asserted, and swapping limited monarchy for despotism. Alexander abandoned the bowing ritual but simmered over Callisthenes' defiance. A few months later, when some of Callisthenes' young admirers were found to have plotted against the king's life, a snare was easily set. Callisthenes died horribly, either tortured and hanged, according to some sources, or imprisoned in a stinking cage and dragged about with the army until lice and disease did him in.

The last challenge to Alexander's authority had been the most serious. In Opis, where Alexander announced he was discharging ten thousand veterans and bringing in Persian replacements, his troops showed open contempt, mocking his high-handedness and delusions of godhood. Alexander responded instantly and brutally. Wading into the crowd, he clapped a hand on the shoulders of those who scoffed the loudest, marking them out for summary execution. Thirteen men, veterans with long and distinguished records, died without hearing or trial, but the muttering ceased. Alexander regained control.

Now it was Perdiccas' turn to face down a mutinous army. Clearly those who had challenged him had to pay the price and pay it in full view of others. But his power to punish was nothing like what Alexander's had been. An immediate attack was out of the question; his authority was still too shaky, and besides, how could he succeed amid Babylon's streets and palaces? Cavalrymen needed level plains on which charges could be mounted. And so Perdiccas, together with his fellow cavalry leaders, hatched a plan.

From its earliest days, the Macedonian army had practiced a ritual called lustration to purify itself in sight of the gods. A dog was killed and cut in two, and the halves were dragged to two sides of a field. The entire soldiery then marched between them in full armor. Sometimes a feigned battle between cavalry and infantry took place after this march was concluded. Perdiccas now ordered that such a lustration be held in the fields outside Babylon, to cleanse the armed forces of the taint of mutiny. All would gather in one place for the ritual, cavalry ranged opposite infantry.

Meleager no doubt suspected Perdiccas' intentions, but a further stratagem secured his cooperation. Perdiccas planted agents to mutter loudly against Meleager's elevation in the power-sharing deal. Getting wind of these grumbles, Meleager complained to Perdiccas that the malcontents must be punished. Perdiccas proposed that the upcoming lustration, when the cavalry would be deployed in an open field with full tactical advantage, would offer a good opportunity to make arrests. Meleager agreed to the plan, hoping it would result in the destruction of his opponents. In fact it was aimed at his supporters.

The infantry marched outside Babylon's walls, into the stronghold of the cavalry, to enact the solemn rite of lustration. From the opposite side of the field, the cavalry came forward in full armor, led by a wedge of war elephants. This exotic weapon had terrified the Macedonians when they first encountered it in India, but they had quickly learned how to check it, then mastered it themselves. Elephants had since become an accustomed sight in Macedonian camps, but to see them marching in a lustral procession was strange and, no doubt, disquieting.

As the distance between ranks closed, Perdiccas sprang his trap. He sent King Philip over to the infantrymen with a prepared speech demanding surrender of the leading mutineers—the very men who had put him on the throne and given him his name—and to threaten a devastating cavalry charge if they refused. Meleager had been double-crossed but could do nothing about it. His thirty staunchest supporters were handed over, bound, and, as the assembled infantry looked on, cast under the feet of the elephants and trampled to death. With a single macabre stroke, the army was purged of its most troublesome members. But Perdiccas' duplicity was not without its costs. From this point on, the chiliarch became "suspected by all and full of suspicions," says Photius, summarizing the view of Arrian in the lost *Events After Alexander.*

Meleager himself escaped the lustration, but a few days or perhaps a few hours later his own reckoning with Perdiccas arrived. When officers appeared accusing him of treachery, Meleager did not bother to defend himself. He fled to a nearby temple, trusting in the ancient taboo against harming those seeking sanctuary at altars of the gods. But such taboos were a luxury that could not be afforded in the current crisis. Perdiccas ordered his troops to enter the enclosure and drag Meleager away. King Philip, indifferent to or barely cognizant of his change of masters, signed the order for Meleager's execution as compliantly as he had earlier signed a similar writ against Perdiccas.

. . .

Having literally stomped on the spirit of sedition in the army, Perdiccas plotted a second purge of a very different kind. We know almost nothing about this plot because only one ancient chronicler, Plutarch, mentions it, and only in a single, short, confusing paragraph. But there is no reason to doubt that it took place. In this case Perdiccas had an unusual collaborator, a woman unaccustomed to political murders: Alexander's pregnant young widow, Rhoxane.

Rhoxane must have realized, during the days after Alexander's death, that she had become presumptive queen mother. But she also knew that her lofty status was a fragile thing. Alexander's two other widows, Stateira and Parysatis, were daughters of the two most recent Persian kings. Alexander had intended to beget children by them, children who, with both European and Asian royal blood, would be ideal rulers of the Perso-Macedonian empire. Now these two Persian princesses offered an opportunity for someone else, one of Alexander's generals presumably, to sire sons who were royal at least on their mother's side. In the new political landscape, with Europe and Asia forced together by Alexander's titanic will, it was unclear whether such children could become candidates for the throne. A more confusing possibility was that one or both princesses were already pregnant by Alexander or would claim to be—a claim that would pose great perils for Rhoxane and her unborn child.

So Perdiccas and Rhoxane, acting together, resolved to murder at least one, more likely both, of the Persian princesses. A letter, tricked up to look as though it came from Alexander, was brought to Stateira. Since Perdiccas had control of Alexander's signet ring, it is tempting to think he used it to seal the forged letter. Whatever Stateira read in that letter drew her to a spot where Rhoxane was waiting for her, and where Rhoxane had her killed, together with another woman, probably Parysatis. Then the bodies were secretly cast down a well and the well was filled in with earth. Rhoxane and Perdiccas meant no one to learn what had happened; they simply made the two women disappear. If not for a single sentence in Plutarch, derived from some unknown informant, the crime would have remained hushed up to this day.

There is a verb, *phthanō,* in ancient Greek that denotes the taking of preemptive action, especially where one harms an enemy to prevent that enemy from doing harm. When Alexander had a high-ranking officer named Philotas tried and executed, on thin evidence of collusion in an assassination plot, he named the city founded at the trial's site Prophthasia, the place where he had gotten the jump on danger. *Prophthasia* had always been the prerogative of Macedonian kings. The safety of the monarch justified the elimination even of anticipated threats. But the murder of the Persian princesses by Rhoxane and Perdiccas took this logic to a new extreme. Heirs to the throne had been rubbed out before, but killing women to prevent them from bearing heirs was unprecedented.

Once this logic of *prophthasia* was invoked, it was hard to limit how it was applied. The violence it seemed to license would, in years to come, claim the lives of all the women who shared Alexander's blood or who had shared his bed. Somehow one unlikely survivor would escape the carnage to help beget a new royal line.

In either July or September—our sources are divided on the chronology—Rhoxane gave birth to a boy. Never before or since, one imagines, was the gender of an infant anticipated so keenly by so many. Most were no doubt relieved, but none more so than Perdiccas. The settlement he had masterminded was secure. His plan for the future of the empire, which, like Alexander's, called for a center of power at Babylon rather than in Europe, could go forward.

The baby was named for his father, as was inevitable given that his counterpart had been renamed after *his* father. A new Alexander was now acclaimed as king alongside a new Philip. History knows the pair as Alexander IV and Philip III (sometimes called Philip Arrhidaeus).

The time had come for Perdiccas to give new assignments to the Bodyguards, since it did not suit their training or temperament to attend a mental invalid or a suckling infant. Perdiccas needed to reward those who had stayed loyal during the infantry uprising and also get rivals off the scene. It was resolved that each Bodyguard, Perdiccas excepted, would leave Babylon and become a satrap, or provincial governor (the Persian name for the office had already been adopted into Greek, and as a result survives today in English). Such appointments conferred power and status, and were strategically important as well, for satraps controlled small armies that could cement the unity of the empire—or, if used for revolt, destroy it. It was essential that the heads of the provinces be reliable men, strong but not too strong, who would follow orders issued by Perdiccas in the name of the joint kings.

The division of these posts, however, posed a complex problem in diplomacy. Perdiccas could not risk offending his comrades by giving them too paltry a province or emboldening them with one too powerful. In the end he made errors on both sides of this delicate balance, errors that would soon threaten the survival of his regime.

The biggest question Perdiccas faced was how to accommodate Ptolemy, the second most powerful Bodyguard. Ptolemy clearly disliked him yet had supported him during the infantry insurrection. Ptolemy wanted Egypt. It was a gem of a province, wealthy beyond measure and friendly to the Macedonians, with borders that were easy to defend—all too easy, in Perdiccas' eyes. Ptolemy could not be denied Egypt without risking a severe breach, but he also could not be allowed to use it as a base for mounting revolt. A diplomatic solution was found: Ptolemy got his wish but was also assigned an adjutant, Cleomenes of Naucratis, an unscrupulous Greek who was already serving in Egypt as finance minister. Cleomenes was clearly meant to watch Ptolemy on Perdiccas' behalf and keep him from misbehaving.

Astride the straits of the Hellespont (the Dardanelles), two other Bodyguards, Lysimachus and Leonnatus, took up new commands. This crossing point between Europe and Asia held enormous strategic importance, bridging the vast Asiatic portion of the empire and the Macedonian homeland. The western side of the divide, Thrace, was a rough place, home to many warlike tribes; Lysimachus was charged with the stern job of pacifying it. To the east, Hellespontine Phrygia, a small and only modestly wealthy province, went to Leonnatus. Leonnatus had already, as part of the bargain Perdiccas struck with Meleager, accepted demotion from the governing board of the empire. Perdiccas

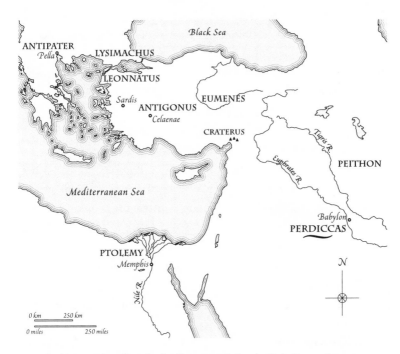

Positions assigned to the leading generals by the Babylon settlement, and the accidental position of Craterus, who was en route to Europe when Alexander died

might have supposed—wrongly, as things turned out—that his longtime supporter would be content with such a paltry prize.

A big winner in this territorial lottery was Eumenes, Alexander's Greek secretary and, recently, a cavalry officer as well. For his diplomacy during the infantry mutiny, and in recognition of the favor Alexander had shown him, Eumenes received cavalry-rich Cappadocia (in what is now eastern Turkey). This was a remarkable honor, for only two Greeks before this had become satraps, and both in the remote East. But there was a hitch. Cappadocia had not been fully subdued by Alexander and was now home to a feisty Persian warlord named Ariarathes. This man rejected Macedonian sovereignty and had an army of fellow resisters. Eumenes would need to fight his way into power, a tall order for a man who had never yet led troops in battle. Perhaps Perdiccas intended a test, to see if this clever Greek, an expert thus far only at paperwork, had the right stuff for armed combat.

To aid Eumenes, Perdiccas directed two neighboring satraps

to bring their troops forward, Leonnatus from one side and
Antigonus One-eye, satrap of Phrygia (today southwest Turkey),
from another. Antigonus, a bear of a man who had lost an eye in
battle in his youth, had long been sidelined from Alexander's
army, left behind to manage western Asia while the campaign
headed east. He and the other generals had not seen one another
in a decade, so it was no doubt with some uncertainty that Perdiccas now wrote to Antigonus, a man twenty years his senior, to
issue his orders. Perhaps he counted on Antigonus' fondness for
Eumenes to ensure his support, for the two men, though oppo-
sites in size, rank, and power, had been friends long ago at the
Macedonian court. Or perhaps this too was a test, for Perdiccas
needed to know whether he could command the respect of existing satraps, who had been absent from the new regime's founding
and had not given it their assent.

Two other powerful men had to be accommodated by the
apportionment plan, though they too were too far from Babylon
when it was drafted. Craterus, making slow progress on his homeward journey, was camped in Cilicia with his supposedly decommissioned veterans, and in Europe old man Antipater, faithful
guardian of the Macedonian homeland, remained in the post
from which Alexander had sought to remove him. Already these
two men were included in the executive council running the
empire, but they had been largely relegated to Europe while
Perdiccas managed Asia. In the final settlement, Antipater was
confirmed as head of Macedonia, Greece, and the Balkan territories. Craterus' assignment was less clear; Perdiccas no doubt left it
vague, wary of offending a general who was both beloved of the
soldiers and, by accident of timing, in control of a huge number
of them. Probably he encouraged Craterus, as gently as he could,
to proceed to Europe and share power with Antipater. He did not
want such a talented general lurking in Asia with an army of ten
thousand.

Perdiccas himself took no satrapy. His role was custodian of
the joint kings and commander of the royal army, the two nodes of
executive power now located in Babylon. He shored up his position by making a trusted subordinate, Seleucus, his second in command, appointing him to the post of chiliarch he himself had once

held. Perdiccas was now the closest thing the empire had to a central authority, with power to disburse funds from the royal treasuries, great depots of precious metals housed in closely guarded forts throughout the empire. This power of the purse formed a crucial prop to Perdiccas' leadership. The army had already made clear, while Alexander was alive, that it would fight only for rich rewards, either pay or plunder and preferably both. Any ruler who sought to retain its loyalty was going to need ready cash.

And so the generals at Babylon, like gods claiming chunks of the cosmos, took charge of the pieces of Alexander's empire that best matched their power, temperament, and rank. The newly crowned king Philip—following Perdiccas around like a spear-carrier, a mute extra, in a play, as Plutarch wryly observes—gave his all-too-ready approval to the apportionment scheme.

Before the generals departed for their new posts, Perdiccas convened an assembly of the army to consider Alexander's last plans. According to Diodorus, Perdiccas had found a document containing these plans among the papers in the royal chambers. It described a set of projects of such astounding scope and scale that some modern scholars believe it a forgery, though most accept it as genuine. Perdiccas wanted these plans quashed, but in the charged atmosphere at Babylon he could not contravene the dead Alexander without the support of the army. And so he had the document read aloud to an assembly of troops, revealing to them the intentions of their now-mummified monarch.

Alexander had wanted a thousand warships built, to be used in a campaign in the West. The coastal towns of western Asia were to supply lumber for these ships, all to be larger than the standard-size trireme with its three banks of rowers. The objective of the new fleet would be Carthage and the rest of North Africa, along with Sicily, the Iberian Peninsula, and the European coastline between them. To support the fleet, a road was to be built through North Africa as far as the Pillars of Heracles (Strait of Gibraltar), with ports and dockyards at intervals suitable for trade and naval operations. Alexander, if we believe the last plans to be genuine, was planning a second, western campaign of conquest as extensive as the first, eastern one.

Alexander further wanted the construction of vast, costly temples at sites in Greece and Macedonia. A temple to Athena, "not capable of being surpassed by any other," was to be built at Troy, the place Alexander had made a monument to Greek aspirations of foreign conquest. Great sums were to be spent on memorials to those closest to Alexander in life, his father, Philip, and his best friend, Hephaestion. Philip's tomb, the document specified, was to be built on a scale rivaling the Great Pyramid in Egypt.

Finally, and most ambitiously, Alexander's plans called for the movement of European peoples into Asia and Asians into Europe, with the goal, as Diodorus transmits it, of "bringing the two major continents, by way of intermarriages and family bonds, into a common harmony and a brotherly affection." It is hard to imagine what this plan entailed or how it would have been carried out. Clearly it represents a new and hugely ambitious stage of Alexander's cultural fusion program, an expansion to global scale of the mixed marriages at Susa.

The reading of the document allowed those present to take the full measure of the leader they had lost. It was an astonishing vision that stood behind the plans: a single world-state stretching from the Atlantic to the Indian Ocean, its cultures severed from continental moorings, its expanses knit together by roads and sea-lanes and bestrode by colossal monuments. It is a vision that inspires both wonder and terror from a distance of twenty-three hundred years, for it anticipates both the Christian New Jerusalem and the warped utopias of Fascist dictatorships.

The troops who heard the last plans, however, felt neither inspiration nor revulsion but fatigue. They had already shown in India that their stamina was the weak link in their king's dream of universal empire. Asked for its response, the army rejected the plans on the grounds that they were, in Diodorus' words, "overly grand and difficult to achieve." Most were never contemplated again.

By the simple expedient of a vote, Perdiccas brought the thirty-five-year expansion of the Macedonian empire to a halt. He would seek merely to preserve what had been won, and that task was already proving immensely difficult.

The Athenians' Last Stand (I)

The European Greek World

SUMMER—WINTER 323 B.C.

News of Alexander's death took several weeks to reach the cities of European Greece. The quickest path was across the Aegean from the ports of western Asia. Probably a ship that left those ports in mid-June, after the first reports from Babylon had arrived there, got to a European harbor by early July. Most likely that harbor was Piraeus, the busiest trade hub in the Aegean, the port that served the Greek world's foremost democracy and greatest military power—the city of Athens.

Many lives, and the collective fate of the city, would be profoundly changed by the arrival of this news. The politicians of Athens, called *rhētores,* or "public speakers," because they wielded influence by speaking in the citizens' Assembly, had defined themselves by their relationship to Alexander and Macedonian power. Some, like Demosthenes and his fiery-tongued colleague Hyperides, resented that power and itched for the chance to resist it; others, like Demades, collaborated. The most senior statesman of the day, the philosophic Phocion,* stood somewhere between

---

* "Foe-see-on" is the best of several possible pronunciations.

these extremes, grudgingly accepting Macedonian power because he thought Athens too weak to do anything else. All four men had made difficult choices over the preceding three decades, as Athens grappled with the reality of its newly humbled status. Now they faced other, harder decisions, as well as a fresh reckoning for those already made.

Not only political leaders but intellectuals as well would soon be called to account for their relations with Macedonian power. Many such thinkers, including the renowned Aristotle, had been drawn to Athens from other parts of the Greek world, attracted by the city's liberal climate and by philosophic schools like the Academy of Plato. But the fate of Plato's teacher, Socrates, had shown that the city's liberality had its limits. To be on the wrong side of a political divide during dangerous times, as Socrates was perceived to be, could, even in the Greek world's most pluralistic society, incur a death sentence.

Times were about to become dangerous once again. For the past fifteen years, the regime of Alexander and his chief agent in Europe, Antipater, though widely resented, had provided stability and certainty. It was the polestar by which the ship of state was steered. Without that fixed point of navigation, Athens was about to be set adrift amid treacherous currents and riptides. Its adult male citizens, who by their votes in the courts and Assembly decided all questions of policy, lacked a reliable compass. The speakers on whom they relied for counsel were divided on the question that had loomed throughout Alexander's reign: whether to revolt from Macedonian control and make Athens again what it had often been, superpower of Europe.

Worse, the city's two most trusted leaders were both off the scene. One had recently died: the brilliant administrator Lycurgus, who with fiscal reforms and a careful military buildup had made Athens stronger than at any time since the rise of Macedon. The other, Demosthenes, had inopportunely been driven into exile and deprived of his citizenship rights. This golden-tongued orator, the man who ordinarily would have been first to step forward in the Assembly in a time of crisis, was not there to offer the Athenians guidance just when they needed it most.

I. DEMOSTHENES (CALAURIA, JULY 323 B.C.)

For Demosthenes, this was an unbearable moment to be away from Athens. For much of his long career in politics, a career begun in boyhood with a rigorous program of public-speaking exercises, he had spoken out against the Macedonians, rallying his fellow citizens to stand up to the power to the north. In 338 he had prodded them into full-scale war, a war they had lost to Philip, Alexander's father, on the fields of nearby Chaeronea. Athens had then stood together with Thebes, the two cities combining to put some thirty thousand soldiers in the field. Demosthenes himself had been one of them, a forty-six-year-old statesman donning infantry armor for the first time. Against Philip's crack veterans, he and other green Athenian recruits never had a chance.

Thanks to Philip's generosity, Athens retained its fabled democracy after its defeat, but lost the option of setting its own foreign policy. Like most other Greek states, it was forced to join the League, a Hellenic alliance pledged to support Macedonia and accept its leadership. Philip, and then his son Alexander, dominated the League and kept Athens in line. But even while watching his city forced to truckle to the Macedonians, Demosthenes had also seen it recover and even surpass its prewar strength. And now, at the very moment Athens was most ready for a fight, a piece of news had arrived more potent than a corps of infantry. Alexander was dead.

Sadly, Demosthenes had to celebrate this news alone. When it came, he was living in exile on Calauria (modern Poros), a tiny, rocky island between Attica, Athens' home peninsula, and the Peloponnese. He had been ignominiously drummed out of Athens months earlier, exiled for the banal crime of taking illicit money. Hyperides, once his partner in opposing Macedon and his closest friend, had helped to secure his exile, using his fiery tongue to lead the prosecution at the corruption trial. Hyperides had won an easy conviction by playing the role of the injured member of a famous partnership gone sour. "You destroyed our friendship," he told Demosthenes in front of a jury of fifteen hundred Athenians. "You made yourself a laughingstock."

In exile, Demosthenes had found refuge on Calauria, in a grove sacred to Poseidon where the defenseless were supposedly protected from all harm. From here he could almost see the shores of his homeland, only thirty miles away but for him inaccessible. His empty days gave him time to ponder the upheavals no doubt taking place there. With Alexander's death, his longtime rivals Demades and Phocion would be cast down, resented for their too-close embrace of Macedon. The city would put itself on a war footing. All would turn for leadership to Hyperides, the man who had often agitated for a military showdown. Hyperides, Hyperides—it would be *his* name, not that of Demosthenes, on every Athenian's lips.

Once before, Demosthenes had seen the political game board overturned by a change of power in Macedon, and that time it was he who had benefited. King Philip, Alexander's father, had been assassinated in 336, suddenly and at the height of his powers, only two years after routing the Athenians at Chaeronea. At Athens a public celebration was decreed, with a state-sponsored sacrifice and feast; Demosthenes appeared dressed splendidly in white, with his head garlanded, even though his daughter had just died and some said he ought to have worn mourning. The new Macedonian king, he told cheering throngs, was a bumbling teenager named Alexander, a nonentity who would quickly lose his father's empire. The sense of vindication, of being on the right side of history, was exhilarating—for a few months. But then Alexander swung into action, and Athens sheepishly put its neck back into the yoke.

Now, as Demosthenes well knew, there was no second Alexander to take the place of the first, only a handful of quarrelsome generals likely to tear one another to pieces. The long Athenian nightmare of intimidation by Macedon might truly end, as it had seemed to do after Philip's demise. His city could win back the honor it had lost at Chaeronea, could beat the Macedonian army and prove to the world that Greeks were masters of barbarians, not the other way around. For Demosthenes regarded the Macedonians as barbarians, a brutish and boorish people, despite the Argeads' claims of Greek ancestry and their buying up of Greek artists and poets. "Macedon!" he had sneered to the Assembly in one of his fiery *Philippics*. "A place where you can't even procure a decent slave!"

Demosthenes could not stand and watch as a great historical moment passed him by. He made up his mind to win his way back to Athens. Eloquence and argument, always his most potent weapons, were now his best hope. He began a series of letters to the Athenians pleading for recall and offering to reconcile with his opponents. In the four letters that have survived, Demosthenes becomes by turns wheedling, outraged, self-righteous, and coldly calculating. At one moment he protests his innocence; at the next he grandly refuses to dwell on past hurts. He reaches out obliquely to Hyperides, though never mentioning his former ally by name. He tries, in every way his forty-year legal career had taught him, to convince his countrymen: *Bring me back.*

It was a short hop for these letters to be ferried over to Troezen, the nearest major port, where ships could easily be found making ready to sail for Athens.

2. PHOCION (ATHENS, JULY 323 B.C.)

At Athens, news of Alexander's death had put the city into an uproar. A man named Asclepiades was the first to bring the report; the Council of Five Hundred was quickly alerted and the people's Assembly summoned into session. No one could be sure whether to trust the news. There had been false reports before, including one twelve years earlier, in 335, that sparked a disastrous rebellion by the city of Thebes. In the Assembly many shouted that this time Alexander *was* dead, and they demanded action. It was Phocion, the city's cautious senior statesman, who stepped to the speaker's platform to dispel the sense of urgency. "If Alexander is dead today, he will still be dead tomorrow, and the day after that," he told the crowd. "We can deliberate then with more calmness and not make mistakes."

It was the same advice Phocion had given through six decades as general and politician, though the people had rarely listened. His approach toward Macedon was too moderate, too watchful of consequences, to suit their rages and passions. Once Demosthenes had taunted him by saying, "If the people ever lose their heads completely, Phocion, they will kill you." "Yes, and they'll kill *you* after they regain their sanity," Phocion replied. Demosthenes and *that* crowd—they were always beating the drum for war, never thinking of the price to be paid. Now Demosthenes was off the scene, but Hyperides, an even more rash war hawk, had the ear of the Athenians. They would make the same mistakes they had made at Chaeronea, unless Phocion and his allies could stop them.

Phocion had just barely stopped them in 335, after the false report of Alexander's death ignited the rebellion of Thebes. Demosthenes had urged Athens to support the revolt, not just with money but with an army. The Assembly thrilled with anger and excitement and was on the point of casting the die for war, but Phocion stepped forward to urge restraint. He turned angrily on Demosthenes and thundered a line from Homer's *Odyssey:*

The speaker's platform of the Pnyx at Athens, from which Demosthenes and Phocion addressed the citizen body (here captured in a nineteenth-century albumen print)

"Rash fool, why wilt thou stir the wrath of a savage?" Those words had been spoken by Odysseus' crew to stop their captain from taunting the blinded Cyclops. Odysseus did not heed the warning; he boastfully yelled to the monster his own name, up to then cleverly concealed. As a result, the entire crew later drowned in a storm sent by Poseidon, who, unbeknown to Odysseus, was the Cyclops' father. Phocion had made his point: it was the people who would pay the price, not Demosthenes, should they join the Theban revolt and the revolt fail. The Assembly pulled back at the last minute.

Alexander's revenge on Thebes was terrible. After capturing the city, he let loose the full wrath of the Macedonian army, allowing his troops to slaughter thousands in their very houses. More than thirty thousand survivors were executed or sold into slavery; an entire Greek city-state suddenly ceased to exist. From across the thirty-five miles that separated them from Thebes, the Athenians looked on in horror at the fate that could have been theirs.

Phocion had carried the day on that occasion; but had he saved Athens or doomed Thebes? Perhaps the rebellion had failed only because Phocion robbed it of support. Some Athenians may have even suspected he was serving Macedon's interests more than those of his homeland. Indeed, only a few days after the Theban cataclysm, Phocion gave ample grounds for this kind of suspicion. In a tense crisis played out before thousands in the Assembly, he showed that his politics could go beyond restraint and caution, into the realm of appeasement.

While the rubble of Thebes was still settling, Alexander, his fury not yet slaked, demanded the surrender of ten Athenian orators who had supported the rebellion. Demosthenes' name was of course at the head of the list. This was a stern test of Athens' famously liberal ideals. The city had never before, in its century and a half as a democracy, seen its freedom of speech threatened by a foreign power. But it had also never seen the obliteration of a Greek state as important, and as close by, as Thebes.

In the hush at the start of the Assembly session, the eyes of all turned to Phocion. With his triumph only days earlier in the debate over Thebes, Phocion had taken first place in the people's esteem, and he was now in a position either to save or to cast out his chief rivals. True to his severe nature, Phocion gave the Assembly stern advice: *Cast them out.* Or, better yet, he said, the men on the list could go voluntarily to Alexander, sacrificing themselves to save their city as the mythical daughters of Erechtheus had once done. Their inevitable death sentences would repay them, Phocion implied, for the troubles they had caused with their demagogy. At his peroration, he grabbed his close friend Nicocles—no doubt planted in the crowd for this purpose—and pulled the man up to the rostrum. "Athenians," he declared, "these men"—he pointed to Demosthenes and his partisans, in the crowd below him—"have so led their city astray that, even if it were my friend Nicocles here whose name was on that list, I would tell you: Give him up."

But Phocion had overplayed his hand. He had advised the Athenians not only to avoid provoking the Macedonian Cyclops but to feed it a banquet of men. With jeers of derision—a powerful weapon of protest in the Assembly—the Athenians drove him off the speaker's platform.

Demosthenes stepped up next, ready to deliver the speech of—and for—his life. Just as Phocion had done with his quotation from the *Odyssey,* Demosthenes drew on Greek legend to make his case. He reminded the Athenians of one of Aesop's tales, concerning a time when sheep were at war with wolves. The sheep held their own for a while, thanks to their alliance with the dogs, but one day the wolves asked the sheep to betray that alliance and surrender the dogs, promising peace in exchange. The sheep accepted the offer. But then, without their guardians, they were devoured by the wolves, one by one. It was a story Aesop had once used to save his own neck, when an angry barbarian king had demanded his surrender. Now Demosthenes gave it his own embellishment. Alexander, he said, was not just a wolf but a *monolycus,* a "lone wolf," the most rapacious and savage kind, an implacable killer.

The Assembly reached an impasse. The citizens would not throw their orators to the wolves, but they also would not court destruction by defying Alexander. A compromise was needed, and it was the notoriously supple and corrupt Demades who provided it. Demades, perhaps paid off by Demosthenes and the others on the list, proposed that an embassy, led by himself and Phocion, be sent to negotiate with Alexander. Perhaps the king would rescind his demand if approached by men who had treated his father's regime with reverence and had even, in the case of Demades, collaborated.

The Assembly enacted Demades' proposal, and the compromise succeeded. Mollified by the words of trusted envoys, Alexander revoked his proscription. He demanded only that one man from the ten on his list go into exile. Demades and Phocion returned to Athens in triumph; the political capital they had won made them the new leading lights in the Assembly. Demosthenes and his partisans were saved, but their policy failure left them weakened. Their voices grew more muted than before and less eagerly heard by their fellow citizens.

Thus, in 335, the question of how to deal with the Macedonians had been settled on Phocion's terms, not those of Demosthenes. The new superpower was not to be defied but bargained with, deferred to, accepted. And so it had gone for the twelve years following. When the Spartans, following in the path of Thebes, went to war in 331 to destroy Macedonian control, Athens stayed neutral, and Demosthenes stayed silent. Without the support Athens could have provided, Sparta's armies were soon crushed.

Phocion grew old, and his city grew wealthy. In 323, after twelve years of the Pax Macedonica, Phocion could look back with satisfaction at the course he had charted. He had steered his countrymen away from the shoals on which first the Thebans, then the Spartans, had wrecked themselves. Now in his late seventies, he had good hopes of finding an honorable grave in his native soil, rather than a grim pyre on some Balkan battlefield. But then the news arrived that Alexander was dead, and everything changed.

3. ARISTOTLE (ATHENS, JULY 323 B.C.)

Phocion was only one of many in Athens who had linked their fortunes to Macedonian power. The philosopher Aristotle had made Athens his home for the past twelve years, arriving, not coincidentally, just after the affair of Thebes. Under the leadership of pro-Macedonian politicians, Athens had been a congenial place for Aristotle to pursue his studies, for he was known to be the former teacher of Alexander and a close friend of old man Antipater, Alexander's surrogate in Europe. Now Athens would likely go to war against Antipater, and Aristotle would be on the wrong side.

Nicomachus, Aristotle's father, had cast his family's lot with the Macedonians many decades earlier, when he became court physician to the Argead royal family. He was a Greek doctor living in Stagira, a Greek city close to Macedon's borders, when King Amyntas learned of his skills and brought him to Pella, the Macedonian capital. Aristotle likely spent much of his childhood in Pella; he may well have played there with Philip, a boy just his own age, and formed a bond with the future king that would one day lead to the most famous tutoring assignment in history.

In 367, when Aristotle was seventeen, he left Macedonia and moved to Athens, to study at Plato's renowned philosophic institute. He stayed in Athens for the next two decades, years that saw growing Athenian mistrust of Macedon—mistrust that spiked in 351 when Demosthenes launched a series of vitriolic speeches against Philip, by then the Macedonians' king. Aristotle, as a noncitizen, could not enter the Pnyx, where the Assembly met, but he could listen from an adjoining hillside as the man he had grown up with was vilified. Athens' mistrust of Philip turned to rage in 347, after the Macedonians destroyed its ally Olynthus, a northern Greek city that stood in their expansionist path. Plato died that same year, and Aristotle left Athens, partly because leadership of the Academy had changed but also because the city had become an uncomfortable place for friends of Philip's regime.

Aristotle crossed the Aegean to Atarneus, a Greek city in western Anatolia, where a man named Hermias, an admirer of Plato and a patron of philosophy, had come to power. Hermias helped support Aristotle's scientific work, and a warm friendship sprang up between the philosopher and the potentate—a bond greatly strengthened after Aristotle married Hermias' niece and adopted daughter, Pythias. Aristotle, now forty, had reached what seemed an ideal haven for his studies, surrounded by fellow scientists and protected by a powerful father-in-law, in a land far from the tensions of Europe. But Macedonian power was still growing, and reaching toward Asia. Philip, by now the most powerful ruler in

Europe, was laying plans for an attack on the Persian empire (the plans that would later be executed by his son Alexander). Hermias, whose territory lay in the path of this invasion, made a secret pact to aid Philip. Quite possibly he colluded with his son-in-law Aristotle, whom he knew to be a fellow supporter of the Macedonian cause.

The Persians somehow got wind of Hermias' machinations. They captured him by trickery and tortured him to get information. Aristotle, perhaps fearing he would be named as a co-conspirator, had by this time gone to Lesbos, safely offshore, to study marine life in the lagoons there. Eventually he received a message from Hermias, who by then was dead, saying that in his last hour he had done "nothing unworthy of philosophy," meaning he had not implicated others, even on the rack. Aristotle was deeply grieved by his father-in-law's fate and moved by his courage. He composed a hymn in honor of Hermias' virtue and had a cenotaph put on display at the religious center of Delphi, where it would be seen by visitors from all Greece—reverent tributes that, he little guessed, would come back to harm him long afterward.

Aristotle spent several years completing field research on Lesbos and then returned to Macedonia, at King Philip's express invitation, to become tutor to Prince Alexander. So began a student-teacher pairing that would become enshrined in Western myth as a longed-for alliance of supreme power and supreme intellect. But whatever the truth about this relationship—evidence suggests it was in fact slight—a warm friendship grew between Aristotle and Antipater, Philip's trusted general and right-hand man. Antipater was at this time in his fifties, already the father of ten children, author of a historical treatise, hero of many wars, and an accomplished counselor and diplomat. To Aristotle, about fifteen years younger, he must have looked like an ideal soldier-statesman, a man whose noble nature was written in his loyal service to King Philip. In later life Aristotle maintained a warm correspondence with Antipater, and a few snippets of their letters survive, speaking, in the words of the great Aristotle scholar Werner Jaeger, "the language of unhesitating mutual trust."

In 340 Aristotle's royal teaching commission ended, but just what he did for the next five years—the years that saw Philip's defeat of Athens and Thebes at Chaeronea and Alexander's total destruction of the latter city—is unclear. Perhaps he remained in Macedonia and used his influence to soften anger against Athens, for the Athenians at some point honored him with a stone inscription thanking him for advocacy at Philip's court. It was one of two such inscribed tributes Aristotle is known to have received. Much later he went to Delphi with his grandnephew Callisthenes and conducted a remarkable research project: together, the two men compiled a list of victors in the quadrennial Pythian Games going back as far as records existed. The gratitude of the governing board of Delphi was recorded on a splendid engraved stone, along with instructions that their list, an invaluable chronological resource, be publicly displayed in a temple. This honorific stone was found in the nineteenth century, in fragments, lying in an unlikely place, at the bottom of an ancient well.

After the crushing of Thebes and the cowing of Alexander's opponents, Aristotle returned to Athens, where in his twenties and thirties he had studied with Plato in a grove sacred to the hero Academus. Now reaching his fifties, he was ready to become the kind of teacher and guide Plato had been for his younger self. But leadership of the Academy was already spoken for; and in any case, Aristotle was no longer entranced by the abstractions he had once debated there, the Forms of things like Goodness and Justice shining down from a distant realm. Increasingly, he wanted to focus on the world around him, the world accessed by experiment rather than Zen-like contemplation. Aristotle set up a new school in a different grove, the Lyceum, and started lecturing to different students. In time, he had a building constructed there and filled it with maps, specimens, and documents—a place to study things that are, rather than those that could or should be.

For twelve years Aristotle lectured in the Lyceum, addressing his students in the morning and the general public in the after-noon. He taught biology, geography, political science, rhetoric, physics, and the science of the human soul. Once he even spoke on comic and tragic drama, art forms invented by the Athenians, explaining how they worked and how to perfect them. He spoke from outlines, and it is these notes that have come down to us as his "writings," for he had long before this ceased to write for publication. The written word, as far as Aristotle was concerned—in this he agreed with Plato—was powerless to convey knowledge.

During these twelve years, while the Athenians followed Phocion's policy of entente with Alexander, Aristotle had not needed to worry that he was, in Athenian eyes at least, a Macedonian. The dark looks he must have received from Demosthenes' partisans did not matter, for he was a friend of Antipater and anyone who harmed him would have to answer to that powerful general or even to Alexander himself.

But now Alexander was dead, and Aristotle's umbrella of security was deteriorating. His friendship with Antipater was now a mark against him, and those active in politics were quick to use it. Dark charges were flung at him in the Assembly: it was alleged that more than twenty years earlier, he had informed on wealthy citizens of Olynthus and had thus given Philip a pretext to seize their estates. An Athenian named Himeraeus, a fierce anti-Macedonian, took it upon himself to ascend the Acropolis, wrench up the stone tablet recording the city's gratitude to Aristotle, and hurl it down onto the rocks below. In Delphi, meanwhile, the stone inscribed with praises for Aristotle and Callisthenes was similarly destroyed, broken up and tossed down the well from which it was eventually recovered.

Aristotle wrote to Antipater about the annulment of his Delphic honors, and, by purest chance, a quotation from that letter survives. "I don't care too much, but I don't *not* care," Aristotle told his oldest friend. It is the candid confession of a thoughtful man, near the end of life, watching his reputation get systematically destroyed.

One other quotation survives from Aristotle's letters to Antipater, also (to judge by the content) from the period following Alexander's death. "It's dangerous for an immigrant to stay in Athens," Aristotle wrote.

4. HYPERIDES (ATHENS, JULY 323 B.C.)

But there were others in Athens, among them the fiery rhetorician Hyperides, in whose eyes Alexander could not have picked a bet-

ter time to die. Athens was ready for war as never before. Better
yet, from Hyperides' perspective, the leadership of the city had
recently changed, leaving *him* the sole head of the anti-
Macedonian cause. His former partner Demosthenes had been
drummed out months before, denounced by Hyperides himself at
a sensational corruption trial. After decades of standing in
Demosthenes' shadow, Hyperides would finally get to call the
shots—and those shots would be aimed right at the heart of
Macedon.

Events seemed to have come together as if guided by gods
who were favoring the city's fortunes. Both resources and opportunity for revolt had arrived at just the same moment, without
Athens doing anything to summon them. To understand how this
happened, to see the moment of Alexander's death as Hyperides
saw it, requires us to look back about two years from July 323. The
chain of events that seemed to promise total victory for Athens
began then, when Alexander, forced to halt by the mutiny of his
troops, had begun his long trek back from the far-off land of
India.

Harpalus Arrives in Athens

By invading India, Alexander seemed to many to have left the
known world behind, and during his absence some of his satraps
acted as though he would not return. Alexander had given them
small armies, but many began to hire Greek mercenaries as well,
an obvious effort to build power. They extorted money from their
subjects to pay for these troops, or skimmed off cash from imperial treasuries. Alexander returned from India very displeased by
what he found. He ordered all satraps to release their mercenaries
and took steps to punish abuses. Those who had committed the
worst offenses fled before Alexander's agents arrived, and among
these was one who was in especially grave trouble, an old and close
friend of Alexander's, a highborn Macedonian named Harpalus.

Harpalus is a unique figure in Alexander's inner circle, no soldier but a hedonist, a sensualist, and a lover of women. Disabled
from birth, he was useless on the battlefield but nonetheless stood
high in Alexander's affections. Even after Harpalus stole imperial

funds and ran away from the Asian campaign, in its early stages, Alexander forgave his old friend, sent envoys to cajole him back to Asia, and put him in charge of the empire's largest treasury, in Babylon. Here, in a city famous for loose morals and sensual delights, Harpalus lost his bearings. He spent wildly on his own pleasures and on gifts for imported Greek courtesans. When Alexander returned from the East, Harpalus was terrified. Once before he had obtained pardon, but this time escape was his only hope.

Because he had sent them grain during a shortage years before, Harpalus had received honorary citizenship from the Athenians, and so, in the spring of 324, he fled Babylon for Athens. He sailed for Piraeus, the Athenian harbor, with a fleet of thirty warships, a powerful force of six thousand mercenary soldiers, and a fortune in embezzled money. He let it be known by messengers that he would use this army and these funds to help Athens revolt from Macedonian control.

But did Athens want to revolt? As Harpalus and his fleet waited off Attica for permission to dock, the Assembly met to consider its options. Debate proceeded along familiar lines: the war hawks spoke in favor of admitting Harpalus, while the entente party, Phocion and his ilk, argued that the danger to Athens would be too great. Demosthenes, unaccountably, switched sides from his customary alignment. The man who had roused his countrymen to fight at Chaeronea fifteen years before, and who had urged them to fight at Thebes, now said that the time was not ripe for war. He said that Harpalus should be sent away, and his support carried the motion.

Hyperides and the other hawks were aghast at this seeming betrayal, and at the thought that Harpalus' flotilla, with its fabulous cargo of military might, would be allowed to pass Athens by. As Harpalus raised sail and headed for Taenaron, at the tip of the Peloponnese, it must have seemed to Hyperides that Athens was destined always to be under the thumb of Macedon and never regain its former glory. But there were other reasons, arising from just the place Harpalus was heading, for Hyperides and his partisans to live in hope.

Leosthenes at Taenaron

Alexander's order disbanding personal armies produced a wave of unemployed Greek mercenaries. Alexander intended to hire many himself, but before he could do so, some crossed the Aegean and landed in Taenaron, where sheer distance from Macedonia, and the buffer provided by Sparta, placed them beyond Alexander's control. Mercenaries returning from all parts of Asia found safe haven in this no-man's-land. In a short time Taenaron was bustling with thousands of them, enough for a sizable army, were they to come together under one leader. And just such a leader emerged in Taenaron in 324: a swashbuckling captain named Leosthenes, an Athenian who had spent his life among the Macedonians—his father had been exiled from Athens decades earlier and had gone to the court of King Philip—but who had, for reasons unknown, become a die-hard foe of Alexander.

Some at Athens, including Hyperides, noted with interest that the captain general of the Taenaron troops was Athenian (by birth at least). For they were aware by early 324 of an edict Alexander was about to issue at that summer's Olympic Games and of the disastrous effect it would have on their city. Hyperides and the war hawks at Athens kept in secret contact with Leosthenes as they awaited the edict's announcement. They could foresee that its terms, if not softened by Alexander, might very well push Athens into war with Macedon, despite any arguments that Phocion and the entente party might raise.

The Exiles' Decree and Harpalus' Return

The Olympic Games of the summer of 324 were unusually crowded. The ranks of attendees were swollen by more than twenty thousand Greek exiles, people thrown out of their home cities for various misdeeds or banished by political enemies. These exiles came not so much to watch the games as to hear the reading of a letter from Alexander, the contents of which had already been rumored in Greece for several tense months. The pronouncement it contained is known today as the Exiles' Decree.

The Olympics were not normally a venue for edicts, but this was no ordinary edict. It represented Alexander's first attempt to set policy for the entire Greek world, not by way of hirelings or puppets, but with his own words. Such arbitrary use of power violated the charter the Greeks had made with Philip fifteen years earlier. They were supposed to make their own laws by votes of the League, not receive them from a distant dictator. But the exiles in the stadium at Olympia had come to cheer this edict. By its terms they would be returned to their homes, homes not seen, in some cases, for decades.

Also in the crowd that day was Demosthenes, himself (though he could not know it) soon to become an exile. He too had come to hear the letter read and then to do all in his power to get Athens exempted from its terms. His city had sent him as its envoy in a bid to keep its proudest overseas possession, the island of Samos. Athens had exiled the native Samians several decades earlier, replacing them with its own citizens in a forcible landgrab. Under the new decree these refugees would be returned and Athens would give the place up.

Alexander had entrusted the reading of his letter to Nicanor, a Greek who enjoyed high standing in the Hellenic world—he was (almost certainly) Aristotle's nephew and adopted son—and high rank in Alexander's army as well. As the crowd hushed, Nicanor took his place at the center of the stadium and declaimed his message. "King Alexander thus addresses the exiles from the Greek cities: It is not we who have caused your flight, but we shall be the cause of your return." A roar went up from the crowd, the voices of twenty thousand exiles celebrating in unison their miraculous deliverance. Demosthenes and his fellow Athenian envoys, however, had little cause to cheer. Their concern was not the public form of the decree but whether Alexander, through his representative Nicanor, was willing to bargain in private.

Demosthenes had another matter to negotiate with Nicanor as well, less momentous perhaps but more urgent: the problem of Harpalus. The Macedonian renegade had returned to Athens some weeks before, though he was turned away on his first approach. This time Harpalus came as a suppliant, seeking protection under religious law, with only two ships and a modest sum of money (still a fortune by Athenian standards). He had gained admittance to the city, probably by bribing the harbormaster in charge of keeping him out. Messengers had soon arrived from the Macedonians, demanding that Harpalus be handed over and his stolen cash returned. On Demosthenes' advice, the Athenians put Harpalus under house arrest until terms of extradition could be arranged. The embezzled money, seven hundred talents (according to Harpalus' accounting), was moved to the treasury for safekeeping, and a negotiating team was selected, with Demosthenes at its head.

Demosthenes found himself in the same role Demades and Phocion had played twelve years earlier, when his own fate was hanging in the balance. Now it was he who advised against confrontation, who sought a moderate path, who agreed to sup with the Macedonian devil. He met with Nicanor in a private enclave at Olympia. What passed between them was kept secret, but the route to a solution was clear enough, since Athens wanted Samos and Macedon wanted Harpalus. Some sort of trade-off was arranged, though final say over the fate of Samos was reserved for Alexander himself.

There was yet another delicate issue that was no doubt discussed at that meeting. For the previous year, the Athenians (and other Greeks) had debated whether to worship Alexander as a god. Most of them found it a repugnant idea, and they punished one of its sponsors, Demades, with a heavy fine. But Demosthenes was a pragmatist, not a religious purist. When he returned to Athens from Olympia, he told the Athenians, "Let him be the son of Zeus, and of Poseidon too if he wants," disguising with dismissive irony his obvious capitulation. If he had bargained with Nicanor over divinization, as seems likely, he at least got a good price. Athens had been granted a stay of the Exiles' Decree, a pause in which to present its case to Alexander in Babylon. The policy of entente, this time as practiced by Demosthenes, had borne fruit once again.

Hyperides, who hated Alexander as either a man or a god, had once again seen his cause betrayed by Demosthenes' inexplicable compliance. The fortunes of the anti-Macedonian party seemed once again to be at low ebb. But the turbulent eddies of Athenian politics had taught Hyperides never to trust in the status quo; things would always change. And in the summer of 324, quite suddenly, they did.

The Bribery Scandal at Athens

Shortly after Demosthenes' return from Olympia, Harpalus escaped from his guards and fled Athens. Who helped him escape, and why, are unclear; many stood to gain from the disappearance of the most wanted man on earth. No one was ever blamed or charged, so presumably all factions were content to see him go. But the money Harpalus left behind was a different matter. These seven hundred talents, stolen from Alexander's treasury and seized by Athens as contraband, had been held in escrow for weeks, but when state officials went to examine the stash, they found only three hundred fifty. Athens went into full crisis mode. Charges and countercharges flew around the city, as politicians accused one another of pocketing the loot. And among those most sternly accused was Demosthenes.

The influence of money on politics had always been accepted, even joked about, as a fixture of Athenian democracy. One public speaker laughed at a poet who had won an award for reciting his verses, saying that *he* could earn ten times as much, from King Philip, for keeping quiet. But the missing half of Harpalus' embezzled funds caused deep anxiety. This was money that belonged to Alexander; the Macedonians had already demanded it back; Athens' fate, especially the question of control of Samos, lay in Alexander's hands. Someone would have to pay the price for the money's disappearance, and Demosthenes was among those selected. The man's recent changes of stance, his sudden willingness to oppose revolt and support Alexander worship, the suspicious sore throat that he claimed prevented him from debating a provocative measure in the Assembly—all this evidence seemed to show that Demosthenes had been bribed.

Hyperides had reason to welcome the idea that his old friend and ally, more recently the turncoat who had abandoned him, might finally fall from grace. Hyperides' fight for freedom from Macedon—once Demosthenes' fight too—might flourish, along with his own political fortunes, if his great colleague was forced from the scene. So Hyperides joined those attacking Demosthenes as a liar and a taker of bribes. He made it clear to the public that he had split from his onetime partner, and they elected him to lead the prosecutorial team.

After a six-month investigation produced the expected indictments, including that of Demosthenes, Athens prepared to watch a thrilling spectacle of political blood sport. Hyperides, the second-greatest orator of the day, was about to turn all his rhetorical weapons on the greatest, his own lifelong friend.

"Don't you dare talk to me of friendship," Hyperides fumed in his speech (partly recovered from a tattered roll of papyrus that turned up in Egypt in 1847). "You yourself destroyed that friendship when you took money to oppose your country's interests and changed sides. You made a laughingstock of yourself. You cast shame on those who, in former times, chose to go along with your policies. To think that together we might have been most glorious in the eyes of the people . . . But you have overturned all that." Hyperides spared nothing in his caricature of Demosthenes' venality. He reduced the man's career to one long quest for bribes. Demosthenes had supported the Theban revolt, said Hyperides, only because he was bought and paid for by Persian gold. Then he had doomed that revolt to failure by pocketing money meant for Thebes.

The rhetorical jabs hit their mark. Demosthenes was convicted, along with only one other defendant, Demades, long notorious both for corruption and for aiding the Macedonians. It was a catastrophe for Demosthenes' political career and a deep humiliation. The Athenians fined him fifty talents, a sum he would be unable to pay unless he revealed that he did in fact have Harpalus' missing money. When he did not pay, he was imprisoned, but friends, and no doubt bribes, helped him get out of jail and into exile.

At about the same moment, word arrived from Babylon. Alexander had rejected the pleas of the Athenian envoys. Samos was to be returned to the Samians. Athens hoped to petition him a second time but never got the chance. Three months later, he was dead.

5. THE OUTBREAK OF WAR (ATHENS AND NORTHERN
GREECE, AUTUMN 323 B.C.)

Even after reports of Alexander's death were confirmed, revolt was not an easy choice for the Athenians. Those with money and property, who would principally foot the bill for the war, did not want to fight. Their lot had improved in the last twelve years, and promised to get better yet if the Pax Macedonica were sustained. Then there were the arguments of Phocion to reckon with. Phocion, as usual, did not think Athens strong enough for war. An experienced military man, now almost eighty with more than forty years of generalship, Phocion had the ear of those disinclined to take risks. Hyperides, who chafed for war, had often despaired at Phocion's cautiousness. "When will you *ever* advise Athens to fight?" he challenged the old man before the Assembly. "When I see the young men willing to keep in formation, the rich to pay war taxes, and the politicians to stop stealing from the treasury," the high-minded Phocion replied, lording it over those implicated in the recent bribery scandal.

Now, though, Hyperides had a way to trump Phocion's caution. Into the Assembly he brought Leosthenes, the mercenary captain of Taenaron, who had secretly been on the Athenian payroll for several months. Here was a general who had all the swagger Phocion lacked, who commanded thousands of mercenaries, men with experience fighting under, or against, the Macedonians. And here was the money to pay for that army: the stash of 350 talents still left on the Acropolis. Alexander's stolen hoard, though mysteriously reduced by half, could now at last serve the purpose for which Harpalus had brought it, revolt from Macedon.

The Athenians were wild with enthusiasm. In a flurry of votes the Assembly elected Leosthenes a state military commander, mobilized all citizens up to age forty, and dispatched envoys to the rest of Greece to seek alliances. The goal of the coming war, according to the Assembly's decrees, was "the common freedom of the Greeks and the liberation of the garrisoned cities," the places guarded by hated Macedonian detachments. A team was sent to northern Greece to make common cause with the powerful Aetolian League. The Aetolians had just as much reason as the Athenians to stop enforcement of the Exiles' Decree: some years earlier they had seized a neighboring city and expelled its inhabitants, just as the Athenians had expelled the Samians. The Aetolians promised to add their troops to Leosthenes' core force of five thousand Athenian infantry and five hundred cavalry, plus almost twice as many hired mercenaries.

Most Athenians rushed to get behind Hyperides and the war party, but Phocion remained cool. Some citizens tauntingly asked him whether he was impressed by the city's armed forces. In reply Phocion invoked a comparison from the Greek athletic games. "They are good enough for the *stadion*," he said, referring to a sprint of about two hundred yards, "but it's the *dolichos* of war I fear"—a footrace several miles in length. Athens was throwing all its ships, soldiers, and money into a single attack force, he said; were these defeated, there would be no reserves to draw on. He might have added rowers to this list, the power supply of Greek battleships. In the end it was rowers, more than any other resource, on which the outcome of the war would hang.

Despite his contrarian views, Phocion's long military record made him valuable to the Athenians. They could not leave him without a command. They appointed him to lead the home guard, the force that would meet a seaborne invasion of Attica were the Macedonians somehow to get past Athens' expert navy. In that post, within sight of Athens' walls, Phocion could help the war effort without getting in the way of Leosthenes. For the two men disliked and mistrusted each other and had sparred bitterly in the Assembly. In a recent debate Leosthenes had challenged Phocion, a man twice his age, to say what good *he* had done for the Athenians in all his many generalships. "Do you think it no boon that they're buried here, in civilian graves?" the old man replied.

6. ARISTOTLE (ATHENS, AUTUMN 323 B.C.)

While Athens was bustling with mobilization for war, a quieter scene was taking place in the Lyceum outside the city's east gate. Aristotle was making ready to leave.

The wolf pack of Athenian public life, those who advanced or got rich from denouncing others, had been drawing ever-tighter circles around him. Now that Alexander was dead, they were snarling and baying for his blood. They hated Aristotle for his ties to old man Antipater and the Macedonian elite, ties recently revealed by the fact that Nicanor, Aristotle's adopted son, had been chosen to read out the Exiles' Decree. But they chose to attack the philosopher on private and religious, not political, grounds. It was Aristotle's devotion to his father-in-law, Hermias, the petty king tortured and killed by the Persians almost twenty years earlier, that gave his enemies the means to blacken his name.

Hermias was easily demonized by Athenian gossip. He was rumored (perhaps falsely) to be a barbarian and a eunuch, and a former slave, yet he had philosophic ambitions and was friends with many of Plato's former students. He thus conjured up stereotypes of both the effeminate Asian and the effete, high-minded intellectual, a grotesque combination. Above all, he had taken the Macedonian side when war loomed between Philip and the Persians. Aristotle's marriage to this man's daughter, Pythias—long dead, but called to mind by their daughter, also named Pythias—could be exploited as proof of moral baseness and philo-Macedonian tendencies.

Aristotle had set up a cenotaph for Hermias in Delphi, inscribed with verses of his own composition. A cruel parodist by the name of Theocritus, an inveterate Macedonian hater, now came forward with a mock epitaph in the same meter:

For Hermias the eunuch, the slave of Eubulus,
Empty-headed Aristotle built this empty tomb.
He honored the lawless ways of the belly, and so moved his home
From the Academy to rivers running with filth.

The second two lines ostensibly describe Hermias but are framed ambiguously so as to refer to Aristotle as well. Theocritus knew a good smear opportunity when he saw one. He neatly grafted onto Aristotle—hardly intemperate in his personal habits—a caricature of Hermias as a corpulent, depraved barbarian.

Aristotle's other tribute to Hermias, a fourteen-line poem celebrating the courage of his dead father-in-law, brought even more trouble down on the philosopher's head. The poem took the form of a hymn addressed to Virtue, personified as a goddess, the shining ideal for which Hermias, according to the final two lines, had died. Like all such hymns, the poem was set to music, and Aristotle saw that it was regularly performed, on some anniversary perhaps, by students at his philosophic school. But such a ritual was easily distorted by enemies into a weird, cultic rite of worship. One such attacker, a religious official named Eurymedon, used the poem to indict Aristotle for impiety, claiming it showed a belief in new gods. The charge was eerily similar to the one the Athenians had used to indict Socrates, and put him to death, nearly eight decades earlier.

Aristotle wrote a defense speech for his trial—the first Greek known to have done so, rather than relying on a hired speechwriter—but in the end chose not to find out whether Athenian juries were more enlightened than in the days of Socrates. Writing to his friend Antipater that he "would not let the Athenians sin twice against philosophy," he gathered up his family and left. He headed for an estate on the island of Euboea that had once belonged to his mother. It was a place he had seldom if ever seen, but the city that had been his childhood home, Stagira, had been destroyed long before, a casualty of Macedon's imperial ambitions. Why he did not go to Macedonia itself, where Antipater would have gladly received him, is unclear.

The Lyceum, his students, his researches, all he had built over the past twelve years, Aristotle left in the hands of Theophrastus, a brilliant botanist who had studied with him since his time in Asia Minor. He could only hope that this young man, who like him had lived well off the patronage of Hermias, would escape calumnies and racial hatred, the dark forces now making his own life in Athens impossible.

7. THE HELLENIC WAR (NORTHERN GREECE, AUTUMN 323 B.C.)

Leosthenes' primary objective was the pass at Thermopylae, the narrow corridor between mountains and sea that connected central Greece with the North. The place was not only strategically but symbolically important. Here, more than 150 years earlier, the Greeks had fought off for days a huge Persian invasion force led by King Xerxes. After all hope of holding the pass was lost, most of the Greeks pulled out, but a band of three hundred Spartans, along with eleven hundred allies from other Greek cities, remained and fought until almost all were slain. Thermopylae had thereafter become a shrine to Hellenic freedom. The monument erected there reminded the Greeks of the high cost of standing up to aggressors. Now, it seemed, they were prepared once again to pay that price.

To underscore what was at stake, the Greeks dubbed their fight against Antipater "the Hellenic War." The name cast the fight as a sequel to that glorious struggle against the Persians. Once again, the Greek cities were in league, fighting to defend their shared Hellenism. Their opponents, by simple logic, must be "barbarians." No matter that the Macedonians too had cloaked themselves in the mantle of Hellenism, portraying their invasion of the Persian empire as retribution for the invasion by Xerxes. The coming war, the Greeks hoped, would redraw the racial boundaries that recent decades had blurred.

Just as in the war against Xerxes, however, the Boeotians, those dwelling in the region around Thebes, held aloof from the Greek cause. They had benefited from the destruction of the regional superpower and now occupied its former land. Were the Macedonians to be defeated, Thebes would be refounded, and the Boeotians would forfeit their spoils. Leosthenes had to fight these holdouts first in order to effect a juncture with Aetolian forces to their north, a sizable contingent of seven thousand men. Once this was accomplished, the combined Greek armies moved into position at Thermopylae. It was the most potent force assembled in Greece since the time of the Persian Wars—more than thirty thousand soldiers, and many of them, unlike in earlier fights against the Macedonians, battle-hardened veterans.

On came Antipater, with a force much smaller than that of the Greeks, perhaps only thirteen thousand. His manpower had been badly drained over the years as Alexander, from Asia, had several times demanded fresh recruits. His best hope lay in his

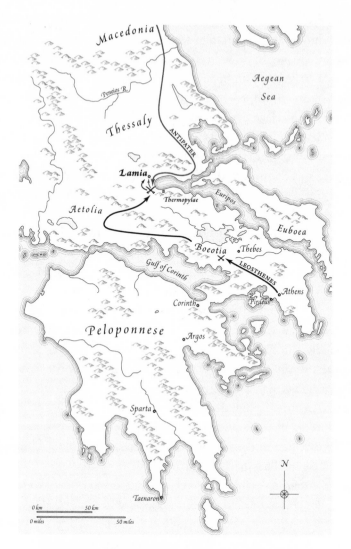

Movements of forces in the first phase of the Hellenic War,
resulting in the siege of Lamia

cavalry, always Macedon's most potent striking weapon, and in
the similarly powerful cavalry of the Thessalians, the stalwart
Greek allies on his southern border. On his march through Thessaly, Antipater levied enough cavalrymen that he was satisfied he
could beat Leosthenes with his horse. Then he hastened to Thermopylae to seek battle.

But Leosthenes had been in secret contact with the Thessalians, urging them to throw their support to the Greek cause.

They were Greeks too, his messengers argued, despite their long alliance with Macedon. They could swing the fortunes of war at the critical moment and crush Antipater for good. As the two armies formed their lines and made ready to join battle, the Thessalians declared who they were. Their cavalry galloped over to Leosthenes' side of the field, defecting to the Greeks.

Leosthenes now held the upper hand, and both sides knew it. Antipater tried a ruse to make his forces appear greater, filling the back lines of his cavalry ranks with troops mounted on donkeys, but such measures could only buy him time. After a brief trial engagement, Antipater bowed to necessity. He led a retreat to a nearby Thessalian city, Lamia, and took it by surprise attack. Then he shut himself and his troops behind its formidable walls.

Lamia was too strongly fortified for the Greeks to storm, though they made several attempts. Its walls were thick and topped by batteries of the Macedonians' superb missile-firing weapons. Some Greek troops, including the Aetolians, became discouraged and departed for home. But Leosthenes' fallback strategy was a promising one. Building a perimeter wall and a ditch around the town, he settled in for a siege. He would wait for hunger to take its inevitable toll on the men inside. It was not a glorious tactic but routine and reliable. All Leosthenes had to do was finish his wall, hold his position, and interdict all supplies, and within a few months the war would be won.

8. DEMOSTHENES (SOUTHERN GREECE AND ATHENS, WINTER 323 B.C.)

Back in Athens, Leosthenes' victory was celebrated with festivals and sacrifices to the gods. The city's new general had achieved a coup that had eluded the Greeks for three decades, the intimidation of a Macedonian army in open battle. Antipater had flinched, and had now put himself in a very tight spot indeed.

Those who had supported the war crowed over the success of their policy. One of them twitted Phocion for his caution, asking whether *he* would be pleased to have done what Leosthenes did. "Naturally I would," said the old warrior, unshaken, "but I'm also pleased with my former advice." Phocion had a more skeptical view of Leosthenes' position than the rest of the city. In reply to the buoyant dispatches that kept arriving from Lamia, he is said to have asked, with weary irony, "I wonder, will we *ever* stop winning?"

With old man Antipater bottled up in Lamia and Leosthenes proving his brilliance, the Athenians sent out new diplomatic missions in the autumn of 323. Sieges, if pursued to conclusion, were lengthy affairs and required huge commitments of money and manpower. Hyperides was dispatched to the Peloponnese to lobby for greater support. Thousands of troops would need to be paid for many more months of service, and the coffers of Athens, even after Harpalus' stolen money had topped them off, were not adequate for the job.

On his way south, Hyperides was reunited with someone he never expected to see again, in life at any rate.

Demosthenes, the fallen Athenian statesman, had followed the war through letters that reached him on Calauria. He knew from informants that envoys of Athens would soon make their way to the Peloponnese. He may even have known that his ally-turned-persecutor, Hyperides, was among those envoys. If so, he chose to forget his wounds and reach out to his old friend. Calauria was separated from the Peloponnese by a narrow channel, only a few hundred feet wide; perhaps, he must have reckoned, the gulf between himself and Hyperides could be crossed as easily.

Demosthenes left Calauria and intercepted Hyperides en route, offering to lend his rhetorical talents to the Athenian diplomatic mission. Officially, Hyperides should never have considered such an offer. The Athenians had stripped Demosthenes of citizen rights such that he wasn't allowed to vote, never mind serve in government. But Athenian rules, always pliable, were even more easily bent in wartime, and breaches were also more easily healed. Hyperides embraced as a partner the man whose conviction he had secured only months before.

Demosthenes had found his route back home. When the Athenians learned of his efforts on their behalf, they happily recalled him from exile and sent a state warship to pick him up. The entire city turned out for his landing in the harbor of Piraeus. Demosthenes used the occasion to publicly thank the gods and invoked the memory of Alcibiades, the great Athenian military leader of the previous century. Recalled from banishment after winning great victories as a privateer, Alcibiades had sailed into Piraeus leading two hundred captured galleys, yet not even he, Demosthenes claimed, had been so wholeheartedly welcomed back into the body politic.

It was a total restoration, beyond what the great orator had pleaded for from exile, beyond what he could have expected or hoped. In his letters from Calauria, he had sought a mere extension of the due date for his fifty-talent fine; he said he would try to collect fees owed to him and make a partial, initial payment. The Athenians had refused even that modest request. Now they eagerly took care of the entire sum on his behalf. By decree of the Assembly, Demosthenes was appointed to a minor religious office and awarded a salary of exactly fifty talents.

With victory over Macedon seemingly imminent, money, and forgiveness, could be freely extended. Athens was ready to reclaim its ancient glory, with its most illustrious leader back at the helm.

4

Resistance, Rebellion, Reconquest

Asia and North Africa

SUMMER 323–SUMMER 322 B.C.

News of Alexander's death traveled outward from Babylon like shock waves from an earthquake. In all likelihood, it was the fastest- and farthest-moving piece of news the world had yet received. Millions heard it within a week's time. Recent discoveries of dated records near Idumaea, beside the Dead Sea, show that Alexander's death was reported there only six days after it occurred.

The news went out along communications lines set up by the Persians and still functioning under Macedonian rule. Criers stationed on hilltops, spaced at the limits of earshot, called it to each other, sending it in one day's time the distance of a month's travel. Mounted couriers, called *astandai* in Persian, carried it at a gallop from one way station to the next, relaying it at each one to a fresh rider atop a fresh horse.

Swiftest of all were the fire beacons that raced along spoke-like lines to the main Persian capitals, Susa and Persepolis. By manipulating poles on which the fires were displayed, the relay crews could transmit coded messages. Almost certainly this system brought word of Alexander's death to Susa during the night of June 11, for Alexander died not long before nightfall on that day, and Babylon was only a few hundred miles from Susa.

At Susa (as far as we know) dwelled much of what remained of the Persian royal family, including two princesses who were now Alexander's widows, Parysatis and Stateira. Also there was Stateira's grandmother, Sisygambis. All three had been captured by Alexander ten years earlier, after the defeat of Sisygambis' son, Darius, at the battle of Issus. Following royal tradition, Darius had brought his family with him and parked them close to the battlefield but took no measures to secure their safety; the Persians had no experience of losing battles on their own territory. After Darius and his officers fled from Issus, Alexander coolly rounded up his royal prisoners, treating the women with a deference that became legendary and sending them to Susa to live as royalty once again. He was particularly kind to Sisygambis, addressing her as "Mother" and refusing to sit in her presence until asked, the same mark of respect a highborn Persian would pay to the woman who bore him.

When in his last year of life Alexander wed Stateira and Parysatis, the granddaughter and grandniece of Sisygambis, the old woman saw her family's fortunes miraculously restored. Though once a prisoner who could expect enslavement or worse, she was again the matriarch of a ruling family. She had every hope of seeing a great-grandson inherit her son's throne and rule Asia as Darius had done, along with much of Europe and North Africa—an empire that had been expanded, not diminished, by defeat.

That hope was dashed, however, by news of Alexander's death. Now Sisygambis' star was sinking again. She knew enough about dynastic politics to foresee what lay in store. Her widowed granddaughter would be easy prey for enemies and rivals (indeed, in Babylon, Perdiccas and Rhoxane would shortly murder Stateira, as we have seen). Without male relatives to look to for protection—purges within her own family had wiped these out— she would be little more than a household slave to the Macedonians. The prospect of facing old age in dishonor was more than Sisygambis could bear. On the night of Alexander's death she stopped taking food and drink, a resolute, slow-motion suicide. In five days she was dead.

Elsewhere in Susa and other great cities of the Iranian plateau, the Persians began the solemn rituals of state mourning. Though Alexander had come as an invader, he was by this time the only king they had, and they marked his passing reverently. Men shaved their heads and donned funereal clothing. At altars across the land, the sacred fire of the Zoroastrian faith, fueled night and day by attendant priests, was extinguished, a sign that the energies that gave life to the cosmos had come to a halt.

The final rite in the Persian cycle of mourning was the slow passage of the king's body through the kingdom, with stops along the way to allow subjects to lament. Alexander's body too would be carried in such a procession, the generals in Babylon ultimately decided. Its destination, though, became a matter of dispute. Alexander had expressed a wish to be buried near the oracular shrine of the god Ammon, west of Egypt, but at some point his request was overridden by the governing regime in Babylon. In life, Alexander had exerted astounding control over his empire and those who ran it; in death, his corpse could again be an instrument of control to those who gave it burial. Such a precious resource could not be wasted in a remote North African desert.

The criers cried, the horses raced, and the beacons flared, bringing news of Alexander's death across the two million square miles of the empire. The report eventually reached all the king's men—satraps, garrison chiefs, and finance ministers who governed the realm's two dozen provinces. Alexander had appointed these men, reshuffled them, and purged their ranks of those he considered disloyal. Now the loyalty of those who remained in power would be put to the ultimate test. Everything depended on their willingness to take orders from an uninspiring triumvirate: a regent, Perdiccas, who was only a man, not a myth like his dead commander, and two kings who were considerably less than that.

I. ANTIGONUS (PHRYGIA, SUMMER 323 B.C.)

The reports from Babylon quickly reached a man dwelling in Phrygia (now southwestern Turkey) who no one yet imagined would be a key player in the contest for Alexander's empire—not even the man himself. Antigonus One-eye had spent the past ten years as satrap of Phrygia, governing this big, unruly province in Alexander's name. But now Alexander was dead, and Antigonus was serving other masters. He soon received word from Perdiccas, the head of the new government in Babylon, that a division of satrapies had been held and that he had been reappointed to command of Phrygia.

No doubt Antigonus was glad to receive this news but less pleased by his first assignment. He was to help Eumenes gain control of his new province, Cappadocia. Antigonus had always liked Eumenes during their years together at Philip's court, but in his eyes the man was a mere bookkeeper, and a foreigner to boot. Was Antigonus, a Macedonian of long service and high standing, really expected to aid such a man? Was the new regime really giving satrapies to *Greeks*?

Antigonus was about sixty, a generation older than the generals in Babylon, a giant of a man with a booming voice and a gruff, boastful temperament. He had lost an eye while helping Philip, Alexander's father, conduct a siege; a bolt fired from the walls of the besieged city had lodged in his eye socket, but with characteristic resolve he refused to have it extracted until the day's fighting was over. To see this enormous figure charging the walls, blood streaming down one cheek and a piece of metal where his eye should have been, must have been terrifying indeed. After his wound healed, his mangled visage continued to inspire fear. Once a Greek orator who had displeased Antigonus, summoned to appear before him, defiantly told the guards who came to fetch him: "Go ahead, feed me to your Cyclops!"

While overseeing Phrygia, Antigonus had raised his only surviving son, Demetrius. Now, in early adolescence, the boy was turning out to be almost as big as his father, and far more dissolute. Antigonus doted on this staggeringly handsome boy and teased him about his appetites for wine and women, both of which were soon to become legendary. On one occasion he had gone to visit Demetrius in his quarters, where the boy had shut himself in, claiming a fever. As he approached his son's bedroom, he spied a beautiful courtesan slipping away from it. Antigonus went in, sat down beside the boy, and pretended to take his temperature. "The fever has left me now," Demetrius lied, to which

Antigonus winkingly replied, "I know, I met it just now on its way out."

On another occasion described by Plutarch, Demetrius one day came into the palace staterooms, fresh from a hunt, without bothering to first store his javelin. Antigonus was meeting with some foreign envoys, and Demetrius blithely seated himself next to his father, weapon still in hand. Antigonus proudly pointed out to his visitors that he trusted Demetrius to bear arms in his presence. The episode prompts Plutarch to offer a pointed comment: one can measure the perils of power, the great moralist remarks, by the fact that Antigonus could make a boast of not fearing his own son.

Service in Phrygia had not been Antigonus' choice, for any general with his talent and temperament would have preferred to go east with Alexander. He had been sidelined here, the first high-ranking officer of the invasion to be left behind in a rear-guard post. Perhaps Alexander thought Antigonus too old for the rigors of the campaign; if so, the years to come would prove him badly mistaken. Perhaps, as one source reports, he mistrusted Antigonus' love of power, a judgment far closer to the mark. Satrapal appointments were a tactful way for Alexander to neutralize ambitious men before they could become threats. Alexander later shucked off Cleitus, another senior officer, by making him satrap of Bactria, just before starting on the Indian leg of his journey of conquest. Cleitus took this as a slight and began grumbling bitterly during his departure banquet, finally becoming so strident that Alexander killed him with his own hands.

Whatever the reason for his stranding in Phrygia, Antigonus had been a good steward of his province. His small Macedonian army had won several battles against determined Persian resistance. He had maintained peace and stability, so much so that his wife, Stratonice, had left her wealthy Macedonian home to join him in the Phrygian capital, Celaenae. This courageous lady became one of the first European colonial wives in Asia, the forerunner of many later memsahibs.

For ten years Antigonus held sway in Phrygia as Alexander receded ever farther toward the horizon. Few orders came to him from the East, and he had gotten used to running his province his own way, with his own troops. But now, that autonomy was being compromised. He had received commands from Babylon, from a new government installed without his consent. The task Perdiccas had set him—helping little Eumenes win his way into power— was a humiliating one, in effect a demand for total submission.

For a man like Antigonus, the choice of how to respond was an easy one. Saying nothing about his intentions or his reasons, he simply declined to show up for the invasion of Cappadocia. It was a passive rebellion but unmistakable in its significance. Antigonus, the first man outside Babylon called upon to support the new regime, had become the first to defy it. One of the last of his generation, the older men thrust aside, left behind, or killed by Alexander, he was not ready to give up his prerogatives and make way for the triumph of the young.

2. THE REVOLT IN BACTRIA (NORTHERN AFGHANISTAN, UZBEKISTAN, TAJIKISTAN, SUMMER 323 B.C.)

More than two thousand miles east of Antigonus' palace, in an opposite corner of Alexander's realm, a different challenge to the new government was taking shape. In the dusty fortress towns of Bactria, the outposts set up by Alexander to secure his northeast frontier, squads of Greek garrison troops received the news from Babylon with keen anticipation. For a long time they had sought a way to leave their posts, landlocked, alien places they found cheerless and barren. Now, with word of Alexander's death, that opportunity was at hand.

Similar news had arrived two years earlier, when the king's lung wound in India was rumored to be fatal. The false report had spurred a mass exodus of the Greeks in Bactria. Longing for home and thinking themselves free of a harsh master, many threw off the chains of garrison duty and organized a march to the West. Three thousand Greeks had crossed most of Macedonian-controlled Asia—a journey fraught with perils, from which no account has survived—and returned to their European homes. News of their escape must have made its way back to Bactria, inspiring new discontent and homesickness among their former comrades. Now these men had a miraculous second chance.

There were more than twenty thousand Greek soldiers scattered across Bactria and its northerly neighbor, Sogdiana (the "upper satrapies," as the Persians called them). Most were infantrymen of the hoplite class, armed with large shields, eight-foot thrusting spears, and metal breastplates and helmets. Some were draftees, forced into service by standing treaties; others were mercenaries, soldiers of fortune hoping to get rich under an invincible leader. Still others had been fighting for the Persians when Alexander launched his invasion, but had been allowed to save their lives by switching sides. Few considered Alexander their king or believed in his cause. To the mercenaries he was merely an employer, if a very well-paying one; to the recruits, brought along largely as hostages ensuring the loyalty of their home cities, he represented the war machine that had robbed Greece of its freedom.

In combat these Greek troops had played only a minor role. The Macedonians, with their longer pikes and lighter, more mobile divisions, regarded them as second-raters, throwbacks to an outmoded style of warfare. All the same they were valuable to the army as cultural capital. Steeped in literature and learning that Macedonians lacked, revered for progressive political traditions, these Greeks offered Alexander a potent propaganda weapon. His rule over Asia would be not another Persian-style despotism but a Hellenic regime, with a king who exercised wise and just (though absolute) power. The presence of Greek contingents in his army, and a few Greek officers among his Companions, helped Alexander maintain his enlightened image.

In the upper satrapies Alexander's Greek troops were especially important as cultural signposts. This was Asia's wild frontier, a rugged, mountainous realm where tough nomads lived by the arrow and the sword. Raiding and counter-raiding had been rife for centuries, and boys learned to ride and shoot almost before they could speak. Attacks by Scythian warlords to the north kept the region unsettled and violent. If Hellenism could plant its flag even here, if the Greek polis could be imported from the Aegean to the Oxus and Jaxartes rivers, then Alexander's campaign of conquest could be seen as a civilizational crusade.

Thus Greek squadrons were culled out of Alexander's army and scattered through the Bactrian wilderness, like seeds from which city-states could grow. That at least is the metaphor invoked by Alexander's admirers through the ages, from Plutarch in Roman times—who in a rapturous pair of speeches imagined plays of Sophocles being staged on the banks of the Oxus—to Sir William Tarn, the great British champion of Alexander in the mid-twentieth century. Alexander's critics, whose views have become predominant in recent decades, have of course taken a different view. To them the new settlements were not beacons of enlightenment but mere bunkers, ensuring control by predators of their prey. The truth of the matter surely lies between these poles. Cultural and economic nurture goes hand in hand with hegemonic exploitation even today, when Western powers once again struggle to tame the wild energies of Bactria.

In any case, the "Athens on the Oxus" glorified by Plutarch was a far cry from the lot of Alexander's garrison troops. Many had spent six years in parched mud-brick towns like Zariaspa and had seen very little else of Asia. At first their duties had been not only toilsome but dangerous. Through the surrounding desert

In southern Afghanistan, the kind of landscape that drove many Greeks to flee the East

rode fast-moving bands of guerrillas, and these tribesmen drew the garrison troops into several deadly ambushes. Alexander had finally pacified the region, in part by marrying Rhoxane, the daughter of its most powerful warlord, but its climate and landscape remained as forbidding as ever. From the walls of Zariaspa the Greeks saw only treeless wastes and arid mountains shimmering in the heat. There was no glimpse of their surest ally and quickest route back home, the sea.

It was the sea the mutineers now sought to reach. Twenty thousand infantry and three thousand cavalry set out westward in the months after Alexander's death, choosing as their captain a certain Philo, otherwise unknown. Probably they were aiming for the ports of Phoenicia or Asia Minor, where ships could be commandeered for the voyage to Greece. They counted on their numbers and weapons for security, and on Alexander's absence. Perhaps they judged that none of the ruling generals, men who had once suffered the rigors of Bactria as they were now suffering, would care enough about that blasted, barren province to stop them from leaving it. If so, they judged wrong.

3. CRATERUS (CILICIA, SUMMER–WINTER 323 B.C.)

Meanwhile, in Cilicia (today southeast Turkey), Craterus, Alexander's most revered general, was contemplating the paths that lay before him. The news from Babylon reached him en route to Europe as he marched at the head of the ten thousand veterans sent home from the army the previous year. Now that his king was dead, Craterus could foresee a change of masters and a change of political destiny, but first, the change from which all the others would flow, a change of wives.

Craterus, almost fifty and the oldest of Alexander's top staff, was married to a highborn Persian named Amastris. Cousin and best friend of Alexander's own bride Stateira, Amastris was one of the most distinguished women Alexander had bestowed in the mass wedding at Susa, a mark of what he owed to the loyal, dutiful Craterus. But the apparent honor also carried a sting. Craterus, as everyone knew, disliked Alexander's embrace of Persian ways. He loved his king—indeed, no one had done more to protect and strengthen Alexander—but he hated the king's policy of fusion, by which the ruling elites of Europe and Asia were being grafted together like shoots from two trees, and several times told him so to his face. Marriage to Amastris meant participating in this fusion plan.

Shortly after the mass wedding Alexander sent Craterus home to Macedonia, perhaps out of dislike of the old soldier's traditionalism. Craterus' assignment was a formidable one. He had to oust Antipater, staunch public servant for nearly half a century, from his position as guardian of the homeland, and install himself instead. The task would be even harder if Craterus brought along his barbarian wife. Alexander himself had recognized that difficulty, for he had forbidden the ten thousand veterans to bring their own Asian wives or mixed-race children home with them. Among the army at Babylon, such hybrid families were common enough, but back in Europe they would cause shock and dismay. Small wonder that Craterus had not hurried to complete his assignment. He had been ill when he departed Babylon, and that slowed his progress, but more recently he had come to a dead stop. Almost a year after leaving, he was still in Cilicia, only about halfway to the Macedonian capital, Pella.

In Cilicia, in the summer and fall of 323, messengers from both east and west kept Craterus informed of the changing world picture. From Babylon came news that Alexander was dead; that the king's last orders had been voided; that Perdiccas was in command of the joint kings; that Craterus had been made sovereign over Europe, along with Antipater, the man he had been formerly told to replace. Then, from Europe, came reports that Athens had revolted; that the Greeks were on the march; that Antipater was besieged in Lamia and desperately needed relief. Finally a letter arrived from Antipater himself. It was a plea for Craterus to cross the Hellespont and prevent the collapse of the homeland. Antipater offered Craterus one of his daughters—his oldest and most prized, the renowned Phila—as a bond of alliance.

Few women rivaled Phila for sagacity, nobility, and warmth. Even in her childhood Antipater reportedly conferred with her about matters of state. Later in life she had the self-possession to manage disputes in camps of armed soldiers, dealing out justice so as to win the trust of all. But Phila was no Athena, devoted only to warfare and statecraft. She had a keen interest as well in matters of the heart. She used her own wealth to subsidize marriages of poor women who lacked dowries, a private endowment in the service of love.

Phila was in Cilicia at the time of Alexander's death, not far from Craterus' camp, and was recently widowed. Her marriage to a Macedonian officer named Balacrus had brought her to Tarsus, capital of Cilicia, but Balacrus had been killed by the Pisidians, a stubbornly autonomous tribe, in a battle the previous year. Accidents of time and place seemed to be bringing Craterus and Phila together, the army's most revered officer and one of Europe's most admired women. The union suited Craterus far better than his arranged marriage with Amastris and also offered him a surer place in the imperial hierarchy. With Phila at his side, he would have a glorious homecoming; if he then rescued Antipater from Lamia, he would become not only the old man's son-in-law but, soon enough, his heir.

Still, Craterus delayed. Month after month he stayed in Cilicia, despite the urgency of Antipater's messages. What was keeping him? Probably he felt the pull of the power vacuum in Babylon, where Perdiccas' regime, as he knew by report, was struggling. Craterus' standing among the rank and file was highest of all Alexander's generals; many no doubt whispered that he, not Perdiccas, should be their new commander. The forces Craterus was leading, more than ten thousand seasoned troops, including the matchless Silver Shields, were more than enough to take on Perdiccas and his loyalists. Any move against Perdiccas, who had gone out of his way to give Craterus a high place in the new regime, would of course be a stab in the back, but one that would almost certainly succeed.

Would Craterus turn east or west, toward Babylon or toward Pella? The choice seemed to hinge on which wife he would have. Wed to Amastris as he now was, he could rule Asia and father children who were royal (in Persian eyes at least). But if he renounced Amastris and took Phila instead, the most powerful man in Europe would be his father-in-law. Each woman seemed to bring with her a continent as her dowry. One was well suited to Craterus' temperament, while the other opened avenues to immense power and wealth, perhaps even an imperial throne.

For the moment, Craterus stayed where he was, in Cilicia. No one who was with him recorded his thoughts or motives, which consequently have remained one of the darkest mysteries of the post-Alexander era. But the competing forces acting on him were enough to paralyze even the most decisive leader. Paths of glory beckoned on either side of him, while right in the middle, only miles away, stood Phila, Antipater's daughter, from whom he might gain sure success on one of these paths, and happiness to boot.

4. PERDICCAS AND PEITHON
(BABYLON, AUTUMN 323 B.C.)

In Babylon, Perdiccas, head of the embattled new regime, was also seeking to become Antipater's son-in-law. Perhaps he had gotten wind of the old man's offer of Phila to Craterus and feared being isolated by this new marital bond. Antipater represented legitimacy, stability, and authority; Antipater's blessing was vital to anyone who sought to take Alexander's place. Thus, shortly after appointing himself regent for the joint kings, Perdiccas wrote to Antipater seeking the hand of his daughter Nicaea, and the old man wrote back agreeing to the match.

Now, as he awaited the arrival of his bride, Perdiccas contemplated the two rebellions on two extremes of Asia. To his west, Antigonus One-eye had rejected his orders, refusing to lend aid to Eumenes in Cappadocia. To his east, the Greek hoplites stationed in Bactria were on the move after abandoning Alexander's garrisons. Perdiccas' authority, reestablished at such high cost after the uprising of Meleager, was under grave challenge in both places. Leaving Antigonus alone for the present, Perdiccas moved to tackle the problem of the Bactrian Greeks. He sent for his one-time fellow Bodyguard and close ally, Peithon.

Peithon had been one of Perdiccas' chief supporters during the tumultuous week after Alexander's death. Too low in stature to vie for command, he had been content to second Perdiccas' proposals for the complex structure of the new government. As a reward he had been appointed satrap of Media, a wealthy and important province. There, Peithon had begun to nourish larger ambitions: dominion over the empire's cavalry-rich eastern sector, the upper satrapies of Bactria and Sogdiana, an ideal place to start an independent kingdom or build power for a takeover of all Asia. For the moment, however, he kept this longing hidden.

Responding to Perdiccas' summons, Peithon arrived in Babylon. There he received an expeditionary force of three thousand infantry and eight hundred cavalry, chosen by lottery from Perdiccas' own forces. Peithon was also given letters allowing him to levy more troops from the other satraps of the East and to serve as *stratēgos*, or "commander in chief," of the whole region. Such letters, sealed with the signet ring Perdiccas carried, were the standard instruments by which the empire was managed. On their directives, troops or funds were moved here and there across its vast expanse. A satrap who received them was obliged to obey or other letters would be sent to the local garrison ordering his arrest, or worse.

The letters given to Peithon were a necessary means of dealing with one rebellion, but Perdiccas worried that they would spawn another. Somehow, Perdiccas had begun to mistrust Peithon, the man he had just appointed to a prestigious command. He feared that the mission to the upper satrapies would place Peithon beyond the reach of central authority. Were Peithon to collaborate with the Greek rebels rather than subduing them, he could easily control the East. Perdiccas decided to take no chances. He gave instructions to Peithon's army that the Greek rebels were not to be taken prisoner but killed, and he granted the right to plunder their possessions as a reward for compliance. None of over twenty thousand former comrades was to be left alive. It was a desperately cynical strategy—the preemptive destruction of an entire army to prevent its use by a rival. The upper satrapies would be largely stripped of colonists, but at least they would not threaten the empire as a whole. If Perdiccas had to cut off a limb to preserve the rest of the body, that was a price he was willing to pay.

And so he sent Peithon off to the East, while he waited for an envoy to arrive from the West with Antipater's daughter Nicaea, his bride-to-be.

5. PTOLEMY (EGYPT, AUTUMN 323–SUMMER 322 B.C.)

Meanwhile, in the south of the empire, in Egypt, yet another of Alexander's generals, Ptolemy, was also about to marry a daughter of Antipater—the old man's youngest, Eurydice. Ptolemy had sought this woman's hand as part of a pact with Antipater, whose support he badly needed. For upon his arrival in Egypt he had taken steps that were sure to bring a momentous consequence, war with Perdiccas.

Ptolemy already had two remarkable women by his side. For years he had kept a famous mistress, the beautiful Athenian courtesan Thais. According to one account, it was Thais who, while drinking and carousing with Ptolemy and other generals in the Persian palace at Persepolis, impishly suggested that they all set the place on fire. Alexander, drunk as well, took the dare and threw a torch at the roof timbers of the palace, starting a conflagration that left it a ravaged shell (the ruin still standing today in southern Iran). Perhaps the fire really did start this way, or perhaps, as a different account suggests, it was a deliberate move by a sober Alexander. But even if Thais was the instigator, she had not thereby lost Ptolemy's affections. The couple had three children born during the Asian campaign, two boys and a girl, now settled with them in their new home in Egypt.

Ptolemy also had a wife, the Greco-Persian noblewoman Artacama, given to him by Alexander at the mass wedding in Susa the previous year. She was the daughter of Artabazus, a great Persian warrior-chief, and sister of Barsine, Alexander's former mistress and mother of his son Heracles. By marriage to Artacama, Ptolemy had been taken into Alexander's extended family, and into the hybrid Euro-Asian elite destined to rule the brave new world.

It was an odd combination of consorts, a highborn Persian princess and a high-priced Athenian courtesan, but then Ptolemy was a man for all seasons, versatile and rangy. Alexander had given him a variety of commands, diverse and sensitive missions, and he had always succeeded. Not by nature a military man—at least he played no major role in the Asian invasion during its first five years—he had learned the art of war from those around him. Perhaps he did not have as much boldness as Perdiccas, nor as much authority as Craterus, nor as much cleverness as Eumenes the Greek. But he had a balance of all three qualities that was stronger than any single one by itself.

Ptolemy was going to need his versatility now that he had arrived in Egypt. His new satrapy was a land of strange and powerful religious passions. In his capital city of Memphis, a glittering temple housed a black-and-white bull calf worshipped as a divine being called Apis. Worship of animal deities was peculiar to Egypt and often hard for foreigners to stomach; once a Persian king had brutally stabbed the Apis in the thigh, calling it a silly god worthy of silly people. The beast later contracted sepsis and died. Alexander had taken the opposite approach: upon entering Egypt, he offered sacrifices at Memphis to gods that conspicuously included the Apis bull. Ptolemy had learned much on that occasion about adaptability, tolerance, and openness to change.

Ptolemy was by nature a tolerant person, not charismatic like Alexander, but reasonable and fair-minded. In years to come his benevolence would earn him the epithet Soter, or Savior, by which he has been known ever since. And the Egyptians desperately needed a tolerant ruler, for in the past few years they had once again, as in the days of the Persians, been oppressed by a cruel foreigner—in this case a conniving Greek named Cleomenes.

Appointed by Alexander as finance minister in Egypt, Cleomenes had come to control all the levers of power and had also become spectacularly wealthy. A record survives of the gangland-type schemes by which he amassed his riches. He extorted money by taking away age-old priestly privileges and then selling them back; he manipulated the price of grain, Egypt's chief export, by cornering the market; he shook down the Egyptians by thuggish bullying. Once, when sailing along the Nile in a region where crocodiles were sacred, Cleomenes lost a slave to an attack by one of these beasts. He promptly declared a roundup and slaughter of crocodiles. The local priests averted this sacrilege only by bringing Cleomenes heaps of gold. He had held their very gods for ransom.

Alexander, while he lived, despised the connivances of Cleomenes but was either unable or unwilling to stop them. Then, in his last year of life, the king bought a favor from Cleomenes at the price of a blanket amnesty. Distraught at the death of his friend Hephaestion, Alexander wrote to Cleomenes requesting that huge memorials be built in the new city then under construction, Alexandria—one in the city itself and another on an island off-shore where it would be seen by all passing ships. "If I find," said Alexander in the letter, "that the temples in Egypt and the shrines of Hephaestion are well built, I will pardon you for any wrong you have done thus far, and if you misbehave in the future, you will meet with no punishment from me." Cleomenes continued his kleptocracy in Egypt, now with the blessing of the king himself.

In the settlement made at Babylon, Perdiccas had assigned Egypt to Ptolemy on the condition that Cleomenes serve as Ptolemy's *hyparchos,* or "lieutenant." It was a patent attempt to trim Ptolemy's sails and keep a close watch on his behavior. But Ptolemy nullified this arrangement soon after his arrival, by arranging for Cleomenes himself to be nullified. Finding some legal pretext—a charge of fiscal malfeasance would have been fitting and all too credible—Ptolemy had the grasping Greek tried and executed, thus taking sole power in Egypt. It was a declaration of independence from Perdiccas and the regime of the joint kings.

Probably it was after this overthrow of Cleomenes that Ptolemy wrote to Antipater, asking to marry one of the old man's daughters. A showdown with Perdiccas was surely coming, and Ptolemy would need help to hold his new seat. Alliance between Ptolemy and Antipater made possible a continental pincer strategy: Europe and Africa, working in tandem, could hold the vast forces of Asia at bay. Antipater, it seems, was happy to take part in this high-stakes triangulation, for he sent his daughter Eurydice to become Ptolemy's wife. And with her he sent the girl's cousin Berenice, a lady-in-waiting who, though no one yet knew it, was awaiting great things.

Cleomenes was not the only problem Ptolemy faced during

his first year in Egypt. Another bold Greek with big ambitions, a Spartan soldier of fortune named Thibron, had begun an attack on Cyrene, a Greek city on the North African coast. Long independent and wealthy, not yet a part of the Macedonian empire, Cyrene made a tempting prize for a warrior with Thibron's nerve. Though his plans did not threaten Ptolemy's domain, they put him right on its borders, and his brashness seemed to endanger the stability of the whole region.

Thibron was among the many talented mercenaries who had become freebooters during Alexander's last year. He had first shipped with Harpalus, the renegade treasurer of Babylon, as part of the hired army brought to Athens to foment revolt. He had watched as Harpalus' efforts at Athens failed, not once but twice, and had then sailed with his hapless paymaster to Crete seeking refuge from Alexander's retribution. There was still a fortune in silver and six thousand armed soldiers aboard Harpalus' ships, enough cash and force to accomplish some bold mission—but what? Poor, lost Harpalus either didn't know or didn't seem likely to succeed. On Crete, Thibron took matters into his own hands by killing Harpalus and seizing command.

He sailed to North Africa and blockaded the harbor of Cyrene. He had the support of some exiles from the city and quickly won a settlement in which the Cyrenaeans agreed to pay him tribute and augment his army. But then things went awry. One of Thibron's subordinates, a Cretan, rebelled against him, split off the other Cretans in the army, and defected to the Cyrenaeans. Thibron was kicked out of the city itself but still controlled the harbor, using confiscated trade goods to fund his war effort. He established a new base in the nearby town of Taucheira, while the Cyrenaeans, for their part, called in neighboring Libyans and Carthaginians for support. An all-out regional war began to take shape, right on Ptolemy's western border.

Thibron, indefatigable like many Spartans, suffered dreadful reverses but would not give up. He lost control of the harbor of Cyrene after a successful Cretan raid; his men, forced to forage in open country, were routed by Libyan tribesmen; his ships, deprived of anchorage, were sunk or driven out to sea by a storm. His only remaining resource was his cash reserve, but this was formidable. Sending envoys to Taenaron, the still-crowded depot for unemployed mercenaries, he hired a new force of twenty-five hundred soldiers and attacked Cyrene again. He defeated a Cyrenaean army said to total thirty thousand—further testimony to the devastating effectiveness of trained veterans—and regained control of the city's surroundings. The seesaw struggle now stabilized into an entrenched, grinding siege, with the fate of much of the region resting on the outcome.

Ptolemy watched this conflagration from the safety of his palace on the Nile. The twists and turns that had created the crisis were truly bewildering. Money that had been collected by the Persians, then captured by Alexander, then stolen by Harpalus and brought to Athens to subsidize a war against Macedonia, had changed hands one last time and landed on North African shores. Like a magnet, it had drawn to the region streams of jobless Greek mercenaries. Surplus cash had combined with free-floating military manpower to form a volatile and explosive mixture. The firestorm it had caused now threatened to spread to Egypt.

But Ptolemy too had a huge cash hoard, thanks to the depredations of his predecessor, Cleomenes. Upon inspecting the Egyptian treasury, he found a handsome sum of eight thousand talents, enough to hire a large army for many years of service, given the going rate of one-tenth of a talent per year per man. Ptolemy put this silver to work hiring a force that could outmatch Thibron's, and when the opportunity came to intervene in Cyrene, he was ready. Called on for help by some Cyrenaean exiles, Ptolemy dispatched his newly purchased soldiers, under the command of his general Ophellas. Thibron was quickly defeated, captured, and turned over to the cities he had attacked for torture and crucifixion. Ophellas was put in charge of Cyrene, which henceforth became a dependency of Egypt—its fate a monument to the power of money.

There was another way to generate power from money, a way pioneered by Alexander but now exploited more fully by Ptolemy in Egypt. Coined money itself, bearing images struck at state-run mints, was a powerful propaganda tool. Alexander had used this tool all across his empire, striking coins showing Heracles, his legendary ancestor, on one side and bearing the legend "Alexander's" on the other. Heracles was shown wearing a headdress made from the impenetrable skin of the Nemean lion, an emblem of Alexander's own seeming invincibility. Ptolemy, during his first two years in Egypt, took this strategy one step further. He minted a coin depicting the profile not of Heracles but of Alexander himself. It was the first time that the image of a human being, rather than a god or a mythic hero, had appeared on any Western coinage.

In place of the lion skin formerly shown on the Heracles issues, Ptolemy's coin showed Alexander wearing a fantastic headdress made from the flayed scalp of an elephant. The beast's tusks protruded from the top of the king's head, and the trunk reared upward like a bizarre, fleshy crest. From the side of the headdress curled a ram's horn, symbol of the Egyptian god Ammon, who had supposedly claimed the king as son. It was not an image ever seen in life but a symbolic one conveying useful ideas. It connected Alexander to the non-European world, an important link for Ptolemy to display to his new Egyptian subjects. It especially evoked the invasion of India, Alexander's greatest feat of power and daring. In India, Alexander had defeated the most fearsome weapon his army had faced, the trained war elephant, and even learned how to use it himself. He had met the wildness of the jungle and made it his own.

It was as though in the crucible of India a new kind of ruler had been forged, blending enlightened, rational Hellenism with something terrifying and monstrous. Ptolemy, by disseminating this ingenious icon on his coins, was investing Alexander with a new power, the power of the East.

6. CHANDRAGUPTA AND CHANAKYA (GANDHARA/INDIA, 323–318 B.C.)

The land of the war elephant, the region the Persians called Gandhara and the Greek world India (today eastern Pakistan), was the last province of Alexander's empire to learn of his death. The news must have arrived there weeks later than in other regions of Asia. Messages that traversed the central satrapies by fleet horsemen or fire signals slowed to a crawl as they crossed the Hindu Kush, carried on foot over the Khyber and Khawak passes. Once the news reached the broad plain east of the mountains, it picked up speed once again, racing from garrison to garrison along the Indus River and its four tributaries. Eventually, it passed beyond the Hyphasis River, the eastern limit of the empire, and was heard on the banks of the Ganges, in the realm of the Nandas, rulers of the great Magadha kingdom.

The news aroused the keen interest of two men who were at that time plotting the overthrow of the Nandas *and* the expulsion of the Macedonians. Within only a few years they would succeed at both ventures and would join the Indus and Ganges valleys under one rule, founding an empire that ultimately encompassed nearly all of the Indian subcontinent. Together they would chase Alexander's governors out of the region and ensure that they never came back. These men were Chandragupta Maurya (Sandracottus to the Greeks) and his brilliant teacher and adviser, a man who goes by two different names in Indian texts, the patronymic Chanakya and the surname Kautilya.

Almost nothing is known for certain about these two men, but legends abound in both Greco-Roman and Indian sources. Justin, in his summary of the Roman historian Pompeius Trogus, claims that Chandragupta was a commoner who offended the Nanda king and was then condemned to death. Somehow he broke away from his captors and outran them, collapsing in exhaustion when he reached the safety of the jungle. He slept where he fell, and as he slept, a lion came and licked the sweat off his face. He woke to see the beast calmly walking away; he knew then that he was destined for rule.

Chanakya, the sage who helped Chandragupta gain his empire, was also a man marked out for greatness, according to Indian legends. Chanakya had been born with a full set of teeth, a sign that local monks explained as an omen of future kingship. But Chanakya's father feared that royal power would mean the perdition of his son's soul, so he ground down the teeth with a file. The monks, seeing the infant's new condition, proclaimed that destiny had been changed. Chanakya would not rule himself but would oversee one who ruled; he would be "a king concealed within an image."

Grown to manhood, Chanakya searched for a youth worthy to be his avatar, finally recognizing Chandragupta by way of yet more omens and signs. Chanakya took Chandragupta with him and trained him in the science of conquest and rule—lessons preserved, perhaps, in the *Arthashastra,* a Sanskrit political guidebook that purports to be the work of Chanakya. The *Arthashastra* in fact dates from later centuries, but its core lessons, including dark teachings about assassination and espionage, may well go back to Chanakya himself.

Chandragupta was in his mid-teens during Alexander's years in India and almost certainly living in Taxila, the university town that the Macedonians used as their base. Chanakya, perhaps thirty-five or forty at that time, had brought the boy here and enrolled him in one of the town's religious schools. It must have been here in Taxila that Chandragupta met Alexander, if we believe the brief record Plutarch made of the encounter. How the two leaders crossed paths, one ending his campaign of conquest, the other not yet having begun, Plutarch does not say. But he reports that in later years Chandragupta was known to laugh when he thought of Alexander and how great an opportunity he had missed. Had the Macedonians kept going to the Ganges, Chandragupta scoffed, they would have found the conquest of the Nanda kingdom an easy matter. He knew whereof he spoke, having by then accomplished that deed himself.

While studying at Taxila, Chandragupta and Chanakya watched the Macedonians devastate their homeland. Alexander's campaign down the Indus to the sea, starting in the fall of 326, cut like a scythe through India's proud, independent tribes, the Malli and the Oxydracae (Sanskrit Malavas and Ksudrakas). Despite outnumbering the invaders many times over, these fierce warriors suffered horrific losses; hundreds of thousands were killed or enslaved. The Malli seemed for a time to have finished Alexander off, hitting him square in the chest with one of their fearsome arrows, but the king miraculously recovered. In the end the two peoples surrendered their ancient liberty to Alexander, lavishing him with gifts and offering their leaders—those few who had survived—as hostages.

Chandragupta and Chanakya learned to revere a man with

the odd-sounding name of Philip as their new master. Alexander appointed this man (no relation to his father or half-brother) satrap of the region and left him a corps of hardened Thracian troops under a captain named Eudamus. Then Alexander and his men departed. They boarded ships in the Indian Ocean or marched back through the Hindu Kush; the least fortunate units followed Alexander himself into the deserts of Gedrosia. The Macedonians' Indian adventure, which had turned the land of the five rivers red with blood for more than a year, was over.

The skeleton crew of Europeans left behind in the Indus valley were not nearly enough to hold it, and they weakened themselves further with internal dissension. Philip was already dead a few months after Alexander's departure, killed by an uprising of his own troops. Eudamus took command in his place, but within a few years he would be pushed out of the region, as Chandragupta and Chanakya, who now had an army behind them, moved to take back the Indus valley (they had already, by that time, taken over the Ganges).

How did such an army materialize in a region depleted by near-genocidal war? Justin supplies our only hint when he says that Chandragupta used "outlaws" to attack Alexander's garrisons. Some have guessed that this refers to the Malli and the Oxydracae, self-governing peoples whose independence might well have looked like lawlessness to a Roman like Justin. It is only a guess, but it suggests that Chandragupta's conquests were fueled by the anger of Alexander's most brutalized victims. The peoples of the Indus valley, in this scenario, rose up and reclaimed the land Alexander took from them, the only Asian nations to have done so. Perhaps Alexander, though he had horrifically reduced their numbers and forced their submission, did not break their proud spirit.

Eudamus fled west, toward the central satrapies of the empire, where we shall meet him again in due course. He took with him a herd of war elephants he had acquired after killing the raja Porus, once Alexander's greatest enemy in the region, more recently his faithful vassal. Gandhara, the land of the five rivers, ceased to belong to Alexander's empire and became part of Chandragupta's. Within a generation the Macedonians would cede control perma-

nently for the price of five hundred more elephants, the heavy
weaponry they needed for their unending civil wars.

7. THE END OF THE BACTRIAN REVOLT
(SUMMER 322 B.C.)

About a year after Alexander's death Peithon, commander in chief
of the East by order of Perdiccas, arrived in Bactria. His forces by
this time had swollen to thirteen thousand infantry and eighty-
eight hundred cavalry. This was the largest army seen in the East
since Alexander had left there, except for the twenty-three thousand mutinous Greeks whom it had been ordered to destroy. Peithon, however, did not intend this order to be carried out. His
plan was to absorb the rebels into his own ranks and amass an
invincible aggregate force. With it he could hold the upper
satrapies against any incursion while making ready for his next
move—perhaps a showdown with Perdiccas, if Perdiccas' troops
would dare fight him.

Somewhere in central Asia, in a place too desolate to have
a name—at least no name was recorded by Diodorus, our only
complete source for these events—Peithon encountered the army
of the mutinous Greeks. He had taken the precaution of cutting a
deal with a Greek subcommander, Letodorus, bribing him to lead
his three thousand troops off the field at the start of the battle. He
was hoping to conclude the engagement with little bloodshed,
since troops killed on either side were ultimately his losses.

The plan worked beautifully. As the two lines engaged,
Letodorus moved off behind a nearby hill and appeared to abandon the Greek cause. The other twenty thousand mutineers lost
heart and broke formation, allowing an easy Macedonian victory.
Peithon ordered the Greeks to ground arms, promising that no
harm would come to them in defeat. They would simply be
returned to their posts in Bactria.

Encouraged by Peithon's words, the Greeks disarmed and
began mingling with the Macedonians. Many recognized comrades from the days of Alexander; many hands were extended in
friendship and trust. But the Macedonians were thinking of the
baggage train in the rear of the Greek lines, rich with the spoils of

Persepolis and Susa, booty they had been promised would be theirs. Many were also mindful of the instructions issued by Perdiccas: *Let no one be left alive.*

Someone gave a signal, and the Macedonians struck. Each man thrust his javelin at the nearest Greeks, who, having put aside their own spears and armor, had no chance to defend themselves. Peithon did not stop the slaughter; he had no plausible reason for doing so. In a few minutes' time an army exceeding twenty thousand—much of the military manpower of Greece, siphoned off into Asia over thirteen years by Alexander's recruiting agents— was annihilated.

So ended the Bactrian revolt. Peithon led his troops back toward Babylon, restoring detachments to this or that satrapy on his way and finally returning the core force to Perdiccas. Peithon's designs on the upper satrapies had been blocked, but he would be back. His bid for control of the East was not over.

For Perdiccas, head of the central government in Babylon, the episode was a grim sort of success. He had prevailed in the unspoken test of wills with Peithon and had headed off a threat before it could emerge. Control over Bactria had been seriously compromised. But the integrity of the empire had been preserved. The reign of the joint kings, in whose name Perdiccas wielded power, went on into its second year.

The Athenians' Last Stand (II)

Athens, Northern Greece, and the Hellespont

AUTUMN 323–AUTUMN 322 B.C.

I. HYPERIDES (ATHENS, WINTER, LATE 323 B.C.)

For the Athenian orator Hyperides, it was the best of times. After decades of urging war against the Macedonians, he had finally gotten his city to listen. His handpicked general, Leosthenes, had led the Athenians and their new allies, the Aetolians, to a stunning victory. Now, even though the Aetolians had left the field, Leosthenes had the foe cornered behind the walls of Lamia. Athens was in a festive mood, marking with celebrations and feasts the return of its lost power. Hyperides enjoyed feasts and all kinds of high living. He was known to stroll through the fish market every day in search of the choicest and rarest delicacies. Born into wealth, he could afford such pleasures, just as he could afford three high-priced courtesans, one in his city house and one each in his two country estates.

While Leosthenes was routing the Macedonian army, Hyperides, back in Athens, was ousting his political opponents. Demades, who had backed the motion making Alexander a god, had been assessed a crippling fine and then stripped of his citizenship when he could not pay. Two other pro-Macedonian orators had bolted and gone over to the enemy, gambling—foolishly, as it now seemed—that Athens would soon be defeated. The fall from grace of Phocion, "Do-good" Phocion, had been softer. Still esteemed by the city despite having opposed war, and valued for his military expertise, Phocion had been appointed to lead the home guard, troops patrolling close to Athens to defend against seaborne invasions. But that posting had effectively sidelined him. In the countryside Phocion could neither take part in meetings of the Assembly nor share Leosthenes' glory at Lamia.

And what of Demosthenes, Hyperides' longtime ally, then briefly his enemy, now his ally once again? The return of Demosthenes to favor, after only a few months in exile and disgrace, had robbed Hyperides of some of his limelight. But the two men seemed able to work together as they once had; Demosthenes showed no need to settle scores over his bribery conviction. The friendship of these political allies had proved resilient over the years, as all such friendships had to be in the volatile Athenian democracy. Once, when Hyperides was ill and in bed, Demosthenes unexpectedly came to call, only to find his friend composing a list of *his* ethical transgressions. Demosthenes howled with outrage, but Hyperides calmly invoked the logic of expediency. "If we remain friends, this list can never hurt you," he said, "but if we fall out and become enemies, it's my assurance that you won't hurt *me*."

All through the winter of 323, Hyperides received encouraging letters from Lamia and had them read aloud in the Assembly. The war effort was on a slow but promising track. The Greeks had been unable to take Lamia by storm; the Macedonians had forced them back with artillery fire from torsion-propelled weapons mounted on the walls. But over time, the siege cordon had held. The Macedonians were hard-pressed by hunger. Old man Antipater, their commanding officer, had sent an offer of truce on terms favorable to Athens, but Leosthenes, holding out for unconditional surrender, replied: "The victors will set the terms." The total collapse of Antipater's position, it seemed, was only a matter of time. But then came a letter with news of a different kind.

One day, while Greek troops were digging the trench that

formed part of the siege perimeter, a squad of Macedonians had rushed out from the walls and attacked. The digging crew had been overwhelmed, and Leosthenes, informed of the skirmish, rode up with reinforcements. As he came within range of the walls, he had been struck on the head by a catapulted stone and knocked unconscious. Carried back to the camp for treatment, he died two days later, the victim of a moment's heedlessness and a fantastically lucky shot. The great mercenary captain and staunch Macedonian hater, the man who had given Athens its first battle-field triumph in a generation, was gone.

The Greeks still held the upper hand at Lamia, but their confidence was shaken. Through the rigors of a winter siege in open country, Leosthenes had inspired them with resolve as no one else could. Back in Athens, Hyperides mourned the loss of a friend and a huge political asset. He and Leosthenes had seen eye to eye on the need to destroy Macedonian power for good. With Leosthenes at his side in the Assembly, he had been able to face down even Phocion, the elder statesman whose long military career made him practically unassailable in discussions of strategy.

With Leosthenes dead, Hyperides feared the Athenians would choose Phocion, their most experienced general, to take command of the Lamia siege. But Phocion had opposed the war and had been skeptical of its chances. If given command, he might well come to terms with Antipater and let the Macedonians slip out of the Greek choke hold. To head off this danger, Hyperides and his party used a devious tactic in the Assembly. They hired an ordinary citizen, someone unknown in political circles, to stand up and claim he was a friend of Phocion's and to urge the city not to send to Lamia a leader whose talents were needed at home. The crowd seemed to approve, when Phocion himself, who was unexpectedly on the scene that day, rose to speak. "That man is *not* my friend," he said, "and I have never seen him before today; but," he added, turning to the man who had spoken, "from this day I shall *make* you my friend, for the advice you have given is much to my benefit." Hyperides and his partisans drew a sigh of relief. Phocion didn't want the command, which went instead to a much younger general, Antiphilus.

Despite the huge setback of the loss of Leosthenes, Hyperides continued to show his old bravado in the Assembly. He even proposed state honors for Iolaus, Antipater's son, once Alexander's wine pourer at Babylon, thought by some to have poisoned the king's drinking cup. It was a roguish move, designed to show confidence about the outcome of the war, for such a motion, which both spat on the memory of Alexander and implicated Antipater's family in regicide, would incur the gravest retribution, were the city's revolt to fail.

2. OLYMPIAS (EPIRUS, AUTUMN 323 B.C.)

Among those watching the Hellenic War with interest, from her ancestral home in the far northern reaches of the Greek world, was Olympias, Alexander's mother.

Her feelings at this moment must have been intense and complex. On the one hand, she despised Antipater, the Macedonian general. She had fought over turf with him for years after Alexander's departure for Asia, and now she blamed him as well for poisoning her son in Babylon, using (as she supposed) his own sons Cassander and Iolaus as henchmen. But she also resented the Athenians. Their freethinking, upstart ways had given many slights to her son's authority and her own. Once, when the Athenians had sent beautiful carved hands and a face, made of gold and ivory, to adorn a statue in nearby Dodona, Olympias had bridled, claiming they had no right to meddle in *her* territory. Her letters to Hyperides on the subject were filled with what the orator called "tragedies and accusations"—the shrill rhetoric of what today might be called a drama queen.

More recently, when the Athenians had taken in the renegade Harpalus and his embezzled money, both Olympias and Antipater had sent envoys to Athens demanding them back. The dowager queen and the aging soldier-statesman had briefly been on the same side, aligned against Athenian intransigence, even though they were bitter rivals. Now that the Athenians and Antipater were at war, it was unclear which side Olympias was on.

By birth Olympias was a princess of the Molossians, a Greek people inhabiting the region of Epirus (now largely in southern Albania). Her royal family claimed descent from heroes of the

Trojan War, Neoptolemus, son of Achilles, and his captive bride, Hector's widow, Andromache. The family advertised this heroic lineage with its choices of names: Olympias' father was another Neoptolemus, and she herself was called Polyxena (among other names) up to the time of her marriage, after a Trojan princess famous for her sufferings. Her brother was called Alexander, after the fair-haired Trojan prince, also known as Paris, who stole Helen to start the legendary war. Later she was to give her son the same name.

Taking mythic names was more than just an affectation for the Molossian royals. Their lives and their culture resembled those of their Homeric namesakes. Unlike that of the urbanized Greeks to their south, theirs was a rural and tribal society, still under the ancient system of hereditary monarchy. Progressive government, literacy, free trade, and walled city-states, the achievements that had transformed the lives of their southern brethren, had passed them by. The Athenians and their ilk regarded the Molossians as throwbacks to an earlier age. They sneered at the lawlessness of these Northerners, who still carried daggers in public places, and shrank from their weird religious rites, especially those involving the god of ecstasy and abandon, Dionysus.

In her teens Polyxena, soon to become Olympias, was married off to the king of her powerful eastern neighbor, Macedonia. Philip was then just beginning his reign and was building power through marriage alliances; this was his fifth bride in three years' time, and his palace was becoming crowded. Olympias quickly distinguished herself by bearing Philip a son, Alexander. The king had already sired a son by an earlier wife—Arrhidaeus, later to be called Philip—but somehow Olympias' boy was considered heir apparent, perhaps after Arrhidaeus' mental infirmity was recognized. As presumptive queen mother, Olympias gained great stature at court, as well as making great enemies, for she did not carry herself with the humility befitting a woman and a foreigner. Among those inclined to dislike her was Antipater. Two decades her senior, long Philip's right-hand man, he was a natural rival for a woman who dared, as she did, to involve herself in politics.

As her son, Alexander, matured, Olympias saw to his upbringing and jealously guarded his succession rights. Rumors circulated that she had fed Arrhidaeus poisons that destroyed his mind. Other rumors, still believed by some today, made her complicit in the assassination of her husband in 336, when Alexander was just old enough to assume the throne. Whether or not she colluded in that murder, she soon afterward arranged the killing of Philip's latest wife and baby girl, Europa, then only a few days old. There would be no new royal line that might someday, even decades hence, rival the claims of her son.

Now Alexander was dead, and the son he had left behind, another Alexander, was just as defenseless as the baby girl she had killed thirteen years before. Olympias knew dynastic politics well enough to know that her grandson was in grave danger. And if the child were not to survive, her own life, and that of her daughter, Cleopatra, would also be forfeit. By the stern code of Macedonian law, the relatives of those killed by the state were likely to be killed as well, to prevent their seeking revenge. Olympias' passionate temper and iron will would make such a precaution essential.

Olympias realized she needed a male protector, and there were few to be found. Her brother Alexander, king of the Molossians, was dead, leaving her daughter, Cleopatra, a young widow (at her husband Philip's behest, uncle had married niece), with two fatherless young children, a boy and a girl. Back in Macedonia, old man Antipater and his son Cassander had become her mortal enemies, foreclosing any hope of a safe haven there. She needed an alliance with one of the generals in Asia, those who controlled her son's invincible army, if she were to survive long enough to get one of her two grandsons onto a throne.

Marriage and fertility were what had brought her power to begin with; now she needed to tap these resources again, through a surrogate this time, her daughter, Cleopatra. Cleopatra's ability to bear children might rescue all three generations of royals. Mother and daughter together hatched a plan: Cleopatra would offer herself as bride to Leonnatus, a high-ranking member of Alexander's Bodyguard and a nobleman of good pedigree. Leonnatus would be asked to return from Asia to Macedonia and take charge of affairs there. He would no doubt accept, lured by the prospect of gaining royal stature as soon as he fathered an heir to the throne.

A letter was sent to Leonnatus in the months after Alexander's death, offering him Cleopatra in marriage and, implicitly, control of the royal house. Olympias played her trump card, indeed the only card she had. But just then, the Hellenic War broke out, Antipater became besieged, and Europe was thrown into confusion. It was no longer clear what would be left of Macedonian power there, even if Leonnatus did agree to return.

3. LEONNATUS AND EUMENES (NORTHWESTERN ANATOLIA, WINTER, EARLY 322 B.C.)

Olympias was not alone in hoping to lure Leonnatus back to Europe; her great adversary Antipater was also in urgent communication with him. For the first time in his half century of generalship, including the twelve years he had managed the troublesome Greeks on Alexander's behalf, Antipater had lost control of events. He could only wait behind the stout walls of Lamia while his supplies ran thin, hoping that a rescuer, either Leonnatus or Craterus, would arrive in time. He had written to both men, promising each of them one of his marriageable daughters in exchange for alliance and support (a third daughter had been offered to Perdiccas and a fourth to Ptolemy).

As the siege wore on, Antipater sent a second message to Leonnatus, the nearest of the generals, reiterating the marriage offer and the urgent plea for relief. He sent Hecataeus, the puppet ruler of Cardia, as his messenger, somehow getting word to this useful Greek from behind the siege curtain that he must cross the Hellespont and find Leonnatus. It was not the first time Hecataeus had crossed into Asia as a Macedonian errand boy. When Alexander had first claimed the throne, it was Hecataeus who carried into Asia, and then executed, an order to rub out one of the king's political enemies.

Hecataeus found Leonnatus across the straits, conferring with Eumenes, Alexander's former Greek scribe, over the coming campaign to pacify Cappadocia. The encounter was an awkward one for Eumenes, since he and Hecataeus, both natives of Cardia, had a long history of enmity. Eumenes was also uncomfortably aware Hecataeus was now working for Antipater, with whom he had also had poor relations during their days together at Philip's court. These old tensions hung in the air as Hecataeus relayed Antipater's plea to Leonnatus.

For Leonnatus, this was the second stunning message to arrive from Europe in the short time since Alexander's death. A letter from Cleopatra and Olympias had already come, inviting him to marry into the Argead family and assume control of its destiny. He had kept that invitation secret as he pondered his response. Now another trophy bride was being offered him and another chance to return home as hero and savior. To Leonnatus, the ironies of his position must have seemed amusing. Slighted by Perdiccas in Babylon, done out of his role in administering the empire, he was now sought as son-in-law by two powerful leaders, the iconic mother and father figures of the Macedonian state.

Leonnatus now saw a way he could advance himself by aiding both these leaders. First, he would cross the Hellespont and, with a dashing cavalry assault, break the siege of Lamia. Then he would return in triumph to Pella, the Macedonian capital, and claim the hand of the waiting princess, Cleopatra. That would mean rejecting Antipater's proffered daughter, for he could not marry both (only a king had the privilege of polygamy). But the slight would mean little once he had rescued the entire army from near-certain destruction and put himself very near the Argead throne, if not actually upon it.

Having resolved on this plan, Leonnatus decided to recruit Eumenes as his accomplice, a man he esteemed as a clever and loyal subordinate. Keeping hidden for the moment his true aim, to seize control of the Argead house and thus the empire, Leonnatus urged Eumenes to go with him to Europe to respond to Antipater's summons. He offered to help reconcile Eumenes with Hecataeus, the messenger who had brought the summons to their camp, so that the two old enemies could work together and prosper in Antipater's service. Eumenes, however, felt the rift could not be healed and feared that Antipater would have him killed as a favor to Hecataeus. Perhaps too he had doubts about Leonnatus, who, like many Macedonian nobles, showed a worrisomely high self-regard and an inordinate fondness for wrestling and hunting.

Stymied in his first approach, Leonnatus took Eumenes fully

into his confidence, revealing his letter from Cleopatra and his plan to join the royal family. This disclosure, which clearly implied disregard of the orders framed by Perdiccas in Babylon, was fraught with perils for Eumenes. He had to choose sides. He must either become Leonnatus' confederate, by concealing from Perdiccas what he had learned, or become his enemy by reporting it. Eumenes knew what path he would choose but for the moment contrived to say nothing. That night, however, Eumenes slipped away. He took with him a small corps of five hundred men and a chest of gold coins, money meant for hiring mercenaries to fight in Cappadocia. He made straight for Perdiccas' headquarters in Babylon.

When Leonnatus woke and found Eumenes gone, it was clear that the die had been cast. The secret of his plans to seize control in Europe would soon be out, and a showdown with Perdiccas was surely coming. But as the favorite of Olympias and Cleopatra, the man they had selected to father the next heir to the throne, he had good hopes of prevailing in that contest. He made haste to cross the Hellespont and return to Europe, where his destiny, and his queen, were waiting.

4. ARISTOTLE (CHALCIS, 322 B.C.)

While this fissure was opening in the ranks of Alexander's Bodyguards, the philosopher Aristotle died in his adopted home on the island of Euboea. Throughout his life he had suffered from a stomach ailment, and this had grown more severe after his departure from Athens. Perhaps the change of diet and routine hastened his demise. He was sixty-two years old.

Aristotle's wife, Pythias, had died long before, while the family was in Athens. Thereafter, Aristotle had shared his bed with Herpyllis, a former slave to whom he had given freedom. Perhaps it was Herpyllis who bore his son, Nicomachus, still a youth at the time Aristotle died; his daughter, Pythias, was also young, not yet in her teens. In his will—a document that survives complete, quoted by the ancient biographer Diogenes Laertius—Aristotle placed both children in the care of his adopted son, Nicanor, the man who had read aloud the Exiles' Decree to the Greeks at

Olympia. The will instructs Nicanor to look after Aristotle's children as though he were both their father and their brother, but, in a shift of roles not uncommon in the Greek world, to marry Pythias as soon as she came of age.

The will contains detailed arrangements for Aristotle's property, including his slaves, many of whom were to be freed. For Herpyllis, the ex-slave who had become his consort, Aristotle made generous provisions. He instructed Nicanor to look after her well, "because she cared for me sincerely," and to provide her with a home, new furnishings, and, should she choose to marry, a dowry and a staff of servants. At the same time he asked that the bones of his wife, Pythias, interred long before at Athens, be exhumed and reburied beside him. This, he points out, had been Pythias' instruction in her own will.

As chief executor of these arrangements Aristotle appointed Antipater, the great Macedonian soldier-statesman whose friendship had been so important to him. He had paid dearly for that friendship, losing his home of twelve years and his precious Lyceum largely because of it. Now, in his last days, he relied on it as a safeguard for the family he was leaving behind. He seems to have been unconcerned that Antipater, at that time penned up in Lamia with supplies running out, had scant hope of living much longer himself, unless one of Alexander's generals returned from Asia in time to save him.

5. LEONNATUS (MACEDONIA AND POINTS SOUTH, LATE SPRING 322 B.C.)

Leonnatus' entry into Pella, the Macedonian capital, must have been a magnificent event. Riding proudly in the vanguard of a splendid cavalry corps, his hair flipped back at the forehead, Leonnatus looked like a second Alexander—precisely what he hoped to be. His own horse, a rare Nesaean, had its bit and bridle cast from glittering gold and silver, testimony to the wealth won in the conquest of the Persian empire. The Macedonians must have gaped. This was the first great general, and some of the first troops, to return to the homeland, of all the tens of thousands that had left it over the past twelve years.

To Leonnatus, by contrast, the royal seat of the Macedonians must have seemed hopelessly provincial. The palace he hoped soon to inhabit was far smaller than the one he had slept in the previous summer, the Southern Palace of Nebuchadnezzar in Babylon, and that had been only one of several palaces in that grand metropolis. Pella was but a town by comparison with the great Asian cities, and the wealth won by Alexander had only just begun to filter back to it. Yet it was from this modest center that the Macedonians had gone forth to conquer the world. Leonnatus could rule that world, if he could gain control of this center.

The princess Cleopatra, Alexander's sister, must have been among those welcoming Leonnatus home, but what passed between the prospective bride and bridegroom we do not know. There was little time for courtship, since Antipater's position in Lamia had become desperate. Leonnatus mustered the overdrawn native troops and levied more from neighboring Balkan peoples, raising an impressive force of twenty thousand infantry. With cavalry, however, he had less success, since the Thessalians, who had most of the horses and trained riders in the region, were supporting the Greek side in the war. Leonnatus had to proceed with only fifteen hundred horsemen, less than half what the Greeks had at Lamia.

With these forces Leonnatus marched south, determined to break the Greek cordon and link up with Antipater. The Greeks, for their part, were determined to prevent any such link. They abandoned their siege and went to meet Leonnatus, hoping to deal with his army before it could join Antipater's. They did not have enough manpower to maintain their guard over Lamia while also fighting Leonnatus. Several contingents had gone back to their home cities, wearied by the long winter siege or pressed by the needs of farms and businesses.

The Greeks hoped for a cavalry battle against Leonnatus to maximize their advantage, and they got what they hoped for. The horsemen from Thessaly, fighting now on the Greek side, came forward to meet Leonnatus, with a commander named Menon leading the attack. They drove Leonnatus' cavalry into a marsh where his horses had little traction. Leonnatus fought fiercely, but cut off from his infantry and mired in swampy ground, he found his position hopeless. Wounded many times by the thrusts of Thessalian lances, he fell, and his comrades carried him back toward the baggage camp. He died before he got there.

Having prevailed in this cavalry engagement, the Greeks hoped also to defeat the infantry phalanx Leonnatus had brought south with him. But the trained Macedonian pikemen knew how to prevent a minor loss from becoming a crushing one. They drew back onto high ground difficult for cavalry operations, holding out their *sarissas* to form a barrier against a charge. The Thessalian horsemen made a few sallies but soon saw these were useless. The Greek infantry, with shorter spears and far less experience than their adversaries, did not even bother to engage. Thus the battle ended.

By any reckoning the day belonged to the Greeks, who collected their dead and set up a monument on the field, traditional markers of victory. But the huge Macedonian phalanx remained unvanquished and undiminished in numbers. The very next day, it linked up with the army of Antipater, which, while the Greeks were otherwise occupied, had broken out of Lamia. Together these two forces escaped north to Macedonia. The Greeks would have to face Antipater all over again.

With the retreating forces, almost certainly, went the body of Leonnatus, on its way to a state funeral instead of a royal wedding. In his glorious career as a cavalry officer, Leonnatus had beaten Persian noblemen, Indian *mahouts* atop elephants, and Scythians who could fire arrows backward while riding at a gallop, but he was finally unhorsed by his own former allies, the Thessalians. Perhaps he had gained too much confidence from sharing Alexander's victories, for he accepted a fight against a corps more than twice the size of his own. Thus, from not having the brilliance of Alexander, perished the first of Alexander's top generals.

6. HYPERIDES (ATHENS, LATE SPRING 322 B.C.)

While in the field at Lamia, the Greeks, following long-standing traditions, cremated their dead, then sent the ashes to the home cities of the fallen for burial. Many such shipments arrived at Athens during the Hellenic War, including the charred bones of

Leosthenes, the great mercenary captain felled by a hurtling stone. According to their city's unique custom, the Athenians chose a leading citizen to give a public oration honoring the courage of those who had died. The speaker they chose during the Hellenic War was Hyperides—fittingly enough, for this was *his* war, and Leosthenes had been *his* chosen general.

Hyperides' speech was delivered outside the city walls, in a section of the Cerameicus, the Athenian graveyard, reserved for war dead. It was early spring, a time of rainy and gray weather in Athens. A sober procession of eleven wagons passed through the city and out the northwest gate; each wagon bore a cypress-wood chest containing commingled ashes of the dead, one for each of Athens' ten tribes and an extra one, empty, for those whose bodies had not been recovered. Accompanying these wagons came the families of the fallen. Arrived at the Cerameicus, the chests were unloaded and interred in the earth, and the crowd gathered around a speaker's platform to hear Hyperides. Grief over personal loss was combined with unease at the course of the war, for, with the siege at Lamia broken and a new Macedonian army in the field, Athens' chances of victory, once so promising, were now no better than even.

Hyperides mounted the platform to give what was to be the last speech of the golden age of Athenian oratory. It was totally unknown to the modern world until 1858, when a copy was recovered, truncated, though otherwise intact, from the scrap papers used to wrap an Egyptian mummy.

"Of the words about to be spoken over this tomb, concerning Leosthenes the general and the men who died with him in this war—words that will show they were good men—time itself will be the proof," Hyperides began. It was an audacious move to name Leosthenes in his very first sentence, but Hyperides had written an audacious speech. Where other such orations dealt in hazy abstractions, or invoked age-old myths, Hyperides was going to extol a hero who was real flesh and blood. He would give the Athenians a Leosthenes to rival the Macedonians' Alexander. He would fashion a cult of personality around Leosthenes, in hopes that, with this undemocratic style of rhetoric, he might inspire democratic Athens to win its stalemated war.

"I will start with the general, for that is only right," Hyperides continued. "It was Leosthenes who saw Greece disgraced and cowering, undermined by those taking bribes from Philip and Alexander . . . It was he who saw that our city needed a man outstanding in leadership, just as the Greeks needed a leading city; it was he who gave himself to his city and the city to the Greeks, for the cause of freedom!" The cynics in the crowd might have balked at hailing Leosthenes as a champion of freedom—a soldier for hire who had spent his life in arms, who had no ideology but hatred of Alexander and love of victory, who had grown up among the Macedonians and once served under them, who had never even lived in the city for which he fought. But for others, who now thrilled as Hyperides retold the triumphs of the past year, these were overly nice calculations. Under Leosthenes, Athens had *won,* and where Athens won, so did the cause of Greek liberty.

"But let no one suppose I ignore other citizens and heap praise on Leosthenes alone," Hyperides continued, aware of the danger of going too far. "For who would not be right to praise those who died in this war, who gave their lives for the freedom of the Greeks? . . . Through them, fathers have become respected and mothers admired . . . , sisters have made and will make fitting marriages; children will have, as their admission to the goodwill of the city, the virtue of these men"—he gestured toward the fresh-dug graves below him—"men who have not died, but have only exchanged life for an eternal battle line." A strange and striking metaphor, well suited to a speech built around a mercenary captain—a picture of the dead as warriors stationed in a ghostly infantry phalanx.

With such words Hyperides sought to comfort Athens' mourners and strengthen the city for the next phase of the war. Because our sole copy of the speech is incomplete, we do not know whether Hyperides acknowledged the difficulties that phase would bring. His one reference to the recent battle against Leonnatus suggests he regarded this as a victory but not one to celebrate; he did not even name its victorious generals, Menon and Antiphilus. He bent all his energy toward glorifying Leosthenes, which meant casting the new team of leaders as lesser men.

A skilled politician knows how to dodge blame by providing

scapegoats, and Hyperides may have foreseen that scapegoats would soon be needed. All would be well, he seems to imply, if only *his* man, Leosthenes, were still in charge.

7. THE WAR AT SEA (HELLESPONT REGION, SPRING–SUMMER 322 B.C.)

The hopes of the antagonists in the Hellenic War now rested on a narrow body of water, in places less than a mile wide. Across these straits, the Hellespont, the primary crossing point between Europe and Asia, reinforcements would need to come if the strategic balance was to be changed. Old man Antipater, now back in Macedonia preparing for a second assault on the rebel Greeks, could not win without more cavalry, and more cavalry could come only from the forces in Asia under Craterus. Antipater had to get control of the straits so Craterus could cross them, and Athens, if it hoped to beat Antipater again, had to prevent such a crossing. The theater of war now moved to the sea.

The Hellespont had always been a vital strategic asset for Athens or for its enemies. In 480 B.C., King Xerxes of Persis, en route to attacking Athens, had bridged the straits with a chain of more than three hundred warships and brought his army into Europe on a road laid across their decks. Rumor had it that when a storm broke apart his bridge, Xerxes flogged the Hellespont and flung shackles into its waters as though to make them his slave. In the end it was Athens, not Xerxes, that mastered the straits, using its formidable navy to patrol them; a large part of Athens' food supply was shipped through them from the grain-rich lands of the Black Sea, and if those shipments were ever choked off, the Athenians would starve. Only once since the defeat of Xerxes had an enemy of Athens gained control of the straits, and on that occasion—after the capture of an Athenian fleet by the Spartans, in 404 B.C.—Athens had quickly been forced to surrender.

Maintaining mastery over the Hellespont was an expensive proposition. The Athenians kept up a large fleet of warships, over four hundred at times, paid for by boards of wealthy citizens. The burden was a heavy one, and many shirked it. Even more expensive than the ships were the crews needed to row them. Four hundred ships required eighty thousand crewmen, each drawing a daily wage. Athens could neither afford so many nor even find them, for the rapid maneuvers of a warship required not just strength from its rowers but skill and experience. In Europe at the time of the Hellenic War, men who possessed these were hard to come by.

Not so in Asia, however. The seafarers who had once served the Persian empire, in particular the Phoenicians, now served the Macedonians, and where money was needed to pay them, their masters could draw on a bottomless treasury. Persian gold had beaten the Athenians once before: funneled to Sparta during the Peloponnesian War, it had built the navy that denied them use of the straits. Now, in the hands of its new owners, Persian gold might beat them again.

Alexander, just before his death, had started spending that gold to build up his navy. Anticipating war in the West, he had sent a fleet of 110 warships to old man Antipater, along with a supply of cash. These ships had already given the Athenian navy a hard time while Antipater was at Lamia, but they were soon joined by a second fleet commanded by Cleitus the White, an officer who had accompanied Craterus out of Babylon. Sailing to the Hellespont in the spring of 322, Cleitus encountered the Athenians at Abydus, the best landing point for troops crossing into Europe, and soundly defeated them. Then he won a second victory at Amorgus in the Cyclades, intercepting an Athenian fleet sent to retake the straits. Though details of these battles are scant, their result is clear: control of the sea passed from Athenian hands into those of the Macedonians. For Cleitus—who took to standing in the prow of his vessel posed as Poseidon, with a trident in one hand—this was a triumph of heroic proportions.

The Amorgus battle had a peculiar denouement at Athens. A prankster named Stratocles, getting wind while abroad of the Athenian defeat, hastened back to Athens before other messengers could arrive there. He falsely reported that Athens had won the engagement and gadded about wearing a garland and proposing grateful offerings to the gods. The people celebrated his news, then turned on him angrily after the truth finally emerged. Stratocles was unrepentant. "What harm have I done if for two days you have been happy?" he asked his fellow Athenians. Thanks to him the city had enjoyed one last, brief illusion that its 150-year-old naval supremacy was intact.

Remarkably, a huge number of Athens' warships sat idle in the Piraeus docks during the pitched struggle at sea. The city had managed to build a vast fleet but lacked rowers and steersmen to man it. The financial windfall it had gotten from Harpalus had been spent on Leosthenes and his mercenaries. Athens had not been able to afford a land and sea war at the same time.

8. END OF THE HELLENIC WAR (SUMMER 322 B.C.)

Craterus, roused at last from his long stasis in Cilicia, crossed the Hellespont with ten thousand infantrymen and a vital squadron of fifteen hundred cavalry. He met Antipater on the march in Thessaly and placed himself at the service of the older man, whom he now regarded not only as commander but as father-in-law-to-be. Craterus had made his choice of wives. He had brought Phila, Antipater's daughter, with him from Cilicia as his intended bride. Amastris, the Persian princess whom Alexander had given him in marriage, he left on the Asian side of the Hellespont, after gallantly arranging her remarriage to a powerful ruler on the Black Sea coast. (The Turkish town of Amasra, on the site of a city she founded, still bears a corrupted version of her name.)

Antipater, having now absorbed the armies of both Craterus and Leonnatus, brought a force totaling almost fifty thousand to a place called Crannon on the Thessalian plain. He made camp a short distance from the Athenian-led coalition. Each morning, for the next few weeks, he made clear to the Greeks he was ready to fight, arranging his troops in formation in the plain between the camps.

Antiphilus and Menon, the Greek field commanders, debated whether to accept this offer of battle. Their twenty-five thousand infantry were badly outnumbered and outclassed in skill and experience, but their thirty-five hundred cavalry had better hopes of success. By waiting, they might increase their infantry numbers; messengers had been sent to the allied cities seeking new recruits and requesting the return of missing contingents, including those of the Aetolians. But the Greeks could not wait indefinitely. Morale was low. More contingents might head for home; their numbers might shrink rather than increase, as would their fighting spirit. Finally, near the beginning of August, the Greeks' need for action overcame their need for reinforcement. Antiphilus and Menon brought their outnumbered army forward for battle.

All their hopes lay in the Thessalian cavalry, the same force that had beaten Leonnatus. As they had done before, the Greeks sent their cavalry out ahead and held their infantry back. But the Macedonians were not about to let the issue again be decided by cavalry alone. Antipater ordered his massive phalanx to advance. The approach of this mile-and-a-half-long wall of spearmen made a deeply unsettling spectacle, and at the first collision the Greeks began to falter. They drew back onto the high ground behind them, where they could defend themselves but could no longer provide protection for the cavalry. The Thessalian horsemen accordingly broke off their attack.

The day ended without a clear decision. The Greeks had prevailed with their cavalry before being bested in their infantry. Even then, their losses had been light, about five hundred killed, thanks to the orderly retreat of the phalanx. If reinforced by the Greek cities to their south, they still had good hope of prevailing in the end.

But somehow that hope was not enough to sustain them. The Athenian general Antiphilus and his Thessalian colleague, Menon, were not confident they could hold the army together until recruits could arrive. Plutarch says these commanders were young and, being *epieikeis*—a complex Greek word blending notions of fairness, rationality, and gentleness—could not retain the respect of their men. Whatever their qualities, they certainly did not measure up to their illustrious fallen predecessor, Leosthenes.

Antiphilus and Menon took counsel together, and on the day after the battle of Crannon, usually reckoned as August 6, they sent heralds to the Macedonian camp asking for terms of surrender. It was a quiet end to an otherwise climactic sequence of events. No bloodbath or rout had crushed the cause of Greek freedom, but simply a sense that with money and morale running low, there was no longer any point in fighting. The Hellenic War had come to an end.

9. ANTIPATER, PHOCION, AND DEMADES (THEBES, SUMMER 322 B.C.)

The Greek generals hoped to arrange common terms of surrender for their entire alliance, but Antipater was in no mood to bargain. He demanded separate arrangements for each Greek city, clearly intending to deal most harshly with the Athenians. While the Greeks debated this matter, Antipater drove his point home by storming several Thessalian towns, then granting easy terms when they surrendered. The message was clear: he had Athens in his sights and would be clement to others if they broke with Athens—which all the Greek allies now hastened to do. Athens stood alone as Antipater, to enforce his demand for unconditional surrender, led his army into neighboring Boeotia and prepared to attack.

Inside the Athenian walls, a panicked Assembly cast about for direction. The political order of the city, violently overturned the previous year by news of Alexander's death, had to be inverted once again. Hyperides was now discredited, along with his fellow advocate of revolt, Demosthenes. It was instead to Phocion, and the even more pro-Macedonian Demades, that the Athenians turned, hoping to find favor with Antipater and escape complete destruction.

But Demades had been stripped of citizen rights amid the war fervor of the previous year. He now played this irony for all it was worth, refusing to reply even when public officials called him three times to the speaker's platform. The Assembly hastily restored his citizenship and removed his fines, and he came forward at last. He relied on a time-tested strategy and proposed that a negotiating party, led by him and Phocion, be sent at once to Antipater. Phocion, for his part, could not let pass an opportunity to point out he had been right about the war. "If you had trusted my advice before," he told the Assembly, "we would not now be debating such proposals." But he agreed to take part in the diplomatic mission.

Demades and Phocion—the same team that had been sent to Alexander thirteen years earlier, when the lives of ten orators were on the line—met with Antipater at Thebes, amid the remains of the city Alexander had destroyed. The setting was a pointed reminder of what might befall Greeks who defied Macedonian rule. Antipater had Craterus with him, clearly now his partner in command as well as his future son-in-law.

The negotiations were an exercise in humility for Phocion and Demades. They had little to bargain with except the goodwill they had earned in more than thirteen years of entente with the Macedonians. For Craterus, who had spent those thirteen years on campaign in Asia, that counted for nothing at all. When Phocion requested that the Macedonians stay where they were and not bring their army of fifty thousand into Attica, Craterus sneered; why should their Boeotian friends, and not their defeated enemies, bear the burden of feeding them? But Antipater took his new comrade by the hand and urged, "We must grant this as a kindness to Phocion." There was a deep mutual respect between Antipater and Phocion, both now in their late seventies, veterans of six decades of combat and political upheaval.

When the Athenian envoys broached terms of surrender, however, Antipater turned icy. He spat back the words Leosthenes had once spoken to him: the victors would set the terms.

Unable to stomach an unconditional defeat, Phocion and Demades returned to Athens. The Assembly sent them out a second time but put a new team member in place: Xenocrates, an aged philosopher, a former friend and fellow student of Aristotle's, and, at this time, head of Plato's Academy. The city hoped to remind Antipater of its great intellectual traditions—a strong argument against its destruction—and also to play on his known friendship with Aristotle. But when the new team arrived in Thebes, Antipater ignored Xenocrates entirely and rudely spoke over him every time the man opened his mouth.

Though initially bent on surrender without terms, Antipater at last laid out steps by which Athens could avoid an invasion. The city was to hand over Demosthenes and Hyperides, along with other instigators of the revolt. It had to change its time-honored democracy into an oligarchy, accept a Macedonian garrison in Piraeus (Athens' harbor), and repay all the costs Macedon had incurred in the war, plus a fine. This was better than Phocion and Demades had reason to expect, and they signaled approval. Xenocrates, who had been excluded from the discussion, was less reconciled. He delivered a bitter parting shot, telling Antipater he was treating the Athenians too generously for slaves but too cruelly for free men.

Installation of the Piraeus garrison was the harshest of Antipater's terms, as far as Phocion was concerned. Other Greek cities had long before submitted to armed occupation, but Athens had always been spared; its proud history conferred special standing even under Macedonian hegemony. Phocion pleaded with Antipater to once again exempt Athens, but the old general replied, "Phocion, we are willing to grant you anything, except what will destroy you and us both." This was a winking acknowledgment of the new realities Phocion faced as Antipater's collaborator. Were the Athenians, left unguarded, to revolt again, Phocion would be as much their enemy as Antipater. Reluctantly, Phocion agreed to the garrison.

Under the command of a certain Menyllus, Antipater's troops sailed into Piraeus a few weeks later, in mid-September, to take up guard duties on the fortified hill of Munychia. It was the very day that a sacred procession left Athens for nearby Eleusis as part of the local religious rites known as the Mysteries. The conjunction of this treasured ritual with the arrival of garrison troops distressed the Athenians, who felt the gods themselves had abandoned their city. Strange portents and visions were seen, giving the day dire significance. A worshipper taking part in the Mysteries, while washing a sacrificial pig in the harbor waters, watched in horror as a shark bit the animal in two and swam away with the lower half. Seers divined that Athens would forever lose the "lower part" of its city, meaning Piraeus, to Macedonian power.

Phocion and Demades became the leaders of an Athenian government refashioned as a broad plutocracy. Only those with property worth at least two thousand drachmas—a sizable upper-middle-class estate—were allowed to hold office or vote. The organs of the old democracy continued to function, but more than twenty thousand, well over half the citizen body, were now barred from participation. Many of these left the city and accepted new lands in Thrace, lands that old man Antipater graciously—and expeditiously—provided. It was in his interest to excise those he called "troublemakers and warmongers" and make Athens a city of the comfortably well-off, the class that had largely opposed the Hellenic War to begin with.

The disenfranchised poor who stayed in Athens chafed at their second-class status. In other Greek cities they would never have tasted power, but having grown used to it, they found its loss hard to bear. Their humiliation embittered them against their burgher neighbors, and especially the man whose aristocratic manner made him the perfect target of their rage—a former student of Plato's, now seemingly Antipater's puppet, Do-good Phocion.

10. HYPERIDES (AEGINA AND CORINTH, LATE SEPTEMBER–EARLY OCTOBER 322 B.C.)

Hyperides and Demosthenes did not wait to hear Antipater's terms before making their escape from Athens. It had been clear for a long time that the old general would seek their lives if he won the war, and that this time, unlike in the showdown with Alexander thirteen years earlier, Athens would not protect them. In the end, Demosthenes' nephew and protégé, Demochares, made a show of defending his uncle, rising boldly to speak in the Assembly with a sword at his waist. But the time for such defiance had passed. The Assembly soon voted, on the motion of Demades, to condemn both Demosthenes and Hyperides to death in absentia, and to forbid their burial on Attic soil. This last clause was an unusually harsh measure, an obvious sop to the wrath of Macedon.

Athens' two greatest living orators, and two lesser ones condemned along with them, had little hope except sanctuary at the altars of the gods. In former days, when Asia still belonged to the Persians, an Athenian forced into exile could find safety there, among the enemies of his enemies. But now the whole known world was in Macedonian hands. There was nowhere to hide.

Together the party of fugitives went to the island of Aegina, where a vast marble enclosure sacred to the mythic hero Aeacus offered protection to suppliants. Close on their heels came a notorious Greek bounty hunter, Archias the Exile-chaser, with a squad of Thracian toughs. This versatile man had abandoned two earlier careers, as a tragic actor and as a rhetorician, to become Antipater's bloodhound, no doubt in exchange for handsome rewards. (At some point he came a cropper in his new line of work, for Arrian, in a lost portion of *Events After Alexander,* told how he ended his life in poverty and despair.)

Hyperides and his two comrades chose to stay on Aegina and await their fate, while Demosthenes went on to the tiny island of Calauria, where he had lived in exile the previous year. The sanctuary of Poseidon there was said to be inviolable. Before his departure, he and Hyperides said their final farewells. Their forty-year partnership had been briefly severed amid the turmoil of the bribery scandal, but it had been miraculously restored in the last few months, when Athens had come agonizingly close to the liberation both men had sought. Now, at the doorway of death, Hyperides apologized for his prosecution of Demosthenes, and the two men parted as friends. Perhaps they paused to consider that, were it not for the chance arc of a stone at Lamia, they might together have become the greatest heroes in Athenian political history.

Archias the Exile-chaser arrived in Aegina not long after Demosthenes left. Undeterred by religious scruple, he had the three proscribed orators dragged out of the sacred enclosure and sent to Antipater, who was then at Cleonae, near Corinth. All three were executed, and Hyperides' tongue, the tongue that had delivered so many speeches against Macedon, was cut out of his head. His corpse was cast out unburied as a warning to his sympathizers and as punishment for his support of the Hellenic War.

Later, though, Hyperides' body was given to a kinsman named Alphinous, thanks to the intervention of a Greek doctor who had influence at the Macedonian court. After honorable cremation, the ashes were secretly interred near the Hippades Gate at Athens, in Hyperides' native soil, in defiance of the Assembly's decree.

II. DEMOSTHENES (CALAURIA, MID-OCTOBER 322 B.C.)

About a week after Hyperides' death, in the grove of Poseidon at Calauria, Demosthenes awakened from a strange dream. He dreamed that both he and Archias the Exile-chaser were actors in competing tragic dramas, and Demosthenes' performance, being much the better, won the greater share of applause. Nonetheless, because his production lacked expensive scenery and fine costumes, the prize was given to Archias. Perhaps Demosthenes took comfort from this dream, in which mere victory was distinguished from intrinsic worth. The moral standing of his cause, Athenian freedom, might after all remain undamaged, despite the triumph of Macedonian power.

His return to Calauria only a few months after leaving it showed how quickly Fortune's wheel could turn. First had come word of the death of Alexander, bringing with it Athens' move toward war. Then Demosthenes' return to favor at Athens—sudden, exhilarating, and maddeningly brief. The failure of the revolt had forced him back into exile, this time under a sentence of death. Athenian politics had never been more stormy or unpredictable than in the past year and a half, but politics was the life Demosthenes had chosen, for better or worse. Once, when some young men had sought his advice about careers, he had wearily observed that if two roads had been shown him as a youth, one leading to the speaker's platform and the Assembly, the other to an early grave, he would have chosen the path to the grave. Now it seemed the other path would lead there as well.

That very morning, a day in mid-October, Archias the Exile-chaser was crossing over to Calauria accompanied by his Thracian spearmen. The search party soon made its way to Poseidon's shrine and, for some reason unwilling to enter, hailed Demosthenes from outside. Archias told his quarry to come peacefully and promised that neither he nor Antipater would do him harm. Demosthenes retorted that he had never before found Archias' acting convincing and did not now. He had surely learned what had befallen Hyperides a week earlier and was determined to make a better end.

When Archias began threatening to use force, Demosthenes, as though acknowledging defeat, asked to compose a letter to his family. Withdrawing into an enclosed part of the temple, he put the end of a reed pen to his mouth as he often did when writing and stealthily sucked out some poison he had hidden there. Then he covered himself with his cloak and put his head down, waiting for death to arrive.

The Thracians looking on from outside mistook his posture for supplication of the god and began to taunt him for cowardice. Archias entered the room and tried once again to convince Demosthenes that his life would be spared. But by now the poison had begun to work. Demosthenes uncovered his head and, with another barb at his captor's former career, suggested that Archias could now play the part of Creon in Sophocles' *Antigone,* the tyrant who exposes the corpse of his enemy for dogs to devour. Then he turned to the statue of Poseidon at the center of the shrine. "Good Poseidon, I will leave your temple still alive, though Antipater and the Macedonians would not have let it stay undefiled," he said, and asked for help getting to his feet. He wanted to avoid polluting the holy precinct with his death, but as he staggered past the altar, he fell and groaned his last.

Plutarch, who like other Greeks regarded Demosthenes' suicide as a heroic act of defiance, notes that there were various descriptions of the event. According to one, Demosthenes took poison not from the end of his pen but from a little cloth bag he wore tied to his waist. Another claimed the venom was contained in a hollow bracelet. Demochares, the nephew of Demosthenes who had tried to rally support in the Assembly, claimed that his uncle had not taken poison at all but had been delivered from his enemies by divine will; some god had sent him a painless death at the most opportune moment. It was comforting to think that after so much neglect of Athens' fortunes, the gods had intervened to spare the dignity of the city's last free man.

It took decades for Demochares to rehabilitate his uncle's reputation, but he finally succeeded, near the end of his life, in persuading Athens to erect a commemorative statue. The portrait

Demosthenes, as depicted in a Roman copy of
the commemorative statue by Polyeuctus

was done in bronze by Polyeuctus, a famous Athenian sculptor of
the day; it survives in several Roman-era stone copies. Demosthenes is shown standing erect but with head downcast; his careworn face wears a pensive expression; he holds in both hands a
papyrus scroll, no doubt a speech to be delivered in the Assembly.
The portrait gives a vivid impression of strength, conviction, and

seriousness of purpose, but also of tragic futility. It depicts a man whose goals are doomed never to be achieved.

The statue's original was set up in the Athenian market square, with a rueful verse inscription on its base:

> *If only your strength, Demosthenes, had been equal in force*
> *   to your judgment,*
> *Greece would have never been ruled by Macedonian Ares.*

A Death on the Nile

Western Asia and Egypt

SUMMER 322–SUMMER 321 B.C.

During the year since his death, Alexander's mummified body had lain in a coffin of hammered gold, covered by a purple cloth embroidered with gold, in the palace of Nebuchadnezzar in Babylon. Throughout that year and most of the next, Arrhidaeus, the officer appointed by Perdiccas, oversaw construction of a magnificent hearse to bear the body to its final home.

Preservation of corpses was new to the Macedonians. Before Alexander, only Hephaestion had been embalmed, and only briefly, to keep his body from decay while an elaborate funeral pyre was made ready. Alexander's case was different. As weeks stretched into months and then past a year, the purple-clad casket must have become an eerie fixture of the palace complex, inspiring comfort or fear in those who passed near it. It seemed to contain a god, yet gods were supposed to dwell beneath the ground or in the sky, not under the same roofs as men.

It was the custom of the Macedonians before Alexander's day to inter their kings in chamber tombs in the royal city of Aegae, usually after cremation. That was the protocol for Alexander's father, Philip, whose remains were found in one of the two tombs discovered at Vergina in 1977 (though just which one, Tomb 1 or Tomb 2, is still debated). It was to Aegae that Alexander's body would finally be sent, not by the king's own wishes but by the will of Perdiccas' government, after the completion of his catafalque.

But Alexander's corpse would never make it to Aegae. A different burial site was being arranged for it by Ptolemy, satrap of Egypt, even as the magnificent hearse was being built. Those arrangements were as yet a secret, and would remain so until the moment they were put into effect, for any disclosure might be reported to Perdiccas, head of the beleaguered Babylon government, and the consequences were sure to be severe.

1. CLEOPATRA (SARDIS, AUTUMN 322 B.C.)

It was not a funeral but a wedding—her own—that was on the mind of Alexander the Great's sister, Cleopatra, as she journeyed from Macedonia to the city of Sardis (in what is now western Turkey). She and her mother, Olympias, had failed in their first bid to arrange a marriage, when Leonnatus, their chosen bridegroom, got himself killed in battle. Now the two royal women, Alexander's closest kin, were determined to try again. This time, rather than lure a potential husband to Europe, Cleopatra herself came into Asia, where Alexander's generals were thickest. Her family's fortunes depended on her attracting one of these, and the sooner the better, for their nemesis, old man Antipater, was quickly cornering the marriage market. Craterus in Europe was already wed to Antipater's eldest daughter, Phila; Ptolemy in Egypt was awaiting the arrival of his youngest, Eurydice; and to Perdiccas, the most powerful of them all, he had promised Nicaea. Antipater had thus gained sons-in-law on all three continents, dangerously isolating Olympias, his ancient antagonist.

But Olympias and her daughter still held the trump card in marital politics, the blood royal. Unlike Antipater's daughters, Cleopatra, now in her early thirties, could beget a legitimate heir to the throne. And, as Alexander's only full sibling, she herself stood closest to that throne. Marriage to Cleopatra would instantly elevate any bridegroom to royal status and might even make him a king. Kingship of Macedon had never before been obtained through marriage, but neither had there ever been joint rule by two kings, nor a king with half Bactrian blood, nor a royal seat in far-off Babylon. The new age ushered in by Alexander had brought unthinkable things to pass, and many routes to the throne might now be fair game.

Cleopatra thus went to Asia, to see whether one of the generals there might marry her. As it happened, the best catch of them all was promised but not yet wed—Perdiccas, guardian of the joint kings and head of the central government.

Cleopatra must have known that the arrival of Perdiccas' bride was expected in Babylon at any moment. She may have been present in Pella when Iolaus, Antipater's son, arrived from Asia to fetch Nicaea, or when the two siblings departed for the Hellespont, accompanied by that most trustworthy of Macedonian agents, Archias the Exile-chaser. If so, Cleopatra must have hastened her own departure in hope of forestalling the wedding. She must have either left in secret or given some pretext to Antipater, who had the means to prevent her departure. Perhaps she claimed only to want to see her infant nephew, the king in swaddling clothes, one-year-old Alexander—a request that Antipater, still a servant of the royals though locked in a desperate rivalry with them, could hardly refuse.

So Cleopatra said farewell to Europe, and the mother she would never see again, and arrived in Sardis, the city she would never leave.

2. PERDICCAS (WESTERN ASIA, AUTUMN 322 B.C.)

To be simultaneously sought by two brides, one of them a princess, might seem to some men an enviable fate, but not to Perdiccas. The unexpected landing in Asia of Cleopatra, at the same time as the long-awaited arrival of Nicaea, posed a delicate political problem. To marry into one powerful family meant, inevitably, to disrespect the other. The question he now confronted was, which would be which?

Perdiccas could see why Alexander had wed no Macedonian women but a Bactrian and two Persians. Though Asian queens in the Argead house had offended the nobles back home, at least all had been equally offended. Alexander had caused no factional splits among the baronial families of Macedon, each seeking favor in the eyes of the king. Now Perdiccas, the closest thing the empire had to a ruler, was staring at a split that would have filled Alexander with dread. The dowager queen Olympias and the aging patriarch Antipater, mortal enemies to each other, both sought him as their son-in-law. He could not accept one without badly alienating the other.

Perdiccas' choice was not just between wives and in-laws but also between two political futures: a limited, Asia-based sovereignty or dominion over the entire empire. Antipater had been given control over Europe in the settlement crafted at Babylon, together with Craterus, now related to him by marriage. Perdiccas had ceded this control because he had been too weak to contest it; merely managing Asia was challenging enough. If he were now to marry Nicaea and ally with Antipater, and by extension with Craterus as well, he would reaffirm that settlement and the division of the world it implied. Cleopatra, by contrast, represented a power that transcended continents and borders. As Cleopatra's husband, Perdiccas could claim a throne in Pella as easily as in Babylon—or, for that matter, in Egypt, where Ptolemy was growing disturbingly strong willed.

Was he to take the lion's share of Alexander's empire, the Asian portion, or rule all three continents together? It was an agonizing dilemma, made worse by the divided counsels of his advisers. Eumenes the Greek, Alexander's former scribe and now Perdiccas' right-hand man, urged marriage to Cleopatra. Eumenes was a monarchist who saw the world in dynastic terms; power, in his eyes, came from a title and a scepter as much as from an army. Perdiccas' younger brother Alcetas kept pulling him in the other direction. Marriage to Nicaea would bless the status quo with amity and concord, Alcetas believed. Antipater would live and let live, his ambitions fulfilled in Europe, while Perdiccas could stay in Asia and harvest its enormous wealth. Perdiccas was still weak, Alcetas argued; he could not afford to throw over Nicaea and risk a clash of continents.

Perdiccas *had* been weak when he first asked for Nicaea's

hand, in those desperate days when he had cast his own troops under trampling elephants. But much had changed since then. Perdiccas had led a campaign in Cappadocia on behalf of Eumenes—Antigonus One-eye and Leonnatus both having spurned their assigned commands there—and had prevailed in a tough fight. Ariarathes, leader of the Persian holdouts looking to undo Alexander's conquests, had put an army of thirty thousand in the field, including large cohorts of Greek mercenaries, but Perdiccas had defeated them in two major battles, and impaled Ariarathes as a lesson to his supporters. Then he had gone to Cilicia and added to his forces the magnificent corps of veterans left there by Craterus, the Silver Shields. This crew of three thousand, led by an oak-hearted captain named Antigenes, were thought to be the best infantry soldiers in the known world. Indeed they had beaten virtually every foe in that world, during three decades of active service.

Perdiccas' strength had increased, and along with it the stature of Eumenes, who had shown he could wield a cavalry lance every bit as well as his secretarial stylus. When trouble had arisen in Armenia from unruly troops, and the regional commander there, Neoptolemus, was making a hash of things, Perdiccas dispatched little Eumenes to set things right. With judicious grants of free horses and tax amnesties, Eumenes quickly raised a decent Cappadocian cavalry force. He drilled and trained these horsemen to fight like Macedonians, and using this cavalry, he soon set Armenia in order. Perdiccas found he had gained not just a devoted ally and wise counselor in Eumenes but a fine field commander as well. Eumenes, for his part, found he had gained a new enemy—for Neoptolemus did not like being upstaged on his own turf by a Greek.

Recently, Perdiccas had claimed yet another victory, over troublesome Pisidian tribesmen who had long defied authority. It was the Pisidians who had killed Balacrus, the first husband of Antipater's daughter Phila, a few years earlier, and now Perdiccas made them pay the price—though in the end they robbed him of the full satisfaction of vengeance. There were two main towns in Pisidia, and after Perdiccas captured the first, he imposed summary punishment, executing all male inhabitants and enslaving women and children. Those in the second city resolved on a more dignified end. As Perdiccas' army attacked, they collected their families into a few houses and set the buildings on fire, then threw into the flames all their possessions. Defenders manning the walls held off Perdiccas' men until this mass immolation was complete, then leaped into the conflagration themselves. The next day the Macedonians entered the smoking ruin and picked through charred bones for puddles of congealed gold and silver.

Despite this dismaying conclusion, the campaign had been a success, making three victories for Perdiccas in the past year. His hand had been greatly strengthened in the contest for Alexander's power, since, to the soldiers on whom power depended, good generalship—and the booty it provided—meant everything. Perdiccas had even begun to plan how he would answer the challenge thrown at him by Antigonus One-eye. That man's refusal to obey orders could not be overlooked. A summons would be sent to Antigonus to appear before an army assembly in Babylon. If Antigonus would not come, he would be attacked; if he fled to Europe, Perdiccas would be rid of him for good.

Perdiccas had other irons in the fire as well, though few as yet knew of them. He had received secret letters from Athens, from Demades, a politician who had long collaborated with Antipater but who was now seeking to change masters. Demades, for reasons unknown—perhaps because Phocion, his partner in the puppet government at Athens, had the lion's share of power—urged Perdiccas to cross the Hellespont and oust Antipater, claiming he would have the support of the Greeks if he did so. "Our cities are held together only by an old and rotting rope," Demades wrote to Perdiccas, referring contemptuously to Antipater. A vigorous new leader, a man like Perdiccas, could easily wrest Europe from that aging and detested warhorse.

Then, too, Perdiccas had control of the body of Alexander, his greatest political asset, and the fabulous hearse that would soon transport it back to the Macedonian homeland. What if Perdiccas were to accompany that hearse, riding at the head of the Companion cavalry, and lead the burial rites of the great king? What if he brought the new kings, the imbecile Philip and the infant Alexander, along with him, like followers in his train? Would it not be clear to all that he, not Antipater, represented the leadership of the empire? Might not even Craterus, who had staged his own heroic homecoming the previous year, acknowledge his supremacy?

Then why should he not also wed Cleopatra and make the triumph complete with an open claim on the throne? The question haunted Perdiccas, even as Nicaea drew nearer. How great was the danger in taking Eumenes' advice, clasping Alexander's sister by the hand and joining the ranks of the royals? It was the same choice Leonnatus had faced when Cleopatra promised to marry him. Leonnatus had seized what was offered, thinking a royal bride worth the cost of universal mistrust.

But Perdiccas, on the brink of a similar leap onto ambition's summit, found he could not make up his mind. He could not break with Antipater and declare a civil war, even if it was a war he was likely to win. But neither could he let slip the chance offered him by Cleopatra. The counsels of Eumenes and Alcetas both had their hold on him; neither could be dismissed.

So Perdiccas married Antipater's daughter Nicaea but also sent Eumenes to Sardis with a covert message for Cleopatra, that he intended to reject his new bride and marry *her* instead. He would bide his time and keep both his options open. The best choice for now was no choice at all.

3. CYNNANE, ADEA, AND ALCETAS (WESTERN ASIA, AUTUMN 322 B.C.)

Just after the arrival of Cleopatra in Sardis, a new entrant in the marital lists landed in Asia, quite unexpectedly. The stratagems of Olympias had pointed the way for another royal mother, Cynnane, to seek power by way of another daughter, a girl in her early teens named Adea. But this mother-daughter team had set their sights even higher than Olympias and Cleopatra. They aimed not to marry a general to a princess but to marry a princess to a king. Cynnane had chosen Philip, the mentally impaired half brother of Alexander (and her own half brother as well), as bridegroom for her daughter (also Philip's niece).

Cynnane knew well the politics of dynastic marriages; she was the product of one. Her mother, a princess of Illyria (today part of

Albania), had come to Macedonia to wed Alexander's father, Philip, and seal an alliance between two contentious nations. Cynnane grew up at the Macedonian court but stayed true to her maternal traditions, for Illyrian women were famously tough, capable of going to war as men did. In her teens Cynnane is said to have accompanied the Macedonian army on a campaign into Illyria and to have slain a queen of that country—perhaps one of her own relatives—in hand-to-hand combat. Unfortunately, no account survives of that encounter between two armed female leaders, the first such encounter known to European history— though it would soon be followed by another.

When she came of age, Cynnane was given in a politically arranged marriage to her cousin Amyntas, an Argead in direct line of succession. She bore him a daughter, Adea. After the assassination of her father in 336 left the throne vacant, Cynnane might easily have become queen, had her husband acted quickly to make himself king, but instead his cousin Alexander seized the throne and had Amyntas done away with. Cynnane became a widow in her early twenties and stayed a widow thereafter, despite other offers of marriage. She focused her attention on Adea, rearing her after Illyrian fashion to be a huntress and warrior who could hold her own among men.

Cynnane was in her early thirties, and Adea barely past puberty, when Alexander died and a new Philip, an imbecilic parody of the old, was put on the throne. Cynnane was herself young enough to marry Philip and bear children, but she handed this opportunity down to her daughter, whose royal pedigree was purer than her own. In the second year after Alexander's death, she and Adea left Macedonia to make their way into Asia, accompanied by a hired band of armed men. Cynnane intended to find Philip and get Adea married to him, thereby advancing her branch of the royal family, the branch sprung from a warlike woman of Illyrian blood.

Such a move would deeply unsettle the already shaky power structure resolved at Babylon. It would add legitimacy to one of the two reigning kings and strengthen the monarchy as a whole, thus reducing the influence of the generals. Indeed it might eliminate the board of four custodians altogether, since Adea, once queen, would be able to speak and act for her royal husband. Antipater, one of the members of that board, determined he would stop the marriage from taking place. He sent troops to turn the two women back as they made their way eastward through Thrace, but in a skirmish at the river Strymon (in what is now Bulgaria) Cynnane and her forces prevailed. The bridal procession continued on its way and crossed the Hellespont into Asia.

Perdiccas was just as troubled as Antipater by the prospect of Adea's marriage to Philip but for different reasons. It was unclear whether Philip, with his mental impairment, was capable of begetting an heir, but should he do so, a son of his by Adea would have far greater legitimacy than Alexander's son by Rhoxane. One of the two branches of the royal family, now poised in a hard-won balance of power, would prevail over the other. Cynnane and Adea would rise in stature, as grandmother and mother of the new monarch; Olympias and Cleopatra, on whom Perdiccas was now resting his own hopes for a throne, would be cast down. Perdiccas determined he could not let that happen. Since Antipater had failed to stop the bridal convoy in Europe, Perdiccas sent his own squad, under command of his brother Alcetas, to intercept it in Asia.

Somewhere on the Asian side of the Hellespont, where Alcetas and his troops met Cynnane and hers, a tragedy occurred that showed how much trust had been lost since Alexander's death. Alcetas and Cynnane were almost exactly the same age and had known each other from childhood. They had grown up together at the palace in Pella, where Alcetas (almost certainly) was one of King Philip's page boys, Cynnane the eldest of Philip's children. They had both come of age at the same moment, she becoming a mother (and soon thereafter a widow), he a soldier in Alexander's army. Under different circumstances, they might have been glad to see each other again, but their paths had diverged greatly in the twelve years of Alexander's reign. Alcetas advanced with his troops arrayed for battle.

Cynnane was outraged by this implied threat. As she came close enough to Alcetas to be clearly heard, she stepped forward and delivered a stinging reproach of his ingratitude and disloyalty. It was the first of several proud speeches delivered by Argead women to Alexander's generals, as the royals defiantly resisted the new realities of their situation. The courtly world Philip had built for them, a world in which soldiers revered Argeads as superhuman beings, was gone. The meteoric impact of the Asian campaign had burst it to bits. Now that Alexander had built an omnipotent army, an army capable of defying its creator, it was no longer clear who was in control of whom.

Alcetas, in this case, was determined to exert not only control but domination. He ended the encounter between his forces and Cynnane's—no account of which has survived—by having Cynnane killed, when he might have taken her prisoner or sent her back to Europe under escort. Perhaps he was stung to fury by Cynnane's reproaches, or perhaps he acted on instructions given by his brother Perdiccas. Both armed columns and the young girl Adea looked on in horror. It was a brutal demonstration of resolve, more brutal even than the elephant-trampling executions Perdiccas had orchestrated two years earlier.

But its very brutality caused the move to backfire. When news of the killing arrived in Babylon, the Macedonian army recoiled from the murder of a daughter of Philip. As they had done in the days after Alexander's death, they rebelled against Perdiccas' leadership and rallied to the royal family. Perdiccas found his new-won military glory slipping away. To mollify the troops, he reversed course and had Adea brought to his camp. At his direction, she married her uncle, the half-wit king, Philip.

No older than fifteen, orphaned by two political murders, Adea claimed the prize her mother had died to obtain for her, a share of the Macedonian throne. She took her place amid a strange assortment of crowned heads: a grown man with the mind of a child, a Bactrian woman with strange manners and speech, and a two-year-old boy, her own cousin, only now learning to walk and talk. She quickly saw that she was the only one among them competent to wield power. She also must have seen, based on the army's support for her marriage to Philip, that the rank-and-file soldiery could be won over to her side. It was they who had put Philip on the throne and given him his name, hoping to reclaim the glories of a greater Philip, his father. They might now embrace Adea, granddaughter of that greater Philip, for the same reasons.

As though to gratify these longings for the past, Adea too changed her name, becoming Eurydice as she took her place on the throne. It was a name with good Argead pedigree, one that had belonged to her grandfather Philip's mother. It was better suited to her new station than Adea, which was (probably) an Illyrian name. She too, like the Philip who had once been Arrhidaeus, was now a standard-bearer of the old Argead traditions, the generations before Alexander's move into Asia. The heritage of her mother and grandmother, Illyrian warrior-women, was put aside in favor of the legacy she had through her grandfather.

But though she might advertise herself as native-born royalty, Adea still retained the warlike ways in which Cynnane had raised her. Her Illyrian roots had not been severed with a mere change of name. Alexander's top generals were about to tangle with one of history's toughest teenage girls.

4. ANTIGONUS, CRATERUS, AND ANTIPATER
(NORTHERN GREECE/WESTERN ASIA
WINTER, LATE 322 B.C.)

Cynnane's murder held particular significance for a man who had been keeping a close eye—the one eye he still had—on Perdiccas' doings.

Proud Antigonus, satrap of Phrygia, had already ignored Perdiccas' orders concerning the reconquest of Cappadocia. That set him at odds with the Babylon government, and since then antipathy on both sides had grown. Perdiccas had issued a summons to Antigonus to appear before a judicial proceeding, intending to settle the question of hierarchy once and for all. But Antigonus was contemplating a different plan. News of Cynnane's death helped further that plan and guarantee its success.

Somehow, Antigonus had learned of Perdiccas' intention to swap wives, trading Nicaea for Cleopatra, Antipater's daughter for Alexander's royal sister. Courtship of Cleopatra was strong evidence of the ambitions of Perdiccas, and the murder of Cynnane—which certainly looked to Antigonus like Perdiccas' handiwork, even if Alcetas had performed it—sealed the case. Antigonus could not stand by and watch one man raise his head above the heads of the other generals, especially above his own. Departing covertly with his family aboard Athenian ships, Antigonus slipped away from the coast of Asia and headed for northern Greece. He made his way to the two generals who would be most alarmed to hear his news, the commanders of Europe, old man Antipater and his son-in-law Craterus.

He found them in Aetolia, hunkered down in snowy mountain camps as they prosecuted the last, grim phase of the Hellenic War. The Aetolians had helped start that war two years earlier, banding together with the Athenians, but had left the front lines before the war's conclusion and had never formally surrendered. They had since retreated to high hills in their native territory, but Antipater and Craterus followed them there and cordoned them off, maintaining pressure even during harsh winter months. The Aetolians were just running out of food, and options, when Antigonus arrived in the Macedonian camp with word of events in the East.

The news hit home and hit hard, as Antigonus intended it to do. Perdiccas' secret pact with Cleopatra spelled betrayal of Antipater in both political and personal terms; it meant the alignment of the Babylon regime with Olympias, Antipater's bitter rival, as well as the insulting rejection of a father's daughter. The additional fact of the murder of Cynnane showed that Perdiccas' regime had lost its bearings and would do anything to strengthen itself. Antipater was livid, and, together with his son-in-law Craterus and Antigonus the bearer of bad tidings, he decided to throw the arrogant, ambitious Perdiccas out of power. Now in his late seventies, having barely prevailed in the Hellenic War the previous year, Antipater steeled himself once more for full-scale conflict. He resolved to invade Asia, a continent he had never set foot on before.

The bond of faith between two great blocs of Alexander's empire was broken. Perdiccas had tried to avoid a showdown by sharing sovereignty, giving Antipater and Craterus control of Europe while he confined himself to Asia. Perhaps this division could have remained stable had Perdiccas not made a play for the whole, or perhaps it was doomed to break down in any case. The blow that destroyed it seemed almost banal, a piece of gossip about a man's interest in a woman other than his wife. But where royal women represented legitimacy, and marital alliance security, the personal and the political had become fused. A bridegroom's change of affection now had the potential to embroil the empire in civil war.

His tale-telling mission accomplished, Antigonus sailed back across the Aegean to rally the satraps of Asia Minor. Their support of the invasion forces, and willingness to abandon Perdiccas, would be crucial. Antipater and Craterus, meanwhile, concluded a hasty truce with the Aetolians. Punishment of the last Greek rebels would have to wait for a more opportune moment. Right now the generals' course was set for Asia, and they began gathering troops for a crossing of the Hellespont.

Antipater appointed a subordinate named Polyperchon, an Alexander veteran who had come west with Craterus, to mind matters in Macedonia while he and Craterus headed east. A mid-level officer with an undistinguished record, now taking up his first command in his sixties, Polyperchon was destined to play a larger role in Macedonia than anyone knew or might have wished. Antipater also sent a messenger south, to Egypt, to firm up his alliance with Ptolemy. He needed to make sure that the two would collaborate, uniting Europe and Africa against Perdiccas in Asia, in the coming war.

5. ALEXANDER'S CORPSE (BABYLON AND POINTS SOUTH, SPRING 321 B.C.)

In Babylon, meanwhile, a team of craftsmen had finished the funeral cart of Alexander. The magnificent vehicle was now ready for its journey through the Asian countryside, bearing Alexander's mummy back to his homeland.

The hearse was built in the shape of a box, about twelve feet wide and eighteen feet long, with a barrel-vaulted roof. This roof was covered in gold plates overlapping like shingles, with precious stones set between them. At each of its corners stood a statue of Nike, the winged goddess personifying victory, also covered in gold. Atop its peak, fashioned from gold leaf, stood an enormous olive wreath, the crown of victory given at Greek athletic contests, glittering so brightly that observers compared it to a flash of lightning.

The roof of the chamber was supported by golden columns in imitation of a Greek temple, except that spaces between columns were not left open but bridged by a meshwork of golden ropes. Each column had a bas-relief acanthus vine climbing up it. Atop this colonnade, where a Greek temple might carry a sculptural frieze, four painted panels displayed the military might Alexander had wielded in life. One portrayed ships ready for combat; another, a squad of cavalry waiting to charge; a third, elephants clad in war gear, leading an infantry phalanx. The fourth panel showed Alexander himself, seated in a chariot ornamented with bas-relief, holding a scepter and surrounded by attendants and honor guards.

Alexander's funeral cart. A model built by the archaeologist Stella Miller-Collett based on the description by Diodorus

Under this image of Alexander, at the rear wall of the chamber, a doorway opened. Golden lions sat on either side, their heads turned as though to watch those entering. Who, if anyone, was allowed inside the hearse at its stopping points has not been recorded, but the space could not have admitted many. Perhaps only the Macedonian elite, the satraps and garrison commanders in each western province, went inside to commune once more with their former commander. Certainly it would have elevated their stature to enter the chamber and stand beside the casket, while their subjects watched from outside, peering through the veil of golden netting.

Below the main chamber, the undercarriage was fitted with a sophisticated suspension system to absorb the shocks of the road. Axles extended out to four iron-rimmed wheels with golden spokes and, at each hub, a golden lion's head holding a spear between its teeth. Four great bells hung from ropes at the cart's four corners, so that its motion created a tremendous sound, broadcasting its approach to the villages of Asia. At the front the cart was fitted with four poles, and to each pole were tied four teams of four mules, sixty-four animals in all, each with a golden crown, two gold bells hanging from its headpiece, and a gold collar set with precious stones.

Accompanying the cart on its journey was an escort of soldiers, engineers, and a road crew, to smooth its path and keep it from harm. The way was long from Babylon to the Hellespont, and then to Aegae in Macedonia, the burial ground of the Argead kings. This was where Perdiccas had instructed Arrhidaeus to bring the magnificent hearse, bedecked with a sizable portion of the empire's wealth. But soon after the convoy left Babylon, it became clear to Perdiccas that something was wrong. Either Arrhidaeus had left too soon, before Perdiccas was ready to lead the funeral procession, or he was headed in the wrong direction, or both. Sensing betrayal, Perdiccas sent a contingent of troops to bring Arrhidaeus into compliance.

These agents caught up with the funeral train in Syria but were confronted there by another armed squadron—one arriving, quite unexpectedly, from Egypt.

Ptolemy had made his move. In a hijacking that was no doubt

coordinated with the leaders of the convoy, he seized control of Alexander's corpse, the most potent political symbol on any of the three continents, and brought it to his own province, Egypt, for burial. It was a brazen bid to steal power from Perdiccas and amass it for himself. Ptolemy would add to his collection of Alexander memorabilia—the coins he had minted, the historical memoir he may already have begun to write—the mummy of Alexander himself, to be displayed in a splendid monument where it could awe the world.

Now it was Ptolemy, not Perdiccas, who marched into his capital city—Memphis, for the newly founded Alexandria was still under construction—at the head of Alexander's funeral cortege. To any who inquired why Alexander's body had ended up in Memphis, not in Siwa as Alexander had requested nor in Aegae with his ancestors, Ptolemy's propaganda machine had an unchallengeable response. A legend was fabricated saying that Ptolemy, during the weeks after Alexander's death, had asked the oracle of Bel-Marduk, the chief god of Babylon, where the king should be interred. "I tell you what will be of benefit to all," the priest responded. "There is a city in Egypt named Memphis; let him be enthroned there." The gods themselves had decreed this change of venue, the legend declared. Ptolemy had merely been their pious servant.

The ease and efficiency of the heist made a mockery of the Babylon regime. After two years of costly preparation, the hearse had spent only weeks, perhaps days, on the road before getting snatched away in broad daylight. Ptolemy had neatly picked Perdiccas' pocket, humiliating the regent before the eyes of the world. Such a brazen insult, added to Ptolemy's earlier provocations—his move against Cleomenes and his expansion into North Africa—was practically a declaration of war. The mistrust between Alexander's two top Bodyguards had widened into a schism that could never be healed.

6. PERDICCAS (WESTERN ASIA, SPRING 321 B.C.)

Perdiccas found himself facing a strategic nightmare, war against two continents at once. Ptolemy's seizure of Alexander's corpse, together with his murder of Cleomenes and his occupation of Cyrene, declared the secession of Africa from the government of the joint kings. The opposition of Europe quickly revealed itself also, as messengers reported Antipater and Craterus were crossing the Hellespont to attack, and Antigonus was already raising support for their cause on the coast of Anatolia. Perdiccas would have to fight on two fronts if he was to stay in power. He stood between the hammer and the anvil, uncertain in which direction to turn first.

His situation was dire, but the example of Alexander—that beacon of strategic success that stood before him always—inspired hope. Alexander too had faced war on two fronts, the rising of Balkan tribes to his north and the revolt of Thebes to his south, soon after ascending the Macedonian throne. He had led his army on a whirlwind campaign, storming the Balkans with terrifying force, then dashing south at unheard-of speed to counter the rebellion of Thebes. The Thebans thought it impossible he could arrive so quickly at their gates; they assumed that it must be Antipater, not Alexander, leading the attack against them. Alexander annihilated their city, a cruel riposte designed to rescue the empire from the double threat it had faced. Subjects on two of his borders had defied him almost simultaneously; he had delivered lightning blows in both directions and prevailed.

Perdiccas resolved likewise to strike in quick succession against two foes, Ptolemy to the south and Antipater to the north. His central position at least meant that his enemies could not combine forces. He had the luxury of dealing with them singly, one after the other. His army was strong enough to hold its own against either: he controlled the majority of Alexander's veterans, including the matchless Silver Shields, whom Craterus had foolishly left behind in Asia. This corps of three thousand, though famous for its headstrong spirit, was fiercely devoted to the royal cause. It would fight under the banner of the joint kings, even against fellow Macedonians, perhaps even against its own former commander, the revered Craterus.

Perdiccas could also count on Eumenes the Greek, his staunch supporter and close confidant, to bring the battle-tested Cappadocian cavalry into the field. Some might take offense at a

Greek commander leading Asian horsemen to defend a Macedonian empire against Macedonians, but these were paradoxes Perdiccas had to accept; this was the world Alexander had created. National and ethnic boundaries had dissolved as Alexander's empire advanced, until all that remained to unite it was the Argead royal house. Perdiccas represented that house, by controlling its two male members. He would take these monarchs with him on his campaign, to bind his armies to him even as he led them against their countrymen.

At an urgent conference in Pisidia (southern Anatolia), Perdiccas and his staff resolved to move first against Ptolemy, perhaps because Ptolemy was the lesser general and had fewer troops. Also, Perdiccas was enraged by the theft of Alexander's body and eager to get it back. Once Ptolemy was defeated, Perdiccas could gain control of his troops, and the Egyptian treasury, and move back northward with cash and forces augmented. Meanwhile, Eumenes would stay in Anatolia to counter the invasion from Europe. He would guard the Hellespont, first and foremost, then fall back into the interior if the Hellespont was crossed. Eumenes would be outmatched by Craterus and Antipater, but he would only need to slow their progress until Perdiccas returned, not fight them head-on. Timing would be critical. Eumenes had to prevent the European forces from reaching Perdiccas while he was still engaged with Ptolemy, or else the hammer would come down on the anvil and smash the royalists to bits. Perdiccas delegated his brother Alcetas and another high officer, Neoptolemus, to support Eumenes in this holding action.

There was one further strategic card to be played, one Perdiccas now saw he should have played already: Cleopatra. Using Eumenes once again as his go-between, Perdiccas sent word to Cleopatra, still residing in Sardis, that he was ready to repudiate Nicaea and marry her instead.

Sardis was dangerous territory for an agent of Perdiccas, now that Antigonus One-eye was in the region rallying the western satraps. Eumenes almost got caught when Antigonus, informed of the Greek's presence in Sardis, set out with a detachment of three thousand to ambush him as he departed. But warned by Cleopatra, Eumenes left the city by an unexpected route, ordering his horsemen not to blow the trumpet or make any sound that would reveal their position. This was the first time Eumenes and Antigonus, former friends at the Macedonian court, had met as enemies, and it set a template for what would follow. There were to be many close calls and covert escapes in the long, tense duel between them.

Eumenes proceeded on to the Hellespont, sending back word to Perdiccas that his proposal had been spurned. Alexander's sister would not now marry him, though she had come to Asia with that very goal in mind. Perdiccas' position had become more tenuous and his future more uncertain; Cleopatra would await the outcome of the coming wars. Meanwhile, Antigonus One-eye, informed by his ally Menander about all that went on in Sardis, sent word of Perdiccas' renewed contact with Cleopatra to Antipater and Craterus. Already enraged by his first report, these two were goaded into fury by the second and went forward to war with renewed determination.

Hapless Perdiccas had twice paid the price for wooing an Argead princess, yet both times had failed to win her. He might well have reflected ruefully on the perils of the middle path. Caught between Olympias and Antipater, he tried to alienate neither but ended by alienating both. His indecision at a crucial moment, when Eumenes and Alcetas were whispering contrary counsels in his ears, had cost him dear.

But there was scant time for such reflections; the empire was collapsing around him. He gathered up his troops and subcommanders—including Antigenes, captain of the Silver Shields; Peithon, his agent against the Bactrian rebels two years earlier; and a junior officer, Seleucus, his second in command at Babylon—and hastened south, toward Egypt.

7. EUMENES, NEOPTOLEMUS, ANTIPATER, AND CRATERUS (NORTHERN ANATOLIA, SUMMER 321 B.C.)

Eumenes' defense of the Hellespont would have been an easy matter with support from the fleet, but the fleet deserted to Antipater.

Suborned by messengers and perhaps by bribes, the Macedonian navy eased the invaders' crossing into Asia rather than barring it. Their admiral was probably Cleitus the White, victor over the Athenians in the Hellenic War, but we know little of what led him to abandon Perdiccas' cause. Perhaps after helping rescue Antipater from Greek rebels the previous year, he could not stomach the thought of helping Eumenes, a Greek, against Antipater, the most iconic of old-guard Macedonians.

Others in Perdiccas' camp also disliked the strange alignment that put them with Eumenes, a Greek and a former scribe, against two of the greatest Macedonian generals. Alcetas, Perdiccas' brother, loser to Eumenes in the debate over whom Perdiccas should marry, was one of those who found this repugnant. Neoptolemus, who still nursed his wounded pride after being upstaged by Eumenes in Armenia, was another. Sensing noncooperation, Perdiccas wrote to both men, restating that they must support Eumenes with all their forces. Alcetas refused, claiming that his troops would not fight Antipater and were so fond of Craterus that they would more likely defect than attack. Neoptolemus, for his part, feigned compliance with Perdiccas' orders but in fact planned to betray Eumenes at the first opportunity. He was in contact with Antipater and Craterus, who had persuaded him to take their side, the side of established Macedonian authority, against an upstart Greek.

Eumenes too had received secret communications from Antipater and Craterus. They offered him complete amnesty, plus rewards and new powers, to join them and abandon Perdiccas. Antipater took a soothing tone in his messages, knowing that Eumenes had always feared him; Craterus, for his part, vowed to help heal this breach. Eumenes replied that friendship between himself and Antipater was no longer possible, but he appealed to Craterus to reconcile with Perdiccas, offering to play peacemaker himself. These probes tested the firmness of alliances on both sides but came to nothing. In the end Craterus and Eumenes both stood by their new masters. There was no hope that those masters, Antipater and Perdiccas, could be reconciled with each other.

Eumenes somehow learned that Neoptolemus, his supposed

ally, was conspiring with his enemies. So he put Neoptolemus to the test by summoning him to move his army forward. Neoptolemus responded by forming up troops for battle, rather than bringing them into camp. His target was clearly not Antipater and Craterus but Eumenes.

Abandoned first by Cleitus and then Alcetas, now facing Neoptolemus as an enemy, with Antipater and Craterus not far off, Eumenes could be forgiven had he reconsidered the offer to switch sides. It was a tight spot for a former bookkeeper, surrounded by generals who mistrusted or scorned him and by their powerful infantry phalanxes. Yet he had confidence in his Cappadocian cavalry and his own strengths as a commander, strengths only recently developed but proved in the field. And he believed in the cause he was fighting for, the sovereignty of the Argead house. He would stick by that house, and by Perdiccas, and fight.

The battle at first went in favor of Neoptolemus but slowly turned. His infantry prevailed over that of Eumenes, as it was sure to do given the excellence and experience of these Macedonians. But Eumenes used his cavalry to get around Neoptolemus' lines and seize the baggage train in their rear. It was a strategy that had been used against Alexander at his greatest battle, Gaugamela, but Alexander ignored the penetration until he had secured victory, thus regaining his troops' lost gear. Not many leaders could keep

The basic unit of the Macedonian phalanx, the *syntagma* of 256 men

their men fighting once their goods had been plundered and their wounded comrades put to death. Loss of baggage usually led quickly to loss of the battle.

For a while, Eumenes' coup went unnoticed by Neoptolemus' infantry. The foot soldiers were advancing rapidly and sloppily, sure of imminent victory. Eumenes' cavalry was well behind them now, unseen—until it charged the unprotected rear of their phalanx. There was a devastating shift of momentum. Many of Neoptolemus' men were killed in the charge, while many more laid down weapons and surrendered. Neoptolemus himself fled with three hundred cavalry to the nearby camp of Antipater and Craterus, abandoning his troops to their fate. These now swore fealty to their new commander, Eumenes.

Eumenes had gained a crack infantry to balance his cavalry and had gained enormously in stature as a general. But his foes were unimpressed by his win. Neoptolemus gave a disparaging account of Eumenes to Antipater and Craterus, who had now been joined by Antigonus One-eye, and the four allies decided to split their vast army into halves. Craterus and Neoptolemus would take one portion to use against Eumenes, while Antipater would take the other east and south, to counter Perdiccas. A critical factor in their strategy was the allegiance Craterus could command from the troops who would face him. These men had not seen Craterus since before Alexander's death. Neoptolemus was sure that at the mere sight of Craterus' distinctive cap, or at the sound of his voice, they would know their true master and switch sides. The luster of Craterus, still bright in the minds of the soldiers, would turn the tide of battle, as though Alexander himself had returned to take command.

Antipater left the war council and set off south with ten thousand men, enough to form a barricade against Perdiccas should he return from Egypt successful. Antigonus One-eye, meanwhile, set sail for the island of Cyprus, where another theater of war had opened up. Neoptolemus, for his part, prepared to face Eumenes a second time, this time backed by Craterus with twenty thousand infantry and two thousand cavalry. The coalition against Perdiccas went into action on land and sea, determined to liberate Asia from the regime forged in Babylon.

8. EUMENES, CRATERUS, AND NEOPTOLEMUS (NORTHERN ANATOLIA, SUMMER 321 B.C.)

As the army of Craterus approached his camp, Eumenes awoke from a curious dream. He dreamed that two Alexanders were arrayed to fight each other, each at the head of an infantry phalanx. The goddess Athena appeared and gave aid to one of them, the goddess Demeter to the other. After a long struggle the Alexander aided by Demeter prevailed, and the goddess wove a crown for her champion out of stalks of grain.

Eumenes looked outside his tent at the rich stands of grain on nearby hills. He felt certain the dream pointed to his victory in the upcoming battle. When he learned from his spies that Craterus had adopted "Athena and Alexander" as his army's password, he felt even more sure. He made his own password "Demeter and Alexander" and ordered his men, as they prepared for combat, to bind grain stalks around their arms and heads.

One Alexander fighting another—Eumenes dared to think this image referred to his looming fight against Craterus. A few years earlier, when Eumenes was a humble scribe and Craterus the greatest of Alexander's generals, he would never have framed such an interpretation. But those years had raised Eumenes ever higher within the king's inner circle. He had been assigned by the king to command a squadron of Companion cavalry, a post no Greek had ever before held. He had been close to Alexander during the king's last months, closer than Craterus, who had been sent home to Macedonia and ordered to remain there. And now it was he, Eumenes, a Greek of obscure origins, first recruited to keep track of royal papers, who fought to protect the rights of Alexander's kin. He would not let Craterus alone invoke Alexander in a slogan to inspire his troops; he too claimed the right to fight in Alexander's name.

But Eumenes did not allow his men to learn whom they would be fighting. He could not, for he knew as well as Neoptolemus that they still revered Craterus as no other and would join his ranks the moment they spotted him. So Eumenes gave word that the new commander who accompanied Neoptolemus was a barbarian warlord named Pigres. To ensure his secret would hold, he stationed only Asian horsemen opposite Craterus' position, on the far right wing, and ordered them to charge the moment the enemy came in view. He kept his Macedonians in the center, well away from Craterus, and bade them hold back during this cavalry charge. He did not want them to engage the enemy's expert phalanx or to find out, from a chance word or cry, who it was that commanded it.

Eumenes stationed his own cavalry facing that of Neoptolemus, on the opposite end from Craterus of the attacking line. This would give each general a chance to charge the other. Eumenes wanted to resolve the conflict begun by Neoptolemus' betrayal some ten days earlier. The animosity between these two generals had made the upcoming battle a grudge match.

As he mounted a hill that separated the two armies, Craterus rode toward battle confident of victory. He trusted assurances from Neoptolemus that the Macedonians serving Eumenes would switch sides as soon as they recognized him. Then he could easily take down Eumenes, whose Asian cavalry would be stripped of the protection of the phalanx. It was a grim surprise when he saw these very horsemen coming at him in battle formation, no Macedonians among them and no one seeming likely to desert. Muttering curses against Neoptolemus, he ordered his men forward to meet the charge. It was the last order he would ever give.

There are three divergent descriptions of Craterus' death. Plutarch says he fought bravely from horseback and slew many foes, until he was speared by a Thracian and fell from his horse. Arrian says likewise that he fought against all comers without care for his own safety, removing his wide-brimmed *kausia* cap to make his face more visible, but was finally killed by Paphlagonians who cared little for his identity. Diodorus gives the least heroic account: Craterus fell to the ground when his horse stumbled and was trampled to death in the melee. All three accounts agree that Craterus lay unrecognized as he breathed his last. Few of the Asians who charged him had ever seen him before, and no one expected him to be there, thinking it was Pigres they were attacking. Plutarch reports that a certain Gorgias, one of Eumenes' officers, recognized Craterus expiring on the ground and dismounted to guard him from the hooves of the horses.

Eumenes' horsemen may not have realized how important a leader had fallen, but those of Craterus certainly did. They broke off attack and rode for the protection of their phalanx, causing the collapse of their army's right wing.

On the left, meanwhile, Neoptolemus and Eumenes were stalking each other amid crowds of clashing horsemen. At last each recognized the other, and an intense single combat was joined. While still on horseback, each dropped rein in order to grab the other's helmet and tear it off. During this wrestling match the horses started from under them, and both tumbled to the ground with a clattering of armor. Though stunned by the fall, Eumenes got to his feet and stabbed Neoptolemus in the back of the leg, a wound that prevented his adversary from standing. Nonetheless, Neoptolemus rose to his knees and slashed Eumenes three times on his arms and thigh. Had he been able to stand, he might have struck a fatal blow. Eumenes, however, was not badly wounded, and with one powerful thrust to the neck he drove Neoptolemus to the ground.

Even then the duel was not over. Eumenes, supposing his opponent killed, began stripping off his armor, the traditional right of a victor. But Neoptolemus still had strength for one sword thrust and, reaching up under Eumenes' cuirass, stabbed him near the groin. It was not a grave wound but, with the others, caused considerable loss of blood. Then Neoptolemus breathed his last.

Having dispatched one of two great opponents, Eumenes now learned the fate of the other. He may even have had a last exchange of words with Craterus as the half-dead senior general was brought into camp. It was an almost unimaginable outcome—a Greek scribbler had vanquished two of the greatest Macedonian warriors in a single day, one by a stratagem, the other by swordsmanship and main force.

The day belonged to Eumenes, but the issue of Craterus' powerful phalanx was as yet unresolved. This block of twenty thousand men remained at full strength, having never joined battle at all. It was still in formation and could repel any attack, even a charge by spear-bearing cavalry. Eumenes sent a Macedonian messenger, Xennias, to offer the leaders of the phalanx a deal. The infantrymen could join Eumenes' side under a blanket amnesty; otherwise, he would surround them with his cavalry and block their access to food, forcing a less advantageous surrender. This bold stroke appeared to succeed when the foot soldiers disarmed and swore to follow Eumenes. But a short while later, when they were allowed to wander about local villages to buy supplies, they broke their oath and struck off to the south, racing to catch up with Antipater. Eumenes was too depleted to lead a pursuit and let them go.

Thus concluded a battle that bears no name, since none of our sources records where it took place. A message was sent to Perdiccas in Egypt, telling of the victory but also of the two potent armies that had slipped past Eumenes and were now heading south.

As he buried his dead, Eumenes had the body of Craterus cremated with all due rites and ceremony. He could not afford to stint the honors for this hero, for many, even in his own camp, were grieved by his fall. Perhaps Eumenes himself felt remorse. There had never been antipathy between the two men; they had merely become enmeshed in the war between their masters, Perdiccas and Antipater. Eumenes would keep the cremated remains with him and saw that they eventually reached Craterus' widow, the noble Phila.

Eumenes had triumphed as tactician and soldier, but had also learned his limitations as leader. In this new kind of war, where allegiances were unclear and a general's best strategy was to draw defections, Eumenes had been on the defensive. Though some Alexander veterans, like those serving under Neoptolemus, might switch to his side in defeat, troops fresh from Europe had refused to do so, even at peril to their lives. And Eumenes' need to conceal Craterus' identity showed how much lower he stood in the soldiers' affections. Had Eumenes not denied him the chance, Craterus could have won the battle simply by revealing his face.

Dream though he might, Eumenes was no Alexander. He never could be, given the deficit of his birth. He had the talent of a first-rate general but none of the stature. His origins barred him from the heights of Macedonian power, certainly from the throne, and he knew that. When, in the aftermath of the battle, he took horses from the royal herds to replenish his losses, he gave receipts for them to the stablemen; he claimed the right only to borrow, not seize, the property of the crown. The humility of the gesture raised a laugh from old man Antipater—a rare moment of levity in what had become an intense and bitter civil war.

9. PERDICCAS (EGYPT, SUMMER 321 B.C.)

While Eumenes was winning glory in Anatolia, Perdiccas and his army were approaching the delta of the Nile. At the apex of that seven-stream triangle was Memphis, and in Memphis was Ptolemy, who had troubled Perdiccas' regime from the start, mocking his authority and defying his orders. In Memphis too was Alexander, now a mummified corpse but still emanating a power that could hold three continents in awe.

The Nile delta had repelled many invaders over the centuries. Perdiccas was determined to penetrate it by crossing its eastern-most branch, the Pelusian. Once across, he could march south to Memphis, bring Ptolemy to heel, and recover the body of Alexander. That talisman of royal might could yet repair his losses and restore his waning ability to exert control.

Perdiccas' control had eroded during the past months at an alarming rate. The treachery of Cleitus at the Hellespont, the defections of the western satraps, the refusal of his officers (his own brother!) to follow orders, the theft of Alexander's corpse—these challenges had come at him simultaneously and from all corners of western Asia. Now even the royal army, the six thousand or so crack veterans he had brought to Egypt, was showing signs of insubordination. When he had convened an assembly near the borders of Egypt to charge Ptolemy with rebellion, the soldiers had listened to Ptolemy's defense and then voted to acquit. They were not willing to give Perdiccas the political cover he so obviously wanted. Perdiccas had been forced to distribute bribes to top officers, buying their commitment to the invasion when he could not inspire it.

And what *could* inspire them to attack their own countrymen or to make war on Ptolemy, whom they had respected and heeded only two years earlier? Perdiccas had brought the joint kings with him as a reminder of their cause, but these hardly commanded reverence: the vacant Philip with his sharp-tongued teenage wife, the toddler Alexander with his babbling barbarian mother. It was a pathetically shaky platform on which Perdiccas rested his authority, yet it was the only source of legitimacy in the post-Alexander world. It would have to be enough, for Perdiccas was already here at the delta, accompanied by infantry, cavalry, siege equipment, and war elephants—enough armed force to take Ptolemy down, if he could only get across the Nile.

Fortunately, Perdiccas had superb training in river cross-ings, for these had been Alexander the Great's choice stratagem. Alexander had brought his army across the Danube, the Oxus, and the Indus, three of the world's largest rivers, and finally, in India, had pulled off a brilliant crossing of the Hydaspes despite a determined foe on the other side. For weeks Alexander had unbal-anced this foe, the raja Porus, by moving in plain sight up and down the bank, making feints and sallies, all the while scouting for a crossing point that would be hidden from Porus' view. When he finally made his move, he marched the army all night through torrential rains and deafening thunder, then led it through the roaring Hydaspes in the dark, with men and horses only barely keeping their heads above water—but got onto dry land and into formation before Porus' forces arrived. Speed and secrecy, as in so many of Alexander's operations, had secured victory.

Perdiccas too needed secrecy for his crossing of the Nile, but he did not have time for the cat-and-mouse games Alexander had played with Porus. His troops were becoming unsteady in their loyalty. Some had already defected to Ptolemy after Perdiccas tried, but failed, to draw off water from the Pelusiac Nile and ren-der it more shallow. Others, he suspected, were passing along information to Ptolemy's forces. When Perdiccas chose a crossing point, opposite a fort called Kamelonteichos, or Camels' Ram-part, he told no one of his destination. He could not trust his own men. He marched the army to this spot under cover of darkness, hoping he would get there unobserved.

At first light Perdiccas' troops began fording the river but were only halfway across when, on the other bank, Ptolemy's forces could be seen streaming toward the fort. The element of surprise had been lost during the night. There was no choice now but to slug it out with Ptolemy's men, and with Ptolemy himself, who had entered the fort and was making ready to lead its defenders in person.

Perdiccas mounted a determined effort to capture the fort. His crack infantry troops, the Silver Shields, were sent up scaling ladders under barrages of spears and arrows. Elephants were brought forward to batter the mud-brick walls with their heads. Ptolemy apparently speared one of these beasts in the eyes and blinded it, then killed its driver, and began boldly knocking men off the ladders into the river below (though this account, like all tales of Ptolemy's heroics, may be the invention of his propaganda machine). Perdiccas' men hurled themselves at the fort for much of the day, but finally, toward evening, Perdiccas gave up. He ordered his troops back across the river to base camp. The Camels' Rampart had held.

Though his men were exhausted, Perdiccas gave them only a short rest before again ordering an all-night march, south along the Nile's bank. He was desperate now to find a way over, or he would face mass defections. His reconnaissance had revealed a spot opposite Memphis where the Nile was split by a midriver island. Both sides appeared to be fordable, and the island was large enough for his entire army to make camp. The opposite bank would not be guarded; no one would expect a crossing upstream from the delta, where the Nile's waters were united in a swift, deep current. It was a daring stroke, much in the manner of Alexander, for Alexander had succeeded, time after time, by suddenly appearing where no one thought he could be.

For the second day in a row, Perdiccas sent his men into the Nile at first light. The first contingents reached the island in safety, though the current was strong and the water came up to their chins in midchannel. Perdiccas tried a new tactic to ease the passage: he sent elephants across upstream of the wading troops to break the force of the current, and had mounted horsemen cross downstream to catch any soldiers who lost their footing. This was a fatal error. The heavy tread of the animals dislodged silt from the riverbed, causing the channel to suddenly deepen. The bewildered soldiers, thinking that Ptolemy had opened a new sluiceway to flood them, could no longer keep contact with the bottom. The crossing was halted. Only half the men had reached the island— too few to defend themselves once Ptolemy arrived, as he no doubt soon would. Perdiccas had no choice but to call them back.

The men on the island cast away their weapons and armor, companions of more than a decade of campaigning, and dove into the swirling current. Stronger swimmers could make it across, but others were pulled downstream, tumbling and flailing as they were swept out of sight. Perdiccas' situation had become nightmarish, but the worst horror was yet to come. The thrashing of drowning men attracted Nile crocodiles, which arrived in swarms and began to feed on both the living and the dead. More than two thousand men were lost, either to the rushing waters or to the snapping jaws of the beasts.

In camp that evening, the surviving infantrymen raised loud, hoarse lamentations for their comrades and shouted curses at Perdiccas. Perhaps a third of their number had been lost that day, comrades who had served beside them for thirteen years or more, without so much as an inch of progress. The Egyptian campaign had come to nothing; and Asia too had been lost, or so the troops feared, for word had not yet arrived of Eumenes' stunning victory over Craterus and Neoptolemus. Had this victory been known, Perdiccas would instantly have seen his authority restored, but in this, as in much else, the gods seemed to be against him. The news arrived just one day too late.

Ptolemy could now be seen on the opposite bank, doing his best to increase Perdiccas' disgrace. His troops were gathering the bodies of the drowned and cremating them with honorable rites. With unerring instincts for self-promotion, Ptolemy was sending a message that he held the soldiers' lives sacred, unlike Perdiccas, who had so recklessly thrown them away. Perhaps he also meant to show he was clement to his enemies and would treat well any who deserted. Almost certainly, he was already spreading that message by way of agents in Perdiccas' camp.

Perdiccas had proved a false Alexander. He had failed at the very maneuver at which Alexander had so brilliantly succeeded.

He had hurled more lives into the river than Alexander had lost in all his great battles. Not even Perdiccas' senior officers, paid off with gifts and favors to support the Egyptian invasion, could countenance its disastrous outcome. Three of these—Peithon, Antigenes, and Seleucus—backed by a hundred followers, went to the tent of Perdiccas that very night and stabbed him to death. First to strike was Antigenes, leader of the Silver Shields. He understood the soldiers' code of loyalty to an officer, but also understood the officers' code that forbade the squandering of soldiers.

So ended the brief reign of Perdiccas, Alexander's top-ranking Bodyguard and inheritor of his signet ring. He had begun his time in power by killing his own men under the feet of elephants and ended by killing them in the maws of crocodiles. The compromise government he had forged at Babylon, designed to preserve the balance and unity of the continents, had been smashed to ruins; the empire was utterly divided and leaderless and spattered with the blood of the generals who had founded it. These men had made all of western Asia their battleground. Soon the violence would spread to Europe as well, engulfing Athens, the Greek world generally, and the Macedonian homeland itself.

The reign of the joint kings went on into its third year.

The Fortunes of Eumenes

Egypt, Western Asia, and Macedonia

SUMMER 321–SPRING 319 B.C.

The empire no longer had a center. Alexander had moved the royal seat from Pella to Babylon, but now Babylon had been emptied of the elements that defined royalty: the royal army, the crowned heads themselves, and Alexander's mummified body. The latter two were now in Egypt but separated by the enormous gulf of the Nile. As for Alexander's army, it had become fragmented as never before. One part was following Eumenes in Anatolia, another was in Egypt, while a third had become mixed with fresh troops from Europe and was now with Antipater in Cilicia. No part was large enough to constitute the assembly that traditionally acclaimed new leaders; and who could propose a new leader for acclamation, a replacement for the fallen Perdiccas, even if a quorum could be gathered somewhere?

Like Babylon, the royal city of Pella in Macedonia had been stripped of its centering figures. No Argeads dwelled there. Olympias had long ago fled to Epirus, and Cleopatra, Cynnane, and Adea had departed into Asia. Old man Antipater too, for years the only general who stayed in a fixed location, had joined the others and gone on the move. His surrogate, Polyperchon, held nominal command in Pella, but he was a second-rank officer with little of Antipater's gravitas, as the years to come would demonstrate all too clearly.

The only real capital the empire now had was the place the joint kings were stationed, wherever that might be. For the moment, that meant the encampment of an exhausted, blood-stained, and leaderless band of men, a desolate spot opposite Memphis on the east bank of the Nile.

I. PTOLEMY, PEITHON, AND ARRHIDAEUS (EGYPT, SUMMER 321 B.C.)

On the morning after the murder of Perdiccas, Ptolemy crossed the Nile to the army that had twice failed to vanquish him. He had almost certainly been in contact with Peithon, his former fellow Bodyguard, to make sure of a friendly reception. Whether such contacts preceded, or even arranged, Perdiccas' murder is not known, but the two men had much to gain by colluding in this deed: Ptolemy wanted to be rid of the army of invasion, while Peithon, the same man who had tried to bring the rebellious Greeks over to his side, wanted more power. The murder of Perdiccas was a good first step toward both goals.

Ptolemy brought with him food for the depleted troops and the cremated bones of the men recovered from the river. These remains were distributed to friends and kinsmen of each soldier, a humane gesture designed to win over the rank and file. Ptolemy knew he had support in Perdiccas' army, for these troops had already refused to condemn him at the trial Perdiccas had held some days before. But they had also agreed to attack him, and many no doubt still resented his theft of their monarch's corpse. Ptolemy delivered a carefully balanced speech before the assembled army, defending his separatist actions of the past two years and assuring Perdiccas' loyalists that they would not be subject to a purge. Perhaps he demonstrated good faith by arranging honorable rites for Perdiccas' body, though there is no record of what became of it or of the ill-omened signet ring it presumably still bore on its lifeless hand.

Ptolemy's speech was a resounding success. The army seemed

about to offer him Perdiccas' old post, guardianship of the joint kings. But Ptolemy had already resolved not to accept. He instead put forward Peithon, leader of the mutiny against Perdiccas, for that job, along with Arrhidaeus, former custodian of Alexander's corpse. The soldiers gave their acclaim to this pair, though only on a temporary basis. They were aware that their decisions were contingent on events in Asia: two far loftier authorities, Antipater and the beloved Craterus, were on the march there, and report had it that Craterus was preparing to fight Eumenes, Perdiccas' Greek consigliere—a battle Craterus was sure to win.

But while Ptolemy was still conferring with the army of invasion, news came that Craterus had been killed in that battle, along with Neoptolemus. A wave of shock and outrage went through the troops. The idea that Eumenes, a humble Greek, had brought down the most revered of Alexander's generals, while serving the now-discredited Perdiccas, was intolerable. The army demanded vengeance. A death sentence was passed in absentia on Eumenes and fifty other leaders of Perdiccas' government, including Alcetas, Perdiccas' brother. His sister Atalante was immediately seized and executed. There would be no mending of fences now, no effort to knit the empire back together. The war would go on until Eumenes, and anyone else who had aided Perdiccas, was destroyed.

Leaving the army to its new crusade, Ptolemy recrossed the river to his palace in Memphis, no doubt glad to return to a less volatile environment. The swings of emotion he had witnessed over the past three days had been bewildering and disturbing. First, Perdiccas' troops had made two determined efforts to penetrate his Nile defenses. Then, with Perdiccas dead, they had embraced *him* as their hoped-for leader, nearly handing him regency over the kings, the keystone of imperial control. Finally, news of Craterus' death had sent them into a murderous rage and turned them back toward Asia to attack their former commanders. It was all too reminiscent of the tumultuous week in Babylon following Alexander's death, the last time Ptolemy had been united with these unruly veterans. Clearly, Perdiccas had failed to tame them during the intervening years.

There was no telling what would happen when this

ungovernable beast returned to Asia, but that uncertainty was not Ptolemy's problem. Undoubtedly, the fabric of the empire would be rent by the collisions and clashes there, but Egypt could remain detached. Ptolemy's Nile defenses had held despite all Perdiccas had thrown at them, ensuring that no Macedonian army would soon attack again. And it had escaped no one's notice that the army was leaving without the prize it had come for, Alexander's body. Neither of the new commanders, Peithon and Arrhidaeus, had dared ask for its return (indeed Arrhidaeus had, not coincidentally, helped Ptolemy obtain it to begin with). Ptolemy's declaration of independence had stuck. He had his own empire, his Egypt, and needed little from the rest of Alexander's realm—except perhaps some trained Indian elephants, a precious resource he took the liberty of commandeering from the departing army.

Ptolemy rejoined his burgeoning household with its two trophy women, Thais, the beautiful Athenian courtesan who had already borne him three children, and now a new bride, Antipater's youngest daughter, Eurydice. One brought him pleasure and the other power, but Ptolemy was still vulnerable to a third impulse, love. By this time he had taken notice of his bride's young cousin and lady-in-waiting, a widow by the name of Berenice. Soon he made this woman his mistress, and ultimately his wife. She bore him his two heirs, Ptolemy II and Arsinoe, a brother and sister who, following an old Persian royal custom, married each other. Through his children by Berenice Ptolemy founded a dynasty that ruled Egypt for almost three centuries, until their great-great-great-great-great-great-great-granddaughter, Cleopatra VII, the lover of both Julius Caesar and Marc Antony, killed herself by the bite of an asp.

2. THE ROYAL FAMILY (EGYPT AND POINTS NORTH, AUTUMN 321 B.C.)

What were the first words spoken by the son of Alexander the Great, just now acquiring the power of speech? Were they in Macedonian or in the Bactrian tongue he presumably learned from his mother, Rhoxane? Or was he tutored in high classical Greek, the language his father had made the lingua franca of the new ruling class? Did he know, at age two, that his words had the power to shape a realm stretching from the Adriatic to the banks of the Indus? Such questions are beyond speculation, since of all the records preserved from this era, not one gives the boy a voice or a consciousness. Though he stood closer to the maelstrom than anyone, we do not have a single utterance or action by which his personality might be judged. The young Alexander, known today as Alexander IV, remains a cipher, even after the opening of his still-unplundered tomb in 1979.

How was the young Alexander told that Perdiccas no longer had charge of him but others he barely knew? What was told to his uncle and co-ruler, Philip, who must have realized, however dimly, that a coup had taken place? Was any attempt made to enlist Philip's support for the new regime? Or was he a mere possession conferring power, like the signet ring given to Perdiccas? One anecdote from later in Philip's life shows that this monarch had a partial understanding of events around him. But his behavior could become erratic and violent, and his keeper on at least one occasion had to restrain him. Peithon and Arrhidaeus could only have given him the illusion of agency, securing his token approval for acts of state as Perdiccas had done.

Philip's new wife, however, was a different matter. Adea, now also called Eurydice, had all her wits about her and all the energies of youth. She was determined to be more than a figurehead. As the army moved north out of Egypt, Adea began to assert herself. She sensed an opportunity to grasp supreme power, an opportunity her mother, Cynnane, had sacrificed her life to give her.

By now Adea had spent several weeks with the royal army and had learned much about the new breed of soldier Alexander had created. Money, she knew, was much on the men's minds. Many of their comrades, those discharged by Alexander but now fighting again under Antipater, had received a handsome bonus at their send-off, a talent of silver per man. The others had gotten no such boon, though they claimed Alexander had promised one. Now the expedition to Egypt had disappointed their hopes of plunder, and even their standard salary was in arrears (Perdiccas' brother-in-law Attalus, on the run from the death sentence imposed on him, had made haste to secure a stash of money from which they would have been paid). For these hardened veterans, fighting not for a cause or country but because fighting was their way of life, money meant everything. It was a measure of prowess, a reward for hard labors, a bond linking them to their commanders. If money was running short, as Adea knew it was, that bond could easily be broken.

As the army made its way back into Asia, Adea began making her voice heard in camp. With her status as granddaughter of the great Philip ensuring an audience, she harped on the theme of owed money, a theme she knew would provoke her listeners to outrage. She was in contact with the outlawed Perdiccan faction, men like Attalus who had access to ready cash. Discontent began to swirl around this teenage firebrand, prompting Peithon and Arrhidaeus, the new heads of the central government, to impose a gag order on her. But Adea refused to comply. She knew that after the near mutiny caused by the murder of her mother, the generals would not dare lay hands on her, and they had no other way to stop her voice.

3. TRIPARADEISUS (WINTER, LATE 321 B.C.)

The army arrived at Triparadeisus, a "triple game park" somewhere in what is now Lebanon, with Adea still insisting on her political rights. Peithon and Arrhidaeus played for time, awaiting the arrivals of old man Antipater and Antigonus One-eye, who were hastening to meet them as they advanced northward. Finally, when Antipater and his army were close at hand, the pressure became intolerable. Not content with freedom of speech, Adea was contesting guardianship of the joint kings, the only source of legitimate power. What more right than she, Adea demanded, did Peithon and Arrhidaeus have to speak for her husband? There was no good reply. Events were slipping out of control. Perdiccas' brother-in-law Attalus had arrived on the scene, with money to attract desertions; the army was seething with sedition. Conceding inability to manage the crisis, Peithon and Arrhidaeus resigned their posts, urging Antipater to come at once to take charge.

Antipater arrived to find the royal army, including the famous

Silver Shields, in an ugly mood. This was his first glimpse of how it had been transformed in the years it had spent in Asia (the decommissioned veterans Craterus had brought him were more tractable men). It was not a pretty sight. These soldiers had tasted the ultimate liberty, the right to kill their own commander, and seemed to no longer revere any authority, except an iron-willed teenage girl. Antipater was their nation's highest-ranking officer, but his arrival made little impression on them. They kept howling for the pay they claimed was due them, spurred on by the irrepressible Adea.

Antipater stood before the assembled army and tried to address their demands. He promised to tally up the royal treasuries and make good what was owed, though he admitted that for the moment his resources were thin. The huge caches of gold and silver won in Alexander's conquests were far away, in the great cities of Persis; it would take time to transfer them to depleted western depots. The troops listened but were not mollified. Adea again stirred up their mistrust and goaded them into rage, speaking openly against Antipater and pointing to Attalus, Perdiccas' brother-in-law, as an alternative. Finally their anger spilled over into full-scale revolt. They seized Antipater and threatened him with immediate stoning if he did not pay up.

As before at Lamia, Antipater needed help from one of his confederates, and the rescue effort this time was led by his new junior partner, Antigonus One-eye. Antigonus had just returned from his campaign in Cyprus and had made camp with Antipater's forces, on the opposite side of a river from the mutinous troops. Watching from this camp across the stream, Antigonus could see that Antipater had been taken prisoner by the rebels and was in grave peril. Given the prowess of the royal army and the invincible Silver Shields, Antigonus had few options except bluff and deceit, but those were his strengths. He donned a full suit of armor, mounted his horse, and rode grandly across the bridge that connected the two camps, accompanied by a few select cavalrymen.

The royal army had not seen Antigonus for more than a decade. The unexpected arrival of the huge one-eyed man, impressively clad in full battle gear, awed the rebels and they parted ranks, making a space for him to address them. As he passed the captive Antipater, he somehow signaled the old man to be ready to make an escape. He then stood before the soldiers and delivered a long speech on Antipater's behalf (seconded by Seleucus, one of their own leaders), drawing out his words filibuster-style until an opening arose. Finally he saw Antipater's guards becoming distracted. At a signal his cavalrymen grabbed Antipater away from them and rushed him across the bridge to safety.

Antigonus and Seleucus nearly lost their lives in the ensuing melee, for the troops saw they had been tricked. Somehow both men managed to escape unharmed. Antipater, now back among his own loyal army, set about to restore order. Summoning the leaders of the rebellion to his side of the river, he browbeat them back into obedience. Probably he had some choice words about the folly of following a teenage girl, even one who happened to be queen of the Macedonians.

Adea had nearly pulled off a coup that would have given her control of the kings and the army. With just a few more soldiers on her side, she might have outdone Eumenes, victor over Neoptolemus and Craterus, and brought down *three* top generals— Antipater, Antigonus, and Seleucus—in a single day. Her contest with old man Antipater, whom she had looked up to since childhood as her grandfather Philip's senior statesman, had been fought with intensity and vigor, the qualities her warlike mother had instilled in her. The bitterness with which she resumed her former role as ward—of Antigonus this time, for it was he who was now made custodian of the joint kings—can only be imagined.

As at Babylon three years earlier, a new order had to be created out of the havoc that mutiny had wrought. Antipater firmed up his control of the state by distributing satrapies to reward friends and dispossess enemies. The officers who had deserted to him from Perdiccas—Cleitus, the admiral of the Hellespont fleet; Antigenes, the captain of the Silver Shields; and Seleucus, who had helped murder Perdiccas and save Antipater from the mob— received satrapies for the first time, while other allies were confirmed in old posts. Back in Egypt, Ptolemy, now Antipater's son-in-law, was given a free hand; North Africa was granted to him as "land won by the spear," in recognition of his defense against Perdiccas' invasion. Rule over Cappadocia went to a certain Nicanor, perhaps Antipater's own son (but it is hard to sort out the ten or more Nicanors who played important roles in this period). Its former satrap, Eumenes, now branded an outlaw and a traitor, could not be allowed to retain power there, or anywhere, for that matter.

Antigonus One-eye, who had in the past year emerged as Antipater's principal ally and most talented general, received two prize appointments under the new order: not only guardian of the kings, but *stratēgos,* or "commander in chief," of all Asia. He was given orders to hunt for Eumenes, Alcetas, and the other condemned Perdiccans and was allotted eighty-five hundred veteran infantry, plus cavalry and elephants. He also received a new junior officer, Antipater's son Cassander, as his second in command. This was in part an honor but also an implicit check. Antigonus would have tremendous power in his new role, and Antipater wanted a reliable pair of eyes to watch over his one-eyed partner.

The bond between Antigonus and Antipater was cemented in time-honored Macedonian fashion, through marriage. Thanks to the death of Craterus, Antipater again had a marriageable daughter. His eldest, Phila, twice widowed and now raising the son she had borne to Craterus, was still of childbearing age. She might have made a good partner for Antigonus himself, but instead she was given to One-eye's debauched teenage son, Demetrius—a horrible mismatch of both ages and temperaments. When Demetrius complained to Antigonus about marrying a woman more than ten years older, a high-minded noblewoman to boot, his father twitted him by spoofing a line from Euripides. In the tragedy *The Phoenician Women,* an exiled king, Polynices, explains how he submitted to a life of poverty, biding his time before trying to win back his throne: "One must become a slave, despite oneself, for the sake of gain." Antigonus quoted the line to Demetrius, whom he by now must have hoped to someday put on a throne, with a change of one word: "One must become a *spouse,* despite oneself, for the sake of gain."

There remained the question of the mutinous royal army and its demands for pay. The Silver Shields, under the command of Antigenes, were dispatched to Susa, the wealthiest of the old Persian capitals, with orders to transfer funds to a fortress at Cyinda in Cilicia. This move had a double benefit for the new leadership: money would be more available, and the Silver Shields, the most headstrong of Alexander's veterans, would be out of their hair. The remaining members of the rebellious army were assigned to follow Antigonus One-eye and the kings and to help prosecute the war against Eumenes. They too needed to be kept busy, and now there was a new enemy for them to fight.

A second blueprint had been drawn up for the post-Alexander world, as though Perdiccas' reign had been only a bad false start. But the great problem that had scuttled the old settlement, the relationship between Europe and Asia, was replicated in the new. The two great blocs of the empire were once again in fatal counterpoise, Antipater holding sovereignty in one bloc, Antigonus controlling the kings and the royal army in the other. The ultimate questions posed by Alexander's conquests had again been dodged: Was the new empire a European state, controlling Asian territory many times its own size? Or was it essentially Asian, a new incarnation of the Persian empire, with a small European appendage? Lacking a clear answer, the architects of Triparadeisus, Antipater and Antigonus, designed a structure that would straddle the straits of the Hellespont. Their sons would still be contesting the issue at the battle of Ipsus in 301 B.C., after two more decades of war.

There was one further development before the leaders decamped from Triparadeisus. Perdiccas had not had the chance to destroy his papers before being murdered in Egypt, and Antipater now got control of these, presumably receiving them from Peithon and Arrhidaeus. Among them he found a letter from Athens, from Demades, one of his two most trusted political agents (the other was Phocion). Antipater discovered in this document that Demades had plotted against him, instigating Perdiccas, by way of a caustic joke, to invade Europe: "Our cities are held together only by an old and rotting rope." Antipater was not amused by this mocking reference to his advanced age, and neither was his hotheaded son Cassander. There would be a score to settle with Demades when Antipater returned home—if the old man lived long enough to do so.

4. EUMENES (CAPPADOCIA, SPRING 320 B.C.)

Eumenes had become the loneliest man in the empire. Word reached him from Egypt that Perdiccas was murdered and that the royal army had condemned him to death; then more reports from Triparadeisus, that Antigonus One-eye had been given a powerful army and a commission to hunt him down. His supposed allies, Perdiccas' former lieutenants, had already proved unwilling to work with him; chief among them was Alcetas, Perdiccas' brother, who had refused to offer him aid even when ordered by Perdiccas himself. Branded a traitor by the royal army, yet despised by those who shared his outlaw status, Eumenes could not expect help from any quarter. He and his troops, the fine Cappadocian cavalry he had trained and the Macedonian infantry he had won in battle, were on their own.

A twisting path had brought Eumenes, a Greek from Cardia in the Chersonese (modern Gallipoli), to this isolated stand in western Asia. Plucked from obscurity by Alexander's father and placed in charge of the royal paperwork, Eumenes did not seem destined for leadership. Alexander had promoted him to a cavalry command only late in the Asian campaign, in India, and even then had used him sparingly. Changing times had forced Eumenes to adapt, to learn the ways of the battlefield rather than archive and chancery. And he had learned them well. Eumenes had won his battles on behalf of Perdiccas, even while Perdiccas was losing his war against Ptolemy. The opposite outcomes of their campaigns had made Eumenes a consigliere without a capo, the right arm of a regime that had got its head cut off.

It was comical to think that only two years earlier, Eumenes had tried to mediate the strife in Babylon, claiming he could be trusted by all because he had no interest in politics. Politics had drawn him in and forced him to choose sides. He had aligned himself with the Argeads, his mentors and benefactors since childhood. Their cause had become his, and he had backed Perdiccas as champion of that cause. He had come within a hair of transforming Perdiccas into an Argead, but the regent's decision to marry Cleopatra had come only just too late.

Eumenes still considered Cleopatra and her mother, Olympias, his patrons, and himself their champion. But the question of who had the right to fly the Argead banner had become tortured and complex. Now the joint kings were in the hands of Eumenes' foes, who likewise portrayed themselves as defenders of the royal house. To them, he was a pretender who had used the kings to advance a bid for power; to him, they were kidnappers who had abducted the kings from their rightful keepers.

Even had he wanted to, Eumenes could not now withdraw from the struggle. The chances of war had fallen out such that he had killed Craterus, a crime that would follow him everywhere. He had no choice but to fight and to hope that the showdown with Antigonus, whenever it came, would be on flat ground favorable to his cavalry corps. But what could Eumenes expect from a victory? Barred from the throne by his Greek birth, without any capo in view to whom he could be consigliere, Eumenes knew his long-term outlook was dim. If young Alexander could survive long enough to rule in his own right, Eumenes might serve as his closest adviser, the post for which he was best suited. But that prospect was still more than ten years off. Could anyone hold out for so long, even with a superior army, if he had no constitutional office and was a declared enemy of the state?

Such was the strange position Eumenes found himself in amid the turmoil of the civil war. He alone of all the leaders in that war had gained a major battlefield victory. Yet he had ended up without a country, cause, or commander to fight for. His cavalry was good enough to win against any challenger—but just *what* he could win was beyond anyone's surmise.

Fearing his soldiers would be panicked by the perils ahead, Eumenes called them together to report Perdiccas' death and their own outlaw status. He did not know how his men would respond and freely offered them the chance to leave his service. Perhaps he also mentioned some pointed details of the mutiny at Triparadeisus and the impoverished state of Antipater's finances. In any case, no one took up his offer. His troops urged him to lead them with all speed against the royal army, vowing to shred its decrees with the points of their spears.

That was all Eumenes needed to hear. He struck camp and

moved westward to await the arrival of his foes. If he could fight for nothing else, he would fight for his own survival, for the moment he surrendered, or ran, he was sure to die.

5. THE PROPAGANDA WAR (EMPIRE-WIDE)

Now that old man Antipater and his son Cassander had thrown themselves into the power struggle, questions about Alexander's death began to resurface. Had Alexander been poisoned? If so, had Antipater and his sons been involved, perhaps with help from Antipater's Greek crony Aristotle? The rumors that had circulated in the Greek world cast a dark pall over the new de facto leader of the empire. Antipater's enemies moved to exploit these rumors, and Antipater himself tried to fend them off, in an exchange of forged and leaked documents designed to win the hearts and minds of the Greek-reading public.

Already by this time the Hellenic world had read the memoir of Onesicritus, a Greek sea captain who had served in Alexander's fleet. This memoir claimed that Alexander was poisoned by the guests at a dinner he attended the night he fell ill, but it refused to name the guilty parties for fear of reprisals. Onesicritus' implication was that the assassins were still at large and able to wreak revenge, an indirect way of accusing the generals then in power—which in the Greek world meant, above all, Antipater.

Shortly thereafter—the exact date is a matter of dispute—an anonymous Greek treatise appeared that named the names Onesicritus had kept hushed. The original version of the treatise, sometimes called *The Last Days and Testament of Alexander*, is lost, but a later Latin translation survives, the *Liber de Morte*. It claims that Antipater, summoned by Alexander to Babylon and certain that his execution was near, sent his son Cassander with poison contained in a hollowed-out mule's hoof; that Cassander met with his brother Iolaus in Babylon; that together they administered the poison at a dinner party given by Iolaus' male lover, Medius. With sober fanfare, the treatise then lists the guests present at the fateful dinner and exonerates seven, including Perdiccas, Eumenes, and Ptolemy. It leaves more than a dozen named guests accused as conspirators. The treatise describes how Alexander drank the poisoned wine he received from Iolaus, felt a stabbing pain, cried out, and retired to his room while the fearful plotters dispersed. In a final act of treachery, Iolaus, asked by Alexander for a feather to help him vomit, gave him one dipped in poison.

This document was almost certainly a propaganda weapon deployed by one of the generals vying for power, but which one? Since Antipater stands accused of Alexander's murder while Perdiccas and Eumenes are cleared, it seems at first glance to be the work of Perdiccas or his allies. But Ptolemy was as much Perdiccas' enemy as Antipater, and Ptolemy is exonerated by the treatise. Perhaps there are different strata of material here, as successive forgers added new elements. Whatever its purposes, *The Last Days and Testament of Alexander* shows that charges of regicide came increasingly into play in the Macedonian power struggle, principally to undermine old man Antipater.

Probably in response to these poisoning charges, someone published the final segment of the *Royal Journals,* a sober, day-by-day eyewitness account of Alexander's illness and death. The original is lost but existed in the second century A.D., when it was read (in differing versions) and paraphrased by both Arrian and Plutarch. The *Royal Journals* depicted Alexander's illness as a gradual descent into fever and coma and made clear that it had not begun with a sudden, stabbing pain as the *Last Days* claimed. Perhaps Antipater himself had the *Journals* published, or fabricated, as a way to dispel the rumors that shadowed his family. No certainty is possible in this hall-of-mirrors world of forged, composite, and anonymous documents.

Meanwhile, in Egypt, Ptolemy was undertaking a different kind of propaganda, a history of Alexander's Asian campaign highlighting his own role and obscuring that of Perdiccas. In all likelihood, Perdiccas was dead when Ptolemy began this history, but probably Perdiccas' supporters, and his memory, were not. There was much to be gained from concealing a wound Perdiccas suffered at the battle of Gaugamela, or blaming Perdiccas' lack of discipline for the onset of fighting at Thebes, or, most important, omitting mention of Alexander's greatest mark of favor, the handing over of the signet ring. Perhaps Ptolemy hoped that, as one of few witnesses present, he could consign that moment to oblivion.

It did not reflect well on him if the man whose downfall he had largely caused was the king's legitimate, handpicked successor.

Many others likewise had an interest in blackening Perdiccas' name—those who colluded in his murder, inherited his power, or joined in the hunt for his partisans. Any or all of these may have helped color the portrait of Perdiccas preserved in the ancient sources. We find in those sources condemnations of Perdiccas' arrogance, high-handedness, and brutality, a portrait that at times verges on slander. Diodorus uses the word *phonikos,* or "man of slaughter," to describe him, an odd barb to throw at a soldier whose stock-in-trade was killing enemies. But when a leader has failed, the very qualities that made him a leader suddenly appear as flaws. Perdiccas' arrogance and bloody-mindedness were no more pronounced than Alexander's, indeed much less so. But Alexander, unlike the hapless Perdiccas, knew little of failure.

6. CLEOPATRA, EUMENES, AND ANTIPATER
(SARDIS, SPRING 320 B.C.)

For two years Alexander the Great's sister, Cleopatra, had stayed in Asia, watching the war unfold from the satrapal palace of Sardis. Perhaps she longed to return to her Macedonian homeland or to Epirus, where her mother, Olympias, was looking after her two young children. But that would be to admit defeat and accept a life of irrelevance that might also be short. The one chance she had of restoring her branch of the royal family, and of safeguarding her mother and her children, was to wed a powerful general and beget a new heir to the throne. But back in Europe there were no such bridegrooms to be found. She had come into Asia to marry, and in Asia she remained, like some fairy-tale princess in a tower awaiting her knight-errant.

Her time was running short. As she reached her mid-thirties, her capacity to bear children, the principal asset she brought to the succession struggle, was fast waning. Worse, she knew that her rival in fertility, Adea, now married to King Philip for more than a year, might announce a pregnancy at any moment. Should that happen, Cleopatra's value in the marriage market would drop precipitously. A child produced by *two* royals, if it were male, would without question become the new heir. Not even Cleopatra, the full sister of Alexander, could trump such a potent union of Argead bloodlines, unless she too married an Argead, and there were none left to marry. Even eligible generals, after the deaths of her first two prospects, Leonnatus and Perdiccas, were starting to run short.

The rise to power of old man Antipater spelled danger to Cleopatra. This ancient foe of her mother bore no love for her branch of the Argead house and now could do it much harm. Antipater had played the marriage game far more successfully than she; his daughters were wed to Ptolemy and Antigonus' son, Demetrius, locking up two of her own potential bridegrooms. The whole empire seemed suddenly to be in Antipater's pocket; with the scope of his power, he could choke off access to Sardis and prevent suitors from reaching her. Perhaps he could even force her to marry his son Cassander—but the thought of union with the man believed to have poisoned her brother was no doubt a disturbing one.

While Cleopatra contemplated her darkening prospects, a troop of cavalry rode up to the walls of Sardis with a commanding figure at its head. It was not, however, her knight in shining armor but Eumenes, her brother's former secretary.

This was an awkward development for Cleopatra. Eumenes was an old friend and loyal servant of her family's and, thanks to the changing tides of fortune, leader of a powerful army. He had always supported Cleopatra and her marital ambitions. But Eumenes was now an outlaw, condemned to death for his role in Perdiccas' regime. Not only could Cleopatra not marry him—he was a *Greek* after all, far below her station—but even to receive him might be a criminal act. With Antipater making his way toward Sardis, Cleopatra could not put herself on the wrong side of the civil war.

Eumenes, for his part, was eager to talk with Cleopatra. He had spent the last several months living off the lands of his enemies, plundering provinces in western Anatolia, but had come to Sardis seeking something more precious than booty—legitimacy. Cleopatra could counteract the ascendancy of his two great nemeses, Antipater and Antigonus One-eye. They had taken charge of the kings and claimed to be stewards of the royal house, but Cleopatra could give the lie to that claim with a wave of her hand. If she would become Eumenes' ally, join her moral authority to his military might, they could yet prevail over their enemies. They had much reason to make common cause: both were excluded from power by second-class status, she as a woman and he as a Greek. Both could thrive only by attaching themselves to a regent or king. Perhaps, until one of them succeeded, they could become attached to each other.

Eumenes chivalrously paraded his cavalry before Sardis, trying to impress the princess within. Mindful of his last visit there, when Cleopatra had spurned Perdiccas because of his uncertain chances in war, Eumenes hoped to show that this time victory was assured. Indeed he wanted to fight the royal army right there, on the plains outside Sardis, as though his men would take inspiration from the watching eyes of Cleopatra. She was closest in blood to Alexander of anyone on earth; in her the virtues, perhaps even the features, of the dead king seemed to have found life once again. "Such was the reverence for the greatness of Alexander that even the traces left behind in *women* could be used to summon the blessing of his hallowed name," writes Justin in his summary of Trogus' history.

But Cleopatra, though she granted Eumenes an audience, was not willing to become his partisan. She was conscious of her duty to the state and did not wish to exacerbate its troubles by taking sides. She asked Eumenes to leave Sardis and seek battle elsewhere, far from her regal presence. Eumenes bade farewell to the princess and, as she had asked, led his army from Sardis.

Old man Antipater arrived in Sardis soon after and paid his own visit to Cleopatra. He had been informed of her colloquy with Eumenes, and he was not pleased. He could surmise what game the princess had been playing, first with Perdiccas and now with Perdiccas' consigliere, and perhaps he knew about the dalliance with Leonnatus before that. With his authority already under challenge—another princess, the teenage Adea, had very nearly gotten him stoned to death—Antipater could not allow Cleopatra to flirt with his enemies. He scolded her for heedlessness of the royal house's interests. He had loyally served that house for six decades, but it was being torn apart, as he saw it, by meddlesome, ungovernable women.

Cleopatra would have none of this. She was too proud to be talked down to by a man who had taken orders from her father and her brother. In a now-lost speech that a medieval reader, Photius, described as "beyond what one would expect of a woman," Cleopatra hit back at Antipater with all the ammunition she had. Perhaps she too, like her mother, held this man responsible for her brother's death and now accused him to his face. Antipater somehow mollified her, for the two parted as friends. The empire's senior commander and its most high-ranking royal still needed each other. Cleopatra was unwilling to be blamed for civil strife, and Antipater had learned, through the wretched example of Perdiccas, the high price a soldier would pay for killing an Argead princess.

Antipater went on his way to prepare for the battle with Eumenes. Cleopatra, the damsel in the tower keep, stayed where she was, once again friendless, husbandless, and alone.

7. PTOLEMY (SYRIA AND JERUSALEM, SUMMER 320 B.C.)

Seeing his former comrades busy fighting one another, Ptolemy, safely ensconced in Egypt, chose once again to pursue his own interests. His new realm was ample, nicely enlarged by the additions of Cyprus and Cyrene, but a choice tract to the east, now nearly vacant of Macedonian forces, seemed the perfect way to complete his empire-in-miniature. His predecessors the pharaohs had long coveted Syria and Palestine and had often occupied them; wealthy provinces with well-equipped ports, they provided a valuable buffer against attacks from the east. Ptolemy had narrowly survived such an attack, and though his father-in-law, Antipater, was for the moment an ally, he might not always be one—especially since Ptolemy planned to insult the old man's daughter by making a queen of her bridesmaid, Berenice.

In the north of the realm that Ptolemy sought lay the small

walled city of Jerusalem, populated by a race of curious monotheists whom the Greeks would soon know as *Ioudaioi*. The Jews had thus far remained nearly invisible to Alexander and his generals, though the Macedonians had crossed right through their territory and even, perhaps, entered the holy city. Not a single historian of the Alexander period mentions the Jews or Jerusalem, an omission that a later writer, the Romanized Jew Josephus, takes as a sign of ill will. Indeed, no Greek writer before Alexander's time shows any awareness of the Jews, except Theophrastus, a student of Aristotle's, and he seems to have encountered only expatriates living in Egypt.

Ptolemy, however, knew a lot about the Jews, enough to use their own religious practices against them. He had learned that their calendar was divided into seven-day weeks, each one containing a Sabbath on which all labor, including the bearing of arms, was forbidden. Ptolemy therefore planned his entry into Jerusalem to coincide with a Sabbath day. The Jews stood by their ancient code and did not raise their hands against him. Ptolemy gained a bloodless victory and a rich new addition to his territory. Alexandria, Ptolemy's new capital, began to fill up with Jewish captives and emigrants, soon becoming the most vital Jewish center outside Jerusalem itself.

Thus do the Jews make their entry onto the stage of European history, as pious dupes, conquered by one of Alexander's generals because they would not abandon Moses' laws.

8. EUMENES, ANTIGONUS, AND ANTIPATER (ANATOLIA, WINTER, LATE 320 B.C.)

There is a legend that circulated in the ancient world, that while Alexander the Great was alive, a captured pirate was brought before him for punishment. Alexander was outraged by the man's depredations and asked what right he had to trouble the seas. "The same right you have to trouble the world," the pirate replied. "Only since I do so with a small ship, I'm called a robber; you use a great fleet and are called a ruler." The anecdote may be spurious but makes an important point. Even while Alexander lived, the political goals of his campaign were not always easy to discern; a cynic might regard it as a global plundering raid. Now that he was dead, the piratical side of the Macedonian army was coming increasingly to the fore.

The three generals now stalking through Asia Minor—Eumenes the outlaw and his pursuers Antipater and Antigonus One-eye—understood the terms on which the coming war would be fought. Strength depended on troop loyalty, and loyalty depended on loot. Soldiers who had served with Alexander already owned piles of loot, their share of the riches stripped from the Persians, and they hauled this around through Asia in great, bulky baggage trains. But somehow their stash never seemed large enough. Lacking any home or national cause, lacking any sense of what the Argead royal house wanted from them, they had only money as their raison d'être. They would fight for the generals who provided it, against others who did not.

Antigonus One-eye had the upper hand in this new kind of warfare, since he had the right, as commander in chief of Asia, to draw from imperial treasuries. His written orders, signed by compliant King Philip, could unlock burgeoning storehouses of silver like the one in Cyinda, guarded by the impassable Silver Shields. With such wealth he could try to buy a victory over Eumenes rather than win one on the battlefield—for there he would have to face Eumenes' highly trained cavalry. That corps had already brought down Craterus, the best field general of Alexander's staff, and trampled him under its pounding hooves.

Eumenes, for his part, was poor, but being an outlaw, he could steal from the rich. Asia Minor was filled with wealthy estates and towns populated by potential slaves. In Alexander's day, the army had been allowed to reap such plunder only on enemy territory. But for Eumenes the whole empire was enemy territory, since the empire had condemned him to death. He began allowing his men to seize estates in Anatolia and sell them back to their owners for extortionary sums, thereby raising a sizable war chest. This strategy had a double benefit in that it embarrassed his enemies Antipater and Antigonus, who were in charge of Asian affairs but unable or unwilling to stop the shakedowns. It was *they* who were held responsible by the peoples of Anatolia, not Eumenes. Indeed the popularity of the outlaws only increased as they picked their enemies' pockets.

Antigonus One-eye tried to fight fire with fire by offering a price for Eumenes' life. One day Eumenes returned to camp to find his soldiers studying leaflets: Antigonus would give a hundred talents for Eumenes' severed head—a prize that would test any man's loyalty, unless Eumenes did something to counter it. The wily Greek hastily convened an assembly of the troops and stood to speak before them. He thanked them for standing by their oaths of allegiance —no one, of course, had yet had time to do otherwise—and "revealed" that he had circulated the leaflets as a test, a test his army had passed admirably. Antigonus could never have written them, he reasoned; any general who offered bounties would create a weapon that could be turned back against him. Perhaps some of Eumenes' listeners bought that logic, and perhaps others admired the cleverness of his ruse; but all were convinced by the recent raids that their best hope of riches lay in protecting Eumenes, not killing him. They voted on the spot to vastly increase their leader's security, supplying him a bodyguard of a thousand picked troops.

Eumenes struck back against Antigonus by moving to Celaenae in Phrygia, One-eye's own vacant capital, and plundering his satrapy all through that winter. Antigonus did not challenge him there, but Antipater, with his more seasoned troops, made several sallies. The contest in Phrygia between Eumenes and Antipater, old enemies since the days before Alexander's march, is known in great detail, thanks to two precious pages of Arrian's *Events After Alexander* found in a medieval palimpsest (a parchment rubbed out and overwritten by economy-minded scribes). The erased passage has just now awakened from its millennium-long sleep, thanks to digital-imaging technologies. It gives a painful glimpse of how much was lost with the extinction of this work.

Eumenes continued his hit-and-run raids on a wider scale than before, striking in many directions at once so Antipater could not pin him down. He gave his captains use of his siege machines to make their job easier. In a short time they collected some eight hundred talents from the hapless peoples of Phrygia and distributed this loot among the delighted rank and file. Eumenes grew in stature as his men grew richer, while Antipater began to look like a paper tiger. "In full view of Antipater and his army, the [Phrygians] were being seized, their estates were burned down, and their goods were sold off as booty," Arrian wrote. "They regarded Antipater as nothing more than a spectator of their misfortunes."

But Eumenes' tactics could not succeed forever. His enemies would eventually corner him, or cut him off from food and plunder, thus robbing him of his army's loyalty. Already he had seen disaffection among his troops; a corps of three thousand infantry and five hundred cavalry had deserted from Celaenae and gone on the move, their camp some distance away. Eumenes, borrowing one of Alexander's signature stratagems, sent an elite force of strong, fleet men on an all-night march. These took the deserters entirely by surprise and captured them without bloodshed. Eumenes executed the leaders of the mutiny but reabsorbed the troops, dispersing them among more reliable units and courting their favor with handouts. With both Antipater and Antigonus coming after him, he could not afford to lose experienced soldiers.

Eumenes' best hope was to join forces with his fellow outlaws, the other former leaders of Perdiccas' regime. Each of them still controlled an army of his own: Alcetas, Perdiccas' brother, had considerable forces, while Perdiccas' brother-in-law Attalus had money to spare from the funds he had seized. Eumenes reached out to these two highborn Macedonians as well as to two other Perdiccans, Polemon and Docimus, all four of whom were gathered in nearby Pisidia. Eumenes' strategy proposal is preserved in the now-legible palimpsest. If all five combined forces, Eumenes argued, they could control western Asia for a long time, living off the land and embarrassing their enemies. Antipater and Antigonus would be despised for their weakness, and defections from their armies would increase. Eventually, these two would negotiate a peace in which the Perdiccans would be pardoned and restored to the posts they held under the Babylon settlement. Significantly, Eumenes envisioned not a final victory but a return to unity and the status quo ante. His crimes, perhaps, were not beyond forgiveness. The Macedonians had condemned him in a fit of rage and might relent; they might cease fighting him once they saw he had no wish to fight back.

Eumenes ended his appeal with deference, saying that anyone who had a better plan should bring his ideas forward. Humility was Eumenes' best hope of success, for the men he was addressing did not like, trust, or respect him. Alcetas had once before refused to help Eumenes, even when Perdiccas ordered him to do so. If Alcetas hated Eumenes then, as a Greek who was too clever and had too much influence over his brother, he hated him more now that Eumenes had won great glory on the battlefield. Similar jealousies gnawed at Attalus, Polemon, and Docimus, members of an aristocratic warrior caste who did not like being put in the shade by an upstart foreigner.

The issue of who would command the joint forces was held hostage to these rivalries. Alcetas sought the top post for himself, aiming especially at control of the native Macedonians in Eumenes' infantry, sturdy Alexander veterans all. But Eumenes was unwilling to concede command. In his own mind he was no longer court Greek, servant to the Macedonian warrior elite, but a high-ranking general with proven talents. He could accept being second to someone of Perdiccas' stature, but surely not to an Alcetas or an Attalus. These men had been *his* subordinates not long ago, or at least so Perdiccas, and Alexander himself, had wanted.

In the end there was no reconciling these divergent views of Eumenes' rank, and the five-way parley broke up without agreement. The coalition that could have saved all the Perdiccans was never formed. All would face their enemies on their own terms, and Eumenes, for his part, would face them alone.

9. ANTIGONUS, CASSANDER, ANTIPATER, AND THE KINGS (ANATOLIA, WINTER, LATE 320 B.C.)

Meanwhile, farther north in Anatolia, dissension and defection were also afflicting Eumenes' enemies, the new custodians of the joint kings. Despite their control of the exchequer, old man Antipater and Antigonus One-eye could not suppress the message that Eumenes' banditry had sent: piracy pays. Antigonus found some of his troops heeding that message and taking to the hills, just as Eumenes had foreseen in his proposal to Alcetas and the others. A troop of three thousand infantry broke away from Antipater's army that winter, with them an officer, Holcias, known to be a Perdiccan sympathizer. They had occupied high ground in Cappadocia, a safe place from which to plunder surrounding lands. Antigonus feared they would join Alcetas' or Eumenes' army, but he could not incur ill will among his loyal troops by massacring their comrades.

In two years of civil war Antigonus had grown adept at covert operations, and the current crisis called for one of these. He sent out a high officer named Leonidas to the rebels, telling him to gain their trust by pretending to join their ranks. Warmly welcomed by the rebel band and even elected general, Leonidas led the men down from the heights and into an open plain. There, by prearrangement, Antigonus' cavalry was waiting. With level ground on which to mount charges, Antigonus easily captured the rebel leaders and forced them to swear an oath: to depart Asia with their followers and never return. It was a shame to lose so many soldiers but better than having them join up with the Perdiccan armies.

A worse problem for Antigonus was the quarrel brewing between himself and old man Antipater. This rift had been brought on by Antipater's son Cassander. The boy had come to mistrust Antigonus, to whom he had been made second-in-command, and had gone to see his father in Phrygia to complain (what his grounds were is unclear). Antipater trusted his son's qualms enough to summon Antigonus to Phrygia and to change the balance of power resolved at Triparadeisus. Then, Antigonus had been given charge of the kings and leadership of the scrappy veterans of Alexander's army. Now Antipater took away both these tokens of authority and brought them under his own control. In exchange he turned over to Antigonus the European recruits he himself commanded, swapping troops so that the royal army stayed with the kings. Antipater also made clear a change in his near-term plans. He would return to Europe and let

Antigonus prosecute the war against Eumenes without him. After tangling ineffectually with that sly Greek for several long winter months, the aged soldier-statesman was ready to go home.

Antipater collected the royal family and his son Cassander and made for the Hellespont. Asia had brought him little but travail and humiliation since he first arrived there, and he was destined to suffer one last indignity on its shores. As his column made its way through Anatolia, Adea, King Philip's grasping young wife, began reminding the soldiers of their long-deferred bonus pay. The royal army mutinied once again. Antipater could appease them only by feigning that money was waiting just ahead at Abydus, on the shores of the Hellespont. Having lured them to that crossing point, Antipater slipped across the straits in the dead of night with the kings and a few top officers. The stranded army had little choice but to follow the next day and return to Europe, where Antipater was better able to control them and their teenage queen.

The joint kings had left Asia for good, together with much of the *grande armée* that had fought under Alexander. What their countrymen made of these unruly veterans on their return, or of the strange Bactrian woman and half-breed toddler, Alexander's next of kin, whom they now beheld for the first time, or of the bizarre living war machines called elephants that lumbered in their train, has not been recorded by any ancient writer. Indeed ancient historians seem not to have marked the significance of this crossing, with the exception of Arrian, who chose it as the end point of his *Events After Alexander.*

It was indeed a terminus, the end of a daring experiment in cross-continental monarchy. Alexander the Great had started that experiment, and Perdiccas had tried, however incompetently, to maintain it. By a unilateral decision, Antipater ended it and repatriated the Argead house, severing it from Bactria and Babylon and restoring it to the foothills of the Balkans. Asia might remain part of the Macedonian empire, but it would never again be the *center,* as Alexander had dreamed and planned.

What was left of that dream was written on the complexion and features of Alexander's son, who, if he could survive another ten years or so, would become the first Asian-born monarch to rule on European soil. But given the whirlwind of events in his first four years, that was likely to be a long and dangerous decade indeed.

10. ANTIGONUS AND EUMENES
(ANATOLIA, SPRING 319 B.C.)

With Antipater off the scene and winter ending, Antigonus One-eye and Eumenes prepared to decide the contest for Asia. It was a duel between two intelligent and honorable men, former friends from their days at Philip's court, but driven by political accident onto opposing sides. Both claimed to fight under the Argead banner, and both headed largely Macedonian armies; they had never harmed each other, and there was no ideological gulf between them. Yet Eumenes had been declared an enemy of the state, and Antigonus, commander in chief of Asia, had been assigned the task of destroying him.

Eumenes, however, was not going to be easy to destroy. His Cappadocian cavalry outnumbered Antigonus' horsemen and outclassed them in skill and experience. Antigonus was not about to make the same mistake as Craterus and face a charge by that cavalry, at least not without softening them up first. Fortunately, he had plenty of money to accomplish that softening. His bribes turned the loyalties of one of Eumenes' cavalry officers, a man named Apollonides. Through covert messages, Apollonides promised Antigonus he would desert Eumenes and draw away an entire unit of horse.

Unaware of this looming betrayal, Eumenes confidently sought battle with Antigonus near a place called Orcynia. He camped on open ground in full view of One-eye's position, a signal he was willing to join combat. Heralds passed freely between the two armies, bearing messages from one general to the other, as they prepared for the death struggle that awaited them.

Antigonus used this interlude to play a demoralizing trick on his former friend. While Eumenes' heralds were in his camp, One-eye instructed a soldier to run up to him breathlessly and call out, "Our allies have arrived!" The heralds who witnessed this scene duly reported to Eumenes that Antigonus had been reinforced.

The next day Antigonus marched his phalanx forward in double-wide formation, as though he had indeed received fresh recruits. This sight eroded the confidence of Eumenes' infantry, who, not perceiving from their vantage that the formation was also half-deep, thought they had lost superiority of numbers.

Two devious ploys, neutralizing both his cavalry and his infantry strength, proved too much for Eumenes. The battle of Orcynia—from which no detailed account has survived—turned quickly into a rout. Antigonus butchered some eight thousand of Eumenes' forces and also captured his baggage train, the booty and belongings of his army. Since booty had made Eumenes a hero to his troops, this was a huge psychological blow.

But Eumenes was not done for yet. He escaped the battle with a portion of his army that had neither deserted nor surrendered, including much of his swift-moving cavalry. After somehow catching and killing the traitor Apollonides, Eumenes doubled back to Orcynia, eluding Antigonus, who was still tracking him in the direction he had fled. He was determined to give his slain soldiers burial, a privilege normally obtained by formal concession of defeat. Since Orcynia was barren of trees, Eumenes ordered wood collected from the doors of nearby houses and had two vast pyres built, one for officers, the other for enlisted men; then he raised a mound of earth over their ashes. When Antigonus finally arrived, the grave was complete and Eumenes was gone. Though he had lost the battle, Eumenes had recovered his dignity, denying Antigonus the right of the victor to set terms for return of the dead.

Eumenes hoped to make a dash for Armenia and there recruit a fresh army. But Antigonus was closing in on him quickly. Eumenes had no choice but to make use of a preplanned, last-ditch escape. On the border of Cappadocia lay a fortress called Nora, a set of buildings atop an impregnable crag only four hundred yards around. Stocked with enough food, salt, and firewood to last a small force for years, it could hold out against any attacker. Eumenes released from his service all but six hundred followers and with these shut himself inside the fort, a tiny island of security in a sea of enemies. Here he could wait for the political winds to shift, or for his would-be allies, Alcetas and the others, to come to his rescue. The prospect of long isolation in a mountain-top prison was dismal, but better than defeat.

Antigonus One-eye arrived at Nora to find Eumenes safely barred within. He prepared to surround the fort with double walls, ditches, and guard posts, positions he might need to maintain for years. Before committing to that expensive alternative, however, he decided to try negotiation. He sent his own nephew into the fort as a hostage guaranteeing Eumenes' safety and persuaded Eumenes to come out and talk.

The two men had not seen each other in fifteen years, not since the early days of Alexander's campaign. But they found it easy to put their conflict aside and recover old bonds of friendship. They embraced each other and spoke kind words of greeting, while Antigonus' troops, recruits of a younger generation, strove to get a glimpse of a famous man—the victor over Craterus, the bookkeeper who had become a general, the general who had become an outlaw. They pressed in so close that Antigonus feared for Eumenes' safety and threw his arms around his old friend to protect him from the overeager—and perhaps hostile—crowd.

The parley between the two leaders revealed the artificiality of their dispute. Far from acknowledging his crimes against the state, Eumenes asked for full restoration as satrap of Cappadocia, even though this would mean joining the regime officially committed to killing him. He did not even mention the death sentence passed in Egypt, as though this had been an obvious mistake. Antigonus, for his part, did not reject Eumenes' proposal, showing that he too was dubious about the grounds for the current hostilities. He offered to refer the request to Antipater for adjudication and sent a messenger to Macedonia for this purpose. Eumenes sent his own envoy as well, a close friend and countryman, to plead his side of the case. This was none other than Hieronymus of Cardia—the man who, with his inside view of the post-Alexander power struggle, would one day write the now-lost memoir on which most surviving accounts are based.

As these envoys headed for Europe, Eumenes and Antigonus parted as friends and resumed their appointed roles as enemies. Antigonus finished walling off Nora to prevent outbreaks from within or rescue attempts from without. Then, certain that his hold over Eumenes was secure, he took his army west in pursuit of the remaining Perdiccans. These were still gathered in Pisidia, and Antigonus prepared to lead his young recruits there by a grueling forced march, hoping to reach his foes before they suspected he was coming.

Eumenes, beaten but unbowed, climbed back into his fortress and barred its gates. After marching some twenty thousand miles with Alexander and helping him rule three continents, after being consigliere to Perdiccas with sovereignty over the whole known world, he now had a scant four acres of rocky crag as his dominion. But his enclave was secure from attack and well stocked with food and fuel. Despite abandonment by his former allies, demonization by the royal army, and a crushing defeat at Orcynia, Eumenes had managed to survive. He settled in for a long stay with his six hundred loyalists and awaited the next throw of Fortune's dice.

The War Comes Home

Greece, Macedonia, and Western Asia

SPRING 319–SPRING 318 B.C.

Life for citizens of Athens went on much as it had before the Hellenic War—that is, for those who *were* citizens of Athens. The city's poor had lost their citizenship rights, and many of these, perhaps thousands, had relocated to Thrace on the wintry northern frontier of the Greek world. Old man Antipater had provided them with land there, after forcing Athens to change its constitution and disenfranchise them. "They were like refugees forced out from a city that had fallen in a siege," says Plutarch, even though Athens had in fact avoided a siege by agreeing to Antipater's terms, with its two chosen representatives, Phocion and Demades, leading the negotiating team.

Only those with estates worth at least two thousand drachmas, a sizable fortune, could now take part in government. This amounted to about nine thousand people, less than half the citizen body under the old democracy. The rest—those who chose to stay rather than emigrate—suffered what the Athenians called *atimia,* or "loss of honor," meaning loss of the right to bring legal cases, to hold office or serve on jury panels, or to vote in the Assembly, the body that debated and decided all matters of state.

Atimia was political excommunication, formerly imposed only on criminals or bankrupts, and the Athenian poor hated it.

Only twice before in nearly two centuries had Athens' democratic constitution been replaced by an oligarchy. Both times, the change was made under pressure of war with Sparta, and both times it was reversed as soon as that pressure abated. In the second instance, in 403 B.C., a garrison of Spartan soldiers had kept the oligarchic regime in power; democracy was restored as soon as the garrison was withdrawn. The poor and landless of Athens had shown they could not be denied a voice for long. Their boisterous energy made the city prosperous, and their strong arms, manning the oars of its warships, made it powerful.

In the wake of the Hellenic War it was again a foreign garrison, this time a Macedonian one, that was keeping the poor of Athens down. Though Menyllus, the garrison commander, had been temperate in his use of force, the daily sight of armed Macedonians in the harbor town of Piraeus reminded the Athenians where they stood. The masses could mount no counterrevolution, find no escape from the disgrace of *atimia,* so long as the fort on the hill of Munychia was held by the world's best infantrymen. Perhaps all of Athens, acting as one, might overcome that fort, but the city was divided. Many of the privileged nine thousand were content with their new oligarchy, and some, especially Demades, one of the politicians leading the regime, were profiting handsomely from it.

1. DEMADES AND PHOCION (ATHENS)

Demades knew what *atimia* was like, for he had once suffered it himself. Convicted five years earlier, along with Demosthenes, of pilfering Harpalus' embezzled funds, he had stayed in Athens but without citizen rights, a political nonentity. But all that had changed. After Athens' defeat in the Hellenic War, his accusers had erased his penalty and begged him to come back into politics. His friendship with the Macedonians had in the end paid off. As one of two Athenians whom Antipater trusted, Demades had come to enjoy vast power under the new constitution. Now and then he might be required to do odious things—like sponsoring the measure that brought death to his former colleagues Demosthenes and Hyperides—but he was well rewarded for such accommodations.

Demades had grown up poor, son of a poor father, but his political career had made poverty a distant memory. A notorious libertine for whom no meal and no bribe were too large, Demades could at last subsidize all his pleasures. Athenian law barred foreign dancers from performing in the state theater, under penalty of a huge fine, but Demades produced a play there featuring a dance troupe made up entirely of foreigners, coolly paying the fine for each one. It was his way of showing the city he could afford to squander his wealth. He had come a long way from where he had started, rowing in the Athenian navy for a bare living wage.

Demades had a son, Demeas, the result of a dalliance with one of the loose flute girls who performed at Athenian soirees. He enjoyed lavishing money on the boy and training him in the family profession, political toadying. Recently the lad had begun speaking in the Assembly, providing a target for those who disliked Demades but dared not attack him directly. One such opponent had interrupted a speech by Demeas with a gibe at the boy's origins: "Why don't you shut up? You're more full of wind than your mother was!" Such remarks showed that old resentments against Antipater, and those who served his interests, were still alive. But with Macedonian soldiers just down the road in Piraeus, those resentments stayed bottled up.

For the past two years Demades had watched events in Asia, the spreading civil war between Macedonian generals, with keen interest. Though he had done well working for Antipater, it was somehow not enough. Perhaps he could rise higher, or grow richer, under a new master or else be rid of the senior colleague, Phocion, who always overshadowed him. Knowing that Antipater and Phocion would soon be off the scene—both were very old men—Demades began writing to Perdiccas, head of the Babylon government, urging him to invade Europe and destroy the "old and rotting rope" holding the Greek cities together. Perdiccas' assassination had ended that little venture, but Demades was not perturbed. He went on about his business, lording it over the Athenians, spending vast sums on a wedding banquet for his son.

"Boy, when I married your mother," he told Demeas, "even the next-door neighbors didn't notice; but kings and rulers will chip in to help you celebrate *your* wedding."

Phocion, Demades' partner in leadership, was cut from a different cloth and used his power to different ends. Sober and austere, high-minded and philosophic, this octogenarian saw Athens' loss of freedom as a crisis to be managed, not an opportunity to be seized. He tried to soften the heavy tread of the Macedonians—for example, by opposing the Piraeus garrison, though he finally acceded to this as a necessary evil. He often intervened with old man Antipater to stop him from deporting dissidents beyond the Ceraunian Mountains, into what is today northern Albania. Recently he had arranged such clemency for Hagnonides, an unreconstructed democrat. Thanks to Phocion's intercession, Hagnonides had ended up banished only to the Peloponnese, not to that terrible wilderness.

The new restrictions on citizenship did not offend Phocion, for he had no love of democracy. His childhood teacher, Plato, had taught him to see the follies of that bizarre system, and he had often witnessed them himself in his sixty years of public life. The Athenians had elected him general for *forty-five* one-year terms yet hardly ever took his advice. Instead, they ruined themselves in reckless battles against Macedon, losing every time. The silencing of the poor, who had most of all agitated for the Hellenic War, suited Phocion perfectly well; in his eyes the poor had listened to fools like Hyperides and hence had brought their troubles on themselves. His own class, the staid and sturdy aristocracy, preferred to soothe the Macedonian lion rather than provoke its fury. Theirs had always been the sensible, moderate path.

Like Demades, Phocion had countless opportunities to profit under Macedonian power, but unlike his gluttonous junior colleague he refrained. Antipater liked to say he had two close friends in Athens, one to whom he could never give enough and one to whom he could never give *anything*. Despite his wealthy background, Phocion disdained luxury—or at least feigned disdain, for it was good politics in Athens to appear impervious to bribes. Once Phocion had even refused cash sent by Alexander the Great himself. When the king's messengers approached bearing chests of silver, Phocion asked why Alexander so favored him. "It's because Alexander judges that you alone are a good and true man," he was told. "Then tell him to let me be as I am, and be regarded so," he replied, turning the money aside. (That last phrase, "be regarded so," showed that Phocion was less a philosopher than a career politician tending his image.)

More recently, Menyllus, the Macedonian garrison commander, had also tried to give Phocion money, insisting he take it for the sake of his son. Phocion, it was well known, was father to a wild and free-spending youth, Phocus, who indulged in upscale drinking parties and in the posh athletic event called *apobatēs*. Phocus became good enough at this event, which involved jumping on and off a moving chariot clad in full armor, to win first place at an Athenian sports festival, and Phocion reluctantly went to the victory party for his son. At the door he saw that the hosts had provided footbaths of spiced wine for arriving guests. That was the last straw for Phocion. He packed Phocus off to Sparta and enrolled him in that city's famously ascetic military training. "If my son changes his ways and learns self-restraint, then his inheritance from me will suffice," Phocion explained to Menyllus as he turned down the proffered funds. "As he is now, nothing will be enough."

Phocion had navigated three decades of his city's conflict with Macedon—years that had seen the exile or execution of many politicians—without a fall from grace. The Athenians had awarded him the epithet *chrēstos,* "Do-good," for his devotion to public service. The Macedonian generals, and Antipater especially, admired him as a warrior, a tough old bird like themselves who did not yield to the rigors of the march or the ills of old age. But even for this most expert of political survivors, the middle path between Athens and Macedon was becoming harder to steer. Events were about to spiral out of Phocion's control, and the moderation that had been the glory of his career was about to be trampled by extremism and rage.

The city's poor, though lacking a vote or a voice, had one cause in common with the propertied class, hatred of the Macedonian garrison. This armed camp posed an implied threat: the city, which relied on food imports shipped through Piraeus, could be cut off from its harbor and starved if it misbehaved. The garrison's presence was a daily humiliation, and now that Antipater was returning to Europe, where he could be easily reached by envoys, speakers in the Assembly began agitating for its removal. This was Athens' first attempt since the Hellenic War to loosen its yoke, and it quickly gained support.

Phocion and Demades disagreed over the garrison. Phocion was unwilling to approach Antipater and ask for its removal. He had come to regard the oligarchy as the new reality of Athenian politics, a fait accompli that should not be tampered with. Demades was more restless and ambitious, and more aware of the impetus for change. The city's longing for autonomy and democracy was a potent force, which might bring him greater power in Athens, could he but harness it.

The Assembly voted to send an embassy about the garrison, but Phocion refused to go. Demades stepped into the breach and accepted the assignment. He took his son Demeas with him and departed for Pella, the Macedonian capital, to pay a visit to old man Antipater, just then returning from Asia. It would be the last road he would ever travel.

2. CASSANDER AND ANTIPATER, DEMADES
AND DEMEAS (PELLA, SPRING 319 B.C.)

Antipater had come home, but the Asian campaigns had wearied him. Shortly after his return he fell ill and began to fail. In his eightieth year, the oldest of the Macedonian old guard, victor in the Hellenic War, architect of the global blueprint at Triparadeisus, custodian of the joint kings, sovereign pro tempore of Alexander's empire, was dying.

By his side was his son Cassander, one of the middle children of his many sons and daughters. Cassander had always been by his side, even during Alexander's campaign when several of his other boys had gone east. Antipater had come to rely on Cassander as his helpmate, and Cassander was equally reliant on him. A frail boy, perhaps tubercular, Cassander did not stand on his own as much as other noblemen's sons. It was a Macedonian custom that young men must kill a boar without aid of hunting nets before they could recline at table like an adult, but at thirty-five Cassander was still sitting upright on his couch, his hunting prowess unproved, beside his reclining father.

Since Alexander's death, Cassander had become especially vigilant on his father's behalf. In Asia the previous year, when he had sensed danger from Antigonus One-eye, he had gone to his father to warn him, prompting the old man to take over the joint kings. Also while in Asia he had become aware of another threat to be fended off, and an insult to be avenged, for he had there read the letter of Demades calling his father "an old and rotting rope" and proposing to Perdiccas an alliance to overthrow him.

Now Demades had arrived in Pella, and Cassander was waiting. It was clear that Demades did not know that his treachery had been uncovered, for he would not have put himself, and his son, Demeas, in Cassander's power. Cassander had the luxury of preparing his revenge in secret. When the two Athenians appeared at the palace to discuss the garrison, they were summarily arrested as enemies of the state.

Accounts differ as to what happened next. It seems Cassander subjected Demades to a show trial, with a Greek named Deinarchus, a loyal agent of Antipater's, serving as prosecutor. A document purporting to be a transcript of this trial has surfaced in a chance papyrus find. It shows Deinarchus producing three letters as evidence, while Demades mocks the whole proceeding, asking why the Macedonians had bothered with a trial when any tavern keeper could have stabbed him to death on his way there. This may be only historical fiction, but the manner is like that of Demades, who had become cynical in a long career serving powerful overlords. It's easy to believe that he decried Deinarchus as a Macedonian shill, "wielding a thunderbolt borrowed from Zeus," as the papyrus represents. Demades knew that role well. He had played it himself four years earlier when, acting as Antipater's puppet, he got Demosthenes and Hyperides condemned to death.

The outcome of the trial was never in doubt, but Demades might have been surprised when he saw his executioner. According to Plutarch, Cassander carried out the sentence himself, and added a cruel touch perhaps of his own devising, forcing Demades to first watch the murder of his son. The spatters of the boy's blood, in Plutarch's lurid account, stained the folds of the father's white cloak. Then Cassander heaped insults on Demades for betraying Antipater's cause, and killed him.

What Antipater thought of all this is hard to say. Plutarch represents him as too ill to take part in the proceedings, perhaps even unaware of them. The larger question facing Antipater, as he neared death, was what he thought of his son generally—whether he deemed Cassander fit to take over stewardship of the kings and control of the empire.

Up to this point, Antipater had entrusted his son only with support jobs, never a command of his own. He had not given Cassander control of Europe when he himself crossed into Asia, but instead appointed Polyperchon, an undistinguished officer in his sixties, to mind the home front. Then, at Triparadeisus, he had made Cassander chiliarch, or right-hand man, to Antigonus One-eye, rather than a satrap in his own right—again entrusting power to an older man and making his son an apprentice. Perhaps he did not think Cassander was ready for leadership, or perhaps he thought that more senior men should have their turn first. He had watched as Alexander, king at age twenty, had begun chasing unheard-of visions of godhead and universal empire. That bizarre spectacle made him wary of the excesses of youth.

Whatever his reasons, Antipater, from his sickbed, made known a fateful decision: custody of the kings would pass not to his son but to Polyperchon. Cassander was to be chiliarch, once again second-in-command, to the new ruler.

Cassander was aghast. In his thinking he had been disinherited: custody of the kings was equivalent to royalty itself and so, like kingship, ought to pass from father to son. As Antipater's life ebbed away, Cassander resolved not to accept the subordinate role to which his father had once again consigned him. He would strike out on his own and claim the patrimony he had worked for so hard and waited for so long.

Even before his father died, Cassander began laying his plans. He dispatched a trusted aide, a certain Nicanor—probably not Aristotle's adopted son, though long assumed to be—to Athens, with instructions to quietly replace Menyllus as garrison commander. Many Athenians, he knew, were unreconciled to the new oligarchy; news of Antipater's death might prompt them to overthrow it. An Athenian revolt would deprive him of a valuable asset, for the fortified harbor of Piraeus was the most important naval base in the region. Cassander would not let it fall into the hands either of Athens' democratic hooligans or of his future adversary, Polyperchon.

At last the day of his father's death, and Polyperchon's accession, arrived. Cassander masked his true feelings as he joined in the rites of burial and transfer of power. But shortly thereafter, making a pretense of going on a hunting trip, Cassander went to the countryside to enlist support for revolt. He sent an envoy to Ptolemy, still lingering in newly won Syria and Palestine, to arrange an alliance. And he secured access to the Hellespont so that, when the time was right, he could make his way into Asia and seek out Antigonus One-eye, now master there. A new partnership could be formed by those who stood to gain by Polyperchon's fall. Cassander could play the grand game of two continents against one, this time uniting Asia and Africa for an assault on Europe.

Civil war, already raging in Alexander's overseas conquests, was about to find its way to the Macedonian homeland. The pattern of mitosis that had beset the empire since Alexander's death seemed to be recurring without end. First the royal army had split into two factions and designated two kings to take Alexander's place; then the designs of Perdiccas had become split between two wives; finally all of Asia had been split by the falling-out of Perdiccas and Antipater, and by the war those two had handed down to their surrogates, Eumenes and Antigonus. Now Macedonia was splitting as well, between Cassander and Polyperchon, and with that split would come a division of the Greek world over which Macedon held sway. At the center of that world, about to become its principal battleground, stood Athens, the violet-crowned city, with the aging Phocion at its helm.

3. ANTIGONUS ONE-EYE (PISIDIA, IN SOUTHERN ANATOLIA, SUMMER 319 B.C.)

News of Antipater's death reached Antigonus One-eye in Pisidia, where he had just won a resounding victory over the Perdiccan coalition. It was an opportune moment for such news to arrive. One-eye's reputation had never been brighter or his army more powerful, augmented now by forces that had belonged to Perdiccas' brother Alcetas and other leaders of the fallen regime.

Antigonus had reached Pisidia by round-the-clock marches after leaving Nora, where Eumenes was safely penned in his craggy fortress. He had kept up the bone-cracking pace of forty miles a day over a grueling week of travel. The leading Perdiccans, Alcetas and his allies, held a strong position in the center of a pass, and Antigonus' best hope was to arrive before they could expect him. At this he succeeded brilliantly. The first warning his foes had of his approach was the trumpeting of elephants from atop a nearby hill—a sound that sent them into panic, for they knew that only Antigonus, the general appointed to destroy them, possessed a stable of war elephants.

Alcetas gamely mounted a counterattack, charging uphill with his cavalry to dislodge the forces on the high ground. He might have succeeded, except Antigonus made a lightning advance and launched a charge of his own at the infantry in the pass. Alcetas, about to be cut off from his phalanx, abandoned the hilltop and dashed back to the pass, only just getting there in time. The elephants and cavalry of Antigonus now descended from the hill and fell on Alcetas' infantry, still struggling to get into formation. It was the first time elephants had been used by one European general against another, and the results were devastating: most of the Perdiccan forces surrendered without a fight. Antigonus made prisoners of three leaders—Attalus, Docimus, and Polemon—and sent them under guard to a fort he controlled. Their troops he attached to his own army, building an aggregate of sixty thousand infantry and ten thousand cavalry, the largest force yet commanded by any European.

Alcetas made it out unharmed and put a predesigned escape plan into effect. A nearby city, Termessus, occupied an impregnable position. Its inhabitants were deeply attached to Alcetas, thanks to his gifts over the years and the invitations he had extended to share his banquet table. They happily took Alcetas in and vowed to protect him. But when Antigonus arrived in the valley below, threatening to feed his massive army there while waiting for Alcetas' surrender, a generational dispute broke out among the Termessians. The older men dreaded the loss of their harvest, while their sons, filled with youthful defiance, vowed to defend Alcetas at any cost.

When the older men saw they could not prevail, they made a secret plan with Antigonus, directing him to feign retreat so as to draw the youths away. Antigonus did as instructed; the young men, as anticipated, set off after him. The elders quickly descended on Alcetas. Alcetas saw he had been betrayed and took his own life. The old men carried his body out of the city, hiding it under a cloth lest their returning sons catch sight of it, and brought it to Antigonus.

One-eye was not normally a cruel man, but he could be cruel on occasion. He subjected Alcetas' corpse to abuse for the next three days, until it showed signs of decay. Perhaps he wanted to send a message to the youths of Termessus, who were simmering with rage at the betrayal of their hero and vowing a guerrilla war. Perhaps he sought to avenge Alcetas' infamous murder of Cynnane, daughter of the great Philip. Whatever his motives, he ended by throwing the mutilated body onto the ground to rot and marching away. The young men of Termessus recovered the corpse and buried it with full rites of honor. A rock-cut tomb, seen today in southern Turkey, its walls adorned with a bas-relief of a charging cavalryman, is almost certainly Alcetas' final resting place.

It was just at this point, while Antigonus was departing from Termessus with his vastly enlarged army, that the news arrived from Europe: Antipater was dead.

The old man's passing left Antigonus with many unanswered questions. What was he to do next, now that the Perdiccan forces were vanquished? What role would he play, with Antipater, who had treated him almost as a partner in rule, off the scene for good? Antigonus might well have hoped to become guardian of the kings in Antipater's place, but that post, he now learned, had mysteriously gone to Polyperchon, a man with no great commands or victories. And what was to be done with Eumenes, penned up at Nora and hoping for restoration to his former rank? Antigonus had sent an envoy to consult Antipater about this request, but

A rock carving found outside a tomb in southern Turkey, almost certainly depicting Alcetas charging into battle

that envoy had arrived in Pella too late. Antigonus would have to decide on his own how to handle his former Greek friend.

At some point these two problems, the fate of Eumenes and his own political future, came together in Antigonus' mind and suggested a common solution. With the world's largest army at his back, he need not obey a second-rater like Polyperchon, but could rule Asia as though it were his own. He could interdict the naval convoys leaving its shores and deprive Polyperchon of much-needed cash. But he might then have to fight Polyperchon, in which case he would need a good consigliere, and Eumenes, as he knew, was the best he could find. Antigonus had never borne any animus against the clever Greek, despite having accepted the task of killing him. Now it seemed better to utilize, rather than destroy, the man's intelligence and talent.

Antigonus arranged for Hieronymus, Eumenes' close friend and countryman, to go to Nora and bring a message into the fortress there. Little Eumenes was offered full restoration of Cappadocia, and all his lost wealth, plus additional gifts and honors. He had only to swear loyalty to Antigonus and agree to become his chief adviser. Together the two men could chart their own course and claim any sovereignty they wanted. The empire would be theirs for the taking.

4. POLYPERCHON AND OLYMPIAS
(MACEDONIA AND EPIRUS, AUTUMN 319 B.C.)

With his dying breaths, Antipater had reportedly spoken one last, stern injunction to his followers: *Don't let Macedonia be ruled by a woman.* Undoubtedly, the woman he feared was his old nemesis, the Molossian queen who had constantly wrangled with him for power before giving up and going home, Alexander the Great's mother, Olympias.

Now in her mid-fifties, Olympias had been outside Macedonian politics for years, but no one thought she would remain there forever. Her bids to marry her daughter, Cleopatra, to one of Alexander's top generals had shown she was still a player in the great dynastic game. Her two hoped-for sons-in-law were now dead and there was no third in sight, but Olympias' shrewd mind might find other routes back into power in Macedon.

Polyperchon, the newly appointed regent, had known Olympias only distantly, if at all, before he left for Asia with Alexander. He did not belong to one of the great Macedonian houses, whose sons became page boys and mingled freely with the royal family. He doubtless knew of reasons to steer clear of the dowager queen: her stormy temper and uncompromising nature, her unwillingness to accept second place. But Polyperchon needed help. In Europe, his rival Cassander had gone into rebellion, recruiting allies among powerful friends; in Asia, Antigonus One-eye had also revealed himself as a threat, arrogantly seizing a treasure fleet bound for Macedonia. Polyperchon could see that a showdown with one of these men was looming—or with both, if, as he had to anticipate, they joined forces.

With no natural allies, no cadre of kin and highborn cronies, Polyperchon reached out to the enemy of his enemies. He defied the last wishes of Antipater and sent a messenger to Olympias, inviting her to return to Macedonia and share his rule. She could become guardian of her four-year-old grandchild, Alexander, he wrote—she had yet to meet the boy, or his mother, Rhoxane—

and thus a kind of co-regent with Polyperchon, who would retain guardianship of the other king, the half-witted Philip.

Olympias received this offer with deeply conflicted feelings. Her fondest wishes, both as grandmother and as queen, seemed granted as if by magic. But the realm to which she had been invited was fraught with danger. Stalking its countryside was Cassander, son of her former rival Antipater and potentially an even more vicious foe. Olympias regarded Cassander as the principal murderer of her son, the man who had brought poison out of Europe and delivered it to Babylon; perhaps she had also heard reports of his cruel killing of the Athenian politician Demades. Then, too, Adea, wife to King Philip, posed a different kind of threat, for Adea's branch of the Argead house could not remain allied forever to that of Olympias, linked by the dual kingship of the two male heirs. One branch would someday eliminate the other. Olympias knew that Adea, a woman forty years her junior, reared in the warlike traditions of her Illyrian ancestors, was a formidable opponent.

Unsure what to do or whom to trust, fearing to cast her lot with Polyperchon yet longing to meet her grandson, Olympias sought the advice of a loyal supporter—Eumenes the Greek. Olympias had never lost touch with him despite the vast gulfs between them—not just the physical divide between Europe and Asia but the political rift that made Eumenes a wanted man. Olympias cared little for that rift, which she saw as one more ploy by Antipater and Cassander to trample on her family's rights. She wrote now to Eumenes as a trusted friend, asking whether she should return to Macedon, where she might protect her grandson's life but also endanger her own. She even offered, either in this letter or in a later one, to entrust to Eumenes the protection of her grandson, the young Alexander, the toddler king.

While this letter made its way to Eumenes, a piece of long-dreaded news came to Polyperchon. Cassander had slipped across the Hellespont and was making common cause with Antigonus One-eye. The prospects for the coming war suddenly became grave. Polyperchon would face an enemy that could draw on the vast resources of Asia, its wealth above all but also the dreaded new weapon, the elephant, which inevitably struck terror into

European troops. Polyperchon was not strong enough to confront his foes in Asia, but if he could at least hold on to Europe, he might raise more forces and someday take them across the straits. Reaching again into his political bag of tricks, Polyperchon found a way to shore up his home base, in particular the Greek states to his south. It was something he had seen Alexander do, when the king first entered Asia and needed support from the Greek cities there. These cities had long been ruled by Persian-backed strongmen, but Alexander had proclaimed they could become democracies and enjoy self-rule as of old. Jubilant over their restored freedom, the Greeks welcomed Alexander with open arms, scarcely registering that the absolute power by which he had freed them ultimately meant their enslavement.

Mimicking Alexander's cynical, but successful, manipulation of Greek sentiment, Polyperchon issued a proclamation—or arranged for King Philip to issue one—that the Greek states, as of a certain date some months away, would be free. Their oligarchic puppet governments would be disbanded; exiled opposition leaders would return; the clock would be reset as if the Greek defeats in recent wars had never occurred. Athens was to have its democracy back. It was also to have Samos back, the colonial possession it had lost after a long diplomatic struggle. In return the Greeks were to pass a decree never to make war or foment revolt against the Macedonians—for Polyperchon's grant of autonomy surely did *not* extend to foreign policy. Nor did it include the withdrawal of Macedonian garrisons, which were not even mentioned in the decree.

Accompanying this proclamation were directives Polyperchon sent to certain Greek cities ordering the execution of their leaders. These men had been installed by Antipater and thus, Polyperchon feared, would naturally incline toward his son Cassander. Now that the new regime had cast its lot with Greek democrats, it sought to thin the ranks of the oligarchs Antipater had put in power. Where this would leave Phocion, leader of the oligarchy at Athens, was still an open question.

While news of the freedom decree swept through Greece, Polyperchon turned his thoughts to Asia, where the blows against him were sure to be launched. He had but one card to play to counter those blows, but he played it with a vengeance. Perhaps he had gotten wind of Antigonus One-eye's attempt to recruit Eumenes to his cause, or else he foresaw that possibility. The thought of an alliance between two shrewd generals, each with a string of battlefield victories, was deeply unsettling. But if these two could be kept at enmity, Polyperchon might forestall an invasion from the East. He had to somehow revive the civil war in Asia, which Antigonus had all but won, by rehabilitating the one surviving member of the old Perdiccan faction, Eumenes.

So, under the authority of his ward King Philip, Polyperchon wrote to Eumenes, proposing an alliance on astonishing terms. Eumenes would receive his old command back; he would get five hundred talents of silver from the royal treasury at Cyinda, as recompense for his sufferings; the Silver Shields guarding that treasure, and their commander, Antigenes, would become Eumenes' personal infantry corps. This was already an extravagant bribe, but there was a kicker. Eumenes himself would share custodianship of the joint kings, should he cross over to Europe; or, if he remained in Asia, Polyperchon would cross over himself, with the joint kings and the royal army, and come to his aid whenever he asked. As he had done with Olympias, Polyperchon offered to give away half his power in order to recruit a partner who could save him from ruin.

Polyperchon's messengers left Europe and crossed the Hellespont, following those already en route—the letter bearers dispatched by Olympias, and Hieronymus of Cardia, the go-between chosen by Antigonus One-eye. All these envoys made their way to a tiny fortress in Cappadocia, an obscure patch of rock that had suddenly become central to the future of the entire known world.

5. EUMENES (THE FORTRESS AT NORA, WINTER–SPRING 318 B.C.)

Eumenes' spirits had not been vanquished by his year of confinement at Nora. He had kept up the morale of the six hundred supporters besieged with him on the four-acre rock, inviting them by turns to his table to share meals of bread, salt, and water. Here, as in all his commands, Eumenes' buoyancy and inventiveness helped inspire his men with hope. It was hard merely to generate new topics of conversation, yet the table talk, as Plutarch reports, stayed lively and cheerful.

The biggest challenge of close confinement was lack of space for exercise, not only for the men but also for their horses. Eumenes recognized that the animals would become useless if they stood idle day after day. So he devised pulleys for lifting their foreparts off the ground, then goaded them from behind so that they struggled and danced on their hind legs. The violent workout covered the animals in sweat and foam, but this was better than inactivity. As for the men, Eumenes set aside the largest house in the fortress—itself only twenty feet long—as a track and personally coached the drill sessions there, giving cues to the runners to keep them increasing their pace.

For a while, escape was the only hope. Eumenes and his men tried several attacks on the perimeter wall and succeeded in destroying small sections but each time failed to break out. Then came word that Alcetas and the other Perdiccans had been defeated in Pisidia, that Alcetas was dead and the others imprisoned under strong guard. Eumenes no longer had anywhere to escape to. All of Asia belonged to Antigonus One-eye. But Fortune was about to turn her wheel once again. Events already in motion would transform an isolated, resourceless fugitive into the most sought-after leader in the empire.

First came Hieronymus, Eumenes' comrade and countryman, bearing a miraculous offer. Eumenes could have full restoration of position and wealth, plus much more, simply by swearing an oath of loyalty to Antigonus One-eye. The officers manning the siege were instructed to release Eumenes as soon as he took the oath, a copy of which Hieronymus had brought with him. Once released, Eumenes would become a free man, a satrap, and a senior officer in Antigonus' army, now the world's largest.

Eumenes looked over the oath with misgivings. He knew that Antigonus had been stripped of control of the kings the previous year, a sign that One-eye did not have the royal interests at heart. Perhaps he also knew—just how much Hieronymus had told him about events in the West is unclear—that Cassander, Antipater's son, had rebelled against Polyperchon and the kings and had approached Antigonus for help. Eumenes discerned that allegiance to Antigonus might well mean betrayal of the Argeads, the family whose rights he had struggled mightily to protect. And yet that allegiance was his path to freedom, to political redemption, and to the only post that made sense for him, consigliere to the empire's most powerful capo.

Which side would Eumenes take, and what would he fight for? Did he care who triumphed in the succession struggle, or was he only seeking to better his own lot? This was a moment of truth, requiring Eumenes to choose between loyalty and self-interest. But with characteristic ingenuity, he found a way to have both.

According to Plutarch's account, Eumenes rewrote the oath so that it featured the joint kings and Olympias more prominently than Antigonus. He then submitted both versions to the guards at the siege perimeter and asked which was more just. In effect, he was asking these troops to support the kings over Antigonus, or at least to reject the idea that the two might be at odds. The soldiers obliged by declaring Eumenes' version the more proper of the two, and Eumenes duly swore his own oath. He was released and restored to his former position as satrap of Cappadocia.

Eumenes quickly set about gathering troops, for he knew he had not much time. Antigonus soon learned of the altered oath and was furious that his conditions had been sidestepped. He sent a hasty message to his guardsmen ordering them to recapture Eumenes, excoriating them for their stupidity. Then he sent an armed cohort under Menander, former satrap of Lydia, to catch the wily Greek. Menander and Antigonus had together plotted an ambush of Eumenes years earlier, outside Sardis, but Eumenes eluded them by taking an unforeseen route. Now he once again slipped through their grasp, leaving Cappadocia with a small band only three days before Menander arrived.

While on the march, or perhaps just before departing, Eumenes received letters from Polyperchon and Olympias offering him a commission as chief defender of the royal house. Eumenes was now to have money, legitimacy, and use of the Silver Shields, the most accomplished infantry corps in the army. Antigenes, veteran captain of the Shields, and a new co-captain named Teutamus were already on their way, with orders to serve Eumenes in the name of the kings. Polyperchon himself would join them, the letters promised, should Eumenes request it, and bring the kings into Asia. Olympias would put the young Alexander, her own grandson, into Eumenes' care.

Eumenes had been thrust in an instant from the most remote fringe to the very center of power. He pushed ahead toward the rendezvous with the Silver Shields. His war with Antigonus was back on.

6. PHOCION AND NICANOR
(ATHENS, WINTER–SPRING 318 B.C.)

The shake-up created by Antipater's death had brought Eumenes from Fortune's depths to her heights, but in Athens, for the oligarchs who had once been favored by Antipater, the reverse seemed likely to occur. Chief among these was Phocion, Do-good Phocion, the stalwart public servant who now, in his eighty-fourth year, found himself caught in a political squeeze that threatened to become a death trap.

For Phocion, the announcement of Polyperchon's freedom decree had come as a cruel betrayal. Phocion had known of course that Antipater would not live forever but never dreamed that his successor would embark on a total reversal of standing policy. The decree gave the regime of the nine thousand only a few months in power, after which the poor would be back in the majority, able to vent their rage on those who had disenfranchised them. Phocion could foresee how his record of service would be distorted by his enemies. He had watched it happen to others who had fallen, time and time again. His efforts to mollify the Macedonians, to win clemency for dissidents like Hagnonides, would be forgotten; the public would see only a collaboration with a hated occupier. His carefully groomed integrity and austere way of life—he still drew water for himself, and his wife baked the family's bread, despite a fortune that could pay for many slaves—would not help him once those passions were unleashed.

Phocion's one hope of ending his six-decade career well was the war brewing between Polyperchon and Cassander, a war increasingly centered on Athens. The fortified harbor of Piraeus, which controlled the sea-lanes of the entire Aegean, was a vital asset for both sides. Phocion had watched as Nicanor, the agent of Cassander, slipped into the garrison there and took command, only days before Antipater's death was announced. Phocion's enemies had been outraged, claiming Phocion knew Antipater was dying and helped Nicanor get control. Phocion did not and perhaps could not deny it. He convinced Nicanor to stage some high-priced athletic games for the Athenians' entertainment, hoping to put a good face on an unpleasant episode.

Phocion had always walked a middle path between Athens and Macedon and tried to keep the two nations at peace, but that middle path had become perilously narrow. When Polyperchon's decree became known at Athens, an exuberant populace again demanded removal of the Piraeus garrison. Nicanor was invited to meet with a government council at a secure location, under a guarantee of safety. But the Athenians had laid a plot to arrest Nicanor as he entered the meeting place. Phocion warned Nicanor of the ambush so that he escaped just in time, and the public again howled with anger. Nicanor too was enraged and threatened to wreak vengeance on the Athenians. Phocion somehow managed to calm both sides, but the tension level in the city was rising fast.

It became clear that Polyperchon was sending an army toward Athens to enforce his decree and that Nicanor's control of Munychia would then be at an end. Indeed, many in Athens were prepared to take up arms and end it themselves. Though his popularity was at a low ebb, Nicanor sent a letter to the Assembly, urging the Athenians to bar the new troops and side instead with Cassander. His arguments made little headway, but while he was distracting the citizens with rhetoric, he was also sneaking soldiers into his garrison by night. Phocion turned a blind eye, allowing the escalation to go on while preserving deniability. The elder statesman had seen by now that he must preserve Nicanor's grip on Munychia, in hopes it would allow Cassander to prevail in the war. He might perhaps have recalled the warning Antipater had given him when he asked that no garrison be installed. "Phocion, we would grant you anything, except what would destroy you and us both," the old man had told him. From the moment he agreed

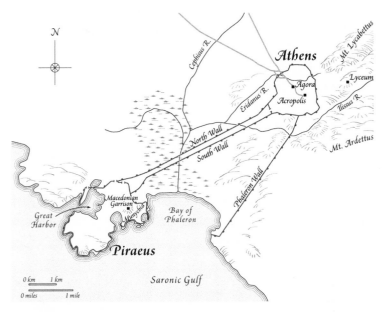

Athens and its harbor Piraeus, with walls protecting the traffic between them

to work with the Macedonians, his fate had hung on their control of his city.

By the time the Athenians realized what Nicanor was up to, it was too late. His forces were large enough to defend the garrison against an uprising. Nicanor tightened his grip by bringing in mercenaries and seizing the entire harbor, along with the booms that controlled its entrance. He could now bar the ships of Polyperchon and admit those of Cassander or, if he chose, bar the food shipments on which Athens depended. Phocion again bore the brunt of the Athenians' anger at their increasing impotence. As he got up to speak in the Assembly, he was hooted down in derision.

At this point a letter arrived in Athens from the dowager queen Olympias, still residing in Epirus but speaking as though on behalf of the Macedonian state. She commanded Nicanor to surrender his position. The Athenians rejoiced when they heard this, believing their troubles were at an end. Nicanor, for his part, seemed disconcerted and promised the garrison would indeed be vacated but again dragged his feet, stalling for time.

For Phocion, the situation had become fraught with peril. The war between Cassander and Polyperchon had become a Panhellenic struggle, with Cassander supporting oligarchic rulers all across Greece while Polyperchon backed democrats. Athens was split down the middle. In the upper city the clock continued to tick toward the freedom decree deadline, and a land army was expected to arrive any day to enforce it. In the harbor, Nicanor fortified his position and waited for Cassander to arrive by sea. Phocion had no way to know who would get there first or which side would prevail. He would benefit from a victory by Cassander, but had to avoid being seen as his ally in case the democrats, backed by Polyperchon, took power. He had to aid Nicanor just enough to ensure the garrison's survival, but not enough to be branded a collaborator.

At last the army sent by Polyperchon arrived at Athens. In its train marched a column of exiled citizens and pro-democracy activists, among them Hagnonides, Phocion's most determined foe. The army's leader, Polyperchon's son Alexander, took control of Athens itself, while Nicanor remained dug in behind the walls of Piraeus. Phocion pleaded with Alexander not to allow the enactment of the freedom decree, at least until the civil war was resolved. He set up negotiations between the two Macedonian generals, but when it was clear these talks were being held in closed chambers, Phocion again fell under suspicion. The people sensed they were being deceived and that Phocion was in league with their enemies. They were not entirely wrong.

Amid anger, paranoia, and demands for retribution, the restoration of the democracy finally came to pass. The Assembly, its ranks now swelled by returning exiles, voted in a clamorous session to depose the existing government and elect a new one. Phocion and his supporters were thrown out of office. Some took flight and headed to Piraeus; some were sentenced to execution; the lucky ones, including Phocion, were merely exiled and stripped of property. Though Hagnonides himself took the rostrum and denounced Phocion, the Athenians did not yet have the stomach to kill their long-serving elder statesman.

Rejected by the Athenians, Phocion looked to the Macedonians for support. He had carefully avoided backing Nicanor in any demonstrable way. Alexander, Polyperchon's son, wrote a letter attesting to this, urging his father to treat Phocion and his friends as valued allies. Bearing this document, a bitter testament to his reliance on the kindness of strangers, Phocion made his way north to find Polyperchon. He had no hope of restoration of power, or even of property; he needed only a sanctuary in which to live out his remaining days. He must by now have hoped that these would be few.

7. EUMENES, ANTIGENES, AND TEUTAMUS (CILICIA, SUMMER 318 B.C.)

Eumenes had arrived at the treasury of Cyinda and rendezvoused with the Silver Shields. Thanks to the letters he bore from Polyperchon, he was *stratēgos,* or "commander in chief," of Asia with power to draw on the royal treasuries, give orders to the royal army, and prosecute the war against Antigonus One-eye—who just a few weeks before had held exactly the same office and powers. Antigenes and Teutamus, co-captains of the Silver Shields, placed themselves at Eumenes' disposal, as Polyperchon had ordered them to do.

The thought of commanding these officers must have given Eumenes pause. Teutamus was an unknown quantity, but Eumenes knew Antigenes well from their years together under Alexander. A tough, unflinching infantryman, more than sixty years old but still in peak form, Antigenes would be a powerful ally but a fearsome adversary. This man had played a large role in Perdiccas' murder—first of the assassins to strike—and had also been among those who, the day following that murder, had condemned Eumenes to death. Despite the reversals of the past weeks, no one had bothered to revoke that death sentence; Polyperchon had not even mentioned it in his directives. Antigenes might regard it as still in effect.

Then, too, Eumenes would face the problem of his origins in dealing with Antigenes and Teutamus, just as he had with other Macedonian generals. Exercising the prerogatives of rank would not be easy for a Greek, no matter what Polyperchon decreed. Letters sent from Pella, half a world away, by a regent only barely hanging on to power, were a slender thread with which to bind these men's loyalty—especially when Antigonus One-eye would eagerly welcome their defection.

Antigenes and Teutamus greeted Eumenes with respect, but soon tensions began to emerge. The two captains were reluctant to come to Eumenes' tent for instructions, regarding this as a form of submission. Eumenes, for his part, was unwilling to go to theirs. Prejudice was once again threatening to set allied leaders at odds. Eumenes tried to use Greekness in his favor, claiming, as he had before in Babylon, that since he was barred from the throne, his motives were beyond reproach. He underscored this point by refusing the five hundred talents that Polyperchon had allotted him from the royal treasury. "I have no need of such a gift, since I have no aspirations toward rule," he told the men now serving— he hoped—under him.

Finally, to avoid the strains he feared would tear his senior staff apart, Eumenes hit upon an invention—the cleverest yet of his many inventions and ruses.

Eumenes had been present the day after Alexander's death, when Perdiccas called a meeting before the king's empty throne. He had heard Ptolemy propose that the leaders form a governing board and convene in front of that throne. Both men had recognized that Alexander, with his colossal force of personality, had knit together a fractious group of determined rivals. If that force could be channeled through the empty throne, the union of those rivals could be preserved.

Inspired by two great models, Eumenes told his officers about a vivid dream that had twice appeared to him. Alexander had returned to life and was sitting in his royal tent, wielding his scepter and administering his empire. The king gave an order to his generals to meet only in *that* tent, which they were to call Alexander's tent. Eumenes then interpreted his own dream. "I think we should construct a golden throne from out of the royal treasury," he told Antigenes and Teutamus, "and place on it the diadem, the scepter, and the crown; then at dawn all the commanders will burn incense to *him,* and convene a council meeting before the throne, and take their orders under the king's name, just as if he were alive and in charge of his own realm." As long as they stayed before this throne, Eumenes assured them, Alexander would be present and would guide their decisions.

This vision of restored authority seized the men's imaginations. They cast a golden throne as Eumenes had suggested and erected it under a magnificent tent. On it they placed Alexander's diadem, scepter, and armor. Beside the throne they stood a set of weapons, and in front of it they erected an altar for burning incense. Every morning they went to this tent, Eumenes and the others together, and took precious incense out of a small golden box, and burned it on the altar, and bowed down before the throne as before a god. Then they sat on silver benches they had placed within the tent and discussed the questions they faced that day.

Dissension among the high command immediately disappeared. Whether or not they believed they were in Alexander's spiritual presence, the daily ritual in "Alexander's tent" restored their sense of a center. They now received willingly orders issued by Eumenes, which seemed, under the penumbra of the tent, to have come from Alexander himself.

With astute psychological insight, Eumenes had given his new subcommanders, the knotty veterans of Alexander's wars, exactly what they needed. They needed their king to come back from the dead.

8. POLYPERCHON, PHOCION, HAGNONIDES, AND KING PHILIP (PHOCIS, SPRING 318 B.C.)

While Phocion was en route northward, the anger unleashed in Athens by the democratic counterrevolution continued to build. Hagnonides, the new leading speaker in the Assembly, fed on this anger and helped stoke it. The Athenians now wanted more than just the exile of the oligarchs; they wanted revenge. Following a long-established pattern, they grew more bitter against absent scapegoats than against those still in their midst. They voted, some days after the departure of Phocion, to send a delegation, headed by Hagnonides, to convince Polyperchon not to give clemency to their fallen statesman.

Polyperchon and his army were on the march in northern Greece, preparing to sweep southward and re-democratize the cities of Hellas. Phocion, exiled from Athens, had not far to go to reach them, but got delayed when a member of his entourage, Deinarchus of Corinth, fell ill. Though Hagnonides had left Athens a few days later, he and Phocion arrived in Polyperchon's camp, near the village of Pharygae, at the same time. The two old enemies were brought before Polyperchon as if for an impromptu debating match.

Polyperchon solemnized the proceedings by installing his ward, King Philip, as presiding judge, seating the half-witted monarch on a throne beneath a golden canopy. Whatever decision was taken could be passed off as the judgment of the king. Polyperchon was discomfited by the problem of Phocion, a man who had faithfully served Macedonian interests for years but who now stood on the wrong side of the freedom decree.

The hearing started on a grim note. Deinarchus came forward to speak on Phocion's behalf, thinking himself a friend of Macedon's; he had managed the Peloponnese well for old man Antipater. But he had not reckoned the depth of the fissures that had opened after Antipater's death. Fidelity to the old man implied loyalty only to his rebel son. No sooner had Deinarchus begun his address than Polyperchon ordered him arrested and led away for torture and execution. The great orator, who had prosecuted Demades in the show trial that got him condemned to death, now found himself in the maw of the beast he had once helped feed.

An uproar erupted as both Athenian delegations, Phocion's party and that of Hagnonides, tried simultaneously to get heard but ended up shouting accusations at each other. Hagnonides sneered that the whole crew should be thrown into a *galeagra,* a cage for trapping wild animals, and shipped back to Athens to sort out their differences. From his irrelevant throne, King Philip suddenly laughed. Did he understand the joke, or was he merely amused by the tumult?

The rest of the hearing played out in a chaotic, even ludicrous, fashion. Order was restored so that Phocion could speak, but Polyperchon, unaccustomed to Athenian wordiness, kept interrupting impatiently. Finally he grew fed up and slammed his scepter on the ground and walked away, fuming in silence. Hegemon, one of Phocion's party, tried to mollify the regent by recall-

ing Phocion's many benefactions, but this only enraged Polyperchon further. "Stop lying to me in the presence of the king!" he
shouted, whereupon King Philip, dimly sensing some insult, rose
from his throne and tried to stab Hegemon with a spear. Polyperchon ran over and threw his arms around Philip to restrain him,
then hastily adjourned the council session.

Before Phocion could leave, an armed guard stepped forward
and put him under arrest. The others in the oligarchic party made
haste to flee, realizing their cause was lost at the Macedonian
court. Polyperchon had committed to the democrats in order to
isolate partisans of the rebel Cassander. Phocion, notwithstanding
his honorable service, would be thrown to the wolves.

9. THE FALL OF PHOCION
(ATHENS, SPRING 318 B.C.)

Phocion and four of his partisans were conveyed back to Athens
by Cleitus the White, the Macedonian admiral who had defeated
the Athenian fleet in the Hellenic War. They were placed on an
open cart for exhibition to the mob and driven through the city to
the Theater of Dionysus. There they were kept in seclusion until
the Assembly could be summoned. The open-air theater was usually used for tragic dramas but sometimes also for political proceedings. The trial soon to take place there would have elements
of both.

In wanton violation of the constitution, the Assembly was
opened to all comers, citizens and aliens, men and women, free
and slaves. The democratic regime did not want procedural
niceties to thwart the will of the people. One brave citizen rose in
protest and urged that foreigners and slaves be ushered out but
was shouted down with cries of "Stone the oligarchs!" The proceeding was then begun by Cleitus, who read aloud a letter from
Polyperchon. The regent proclaimed that in his view, Phocion
and his party were traitors, but, in the spirit of the new Greek freedom, he would leave their fate to the Athenians. In other words,
he washed his hands of the matter.

Phocion and the four members of his party were led into the
theater. Some of Phocion's admirers were moved to tears, covering

224 GHOST ON THE THRONE

their faces with their hands to hide their emotions from their neighbors.

Phocion attempted to speak but was shouted down by the mob. Whenever the hoots and catcalls grew fainter, he tried again to defend himself but each time was drowned out. At last he succeeded in shouting a question above the uproar: "Do you want to execute me justly or unjustly?" When a few answered "Justly!" Phocion replied, "How will you know which you do unless you hear me out?" But this only provoked more heckling. The poor and downtrodden of Athens had been disenfranchised for too long. They would exact every ounce of vengeance they felt was their due.

In a last effort to save others by sacrificing himself, Phocion shouted, to any who could hear, that he freely accepted the death sentence but that those in the dock with him were innocent. "Athenians, why will you put *them* to death?" he implored, to which the answer came: "Because they are your friends!" Phocion fell silent, and Hagnonides stepped onto the stage. He proposed a vote on the guilt or innocence of the accused, with death the automatic penalty if they were deemed guilty. Some in the crowd demanded torture on the rack, but Cleitus, the Macedonian overseer, signaled his disapproval. Hagnonides brushed aside the demand, vowing that torture would be reserved for a worse criminal than Phocion, a man known as Callimedon the Crab. A cynic called out that the rack would someday be brought for Hagnonides himself.

The proceeding now moved to a vote. For all their love of dissent and free speech, the Athenians used an unfree method of voting, the public raising of hands. Secret balloting was known to them and was widely used for polling juries, but political decisions were taken openly, and votes were often lopsided as a result. In this instance, according to Plutarch, not a single hand was raised in support of Phocion. Many no doubt regretted the fate of a leader whose service stretched out longer than their life spans. But the anger of their neighbors made them ashamed to declare themselves.

Phocion and his colleagues were taken to the *desmoterion,* the little prison house where men awaiting execution were kept under guard. The philosopher Socrates had been jailed here more than eighty years earlier, condemned in large part as a scapegoat after Athens had lost a long and costly war. Now Phocion too bore the brunt of a defeated city's rage. The lost battles of Amorgus and Crannon four years earlier, the battle of Chaeronea before that, the two decades Athens had spent appeasing Macedonian Ares— all these accompanied Phocion as he was led away for execution, jeered at and spat on by the crowd that ran alongside.

On the nineteenth of Munychion (mid-May by our calendar), the day of the Olympieia festival honoring the god Zeus, Phocion's death sentence was carried out inside the *desmoterion*. Quantities of poison had been prepared by bruising the leaves of the hemlock plant; the foul-smelling juice induced a creeping paralysis that started at the feet and finally froze the heart and lungs. Phocion was the last of the five condemned to drink the poison, and there was an agonizing delay when it was found that not enough had been prepared. In a last, grim act of public service, Phocion himself arranged the payment of twelve drachmas to the state poison master, who had not been given enough money to purchase more hemlock leaves.

A band of horsemen, riding past the prison house as they led the festal procession of the Olympieia, stopped to reflect on what was taking place inside. Wealthy men, members of Phocion's social class, they and their peers had stood aside from the proceeding that condemned the oligarchs, bowing to the new democratic order in the city. Now they paused in silence outside the place of execution and removed the ceremonial wreaths from their heads. It was a small, passive gesture of sympathy, probably unseen by the dying man within.

The fury of the radical democrats was not slaked by the death of Phocion. A subsequent Assembly passed a motion denying him burial on Attic soil and forbidding any Athenian to kindle his pyre. Undeterred, his relatives managed to get his body cremated in a remote location by hiring an underground agent. Phocion's wife smuggled the ashes back into Athens hidden in the folds of her cloak and buried them secretly inside her own house, beside the hearth. Later the remains were reinterred in the Cerameicus, for it was not long before the city repented the fall of Phocion and restored him to honor, voting him a memorial statue and a public burial.

In 1948 a fourth-century grave monument was unearthed in Athens, a somber marble relief bearing no inscription or identifying marks. Recently one expert has proposed that it is the tombstone of Phocion. It shows a powerful, magnificent horse only barely controlled by a small African boy, quite clearly a slave. There is no rider or owner in the scene, only the horse and the diminutive, hard-pressed groom who holds its reins.

Whether this stone marked Phocion's grave remains a matter of speculation, though one cannot help but see in it a marker of his times. With the passing of the two grand old men of Europe, Phocion and Antipater, the political order that had stabilized the continent for a generation had collapsed. All Greece was ablaze

A late fourth century funerary monument found at Athens, possibly that of Phocion

with factional fighting. Long-standing rivals, the partisans of democracy and oligarchy, could now call in opposing champions, Polyperchon and Cassander. Athens, the only major Greek power as yet undestroyed by the Macedonians, was split in two, its politics volatile and chaotic. Hellas was riderless as never before.

10. CASSANDER AND POLYPERCHON
(ATHENS, SUMMER 318 B.C.)

Soon after the death of Phocion, the rebel Cassander sailed into Piraeus with ships and troops supplied by Antigonus One-eye. He relieved Nicanor of his garrison command and assumed control of the port. His forces were still tiny compared with what Polyperchon could muster, but he held an impregnable base and could be resupplied by sea. The Athenian populace, deprived of their harbor, would need to rely on their own thin soil for nurture and share that meager resource with the army camped outside their walls. The democrats had enjoyed their counterrevolution, but they would have to go hungry as a result.

Polyperchon himself at last arrived outside Athens with another, larger army but found he could accomplish little except consume the food supply more quickly. His chance to take Piraeus had slipped past, for the forces Cassander had brought in had made the place unassailable. He marched on into the Peloponnese to deal with matters there, leaving his son Alexander behind to guard the countryside.

Cassander had gained his toehold in Europe. Phocion had lived just long enough, and had given Nicanor just enough support, to ensure that the rebellion against Polyperchon would survive. The European civil war would go forward to a new and more violent phase, and Phocion would be only one in a long line of its victims.

9

Duels to the Death

Europe and Asia

SUMMER 318–WINTER, LATE 317 B.C.

Alexander the Great had taught his disciples well. During his twelve-year Asian campaign, his officers had watched him manage with surgical skill the world's most complex army. They had seen him orchestrate the phalanx bristling with spears, the cavalry strike force, and the quick-moving Hypaspists, or Shield Bearers; draw on one force or another, or combine the three, depending on terrain and opponent; synchronize their rates of travel; and keep them fed and provisioned by despoiling the route of their march. In India they had seen him master the only known war machine his army then lacked, the trained elephant. Alexander had brought some two hundred of these fortresslike beasts out of India, to terrorize the enemies he never got to fight—Arabs, Carthaginians, and other targets historians can only guess at.

After Alexander's death his generals practiced, with all too great a fidelity, the lessons they had learned. They put cloned armies in the field, each with its phalanx, cavalry, and Hypaspist components, some also with elephant herds. They gave familiar names to these units—"foot companions," "companion cavalry"— to remind veterans of their old assignments. They followed the routes and seasons of march Alexander had laid out, through fertile plains and valleys that could provision vast numbers, making campaigns across the length and breadth of Asia a routine affair. A new era in warfare had begun—the age of professionalized, internationalized, numerically supersized Hellenistic armies.

Alexander had also nurtured in his staff an endless appetite for command and conquest. Of his seven Bodyguards, only one, Aristonous—an older man who likely held his post from before Alexander's reign—attempted something like a retirement, and that turned out to be short-lived, as will be seen. The other Bodyguards never ceased to build power, enlarge armies, and undermine rivals on the model of their master. Ptolemy seized North Africa, and Lysimachus Thrace; Peithon made a try for Bactria and failed but had not given up his ambitions there; Peucestas was enlarging power and popularity in his satrapy, Persis. Leonnatus and Perdiccas had been killed in attempts to gain, or preserve, control of the entire empire. Craterus, whose stature equaled theirs, though he did not belong to the Bodyguard, died trying to deprive Perdiccas of that control.

New contestants had emerged to replace those carried off the field. Antigonus, only a sidelined satrap at the time of Alexander's death, established himself through shrewd generalship as the leading power in Asia. Polyperchon, another mid-level officer, was battling Cassander for control of Europe. Waiting in the wings was an even newer contender, Seleucus, as yet only satrap of Babylon serving more powerful masters but destined to fight Antigonus for almost two decades to come. And then there was Eumenes, anomalous Eumenes, the Greek who had gone from scribe to soldier to general to outlaw and finally to head of the royal army and standard-bearer of the kings. Though Eumenes claimed not to share the ambitions of the Macedonians, he somehow found himself in constant conflict with them, fighting in part for the royal family, in part for his own survival, and in part for the ghost of Alexander, whom he had enthroned as the spectral leader of his cause.

By the strange peripeties of the civil war, Antigonus and Eumenes had by turns held the same high office, commander in chief of Asia. Each could, and did, trumpet his own authority and attack that of the other. Eumenes bore letters carrying the seal of the kings, as well as others from Olympias, ordering the imperial bureaucracy to follow only *him*. Antigonus derided these orders, reminding all who would listen that Eumenes was a foreigner and a condemned criminal besides. At the heart of the dispute was the problem old man Antipater had created with his choice of successor: Did Polyperchon, the official appointee, speak for the monarchy? Or did Cassander, Antipater's son, who claimed his father's office as a kind of natural right?

In the five years since Alexander's death the issue of legitimacy had become so vexed that, to some, it had no doubt ceased to matter. Yet the monarchy still existed; the joint kings possessed a legitimacy that would not die. The orders issued in their name opened the treasuries of Asia, and the years of their "reign" furnished the dates atop imperial documents. Their fate was central to the future of the empire, and that fate now rested on two pairs of antagonists, fighting parallel duels for control of two continents: Polyperchon and Cassander in Europe, and in Asia, their respective allies, the two greatest generals to emerge from Alexander's military academy, Eumenes of Cardia and Antigonus One-eye.

I. THE ROYAL FAMILY (GREECE, SUMMER 318 B.C.)

Alexander's son had reached his fifth birthday. He was old enough to be aware of his surroundings and his unique place in the world. He knew now why he had three armed noblemen stationed around him as Bodyguards, as well as highborn children who behaved more like servants than playmates. Perhaps he understood something of the turbulent currents that had swept him from one guardian to another and landed him with Polyperchon, the careworn general who now dragged him along on his campaign through Greece.

Alexander had been paired throughout his young life with his bizarre counterpart in joint rule, the half-witted Philip. That senior monarch held a higher rank and possessed four Bodyguards to Alexander's three (the canonical number, seven, was split between the two). Some officials spoke and acted as though Philip had sole rule, with young Alexander his designated heir, but the situation was far from clear. At five years old Alexander perhaps already had more cognitive function than his debilitated half uncle.

It was inevitable that the two monarchs would come into conflict, especially after Philip wed the grasping, willful Adea. Philip's interests, as Adea insistently defined them, diverged from his nephew's. If Adea could but conceive—as she no doubt tried fervently to do—the hopes of the royal house would rest on her unborn child, a full-blooded Argead, rather than on the half-breed son of the dead conqueror. And if her child should then be born male, the young Alexander and his barbarian mother would be instantly disinherited, or killed.

But after three years as King Philip's queen, Adea had not conceived. She clearly needed a new strategy in the great dynastic game. Events around her were moving fast, bringing opportunities as well as dangers. She knew that Polyperchon had written to the dowager queen Olympias, urging her to leave Epirus and take charge of her grandson in Macedon. Olympias had so far declined but might change her mind at any moment; Adea had no wish to compete with the only woman in Europe as tough as herself. But the offer also showed that Polyperchon was unsteady, set back on his heels by the rebellion of Cassander. That rebellion might in the end unseat him—especially if Adea threw her husband's royal weight behind it. To Philip, all masters were alike, but to cunning Adea, a shift of allegiance might mean the difference between servitude and sovereignty.

Just how Adea got her husband out of Polyperchon's grasp is unclear. The regent had initially toted Philip with him as he made his way into Greece, fighting now here, now there to install his allies and evict Cassander's. Perhaps Polyperchon was distracted by these fights and neglected to watch his royal ward. Or perhaps he was glad to let Philip go after the disturbing episode at Phocion's hearing, when he had prevented violence only by forcefully restraining the maddened monarch. However it happened, Adea got her husband clear of Polyperchon's power and returned him to Macedonia. Working as his agent, she laid plans to ally with the rebel Cassander, now hunkered down behind the walls of Piraeus.

Perhaps the son of Antipater might be her route to supreme power, in place of the son she now feared she would never have.

2. POLYPERCHON (THE PELOPONNESE, SUMMER 318 B.C.)

Polyperchon began his campaign through Greece with many reasons to be confident. He carried with him the legitimacy bequeathed by Antipater and an army of more than twenty thousand Macedonians. He also brought with him, across the isthmus of Corinth and into the Peloponnese, his supreme weapon, a lumbering, trumpeting herd of Indian elephants, each ridden by its own *mahout*.

These stalwart beasts, acquired in India by Alexander, had over the past eight years walked the entire length of the empire. They had been brought westward by Craterus over the mountains of what is now Pakistan and through the deserts of Afghanistan and Iran. While Alexander lived, they stood in a circle around his tent, one of the concentric rings of his spectacular honor guard. In Babylon, Perdiccas had used them to trample the leaders of the infantry rebellion; in Egypt he sent them into the Nile, causing the erosion that destroyed his army and his reputation. After Perdiccas' murder the herd was split between old man Antipater and Antigonus One-eye at Triparadeisus, and Antipater brought his half across the Hellespont. The survivors, sixty-five in number, now made the journey into southern Greece in the train of Polyperchon, the first of their species ever seen on European soil.

Alexander's soldiers had been terrified of elephants when they first faced large numbers of them in combat, at the battle against Porus in India. But Alexander coolly devised special weapons and tactics to neutralize the beasts. His phalanx was taught to part ranks before the charging elephants, then hack at their trunks and bellies with long scythes while also using *sarissas* to kill or dislodge the *mahouts* who rode them. These harassments drove the elephants into a frenzy of pain and anger, making them more dangerous to their own side than to the enemy's. Porus had been defeated with only small Macedonian losses, and the war elephant had never again so intimidated Alexander's troops.

The only known depiction of elephant warfare from Alexander's own time, on a medallion apparently struck by Alexander. The drawing by historian Frank Holt shows details of the coin's image

One veteran of that battle, a Greek named Damis, had since retired from service and returned home, bringing with him many tales about the elephants of India. At the time of Polyperchon's invasion he was living in the Peloponnese, in Megalopolis, the region's last bastion of support for the rebellion of Cassander. A determined population there had armed fifteen thousand men, strengthened the city walls, and built catapults and torsion weapons with which to fight off a siege. The most potent weapon the city possessed, however, though none of its defenders yet knew it, was Damis' expertise.

Things had gone well for Polyperchon before his approach to Megalopolis. The cities of the Peloponnese had come over to his side, installing friendly regimes and exiling or executing Cassander's partisans. His clean sweep of Greek politics was almost complete, except for Cassander himself in Piraeus. But that rebel was growing more isolated with each city that abandoned his cause. He could not hold out forever, even in a secure position with access to the sea.

Polyperchon began his siege of Megalopolis using Alexander's proven methods. Mobile wooden towers, filled with men firing arrows and artillery, were wheeled up to the walls to clear them of defenders. A sapping team, meanwhile, dug a mine beneath the wall and set fire to the beams propping up its roof, causing a time-delayed collapse. A long stretch of wall gave way, and the Macedonians rushed forward with a shout, believing their labors to be at an end. But the Megalopolitans rallied and fought back. Placing wooden stakes to form a palisade and hurling building materials behind it, they managed to erect a second wall to seal off the breach. From the parapets their torsion weapons, hurling metal bolts at the attackers, began to find their mark. Reluctantly, Polyperchon called off the attack for the day and returned to camp.

Inside Megalopolis, Damis counseled his fellow citizens on what would happen the next morning. Polyperchon would bring his elephants into play, using them to pound the newly built wall into rubble. Damis instructed the city's defenders to feign lack of planning and leave an open corridor for the beasts to approach. In the ground of that corridor, he had them place wooden planks studded with sharp, protruding nails and conceal these under a layer of loose earth. The next day, everything went according to Damis' plan. Polyperchon sent his elephants charging through the unprotected lane leading to the breach—only to see them halt and roar in agony as the concealed spikes drove into their feet. Maddened by the pain and harassed by archers and spearmen who sprang from ambush to attack them, they began rearing and flailing, trampling their own keepers and troops.

It was like Alexander's battle against Porus but in reverse, with Macedonians now on the losing side. Polyperchon had utterly lost control of the weapon that was meant to seal his victory. He broke off the siege and retired from Megalopolis, his reputation irretrievably damaged. From that day forward, the allegiance of the Greek world began to swing toward Cassander.

3. EUMENES, ANTIGENES, AND TEUTAMUS (PHOENICIA, AUTUMN 318 B.C.)

In Asia, meanwhile, Eumenes the Greek, appointed to defend the Macedonian royal house, had used his power of the purse to hire mercenaries of all stripes. His letters from Polyperchon entitled him to draw freely from Cyinda, the fortresslike treasury that at this point housed more silver than any other royal depot. He made sure to pay well enough that reports of his largesse would spread rapidly. In a short time a force of ten thousand infantry and two thousand cavalry had come to the bait. These were added to a core army that, above all, included the incomparable Silver Shields.

Eumenes' army went south to Phoenicia, setting up at each new camp the Alexander tent and its numinous empty throne. Phoenicia had been seized the previous year by Ptolemy, who was now openly supporting Cassander against Polyperchon and the kings. It was thus an important place for Eumenes to plant the royalist flag, as well as a valuable naval base from which to control the Aegean. For it was vital that Eumenes secure a link to Polyperchon in Europe. He had to support his new ally there but also enable him to cross over into Asia, where together they could someday challenge the defiant, dangerous Antigonus.

Antigonus and Ptolemy, coordinating tactics from their separate bases in Anatolia and Egypt, plotted a way to check this troublesome Greek. They would bring him to battle if they had to, but they first tried to neutralize him by indirect means. Ptolemy sent messengers to the captains of the Silver Shields, Antigenes and Teutamus, urging them to overthrow their commander, pointing out that he was still under a death sentence. Other envoys went to the treasury of Cyinda with a similar message, telling the guards not to disburse money to an outlaw and a foreigner. It was a shrewd attack, undermining Eumenes' authority and that of Polyperchon as well, for it was Polyperchon's letter of appointment that had put a condemned man in charge of an army. For the moment, though, that letter stood the test.

Antigonus made a more determined effort along the same lines as Ptolemy. He dispatched a letter bearer named Philotas, along with thirty fast-talking Macedonians, to the camp of Eumenes. These thirty met secretly with Antigenes and Teutamus to organize an assassination plot. They also infiltrated the Silver Shields, hoping to sway former friends and comrades. They leveled the now-familiar charges against Eumenes and promised silver and satrapies to those who would betray him. These inducements opened a breach in Eumenes' wall of loyalty: Teutamus was won over and went to confer with Antigenes, his co-captain, in an effort to turn him as well. But Antigenes argued that Eumenes, being a foreigner, was reliant on subordinates and would have to reward them; One-eye, on the other hand, was strong enough to kill his underlings whenever he chose. Teutamus accepted this reasoning and agreed to stay on Eumenes' side. Eumenes' Greek origins, held out by his foes as a mark against him, were suddenly a point in his favor.

But Antigonus' envoys had not yet given up. Philotas displayed the letter he was carrying, and the Silver Shields demanded to know its contents. At a secret conclave of the platoon this mysterious letter was read aloud. Antigonus addressed the Shields in grave tones and gave them an ultimatum: they must seize Eumenes immediately and put him to death, or Antigonus would regard *them* as traitors and come against them with his army. It was "with me or against me," an agonizing position for the Silver Shields, who had been ordered by the kings to follow Eumenes as their commander and treat One-eye as the rebel.

As the men wavered, uncertain where their loyalties lay or whether loyalty outweighed fear, Eumenes himself entered and read the letter. It was a moment of truth for the wily Greek, similar to one he had faced years earlier, when he had found his soldiers reading Antigonus' offer of a bounty for his head. Back then, he had resorted to deception; this time he played it straight, speaking in earnest tones about the duty owed to the Argeads. Perhaps he was sincere, or perhaps, drawing on the eloquence for which Greeks were both envied and mistrusted, he crafted the argument that would best sway his audience. Whatever the case, he prevailed. The Shields left the meeting with their allegiance to Eumenes strengthened, and Philotas and his men returned to Antigonus with nothing to show.

Eumenes set about building ships and hiring Phoenicians to sail them. He still had an experienced admiral at his side from the days of the Perdiccas regime, a Rhodian named Sosigenes. There was no time to lose. Control of the Aegean was already being contested by fleets of the European combatants, Polyperchon and Cassander, with Antigonus' few ships trying to aid the latter. Cassander, hunkered down in Piraeus, needed to get supplies by sea and preserve his link to Antigonus. Polyperchon sought to break that link and secure access to money, for most of it remained in Asia and had to be sent westward by ship. Antigonus had already seized one such shipment, leaving the government in Macedon starved for cash.

At last Eumenes' fleet was ready, and chests of coin were loaded on board. Sosigenes left the Phoenician crews riding at anchor and climbed a hill to get a better view of currents in the bay. While he was gone, a squadron of warships sailed into view, prows and masts splendidly adorned with trophies of victory. It was the fleet of Antigonus One-eye, fresh from a triumph at the Hellespont, proclaiming to the whole coast, as instructed by Antigonus, its mastery of the seas. Phoenicians had always been quick to back winners, and on this occasion they did just as Antigonus had anticipated: they drew alongside the incoming ships and climbed on board to desert, bringing their cargo of precious metals with them. Sosigenes returned to find his ships empty and all hope lost of control of the sea.

Eumenes' plans in the West had been dashed. He could no longer offer assistance to Polyperchon and the kings, nor they to him. He had no choice but to turn to the East, to Bactria and Sogdiana, where he might raise enough troops and horses to confront the massive army of Antigonus. If he could somehow prevail in that fight, he could return to the West and help his European allies. It was a slender hope, but it was all he had left. In any case, he could not stay where he was, for Antigonus would soon be upon him in Phoenicia. He mustered the Silver Shields, folded up the Alexander tent, and headed for the region that had for centuries been the refuge of the desperate, the upper satrapies.

4. POLYPERCHON, CASSANDER, AND THE ROYAL FAMILY (GREECE, EPIRUS, AND MACEDONIA, SUMMER 318 B.C.)

Eumenes could not yet have known the story behind this triumphant arrival of Antigonus' ships. Polyperchon had been dealt a crushing setback at the Hellespont, in another episode, like the one at Megalopolis, where near victory turned suddenly to defeat.

Cleitus the White, Polyperchon's admiral, had easily prevailed in an initial engagement at the Hellespont, routing ships captained by Cassander's officer Nicanor. Confident that Nicanor was beaten, Cleitus pulled up his ships onto the beach, on the European side, and disembarked his crews for the night. But he did not reckon with Antigonus One-eye, whose army seemed safely removed across the straits.

Ever alert to the complacency of his foes, Antigonus hired vessels from nearby Byzantium and conveyed his best archers, slingers, and javelin men across the straits in the dark. Before dawn this force arrived at Cleitus' camp. The royalists were still asleep, under light guard; they awoke in a hail of projectiles. Cleitus' panicked crews threw gear and booty aboard their ships and launched in disorder. That made them easy prey for Nicanor, who, forewarned of the plan, hurried back to the scene with his surviving vessels. Antigonus sent his fleet as well to take part in the slaughter, his first direct clash with the government of the kings. Unsure whether his men would attack the royalists, he placed a trusted confederate aboard each ship to observe crew members and threaten them with death if they did not row well.

The rout of Cleitus' navy was total. Only one ship escaped, that of Cleitus himself, but it was later seized in Thrace, where Cleitus was put to death. Polyperchon had lost his navy, only a few weeks after losing his elephant herd, and his support in the European theater of war began to crumble. Military failures could be pardoned in a king, who had the sanctity of Argead lineage to protect him. But for a mere general they were fatal, as Perdiccas had proved. Greek and Macedonian leaders alike left Polyperchon's side and went over to Cassander. The democracies installed by the freedom decree began to topple as exiled oligarchs returned.

The democracy at Athens was, as it had often been, a lone holdout. Hagnonides and his followers were loath to give up the counterrevolution that had cost so much effort and that had killed Phocion in its exuberant strength. But the army of Polyperchon's son Alexander, the crucial military prop of the democratic regime, had left. Cassander was no longer penned up in Piraeus; he sallied forth into Attica and took control of Athens' already meager food supply. In the Athenian Assembly, a single brave pragmatist—his name has gone unrecorded—proposed that the city come to terms with Cassander and return to oligarchic government.

Shouted down at first by democratic ideologues, he soon found his proposal gaining support and, finally, grudging approval.

The Athenians opened talks with Cassander, though they had little to bargain with. Cassander insisted on restoring the oligarchy imposed by his father, again disenfranchising the poor. Hagnonides and his followers, now out of power, were tried and put to death. A new leader, one of Phocion's partisans who had managed to escape when the oligarchy fell, was brought back and given plenipotentiary power over the city. Athens underwent its third change of government in as many years, and its chain of metamorphoses was not nearly at an end. In decades to come, each fresh attempt to dominate Europe would start with yet another purge of weary, battered Athens.

Nicanor, victorious at the Hellespont and in higher repute than ever, sailed back into Piraeus to resume his former command there. But his very success made him suspect to Cassander, who knew the strength of the fortified harbor Nicanor would soon control. He resolved to get rid of a threat before it emerged, and to do so quietly, without commotion. Cassander made ships ready as though to sail for Macedonia and instructed a messenger to bring him forged letters while he was walking with Nicanor. The letters invited him to assume the Macedonian throne. Cassander read these missives aloud and excitedly embraced Nicanor, promising to make his faithful lieutenant a sharer in his new power. Then, at this moment of ebullience and feigned partnership, he conducted Nicanor into a nearby house under pretense of holding a parley. Picked troops were waiting there; Nicanor was arrested and sentenced to death.

Though Cassander's letters were forged, their message contained a certain truth. Antipater's old allies in Macedon were indeed urging Cassander to return there, while Polyperchon was bogged down in the Peloponnese. Cassander gratified them by staging a brief, defiant visit to his homeland, a demonstration of political strength. New adherents flocked to his side, including, above all, King Philip and his grasping queen, Adea. This royal pair now openly proclaimed themselves Cassander's partisans. Adea made so bold as to write to Polyperchon in Greece and strip him of all administrative powers. Though her words had no effect, she ordered him to stand down and hand over his army to Cassander, whom she had appointed the new custodian of King Philip.

Cassander now had half the monarchy in his camp, while, with fatal symmetry, the other half declared firmly for Polyperchon. Olympias, the dowager queen, at last gave up her neutrality. She agreed to become Polyperchon's partner and steward of the young Alexander, her grandson. The fissuring of the royal family was complete. Two monarchs, each with his own queen as surrogate and his own general as champion, had ended up on opposite sides of the civil war. There was no alternative now to a direct clash between them. Polyperchon, who seems at this point to have gone to Epirus to join Olympias, began preparing to lead a march eastward to Macedonia, to unseat Philip and install the young Alexander in his place.

As if throwing a new gauntlet at Adea, Olympias chose a member of the Molossian royal family, her young grandniece Deidameia, as a future bride for her grandson. She aimed at winning the hearts and minds of the Macedonians: Alexander and Deidameia could look forward to children and the preservation of the royal house; Adea and Philip were barren. She also aimed at enlisting her nephew Aeacides, king of the Molossians and Deidameia's father, in the upcoming struggle.

What could the five-year-old Alexander, united for the first time with Olympias and her family, have made of his new surroundings? He had lived all his life in a military camp, dragged about first through western Asia, then Egypt, then Asia again, then Greece, and now a mountainous wilderness called Epirus, covered in unfamiliar pine trees. The one constant in his life had been the person least able to help him, his mother, Rhoxane. He had had four generals in five years as his keepers and finally had landed with his grandmother, only to find that she too, like the others before her, was girding for battle. Somewhere across the mountains and the seas beyond, a man they called Eumenes—one whose name he had often heard but whose face he had long forgotten—was fighting a man called Antigonus and would, if he won, make everything much better. Everyone seemed to be at war with one another, and somehow it was all over *him*.

5. EUMENES (BABYLONIA AND POINTS EAST, AUTUMN 318 B.C.)

Eumenes was headed to the East, where he had not set foot since the days of Alexander. He had with him the Silver Shields and a large corps of mercenaries, but he would need to raise more troops, and find cavalry horses and elephants, to have a chance against Antigonus. He would have to win allies from among the satraps in these regions, even though he was holding on to his current subcommanders only by the ritual in Alexander's tent. The men whose realms he was now entering had their own agendas and rivalries, and little reason to support Eumenes, whom they regarded as an outsider, if not a condemned outlaw.

Peithon, a former Bodyguard, was powerful in the East, indeed all too powerful for the liking of his neighbors. Peithon had first gone to the region as Perdiccas' agent, to put down the revolt of the Greek settlers; he had held a commission then as commander of the upper satrapies and felt, rightly or wrongly, that his term had never expired. Upon his return Peithon had begun to assert old prerogatives, to the point of executing a fellow satrap and installing his own brother in his place. Peithon's presumption had aroused the ire of neighboring satraps. They had raised an army and dealt him a serious defeat the previous year, driving him out of the area and into the arms of an old comrade, Seleucus, satrap of Babylon.

As his army approached Babylon, Eumenes sent messages to Seleucus and Peithon, enlisting their support for the fight against Antigonus One-eye. As always, he invoked the power granted him by Polyperchon to defend the government of the kings. The reply of Seleucus was curt. He was quite happy to help the kings, but not to serve under Eumenes, whom the army had condemned to death. It was the same condescension Ptolemy and Antigonus had shown in Phoenicia, and soon Seleucus and Peithon began imitating their tactics as well, sending messages to the Silver Shields urging them to revolt. The captain of that regiment, Antigenes, had been an ally of Peithon and Seleucus in Egypt, where he conspired with them to murder Perdiccas. Their bonds had been forged in blood, but nonetheless Antigenes turned a deaf ear to their demand that he once again kill his senior officer.

Eumenes moved his army to the Tigris River and prepared to cross. He intended to make for Susa, where a large cache of money was stored. But as he readied boats for the crossing, Seleucus and Peithon sailed down the river in person and landed close by. In a tense parley with Antigenes and other officers of the Silver Shields, they pressed their case that Eumenes must be overthrown. Again their appeals went unheard. Rebuffed, and foiled in an attempt to drown Eumenes' army by flooding the plain where it was camped, Seleucus had little choice but to grant Eumenes safe passage out of the territory. He had too few troops for a battle and badly wanted Eumenes to take his hungry army, and his impending war, far from Babylon.

Antigenes, captain of the Silver Shields, had by now been coerced and threatened by four of his nation's top generals. Inexplicably, none had shaken his loyalty to Eumenes the Greek. Perhaps Antigenes was simply pursuing his own interests, as he explained to his co-captain, Teutamus, in Phoenicia: since Eumenes, a foreigner, needed allies more urgently than his rivals, he could be counted on to treat them well. Perhaps he mistrusted Antigonus One-eye, as most men did, and doubted his prospects if that man emerged triumphant. Perhaps he felt bound by the orders he had received long ago from Polyperchon, under the seal of the kings. Whatever his reasons, Antigenes had made his choice. He and his Silver Shields would stand by their Greek commander, to see what the showdown with One-eye would bring.

6. THE ROYAL FAMILY (MACEDONIA, AUTUMN 318 B.C.)

Meanwhile, in the hill country between Epirus and Macedonia, two armies advanced toward each other, each led by a queen. Only one description survives of the world's first known battle between female leaders. According to this no doubt sensationalized report, Olympias, on one side of the field, appeared in the fawn-skin wrap and ivy headdress of a bacchant, as though leading an ecstatic procession for the god Dionysus, and marched to the beat of drums. On the other, Adea came forward in full Macedonian infantry gear. It is an unverifiable but unforgettable image, almost an allegory of the different kinds of power the two women possessed.

Olympias was returning to Macedonia with her grandson Alexander, and Adea was determined to stop her. Olympias was accompanied by her top general, Polyperchon, but Adea did not have Cassander, who was at that moment in the Peloponnese shoring up his Greek support. Adea had urgently sent for him when she learned Olympias was on the march but in the end could not wait, or else thought he wasn't coming. She chose to play the role of field general herself, distributing gifts to her top officers to secure their loyalty. But all her bribes were wasted. Her soldiers, young recruits who had not known Alexander and in whose eyes the conqueror was already a myth, were awed by the sight of his mother, Olympias, and instantly switched sides. The battle ended without a blow being struck. Philip was captured immediately, Adea a short while later while attempting to flee. Olympias, Polyperchon, and the young Alexander marched on to Pella to take control of the riven state.

Olympias had seized power in Macedon at last, the prize for which she had grappled with old man Antipater for so long. Her first order of business was the captured king and queen, Philip and Adea. Olympias walled them up in a cell, supplying rations of food and water through a small opening. Perhaps she thought the Macedonian people, who had deserted the royal pair so readily, would enjoy seeing them treated like beasts in a cage. But she overplayed her hand. Opinion was outraged at her abuse of members of the Argead house. Adea played on her countrymen's sympathy, crying out from her cell that she, daughter and granddaughter of Macedonian kings, was true queen of the realm, not an outsider from Epirus. Olympias could not allow this shrill voice to go on making itself heard.

Argead monarchs had often killed their kin to secure rule, but they tried to do so covertly. Olympias no longer had this option; her murders of Philip and Adea would have to be done in plain view. A gang of Thracians was hired to stab Philip to death, perhaps because no Macedonians would undertake such a deed.

Adea, meanwhile, being a woman, was given the right to kill herself and offered a choice of methods. Olympias sent to her cell a sword, a noose, and a cup of poison, with orders to employ whichever she preferred. Defiant to the end, Adea removed one of her own garments and hanged herself with that, rather than use her captor's noose. Her guards reported that she died a brave death, worthy of a tragic heroine, first praying that Olympias might herself receive gifts like the ones she had sent to the cell. As a final rebuke to her royal rivals, Olympias hid their bodies and refused to accord them proper burial.

With these two off the scene, Olympias set about settling scores with the family of Antipater, which she held to blame for the poisoning (as she saw it) of her son. Antipater was dead, as was his son Iolaus, who had allegedly slipped the toxin into Alexander's drink. But Olympias took revenge on the son anyway, opening his grave and scattering his ashes to the elements. She then killed another son of Antipater's, Nicanor (a different person from the Piraeus garrison commander); he had never been implicated in Alexander's death but, by long-standing Macedonian custom, was presumed an enemy because of his blood ties to other enemies.

Cassander was out of reach in the Peloponnese, where Olympias could not get at him, but she selected an even hundred of his partisans and had them all executed. She felt she must eliminate his base of support before he attempted to invade, as he was sure soon to do.

7. EUMENES AND THE EASTERN COALITION (SUSIANA, SPRING 317 B.C.)

As yet unaware of Olympias' victory in Europe, Eumenes made his way farther east into Asia, seeking new troops and new partners. His anabasis now brought him into contact with yet more satraps disinclined to accept his authority.

One in particular, Alexander's former Bodyguard Peucestas, presented Eumenes with a daunting prospect. A crafty and ambitious man, beloved by his subjects for learning to speak their language and dressing in indigenous clothes, Peucestas had steadily built up power in his satrapy, Persis, the heartland of the old Persian empire. Peucestas had trained and equipped a force of ten thousand Persian archers along with a smaller phalanx and cavalry. With this huge resource he had assumed leadership of a regional coalition that had come together to stop the presumptuous Peithon.

Eumenes rendezvoused with Peucestas and his allies in Susiana, where, at his suggestion, they had brought their coalition army. The camp Eumenes found there was a truly breathtaking sight: more than eighteen thousand infantrymen and forty-six hundred cavalry, the largest force seen in the East since the departure of Alexander. Among them was Eudamus, newly arrived from India with 120 precious elephants he had stolen from a murdered raja, Porus. If this army were joined with the comparably large force under Eumenes, an aggregate would be formed that could easily best either Peithon or Antigonus One-eye, or even the two together, should they also join forces.

But melding troops led by proud Macedonians with others led by a Greek was a complex matter, as Eumenes well knew. Peucestas already had command of the coalition army and was reluctant to accept a lesser role. Yet it was Eumenes who bore the commission of the kings, had control of the Silver Shields, and was entitled to tap the royal treasuries. Compromise between these two leading generals seemed impossible to achieve. The infantry captain Antigenes tried a diplomatic solution, suggesting that the Silver Shields, by right of their enormous value as a military asset, ought to choose the commander. But to accede to this seemed tantamount to selecting Eumenes, so the debate went on.

As the rivalry continued, threatening to become an insurmountable rift, Eumenes reverted to an old but still effective device. He once again set up Alexander's tent and introduced to his new comrades the daily worship ritual he had first shared with Antigenes and Teutamus. As it had done before, the spectral presence of Alexander dispelled tension and knit the factions together. Somehow, in the sanctuary of the tent, Eumenes was able to assert leadership without troubling stiff-necked Peucestas.

With the conflict over command thus defused, the two great armies were merged into one. Each leader was made responsible for paying his own forces, to prevent the practice of influence buying from spiraling out of control. Eumenes, however, exempted himself from this rule in one instance, paying a special grant of two hundred talents to Eudamus, allegedly for upkeep of his elephants. Such a valuable, and treacherous, ally could not be left unbribed.

8. ANTIGONUS AND EUMENES (THE RIVER COPRATES, SUSIANA, SUMMER 317 B.C.)

By contrast with Eumenes, now head of a kind of board of joint chiefs, Antigonus was imperious and solitary in command. He shared counsels with no one and entrusted no one with his plans, not even the son Demetrius whom he cherished. Once when the two were on campaign together, and Demetrius asked what time in the morning the soldiers should break camp, his father withheld even this banal information. "Are you worried that you alone will fail to hear the trumpet sound?" he upbraided the boy. Such secretiveness was to be a key weapon in the campaign ahead.

Antigonus headed east, undaunted by news that Eumenes had joined forces with Peucestas and the other satraps. He could surpass their newly increased numbers by recruitment, and by troop contributions from Peithon and Seleucus in Babylon (with whom he had by now forged an alliance). A bigger deficit, though, was the money he needed to pay for those troops. Eumenes alone could tap the royal treasuries, as was now demonstrated at Babylon: the guardians of the citadel where the imperial coin was stored refused to admit anyone but Eumenes, defying the wills of Antigonus and Seleucus both. Much the same happened when Antigonus' army arrived at Susa. A guard captain named Xenophilus stuck to Eumenes' orders, not to disburse money to Antigonus or even enter into conversation with him. Inside the Susa cache lay twenty thousand talents in coin and treasure, including the "Climbing Vine," a stunning representation of a grapevine with ripe fruit, done all in fine gold, that had once curled around King Darius' bedposts. Antigonus left Seleucus to put the place under siege, and moved eastward to find Eumenes.

Antigonus was on unfamiliar terrain, having never gone east with Alexander as other generals had. As he moved out of Susa, he found himself at the mercy of geography and climate. It was midsummer, and though he marched only at night, he lost some troops to extreme heat. Worse, he was traveling blind, blocked by a river called the Coprates from ascertaining Eumenes' position. His adversary was in fact less than ten miles away, across an even larger river, the Pasitigris.

Eumenes had chosen the Pasitigris as his line of defense. He knew that Antigonus must cross it to follow the easy route to the East, along the coast. His plan was to force Antigonus to instead go the long way around, through the mountains of Media. If Antigonus headed this direction, Eumenes planned to wait until he was safely out of range and then bring the entire coalition army back toward the West, into regions that were now nearly emptied of foes, Anatolia and Phoenicia. From here he could open a naval link with his allies in Europe, Polyperchon, Olympias, and the young Alexander. Antigonus would be cut off from his home base, starved of reinforcements, and, if Cassander could be defeated for good, robbed of his political raison d'être.

Eumenes lined up his troops across a wide stretch of the Pasit-

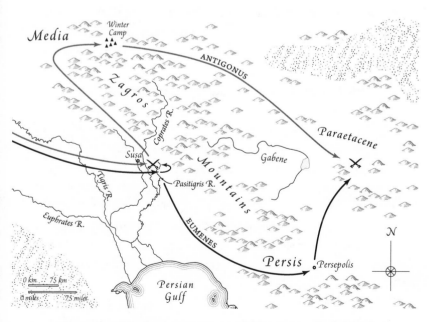

Movements of Antigonus and Eumenes leading up to the battle of Paraetacene, in what is now Iran

igris, knowing Antigonus would do his utmost to cross unobserved. When even forty thousand coalition troops did not stretch far enough, he asked Peucestas to recruit ten thousand more from his home satrapy, Persis. The request implied superior rank and caused Peucestas to bridle, but in the end his mistrust of Antigonus bested his pride. Peucestas gave the order for Persian reinforcements, sending it echoing from one mountaintop to the next by a relay of criers, so that it reached Persepolis, almost a month's travel to the east, in only a day.

Before reaching the Pasitigris, Antigonus had to ferry his men across the Coprates, a river too deep to ford. Here Eumenes, knowing Antigonus was advancing blind, had planned a trap. Antigonus would have to use relays of boats, meaning that, in mid-crossing, his army would be split on two sides of the river. Eumenes waited in hiding until about ten thousand had reached the eastern bank, then signaled a charge. Antigonus' men tried briefly to resist. Then all fled at once for the boats, some of which sank under the weight of those cramming onto them, or dove in panic into the river, which carried away all but the strongest swimmers. Their comrades, out of artillery range across the Coprates, could merely look on in dismay. More than four thousand men finally surrendered and became prisoners of Eumenes, to be incorporated into his army. That put a dent in Antigonus' troop strength, but greater still was the damage to his reputation. Formerly master of the smart surprise attack, Antigonus had been outsmarted.

Antigonus gave up on crossing the river and headed north along a hard road into Media. Eumenes' grand plan was working, but it required the joint commanders, including the eastern satraps, to agree to head for the West. The Silver Shields and Eumenes' own staff backed the plan wholeheartedly, but Peucestas and his partners refused to leave their satrapies to the ravages of Antigonus. They were even less inclined than before to follow Eumenes' lead, having been upstaged by him at the Coprates, a victory in which they apparently played no part. Reluctantly, Eumenes gave up his grand strategy and agreed to fight in the East. It was that or watch the combined army split into its constituent halves, either of which would make easy prey for Antigonus One-eye.

9. THE ROYAL FAMILY AND CASSANDER (MACEDONIA)

Greek writers loved to contemplate women who resembled tragic heroines, and in Olympias they found all the parallels they could ask for. Born a neo-Trojan princess named Polyxena, she seemed to them to have lived her whole life in mythic roles. As Philip's wife, she had morphed into Medea, murderess of the princess who stole her husband's affections; as mother of the dead Alexander, she resembled Hecuba grieving for fallen Hector. As ruler of Macedonia, she evoked Clytemnestra, the iron-fisted queen of Argos, as well as Antigone, but an Antigone in reverse, driven by her passionate devotion to kin to *un*bury the dead.

Whichever of these roles we cast her in—or whether, following biographer Elizabeth Carney, we reject them all as gender stereotypes—Olympias was undeniably a tragic figure. With her triumphant return to Macedon, she seemed to have come safely through the perils that surrounded her, and rescued her grandson as well; she no doubt had plans to bring her daughter Cleopatra, still stranded in Sardis without prospects, back into the palace and the restored royal family. But her time in power was fated to be brief. An avenging Orestes was stalking her from across the mountains, from Greece, and though she knew he was coming, she somehow proved unable to stop him.

Olympias' political leadership was forceful to the point of despotism, but her command of the army did not have the same strength. When the long-awaited Cassander appeared with his forces, key passes and choke points had not yet been sealed off. The soldiers following her chief general, Polyperchon, wavered in their allegiance; some accepted bribes to desert to Cassander. The armies of Olympias' nephew Aeacides also abandoned her cause and, returning home to Epirus, overthrew Aeacides, unseating a royal dynasty that had ruled (according to legend) since the Trojan War. Olympias, despite having custody of the only surviving

Argead monarch, found her position eroding rapidly, undermined by the ill will she had bred in killing the other.

With military resources dwindling, Olympias reached out to Aristonous, a former member of Alexander the Great's Bodyguard come home to Macedonia to retire. Enlisting this man in the defense of her regime, she withdrew to the coastal city of Pydna. There, even if her generals were defeated, she might hope to be rescued by sea by her supporters, perhaps by Eumenes, whose position at this moment she could not know for certain. She brought with her the most helpless hostages to Fortune: the six-year-old Alexander and his equally young consort, Deidameia, and Rhoxane, the Bactrian queen mother. Other members of the court accompanied them, along with a cohort of loyal soldiers and the few precious elephants not done in by the spikes at Megalopolis.

The royal refuge had not been stockpiled with stores of food, and Cassander knew he could make short work of a siege. Arriving outside Pydna with his army, he ordered a firm palisade built across the headland on which the city sat, cutting it off from relief by land, and requisitioned ships and ship-mounted siege machines to attack it from the sea. Nearly two years after his father's death and the accession of Polyperchon, he had finally seized his patrimony. His enemies were cornered quarry, and he did not intend to let them escape.

10. EUMENES AND PEUCESTAS
(PERSEPOLIS, AUTUMN 317 B.C.)

Eumenes' army marched east into Persis. This was Peucestas' home province, and he played the gracious host, feeding the army liberally from cattle herds it passed en route. Dismayed at Eumenes' popularity, Peucestas determined he would win back the esteem of the troops. Food, as he well knew, was an important magnet that drew their allegiance, along with money, victory, and marks of favor from Alexander the Great. Since Eumenes could best him in the other three categories, Peucestas staked his claim to the first.

In Persepolis, his satrapal capital, Peucestas sponsored an

enormous banquet for an army of more than forty thousand. A vast set of four concentric circles was laid out in open ground, the outer one more than a mile in circumference, and dining couches were built out of heaped-up leaves covered with carpets. The troops were assigned to various rings according to their status: rank-and-file infantry in the outermost, Silver Shields and other Alexander veterans next, then cavalrymen and lower officers, and top generals in the inmost ring. At the center of this military cosmos stood altars of the gods, with two new ones added for the divinized Alexander and his father, Philip. This was a banquet of unprecedented grandeur. The admiration of the troops, and the growth in Peucestas' power, were palpable.

Eumenes was hard put to respond. It was clear now that Peucestas wished to contest leadership of the army, but for Eumenes even to acknowledge this rivalry, never mind counter it, might lead to an open split. He did not want a showdown over the right to invoke Alexander's ghost, like the showdown over Alexander's corpse in which his master, Perdiccas, had been wrecked. Eumenes sought a different solution, drawing not on his military skills but on those he had learned in his first career, as secretary to the Macedonian kings.

From Persis to Macedonia was a journey of weeks, and news that traveled between the two places was old by the time it arrived. Eumenes took advantage of this time lag by forging a letter that gave news of dramatic events in the West. Olympias had defeated Cassander and killed him, his letter reported; the young Alexander was securely ensconced on the throne; Polyperchon and his army had crossed into Asia with able troops and elephants, and were moving eastward at that very moment. Eumenes tricked the letter up to look like a report from Orontes, the Persian satrap of Armenia, a known friend of Peucestas, whose word would be trusted by all. For added authenticity he composed it in Aramaic, the lingua franca of the old Persian empire.

Eumenes had the forged letter sent round to all the commanders, and word of its content spread quickly. The camp came alive with ebullience, elation, and esteem for Eumenes. *His* allies, the men believed, had triumphed in the West and were headed east to help *him* in his fight with Antigonus. Because of Eumenes, they would all be redeemed; after an easy victory, they could count on rewards from a grateful monarchy and an end to the civil wars. It was Eumenes, they foresaw, who would dominate the postwar era. He could obtain promotion or punishment for any of them, based on how loyally they followed him now. The little Greek's stature among the troops soared to new heights.

With a masterstroke of deceit, Eumenes had eclipsed the public relations coup Peucestas achieved with his grand banquet. He pressed his advantage by charging Sibyrtius, one of Peucestas' close allies, with secretly aiding Antigonus. Whether or not there was substance to this charge, it was clearly a shot across Peucestas' bow. As for the other coalition satraps, who, as he knew from experience, would hate him more the higher he climbed, Eumenes devised a new measure to guard against betrayal. He asked each of them to lend him a large sum of money, amassing more than four hundred talents in all. As his creditors could well guess, this cash would be paid back only so long as they remained in his good graces, and he remained alive.

No sooner had Eumenes shored up his command than deserters from Antigonus arrived in his camp. Antigonus had left Media, they reported, and was headed south. Eumenes decided to go north to meet his foe; to wait longer would risk a splintering of the coalition or discovery that his letter was a fake. He mobilized his troops and led them into Paraetacene, today part of western Iran. The time for battle was at hand.

II. THE BATTLE OF PARAETACENE
(AUTUMN 317 B.C.)

Antigonus approached Paraetacene with almost forty thousand men, Eumenes with slightly more. It was the biggest aggregation of armed force since the battle of Gaugamela, and the biggest showdown ever between two European commanders. It was also the first time two Europeans had both brought war elephants against each other. Eumenes had 120, thanks to Eudamus, while Antigonus still had 65 of the 70 he had received at Triparadeisus, the well-traveled veterans of Alexander's original herd.

Eumenes approached his foe with high hopes, riding the wave

of support generated by his forged letter, but now, when he most needed to inspire confidence, he had fallen ill. He delayed the march for some days while he tried to rally strength, then finally handed command over to Peucestas and Antigenes so that the army could move forward. For a while he had to be carried, barely conscious, inside a covered litter in the rear of the column, while his men fretted over his condition. Antigonus, for his part, got word of Eumenes' ailment from some scouts he had captured and made haste to seize his opportunity.

The two armies took up opposing positions in miles-long lines, only a quarter of a mile apart. They had anticipated this meeting for two years, but now that it was at hand, both sides were strangely unwilling to commence battle. Eumenes was still recovering from his illness; Antigonus, perhaps, was hoping for a fracturing of the coalition, or a defection of the Silver Shields from Eumenes' side. More than eighty thousand men stood at arms for four days on the rugged plain, while the food supply of the region was picked clean by their foragers.

On the fifth day Antigonus sent envoys to the coalition satraps and the Shields, urging them yet again to abandon Eumenes and promising amnesty and rewards. The satraps could keep their satrapies, he said, while the Shields could choose grants of land in Asia, repatriation to Macedonia with cash bonuses, or high rank in Antigonus' army. It was his third attempt to bribe or threaten Eumenes' men, but it had no more success than the others. The Silver Shields repulsed the envoys and threatened to kill them. What Peucestas and his fellow satraps thought of the offer is less clear, but they stood their ground for the moment.

Eumenes, now recovering his strength, came before his troops and praised their fidelity. Antigonus, he told them, was just like the man in the fable whose daughter is wooed by a lion. The man tells the lion he fears for his daughter's safety, so the lion pulls out its own claws and teeth to gain approval. The man then seizes his chance and clubs to death the helpless beast. "Antigonus is doing just the same thing," Eumenes told them. "He will abide by his terms only until he gets control of your forces, and then he will punish your leaders." "That's right!" the troops cried.

Deserters informed Eumenes that One-eye was planning to

break camp and march away in the night. They did not know his destination, but Eumenes guessed he would head for Gabene, a nearby region with plentiful food, to refresh his troops and fight from better ground. Eumenes determined he would occupy the place first and sent "deserters" of his own to stall Antigonus by telling him of an impending night attack. Antigonus believed the tale and had his troops stand under arms through the night, until his scouts reported that Eumenes had broken camp and was marching toward Gabene. Antigonus hastened after him with a flying force of cavalry, trying to close a six-hour head start.

Antigonus' advance force caught up to Eumenes' army around dawn. Riding up to the edge of a high ridge, they glimpsed Eumenes' column in the plain below, and Eumenes' soldiers likewise spotted them. Luckily for Antigonus, the men looking up from below could see only the front of the ridge and could not tell whether Antigonus' cavalry was accompanied by the entire army. Eumenes could not take that chance; he called a halt to array for battle. This gave Antigonus time to bring up his slower-moving contingents and assemble his forces. Several hours later, after his infantry had arrived, Antigonus led his army down the ridge to join combat.

Antigonus rode in the place of honor on the extreme right of his line, with his son, Demetrius, now old enough for his first battle, beside him. On the left, at the head of a unit of light horse, rode Peithon, hoping to at last win mastery of the East. Plans called for Antigonus to mount the first charge, as right-wing cavalry had always done under Alexander. But for some reason Antigonus stopped his advance before reaching Eudamus and the coalition satraps, whose forces were opposite his. Instead, Peithon, on the left, was first to engage the enemy, dashing forward with his light horse and firing arrows and spears at the elephants surrounding Eumenes.

Eumenes, on the right wing of his own line, watched this movement with concern. His elephants might be goaded into fury if hit too often by barbs. When he sensed Peithon was getting too close, he called for his own light horse, then stationed on his left wing, to ride across the lines and attack Peithon. Peithon's horsemen, who by now had gotten far from the protection of their allies, were driven back to the hills from which they had descended, pursued by the light cavalry of Eumenes.

Meanwhile, the center of Antigonus' line, with its massive infantry phalanx, made contact with the infantry of Eumenes. Antigonus' forces were attacking from higher ground and had a huge numerical edge, but as had been proved many times in the Macedonian wars, nerve, not numbers, decided infantry clashes. The Silver Shields in Eumenes' line had fought together for decades. The young recruits they faced, for the most part, had never before been in a pitched battle. As swords and *sarissas* clashed, the Shields bored into their opponents and began inflicting massive casualties. Antigonus' phalanx broke and fled toward the hills, pursued by the Shields. The tide was turned, and One-eye's army was now in trouble.

The safe move for Antigonus, and what his advisers counseled, was retreat of all forces to the high ground, where they would be safe from further attacks. But Antigonus, watching coolly from his right wing as his left and center collapsed, spotted a gap in his opponent's line. The light cavalry that Eumenes had shifted to meet Peithon had left a hole, and that hole had widened as Eumenes' phalanx advanced. Antigonus charged into it with his cavalry, his son, Demetrius, close behind. They struck Eudamus' forces sharply in the flank. The sudden blow stunned Eumenes' army, and momentum shifted. Eumenes called back his victorious phalanx, ordering it to break off pursuit and aid Eudamus. Antigonus sent swift riders to stop his fleeing troops and get them formed up again for battle.

The fight had gone on for much of the day without resolution, and neither general was willing to break off. Both Eumenes and Antigonus, now three miles from their original positions, once again drew up their lines, this time only four hundred feet apart. The full moon gave enough light for night combat, and it seemed that the battle would begin all over again. Then, suddenly, both sides stood down and grounded their weapons. They were exhausted and starved, having had no real provisions for days. The engagement was ended by mutual consent.

Who had won? Eumenes had inflicted greater casualties and had prevailed in the crucial infantry clash. But when he ordered

his men to return to the battlefield and camp there, the prerogative of the victors, they refused. Their worldly goods were with
their baggage train, in a different location, and they did not want
to be far from these. With rival leaders vying for his men's favor,
Eumenes had to accede. Antigonus, with no such constraints on
his authority, marched his weary troops three miles back to where
the bodies lay strewn and pitched camp. "Whoever is master of
the fallen is winner of the fight," he declared, though he made
haste to cremate his dead the next day, before Eumenes could
learn their number.

Even if they had won by a technicality, Antigonus' troops felt
defeated. Antigonus was determined to get them out of the area,
lest they need to fight again with low morale. When Eumenes'
heralds arrived to arrange recovery of the dead, Antigonus set the
ritual for the following day, but broke camp during the night and
marched off at top speed. It was the final trick in a campaign that
had seen many tricks, feints, and night marches. Eumenes, told by
his scouts that Antigonus was gone, did not attempt to pursue.
His men were exhausted. He would let them rest for the winter
and prepare for the next showdown.

Antigonus and Eumenes had shown in Paraetacene they were
well-matched opponents, both shrewd and inventive men. Each
by now knew the other's strengths and weaknesses. Their record
against each other was dead even, counting Orcynia as a victory
for Antigonus, the Coprates River as a victory for Eumenes, and
Paraetacene as a tie. There was a collective sense in their two
camps that a great duel was under way, with the future of the
Argead dynasty hanging in the balance. Eumenes, it was understood, backed Olympias and the young Alexander. In victory he
would defer to the Argeads, if only because he could not become
one himself. Antigonus, as was equally well known, deferred to no
one. His plans for the empire, were he to prevail over Eumenes,
were unclear, but they surely did not include taking orders from a
seven-year-old half-Bactrian boy.

As the troops of both men went into separate winter quarters,
it was clear to all that a resolution of the duel was not far off. But
just how close it was, or what form it would take, could not have
been foreseen by any of them.

The Closing of the Tombs

316–308 B.C.

More than six years after his death in Babylon, Alexander still held the world in thrall. In Europe, Olympias and the young Alexander had briefly been thrust to the peak of power, largely by virtue of their kinship with him. In Asia, Eumenes had won crucial allies by meeting with them in the presence of Alexander's ghost. In Egypt, Ptolemy guarded Alexander's corpse, the sacred object he would soon house in an enormous memorial called simply the Sema, or Tomb. The body would continue to attract pilgrims at this site until the third century A.D., after which it disappeared, perhaps destroyed in the religious riots that were then roiling the city.

Everywhere in the empire, veterans of Alexander's campaign found they were regarded as heroes and supermen, and none were more heroic than the Silver Shields. The whole world knew of the trust Alexander had placed in them, the perilous assignments he had given them, the honor he had paid them by coating their gear with silver. Six years after the king's death, they were the last unit of his veterans that remained intact, undiluted by more recent recruits. Their unity gave them political power. In army assemblies, the Shields made their voices heard loud and clear, all three thousand seeming to speak as one through their captains, Antigenes and Teutamus. Their privileges were beyond dispute. So was their devastating effectiveness in battle, the result of decades of fighting together as a corps d'elite.

By the time of the battle of Paraetacene, the Silver Shields were old men. Alexander had sent them home eight years earlier, along with the other veterans decommissioned at Opis, but they had not gotten far before the king died and the resulting power struggle brought them back into action. There was no longer any retirement in view for them, nor any home or family to return to. The army camp had become their home. It was their family as well, for many of them had wives or mistresses, and a few had children, accompanying them on their marches. These were toted along behind the army in a vast baggage train, which also held piles of treasure they had amassed from plunder, pay, and the rewards bestowed on them by commanders, some by Alexander himself.

The Shields had followed Eumenes for almost three years before the battle of Paraetacene, ever since Polyperchon first ordered them to do so. Their allegiance had withstood threats, bribes, and challenges, a striking example of constancy in a treacherous era. Some followed Eumenes out of reverence for the joint kings; others, because he paid well; others, because they thought he would win in the end and improve all their fortunes. But true loyalty was not among their motives. They revered no commander except the dead Alexander; indeed, they scorned others for failing to compare with him. Eumenes had resorted to flattery to control them, addressing them as "my protectors" and "the last hope for my survival," and reminding them constantly of their glorious past. It was *they* who had made Alexander great, Eumenes told them. Above all he used the Alexander tent, the penumbra of the conqueror's spiritual power, to bind their two senior officers, Antigenes and Teutamus, to his service.

By thus wheedling, fawning, and manipulating, Eumenes had retained the right, granted to him by Polyperchon, to lead the Silver Shields. But it was a strange sort of leadership, provisional and weak. It had to be reinforced by oaths of allegiance, administered by Eumenes to the Silver Shields at regular intervals. The bonds that tied Alexander's greatest warriors to a Greek, a former book-keeper, a man two decades their junior, were not adamantine. The bribes and threats of four Macedonian generals had thus far failed to break them. But the greatest of those, Antigonus One-eye, had not yet given up the attempt.

I. THE BATTLE OF GABENE (WINTER, EARLY 316 B.C.)

As he rested his army in Media, Antigonus looked back on the battle of Paraetacene with misgivings. He had been outfought and was now outnumbered as a result. His infantry phalanx had given way at its first contact with the Silver Shields and hereafter would be even more intimidated by them. Antigonus faced uncertain odds in another open-field battle—but perhaps that was a risk he didn't have to run. He still had recourse to his favorite stratagem, already used against other foes to great effect: the surprise attack.

From Antigonus' winter quarters to those of Eumenes was a march of almost a month through arable country but only nine days through a sulfurous wilderness where nothing grew or lived. No one could expect an army to come through that desert, and no one would expect an attack during winter, a piercingly cold season in these parts. Eumenes was so sure of his safety that he had divided his army into widely spaced camps stretching more than a hundred miles, as Antigonus had learned from his spies. If taken by surprise, the troops in these camps would never have time to combine forces. Unit by unit, they would surrender, until Eumenes, and his incomparable Silver Shields, could be ensnared.

Antigonus ordered the building of wooden casks and the gathering of ten days' provision for the army. To avoid informa-tion leaks, he told his soldiers they were marching west to Arme-nia but then veered suddenly and led his men into the desert. His secret was then safe, since no spies or deserters could escape notice in an open, blasted plain. To further cloak his route, he ordered his troops to light campfires only by day, for the desert was sur-rounded by high hills from which night fires would easily be spot-ted. This order was obeyed for the first half of the march, but finally the troops could no longer stand the nighttime cold and cutting wind. Some of them kindled fires, and that gave their presence away.

From the distant mountains, herdsmen spotted strange lights in the desert and sent messengers on galloping camels to inform Peucestas, the nearest of the generals in Eumenes' coalition. Peucestas was roused from sleep by the news and hastily summoned the other generals, convening an emergency council. Peucestas urged a retreat deeper into Gabene in order to buy time. Eumenes, again wrestling with Peucestas for control of strategy, countered that the army should stay where it was. He promised that by means of a trick, he would stop One-eye's progress for at least three days, enough time to allow the scattered forces to assemble in one spot. His fellow commanders decided to let him try.

Eumenes immediately sent messengers to all the camps in Gabene, urging his men to join him on the double. Then he took a contingent of troops up to some high ground, measured off stations about thirty feet apart, and at each station posted a crew of fire tenders. Their orders were to light fires each night, letting them blaze up for a few hours but slowly die down toward dawn, just as the watch fires of an army on campaign would do. Eumenes knew how Antigonus, with his fear of deserters and moles, would react, and he was right. Seeing the fires on the ridge, Antigonus assumed that his plans had been divulged and that the entire coalition army was waiting for him. Disheartened, he turned aside from his desert route and took his men into country where they could rest and provision themselves. He assumed they would have not an ambush but an open-field battle ahead.

The stratagem bought Eumenes just enough time to assemble his units. The last to arrive, the slow-moving elephant herd, only barely made it, and Eumenes had to send troops to rescue it from attack, for Antigonus had by then discovered he had been tricked and had brought his troops to Gabene.

For the second time in six months, two great armies, each more than thirty thousand strong, came together for battle on the dry, dusty plains of what is now Iran.

Eumenes put himself and his best cavalry units on the left wing this time, facing Antigonus and Demetrius. He would confront his nemesis face-to-face. He put Peucestas directly on his right, perhaps as a way to ensure he could keep an eye on his troublesome colleague during the battle. It seems Eumenes realized that his fractious coalition was not in good repair. Plutarch reports that rival generals were plotting against his life and that Eumenes himself knew this, but the story lacks confirmation in other sources. In any case, Eumenes had tangled with Peucestas often enough to know not to trust him.

In front of his strong left wing, Eumenes placed a screen of his best elephants. They would attack the elephants of Antigonus while also fending off frontal cavalry charges, for horses were wary of the sight and smell of elephants and would not approach them. At the center of his line, Eumenes stationed his infantry phalanx, spearheaded by the Silver Shields, his greatest asset and best hope of victory. He kept his right wing weak and ordered it to stay out of the battle as long as possible. He would try to score a knockout blow from his own wing, aiming his best units squarely at the enemy leader. It was what Alexander had done in his battles against the Persians, and his model had already become the gold standard of military heroism.

As the two armies drew within a few miles of each other on the barren plain, Antigenes, the Silver Shields' commander, ordered a lone rider to gallop forward and deliver a message. When this man came within earshot of One-eye's lines, he shouted: "Villains! It is your own fathers you are wronging, men who marched with Philip and Alexander and conquered the whole empire!" The boast and the reproach had come, unmistakably, from the Silver Shields. The message unsettled Antigonus' men, who had no great wish to fight the most revered—and most deadly—soldiers of their age. But it raised a cry of approval from Eumenes' side, as a report of its content passed from unit to unit. Hearing that cry, Eumenes led his cavalry forward, and Antigonus, on his side, did the same.

The soil on which the troops were moving was dry and laden with salt. The tramp of horses, elephants, and tens of thousands of men raised a choking cloud of dust that quickly enveloped the field. As the two sides drew nearer to each other, Antigonus, a master at cloaking strategies, spotted an opportunity. He sent some light-armed Tarentine cavalry to ride past the flank of the oncoming army and attack the baggage train behind it. From within the shroud of dust, no one in Eumenes' line saw them coming or noticed them passing by. The Tarentines easily overcame a few token guards and seized the whole train, including the families and worldly goods of the Silver Shields. These they led back around the line of battle to Antigonus' side, still unseen.

Before Eumenes had learned of this setback, another blow landed, even more devastating for his chances. As the elephants engaged and began to gore one another, and Antigonus' massive cavalry wedge began a flanking maneuver, Eumenes saw Peucestas, stationed immediately to his right, leave the field with his fifteen hundred horsemen. This was either an act of cowardice or, more likely, a prearranged move to sabotage Eumenes' efforts and end his life. Eumenes was now stranded, cut off from his own line with only a small corps of elite cavalry. Peucestas, always an unwilling subordinate, had gone his own way at last.

Peering through the whirling dust, Eumenes spotted the huge figure of Antigonus in the oncoming throng of cavalrymen. His chance for a masterstroke, a bold charge that would decapitate the enemy with one sword thrust, was at hand. Eumenes spurred his cavalry on toward Antigonus. But his numbers were too few to penetrate and give him a chance at single combat. The deed he desperately needed, the coup de grâce that would have made a Greek scribe into a second Alexander, was just out of reach. After watching his lead elephant fall, sensing his position was collapsing, Eumenes rode his troops out of the fray and around to the right wing, which had not yet come into contact with Antigonus' left.

Meanwhile, the Silver Shields were moving forward in the center, wielding their eighteen-foot *sarissas* with customary resolve. They cut a deep swath into Antigonus' ranks, quickly sending his infantry fleeing in a disordered mass. The resulting rout was total. Diodorus reports that the Shields inflicted five thousand fatalities without losing a man. Perhaps that is an exaggeration, but there is no doubt that here, in the last battle they were destined to fight together, the Shields proved their prowess once again. "Like athletes of war, without a defeat or a fall up to that time, many seventy years old and none less than sixty—the oldest of those who had served with Philip and Alexander," Plutarch eulogizes them. Thanks to their victory in the center, the outcome of battle was once again hanging in the balance.

Eumenes sought to rally his cavalry and sent a message to Peucestas demanding he come back to the fight. Peucestas sullenly withdrew even farther, taking refuge by the banks of a nearby river. Meanwhile, Eumenes' victorious infantry had come under attack by Antigonus' horse, but had formed a hollow square with lances pointing outward, a sure defense for those who could hold to it unshakably. With consummate sangfroid they retreated to the safety of the river, where they began berating Peucestas for his desertion of the left wing. If not for that, it was clear, the battle would already be won and the army would be reclaiming its baggage—the loss of which had now been learned and was causing considerable anguish.

It was growing dark by the time Eumenes arrived at the river. Another in a long series of command conclaves was held, and as usual opinions were divided. Eumenes wanted to fight again the following day. His infantry was undamaged and totally victorious; his cavalry and elephants had held up well despite desertion by Peucestas. The coalition's chances looked good, easily better than those of Antigonus. The satraps, however, wanted to retreat to home turf, the upper satrapies, and repair their losses.

In previous strategy disputes the Silver Shields had backed Eumenes, but now they were distraught at the loss of their families and fortunes. Eumenes told them they had every chance of recovering these, and seizing more besides, if they would make just one more effort. But their disappointment in him, the sense that they had been seduced by a false Alexander, turned them scornful. They shouted that Eumenes had led them on with false promises, had troubled their lives with constant wars, had brought them into the East when they could have gone home, and finally had lost all they owned, dooming them to an impoverished and lonely old age. The bonds between Eumenes and the Silver Shields had finally given way.

The conclave broke up without choosing a course of action. As soon as it did, Teutamus, junior captain of the Shields, took action on his own. Long dubious about Eumenes, only barely prevented from selling him out once before, Teutamus now secretly contacted Antigonus One-eye looking for a deal. This time he did not consult his senior partner, Antigenes, who had talked him out of betrayal the last time. A trade-off was easily arranged, Eumenes for the baggage train, with Antigonus also promising amnesty and cash rewards. The bargain was struck, and Eumenes' fate was sealed, that very night.

2. EUMENES AND ANTIGONUS
(GABENE, WINTER, EARLY 316 B.C.)

It was no simple matter to arrest Eumenes. He had devoted followers, those whom he termed "companions" in imitation of Alexander, who might try to defend him. Word of Teutamus' betrayal might have already leaked out—indeed there is some indication it had—and Eumenes might have an escape prepared. A group of Silver Shields surrounded Eumenes and distracted him with chatter, some complaining about their lost baggage, others telling him to be confident since he had clearly won the previous day's engagement. When they had hedged him off from his supporters, they pounced, seizing his sword and binding his hands with cloth from his own garment. In a moment it was over. Peucestas and his ten thousand archers, who could have made trouble even for the Shields, saw which way the wind was blowing and declared allegiance to Antigonus. Other satraps did likewise.

Two days later, Antigonus' officer Nicanor arrived to take possession of the prisoner. As he was being led out through the camp, Eumenes asked permission to address the Silver Shields, and this was granted. Eumenes, standing on high ground where he could be heard by all, holding out his bound hands, made his valedictory speech. He began as though to reproach his men but stopped himself; all he really wanted, he said, was their help. "By Zeus, who protects soldiers, and by the gods who enforce oaths— kill me yourselves," he implored, according to the report of Plutarch. "Antigonus will not blame you . . . If you are reluctant to do it with your own hands, free up one of mine so that it can do the deed. If you don't trust me with a sword, then throw me, bound as I am, under the elephants. If you do as I ask, I release you from all blame; I consider you to be the most reverent and most just of men in your treatment of your general."

His pleas went unheard. The Shields yelled to the guards to lead Eumenes away, and as he passed by, they vented their scorn. "Don't listen to his drivel," they muttered. "Why should we care for the sufferings of a pest from the Chersonese, who vexes the Macedonians with endless wars—when we, the best of Alexander's and Philip's soldiers, are stripped of the rewards of our labors and forced to depend on handouts, while our wives are about to pass a third night in the beds of our enemies?" Their losses had filled them with hate, and Eumenes' foreign origins, so often touted by Eumenes himself as a reason the Macedonians should trust him, was the focus of that hate. In the end, Eumenes remained an outsider, an alien who had connived his way into their power structure. He could be more easily demonized when branded a "pest from the Chersonese."

The guards pushed Eumenes forward and prodded him toward Antigonus' camp. A huge throng of onlookers went behind, so great a number that Antigonus, seeing them approach, called up a column of elephants and Median spearmen to disperse them. The two armies were still in a state of war, even if a negotiated stand-down was clearly in the offing. Then Eumenes was put in chains and thrust into a cell under close watch. Antigonus insisted on maximum security—"Guard him as you would a lion or an elephant"—fearful that the man of many wiles would somehow manage another escape. But after a few days he relented and ordered the chains removed. Eumenes' personal servant was allowed to attend him in the cell and his friends to enter and offer comfort.

Antigonus himself did not visit Eumenes. He avoided laying eyes on his adversary after the arrest. Both Plutarch and Justin attribute this to "respect for former friendship," which might mean either that he did not want to shame Eumenes or that he did not want his own compassion stirred up by a face-to-face encounter. For the truth was, now that he had Eumenes in his power, he was finding it hard to destroy him. Though his officers demanded immediate execution, several days went by while Antigonus remained undecided. Antigonus' son, Demetrius, ever his father's closest confidant, stepped forward to plead for Eumenes' life, as did Nearchus of Crete. It seemed entirely possible Antigonus might grant amnesty as he had before, at the siege of Nora, and take Eumenes on as consigliere—an extremely talented one too, as Demetrius no doubt pointed out.

As the debate continued, Eumenes grew perplexed. He asked his keeper, a man named Onomarchus, why Antigonus did not either kill him or set him free. Onomarchus spitefully replied that if Eumenes was so impatient for death, he should have sought it on the battlefield. It was an undeserved reproach, as Eumenes hastened to point out. Whatever else he may have been in his long and morally complex career, he was no coward.

Antigonus turned the question of Eumenes' fate over to his council of senior commanders. These men were adamant in their judgment: if Antigonus pardoned Eumenes, *they* would no longer fight in his service. Even after receiving this ultimatum, Antigonus spent another week in indecision. His army grew seditious. The soldiers, fearing they might be cheated of vengeance, threatened mutiny.

Finally, after more than two weeks, Antigonus made his choice. Perhaps, as the sources represent, he felt compelled by the demands of his soldiers; more likely, he opted for what he thought safest, knowing that a dead Eumenes could never harm him and the message he would send with the execution might do considerable good. He sealed off Eumenes' cell and began denying the prisoner food and water, claiming he did not have the heart to order a violent death. After several days, though, when it was time for the army to break camp and Eumenes had not succumbed, he sent a man to kill him by a silent, and merciful, strangulation.

Thus ended the strangest, longest-odds, least likely bid for power of all those mounted by Alexander's generals. Through sheer talent Eumenes had risen through the ranks; despite his Greek origins, he had come desperately close to gaining supreme power. Few Macedonians liked him or trusted him, but those who

did, including Perdiccas, Olympias, and Alexander the Great, had
done so with all their hearts. In the end, even Antigonus One-eye
seemed to revere him, granting him an honorable cremation and
returning his ashes to his widow. It was just what Eumenes himself had done for Craterus, whose death he had indirectly caused
five years earlier. Eumenes had kept Craterus' ashes ever since,
a burden as heavy as the Macedonian hatred they had brought
him, and as his own death approached, he arranged for the ashes
to be given to the widow Phila, now remarried to Demetrius,
Antigonus' son.

Most of Eumenes' coalition entered the service of Antigonus,
giving the one-eyed general a fantastically potent army. Peucestas
and Teutamus, who in different ways had secured Eumenes'
downfall, both received high appointments, though Peucestas—
whose ambitions were transparent—was also stripped of his power
base in Persis. Coalition leaders who could not be reconciled to
Eumenes' defeat were eliminated. Eudamus the elephant master
was among these, as was another officer, otherwise unknown,
named Celbanus. Antigenes, the captain of the Silver Shields, who
had backed Eumenes on many occasions and had taken no part in
betraying him, received the cruelest death of any who landed on
the wrong side of the succession struggle. One-eye had him
burned alive in a pit.

As for the Silver Shields, who had at Gabene shown all their
qualities in high relief—arrogance, willfulness, and invincible
combat prowess—Antigonus brought their illustrious history to a
close. He felt that the empire, now practically *his* empire, would
be safer without this ungovernable band of supermen. The platoon was broken up, and most of the men were dispatched to
remote garrisons throughout Asia. The most unruly were sent to
Arachosia, what is now eastern Afghanistan and western Pakistan.
The satrap there, Sibyrtius, was given secret orders by Antigonus
to send these men out, in ones and twos, on missions from which
they would never return. Like the man they betrayed, they were
denied the battlefield deaths that would have suited their glorious
careers. Their strength merely seeped away into the dry sands of
the East.

3. OLYMPIAS AND CASSANDER
(PYDNA AND PELLA, WINTER, EARLY 316 B.C.)

Though she was too far from Gabene to know yet what had taken place there, Olympias had suffered a huge setback with Eumenes' defeat and death. During the days that Antigonus had wavered over the Greek's fate, the fate of the royals too was hanging in the balance, for Eumenes was the last general in the field with the ability, and will, to defend them. Perhaps, had Antigonus leaned a hair further toward clemency and taken Eumenes on as consigliere, things might have turned out differently for the Argeads. Eumenes had a gift for argument and persuasion, as well as for deception and manipulation. He might have convinced Antigonus that the united empire could be sustained only under a thriving Argead house. He might have once again erected his magical tent and initiated Antigonus into the cult of Alexander, opening a path toward relief of the conqueror's mother and son.

But as things were, relief was nowhere in sight. The royal family was beginning to starve. The grim logic of warfare by famine was making its inexorable progress through the city of Pydna. Olympias' indomitable will meant that the entire population, combatants and civilians alike, was doomed to see the ordeal through to the end, and the end would be terrible indeed.

The town's meager supplies were stretched to their utmost to permit the survival of the royals and their troops. Enlisted soldiers were allotted about a quart of grain each week, only a few mouthfuls a day. Irregular troops and civilians were given no grain at all. Some survived on butchered horses and pack animals, others on the flesh of those who had already perished. The fodder of the elephants proved the greatest challenge to Pydna's defenders. Desperate not to lose a precious military resource, they sawed up wood and fed sawdust to the wretched beasts, then watched helplessly as they weakened and died.

At last there was no food at all for the soldiers, and with touching deference they asked Olympias for release from service in order to surrender to Cassander. The queen granted their request. There was not much for them to do anyway, except to hoist dead bodies over the walls when these became too numerous to bury.

What comfort could be offered now to the young Alexander as he stared out at the sea, watching for the masts of a rescue fleet? In theory, his power was such that he could command that sea to drain away, leaving a path of escape back to Asia, the place of his birth. But now his circle of empire had shrunk to a walled-up town filled with bloated, stinking corpses. He was surrounded by a thousand shapes of death, barely preserving his own life with a tiny ration of grain. He was not yet seven years old.

Communications with the royal family's two principal generals, Polyperchon and Aristonous, were difficult to maintain behind the siege curtain. Aristonous was ably leading the defense of Amphipolis, a Greek city not far to the east, and had inflicted a severe defeat on Cratevas, the general sent by Cassander to attack him. At last, but too late, Olympias had found a soldier with real skill. Polyperchon, her less competent senior commander, continued to hold out in the mountains west of Macedonia but was unable to make headway. His son Alexander, whose name belied both his talents and his fortunes, was still battling fruitlessly in the Peloponnese, trying to enforce his father's freedom decree. The royalist forces were thus widely scattered, unable to link up with one another or with the Argeads.

As the situation in Pydna grew desperate, Polyperchon devised a plan for the royal family to escape at night in a single warship. He sent a courier to sneak past Cassander's cordon and deliver a letter to Olympias, informing her when and where the ship would land. This man either was caught or abandoned Polyperchon as so many had done; in either case, his message was intercepted and brought to Cassander. An adept at the use of disinformation, Cassander had the message resealed and delivered to Olympias but also seized the warship on its way to the rendezvous. He aimed not merely at preventing Olympias' escape but also at destroying her will to resist. The queen went out at night to meet her rescuers, only to find the beach deserted. Her hopes were crushed. She no longer knew whether Polyperchon, whose seal was on the letter, had gone over to the enemy and was leading her into a trap.

Hunger, despair, and isolation finally conquered the proud will of Olympias. Shortly after the night of the missing warship, she sent envoys and opened negotiations with Cassander for surrender. She had nothing to bargain with yet insisted on receiving a guarantee of her own safety. What arrangements she sought, if any, for the young Alexander are not mentioned in our sources. Perhaps she thought her grandson's chances already so meager that there was no point.

Cassander granted the queen's demand, presumably swearing an oath that she would not be harmed. Despite all the treacheries of the previous six years, the Macedonians still stood by the value of oaths, fundamental buttresses of the social contract. After his recent victory outside Amphipolis, Aristonous had released his defeated enemy, Cratevas, on the strength of his oath that he would not fight again for Cassander. Even Eumenes, master of deceptions and ruses, prided himself on fidelity to oaths; to win release from the fortress at Nora, he had rewritten the oath of Antigonus rather than swear falsely to the original. Olympias thus had reason to trust that Cassander's promise would preserve her life. The same could be said of Aristonous, who, after Cassander likewise guaranteed his safety, agreed to surrender Amphipolis.

But the pledges made to these two prisoners were short-lived. Cassander moved quickly to eliminate Aristonous, fearing that the prestige of a former Bodyguard might stir up resentment against him. He turned Aristonous over to the relatives of Cratevas—ironically, the very man whom Aristonous had spared—for judgment. A death sentence was easily obtained and carried out. This aged veteran, the only one of Alexander's generals who had sought a return to private life, had in the end been drawn back into the power struggle and destroyed by it. There were to be no peaceful retirements for any of Alexander's top staff.

The fate of Olympias proved harder to resolve. In two recent cases where royal women had been killed—Alcetas' murder of Cynnane, and the suicide forced on Adea by Olympias—their murderers had paid a steep political price. Cassander was determined to get a jury to condemn Olympias rather than execute her outright. But he took the precaution of arranging the trial such that Olympias could not speak in her own defense; the relatives of her victims were allowed to address the jury unanswered. Even then, a guilty verdict did not seem assured. In the midst of the proceedings Cassander grew anxious and tried to lure Olympias into an escape attempt, hoping the queen could be killed while fleeing. Olympias, however, did not take the bait.

Finally, after a second trial, or perhaps a resumption of the first, Cassander obtained the death sentence he sought. The question now was how to enforce it. Cassander sent no fewer than two hundred armed troops to the royal residence where Olympias was under house arrest. But the queen put on her finest attire and appeared before them in regal splendor, seemingly unafraid. The men were so awed by the grandeur of the mother of Alexander that they were unable to use their weapons. Cassander found a more hardened crew of assassins, as Justin reports, to run her through with their swords, or else, according to Diodorus, turned her over to the families of her victims for punishment. A third source concurs with Diodorus' version and adds the chilling detail that Olympias was stoned to death.

Olympias died at age fifty-six or fifty-seven. She had exercised more power than any woman in Europe up to her time, with the possible exception of her rival and victim Adea. It was power attained through her son and grandson but exercised, in the final chapter of her life, in her own name and by her own adamantine will. Her hatred of Antipater and his sons had driven her to grotesque acts of violence. In the end her nemeses had won. Cassander took a final revenge on her corpse, casting it out unburied to be ravaged by carrion beasts.

4. RHOXANE, THE YOUNG ALEXANDER, AND CASSANDER (MACEDONIA, SPRING 316 B.C.)

The death of his grandmother meant that the young Alexander was entirely without guardians. His mother, Rhoxane, now his fellow prisoner, could provide nurture but no protection, for she was powerless, as much a hostage to Fortune as her ill-fated son. They were now in custody of Cassander, and we can only guess at how these two regarded him, or he them, during their brief time together. To him, they embodied the most perverse and dangerous tendencies of Alexander the Great: acceptance of things Asian and alien, mixing of races and cultures. To them, he was the murderer of a husband and father, the man who had brought Antipater's poison to Babylon contained in a mule's hoof. It is hard to say which side felt greater hatred for the other.

If it had been risky for Cassander to act against Olympias, the young Alexander was an even more delicate case, a helpless boy and the last slender thread on which the future of the monarchy hung. Apart from the high political cost of killing him, Cassander had reasons for wanting him alive. He did not yet know the outcome of the battle in the East between Antigonus and Eumenes. If Eumenes had won, Cassander would need a hostage to deter an invasion of Europe, or a pawn to trade in some grand, transcontinental power-sharing deal. So for the moment Cassander kept the boy and his mother safe, but stripped them of their entourage and privileges and sent them to Amphipolis under guard of a man named Glaucias. He ordered Glaucias not to treat them as royalty and hoped that his countrymen would cease to so regard them. He had his own plans for the continuation of the Argead house.

Among the prisoners brought out of the devastation at Pydna, Cassander had found Thessalonice, a half sister of Alexander the Great, a daughter of Philip by a Greek woman named Nicesipolis. Somehow Thessalonice had thus far stayed invisible during the succession struggle, despite being unwed and still of childbearing age. Cassander seized on this windfall and immediately married Thessalonice. The match could hardly have brought joy to a woman who, in the siege of Pydna, had stuck by Olympias to the last, but Thessalonice's wishes did not enter into the equation. Olympias' exposed corpse showed that Macedonia's brief experiment with female power was at an end.

Cassander set about begetting heirs. He was determined the monarchy would continue through *him,* not through the line of his father's hated rival Olympias and that of his own great enemy, the man whose portrait bust reportedly caused him to tremble with fear even twenty years later, Alexander the Great.

Cassander's long winning streak held. Thessalonice would bear him three sons in years to come, boys who were at least marginally Argeads and are sometimes shown in the dynasty's genealogical table (more often they are excluded). With the obvious goal of merging his own line with that of his country's most renowned kings, Cassander named these boys Philip, Alexander, and Antipater. Meanwhile, he used his wife's name to christen a city he had founded on Macedonian soil, a token of gratitude for her passivity and her fertility. Today it is the thriving city of Thessaloniki, in northern Greece.

5. PHILIP ARRHIDAEUS AND ADEA EURYDICE (AEGAE)

The Macedonian civil war had ended, for a time. Cassander had eliminated his enemies and secured control of Europe; his ally Antigonus had likewise attained sole sovereignty in Asia. In just a year or two, old patterns of rivalry would reemerge, and these two would go to war with each other, but in the brief calm that followed the cataclysmic violence in the winter of 316, it seemed possible the post-Alexander world might stabilize and begin to heal.

During this hiatus, Cassander honored the dead monarchs Philip and Adea with a lavish royal burial. Olympias, their killer, had denied them proper rites and perhaps (our sources are unclear) had even exposed their corpses. Cassander now cremated their bodies, or what was left of them, according to time-honored rituals and had the ashes interred in a magnificent tomb in the royal cemetery at Aegae. According to one report, he reburied with them Cynnane, the mother of Adea, whose body must also have lacked royal honors following her murder years earlier. Cassander staged funeral games to honor the dead, including single combats between armed soldiers. He had sacrifices performed atop the sealed tomb, then covered it over with earth.

Many believe it is this tomb that the archaeologist Manolis Andronikos found in November 1977, buried at the center of the Great Tumulus in the Greek village of Vergina. With unintended ambiguity, Andronikos called his discovery "Philip's Tomb," thinking it belonged to Philip II, father of Alexander the Great; the young woman in the antechamber he identified as the last of that king's seven wives. But others soon tried to correlate the tomb with a different Philip, Philip III, and his wife, Adea. They claim

that the bones in the tomb had undergone "dry" cremation, after
the collagen inside had already broken down—that is, after Cassander recovered the bodies from wherever Olympias had stowed
them.

The attribution of the tomb to Philip III is far from certain.
To accept it is to believe that Cassander buried awesome symbols
of power with a king who, in life, was utterly powerless. For in
Tomb 2 were found a silver diadem and a scepter, perhaps the very
ones once used by Alexander the Great, and magnificent armor
and weaponry of every kind—gear that Philip III could have
wielded only in hollow mimicry. Indeed this very incongruity
helped convince Andronikos that "Philip's Tomb" could not
belong to Philip III but must be that of his glorious father, Philip
II. It strained credulity that a nonentity, a mentally disabled man
who was the mere tool of Alexander's generals and of his own
wife, had received the most lavish burial ever uncovered in the
Aegean world.

Perhaps, though, it was the monarchy itself that Cassander
was burying, not merely the remains of a monarch. Scepters and
diadems, after all, are normally not interred with their owners but
passed on as dynastic emblems. Indeed this particular diadem was

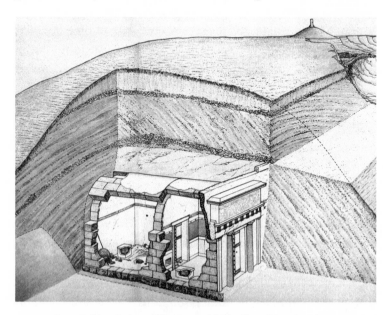

An artist's rendering of Tomb 2 inside the Great Tumulus, Aegae

designed so that its diameter could be adjusted, as though a series of kings, each with a differently sized head, was destined to wear it. But Cassander did not want such continuities, or links to Alexander the Great. Objects that evoked that dreaded specter were best hidden from view, or so it must have seemed to a man who had killed the king's mother, who was suspected of killing Alexander himself, and who was now contemplating the murder of the king's eight-year-old son, the last of the Argeads, Alexander IV.

6. RHOXANE AND THE YOUNG ALEXANDER (MACEDONIA AND AMPHIPOLIS, 316–308 B.C.)

The Greek city of Amphipolis, in the wintry land of Thrace, was the last home Rhoxane and her son would occupy. Together this tempest-tossed pair had been conveyed through the whole of western Asia, into Egypt, across the Hellespont to Europe, and through many parts of Greece and the Balkan lands, in the care of seven successive guardians. In the end they became all too settled. For six years or more, they did not leave their castle keep. Under the fiction that they were merely sequestered until Alexander came of age, they had become Cassander's prisoners.

Nothing is known of their life in Amphipolis, except that they were denied royal privileges. One would hope they enjoyed a peaceful and companionable retreat from the world, like that which Lear envisions for himself and Cordelia: "Come, let's away to prison. We two alone will sing like birds i' th' cage." Perhaps they were glad to be out of the power struggle, though the power struggle would not leave them be. Only a year after their sequestration, Antigonus One-eye, already at odds with Cassander and his other former allies, swore he would cross over from Asia to Europe, release the pair from Amphipolis, and restore their royal rights. Whether he really planned to champion the monarchy, or was only seeking a pretext for invasion, his vows came to nothing. Rhoxane and Alexander went on as before, living as private citizens rather than royalty, their guard Glaucias their closest companion.

Alexander grew up and reached puberty. The idea that he was

king and would someday rule was still widely promoted, though how widely believed is hard to know. Four leading generals signed a treaty in 311, when Alexander was twelve, agreeing to give up power as soon as the young king took the throne. Scribes across Asia dated documents by the year of Alexander's reign (though they sometimes shifted over to Antigonus, or later to Seleucus, as their reference points). Coins in certain Greek cities were minted bearing the legend "BASILEOS ALEXANDROU," "King Alexander's" currency.

What was Cassander waiting for? Or what prompted him finally to act? There were no known pressures on him, except that Alexander was getting ever closer to majority. Probably that alone was enough. An order was sent to Glaucias to do away with the mother and son but not to let their deaths or their bodies be discovered. Glaucias preserved his mission's secrecy so well that the date of Alexander's and Rhoxane's deaths is not even known. The boy was either thirteen or fourteen at the time, Rhoxane perhaps thirty. According to a report, they were poisoned.

Cassander did not desecrate the remains of Alexander, as he had earlier done the body of Olympias, and as Olympias had done the remains of Cassander's brother Iolaus. The enmity between the two most powerful families in Europe had at last run its course, though only after the total destruction of one by the other. Enough stability had returned to Macedonia that civilized norms could resume. After the death of the young king became common knowledge, Cassander prepared a fine chamber tomb in Aegae for his victim, the structure discovered by Andronikos in 1979 and labeled by him the Prince's Tomb. An illustrated frieze, now entirely lost, was placed over the entrance, and a colorful scene of racing chariots was painted all around the walls of the antechamber. It was an apt motif, for what teenage boy does not love the sight of racing chariots?

The body of Alexander was cremated and the ashes placed in a silver vessel, a hydria, typically used for pouring water—an unusual ossuary, more modest than the two gold boxes in Philip's Tomb. A purple cloth was draped over charred remains, and the vessel was sealed. Around its shoulders was hung a delicate wreath of oak leaves and acorns, all wrought of fine gold. Then the vessel

The silver hydria containing the last remains of Alexander IV

was placed in a hollow space inside a kind of stone table, perhaps an altar. Gilded weapons, fine clothing, and silver tableware of all kinds were laid on the floor around the dead monarch. These were the trappings of royalty Cassander had stripped from him in life, now restored in death.

A marble door between the antechamber and main tomb was closed and sealed. A sacrifice was held on the roof of the building, as though to a god. Then the whole structure was covered with earth, just as the tombs adjoining it had been covered. The dead king would have no visitors, in contrast to his mummified father, by this time housed in the Sema at Alexandria, a shrine designed by Ptolemy for throngs of pilgrims to enter and stand amazed.

It was perhaps forty years later, after invaders had vandalized much of the royal burial ground, that the mound covering the Aegae tombs was itself buried under the Great Tumulus. Hundreds of workers heaped on thousands of tons of earth, clay, sand, and gravel, not to hide the tombs but to make them forever inaccessible. The Macedonians were resolved to protect the successors of Alexander the Great, even if that meant never seeing again the beautiful buildings that sheltered them. They would at least know that somewhere at the heart of the mound, wrapped in purples and encased in gold and silver, the bones of the last Argeads lay at peace, in darkness and silence. Absent the corpse of Alexander himself, these were all that remained to them of the monarchy that had made them masters of the world.

Epilogue

The slow-motion execution of Alexander the Great's family required one or two more years to complete. Once the death of the young Alexander was known for certain, two surviving members of his family, both long sidelined from the succession struggle, suddenly came into prominence once again. It was clear now that they preserved the last, slim hopes of the survival of the Argead house.

The boy named Heracles, fathered by Alexander the Great perhaps a decade before his death but never acknowledged by him, had grown up untouched by politics. He lived a quiet life with his mother, the half-Persian, half-Greek noblewoman Barsine, in the city of Pergamon. Only once had he been mentioned as a possible heir to the throne, in Babylon on the day after Alexander's death, and that suggestion had been quickly dismissed. But as Alexander's only living descendant, he could not have stayed out of the power struggle forever. It was only a matter of time before one of the generals used him to advance his cause. As luck would have it, the first to do so was the one least apt to succeed, the hapless former regent Polyperchon.

Polyperchon had survived the defeat of his coalition partners, Olympias and Aristonous, and had gone to Asia to join with Antigonus One-eye. In 309 or 308, Polyperchon, now past seventy, made one final bid to knock his old enemy Cassander out of power in Macedon. He summoned Heracles, then in his late teens, from the seclusion of Pergamon and brought him to

Europe, after writing ahead to his former allies to revive the royalist cause. They lined up an army of more than twenty thousand in Europe to await Heracles' arrival.

The power of the Argead name was still strong in Macedonia, and Cassander had reason to be concerned. He took his own forces to meet Polyperchon's on Macedonia's borders, and there, as the armies prepared for battle, he offered a bargain to his enemy: if Polyperchon would murder Heracles, Cassander promised to make him a firm ally and bestow high honors and office upon him. Polyperchon accepted the deal.

Plutarch records a chilling account of the assassination, though there is no way to gauge its veracity. Polyperchon invited Heracles to a dinner party, an ominous move on the eve of a battle. Heracles was suspicious and came up with a pretext to avoid attending. Polyperchon sent a message that he knew could not fail to sway the boy: "Young man, the first thing you should learn from your father is how to be adaptable, and how to oblige your friends." Heracles came to the dinner, ate well, and was strangled to death.

Cassander had Heracles' body buried secretly so as not to arouse an outcry. Then he gave Polyperchon an inglorious position as major general in the Peloponnese. It was a small prize Polyperchon had won in return for the irrevocable extinction of the Argeads. Presumably, he did little in his new post or did not live much longer, for our sources know nothing more of him.

At around the same time as Heracles' death came that of Cleopatra, Alexander the Great's sister. She had remained at Sardis, a widow separated from her children, for more than a decade following her journey there in pursuit of marriage to Perdiccas. Her adoptive home had long since come under the control of Antigonus, a general whose interests were not served by her survival. Even so, she lived on, perhaps under some kind of house arrest, a mere spectator of the struggle to dominate her brother's empire. She and Antigonus seem to have struck some sort of bargain, for she had not attempted to marry any of his rivals, nor had he attempted to marry *her*.

While she remained a virtual prisoner in Sardis, Cleopatra's fertile years slipped away. At the time her two nephews, Heracles

Alexander wearing elephant-skin headgear, as depicted on Ptolemy's coinage,
starting in 321 B.C.

and the young Alexander, were killed, she was already in her late
forties. She was past childbearing but could still perhaps lend
royal stature to any general she married. It was this prospect that
led Ptolemy, lord of Egypt, to seek her hand, and in 308, for some
unknown reason, she accepted his offer and attempted to leave for
Alexandria.

A city official in Sardis reported her plans to Antigonus. One-
eye immediately sent his agents—women in this case, perhaps to
avoid arousing Cleopatra's suspicions—to kill her. Then, just as
Cassander had done for the young Alexander, he provided her
with a magnificent funeral and tomb, and executed the assassins
he himself had hired.

The end of the Argeads brought the first era of the post-
Alexander world to a close. The contest for power among Alexander's generals would continue and would be passed on to their
sons and grandsons. But the question of succession had at last
been answered. Legitimate monarchy was dead; sovereignty
henceforth would indeed belong "to the strongest," to those who
had the military muscle and bravado to *make* themselves kings.
Within a few years Antigonus, Ptolemy, Lysimachus, Seleucus,
and Cassander had done just that, placing crowns on their own
heads, creating five royal dynasties to replace the one they had
lost.

The diaspora of Alexander the Great's power became irreversible with the near-simultaneous deaths of Eumenes and Olympias. The empire broke up into parts that were kept in balance by the jealousies and suspicions of the men who ruled them. Whenever one seemed to be gaining in strength or ambition, the others banded together to counterweight him. A new political order had emerged, not at all the world-state that Alexander had hoped for and planned but a multipolar world marked by rivalry, shifting alliances, and long-running small-scale conflicts—in many ways, a world like our own.

EUROPE

Danube R.

Black Sea

CASSANDER
Macedonia
LYSIMACHUS
Pella

Epirus

Thrace

Aegean
Hellespont

Thebes
Sparta
Athens
Sea

Sardis
Celaenae
Phrygia
Cappadocia

Cilicia

Mediterranean Sea

Euphrates R.
Tigris R.

Cyrene

Phoenicia

Opis

Babylon

Alexandria

Arabian Desert

Shrine of
Ammon
Egypt
Memphis

Libyan Desert

PTOLEMY

Nile R.

AFRICA

Red Sea

The Breakup of Alexander's Empire
c. 315 B.C.
showing territories controlled by the leading generals

ASIA
Sogdiana
Zariaspa
Bactria
Hindu Kush
ANTIGONUS
Persepolis
Gedrosia
India
Indus R.
Hyphasis R.
CHANDRAGUPTA
MAURYA
Gulf
Arabian Sea
0 km
500 km
0 miles
500 miles

Notes

Preface

xiii *"Diadochs":* The word has ancient authority as a proper noun used to designate the group of men who competed for power after Alexander's death; it appears once in Diodorus' history.

xiv *valid evidence:* The best recent review of the welter of chronological data for this period is Wheatley's "Introduction" (in the bibliography under "Chronological Problems").

xiv *recently proposed hybrid:* Boiy's chronology, which he claims is "between high and low," is laid out in the book whose title begins with that phrase, listed under "Chronological Problems" in the bibliography.

xvi *perhaps even his kinsman:* Eumenes' father was also named Hieronymus, and since names in the Greek world tend to run in families, it has been thought that Eumenes and Hieronymus were somehow related.

xvi *Modern historians:* See especially Bosworth, "History and Artifice" (in the bibliography under "Eumenes").

Introduction: The Opening of the Tombs

3 *"Be as calm as possible":* The quotation, and other details of the discovery of Tomb 2 at Vergina, are taken from Andronikos' own description in "Regal Treasures."

7 *one leading theory:* The attribution of the tomb to Philip III and his wife, rather than to Philip II and *his* wife, has been gaining support in recent years and was vigorously defended by a panel of experts at the January 2008 meeting of the Archaeological Institute of America. Eugene Borza and Olga Palagia, the leading proponents of the theory, have summarized their arguments in "Chronology of the Macedonian Royal Tombs at Vergina." The attribution to Philip II, however, first asserted by Andronikos, is still supported by many Greek and some European and American scholars (most recently by Ian Worthington in *Philip II of*

Macedonia, New Haven, 2009, app. 6). The bibliography on the subject is vast, and can best be accessed through the article by Borza and Palagia.

7 *one expert judged:* The paleoanthropologist Antonis Bartsiokas reported evidence of "dry" cremation in "The Eye Injury of King Philip II and the Skeletal Evidence from the Royal Tomb II at Vergina," *Science* 228 (2000), pp. 511–14. His conclusions have been accepted by some scholars, but just as this book was nearing completion, a challenge was mounted by a team led by Jonathan Musgrave; their arguments appeared in the *International Journal of Medical Sciences* for 2010, http://www .medsci.org/v07p0051.htm. The debate is likely to continue for some time, since it can be conducted only by experts in forensic pathology and these disagree among themselves.

Chapter 1: Bodyguards and Companions

8 *their thoughts went back:* The recollection is reported by Arrian (*Anabasis* 7.18.6).

9 *an interloper never seen before:* The episode of the stranger who took the throne is recounted in different versions by several ancient writers. Arrian (*Anabasis* 7.24.1–3) reports that the man was tortured by Alexander and claimed only to have acted on a whim. Diodorus (17.116) says that the man refused to explain his actions, while Plutarch (*Alexander* 73.6–74.1) says he attributed his act to the promptings of Serapis. Both Diodorus and Plutarch say Alexander had the man killed.

10 *Belshazzar, his descendant:* The feast of Belshazzar is described in the Old Testament book of Daniel 5.

10 *The prophecy came to pass:* According to a curious tale related by the Jewish historian Josephus, Alexander was shown the passage from the book of Daniel on the occasion of his visit to Jerusalem and interpreted it as referring to his own conquest of the Persian empire (*Jewish Antiquities* 11.8.5).

10 *"To the strongest":* The word *kratistos* in the saying, as reported by Arrian (*Anabasis* 7.26.3) and Diodorus (17.117.4), is usually translated "strongest" but can also mean "best," and indeed Diodorus elsewhere quotes the same saying with a different word, *aristos,* unambiguously meaning "best" (18.1.4). Quintus Curtius uses the Latin word *optimus,* "best," in his version of the story (10.5.5).

11 *the Babylonians welcomed him:* Their exuberance at the arrival of Alexander is most fully described by Quintus Curtius 5.1.17–23. The Persian-appointed governor of the city, Mazaeus, took the lead in switching sides.

13 *Perhaps he began to believe himself:* Alexander's own beliefs about his divine nature are probably unrecoverable, but we do know that his troops twitted him about his descent from Ammon (see Arrian's *Anabasis* 7.8.3) and that, in the last year of his life, several Greek cities were debating a proposal to grant him the rites appropriate to a god (see p. 74).

13 *they reached their breaking point:* I follow the traditional understanding of the events at the river Hyphasis. An alternate theory that the so-called mutiny was in fact a staged event designed to allow Alexander to reverse course without losing face has recently been advanced and is to my mind unconvincing.

14 *Panic seized the army:* The details that follow are taken from Arrian, *Anabasis* 6.12–13, where it is clear that Alexander needed to take extraordinary measures to calm his own troops. Quintus Curtius, by contrast, stresses his need to make a show of his strength to the surrounding hostile peoples (9.6.1).

15 *On the seventeenth of the Macedonian month Daisios:* The date is arrived at by starting from the date of Alexander's death, generally agreed (on Plutarch's testimony) to be Daisios 28, and counting backward by the days of illness Arrian records in *Anabasis* 7.25–26, apparently eleven (though the text is somewhat unclear). Plutarch, however, has a different count of sick days, and records the date of the first sign of illness as Daisios 18 rather than 17 (*Alexander* 76.1).

15 *the first of June 323 B.C.:* This date has been arrived at by another backward count, starting from the date of Alexander's death, which has been fixed at June 11 by the use of a Babylonian astronomical text (see Depuydt, "Time of Death of Alexander the Great"), and again reckoning Arrian's illness days at eleven. It is not possible to make hard-and-fast correlations between Greco-Macedonian dates like Daisios 18 and modern ones. Peter Green uses a different set of modern dates from mine in *Alexander of Macedon*, pp. 473–75, in part because at the time he wrote, the Babylonian text in question was thought to indicate a date of June 10; the interpretation has since changed.

15 *their rock-solid loyalty to Alexander:* In portraying the Bodyguards as a cadre loyal to Alexander, I am clearly rejecting the hypothesis that they collectively acted to bring about his death, either by poisoning him (asserted by Bosworth in "Death of Alexander") or by denying him moral support or medical attention (Atkinson's scenario in "Alexander's Death"). The evidence supporting a broad conspiracy is very slim. Only one ancient document, the *Last Days and Testament* (preserved as part of the *Liber de Morte*), indicts a large number of insiders in a murder plot, but the testimony of such an otherwise unreliable text is nearly worthless. Conspiracy theories have always flourished after the sudden demise of a great leader. The question in Alexander's case, to my mind, comes down to this: Would an aristocracy that had never known any system but hereditary monarchy, recognizing that its king had no viable heir, take a blind leap into the unknown by committing regicide? To answer yes, one could have to assume that Alexander had become so unstable as to make the status quo unbearable (a situation like that which prompted the Praetorian Guard at Rome to assassinate Caligula). I see no grounds for this assumption, even if Alexander was undeniably impetuous and prone to suspicions in his final year. The Bodyguards and other insiders could

never have imagined that their fortunes would be improved by his death. There are better grounds for thinking that a small number of outsiders, Europe-based generals like Antipater and Cassander (always the ancient world's prime suspects, as I discuss later), killed Alexander to prevent him from taking the Asianization of the empire any further, but even this hypothesis cannot be supported by evidence, despite the assertion by Adrienne Mayor ("Deadly Styx River") that the river from which Antipater was said to have collected his poison may in fact have contained toxic bacteria.

16 *a man perhaps a few years older:*   There is no firm evidence for the date of Ptolemy's birth. It is often given as 367 B.C. on the basis of one very dubious ancient report (Pseudo-Lucian *Macrobioi* 12), but many historians feel that the relationship between Ptolemy and Alexander seems to be that of two men close in age. Helmut Berve dated Ptolemy's birth not earlier than 360, making him no more than four years Alexander's senior.

16 *legend later reported:*   Diodorus 17.103 and Quintus Curtius 9.8.22–27.

16 *Perdiccas was perhaps a few years older:*   There is no evidence at all on which to date Perdiccas' birth, but it seems probable he was in his twenties, as Berve speculates, at the time of Philip's assassination.

17 *Greeks were a kindred but foreign race:*   The question of the Greekness of the Macedonians is a vexed one, both in classical scholarship and in modern Balkan politics. I make no claims here that the Macedonians were, or were not, a branch of the Greek people, as I think the evidence is not decisive. But at many points in the ancient accounts of Alexander's army, both before and after the king's death, it is clear that Greeks were regarded by the Macedonians as a separate race. Many Greeks believed the same about the Macedonians, though there were also some, like Isocrates the Athenian, who endorsed the Greekness of the Macedonian royal house—not the entire people—in order to advance a political agenda.

17 *then took his hand, shedding tears of relief:*   Recounted by Arrian in his chronicle of Nearchus' voyage, *Indica,* chap. 35.

17 *Philip had simply liked the look of the boy:*   Perhaps this is only a legend contrived to highlight Eumenes' humble origins, like the even more dubious report that Eumenes' father was a wagon driver or a funeral musician (both found in Plutarch *Eumenes* 1). Anson, in *Eumenes of Cardia,* assumes that Eumenes could only have found his way into Philip's employ had he belonged to a noble and well-connected family.

17 *In India, Eumenes received:*   The episode is recounted by Plutarch *Eumenes* 2, and possibly referred to by Arrian, *Anabasis* 7.13.

18 *appointing Eumenes as commander:*   Plutarch *Eumenes* 1.5. The appointment is not discussed in any of the Alexander histories, and nothing they tell us adequately accounts for it.

19 *In the royal pavilion he set up in Persis:*   Described by Ephippus of Olynthus, as quoted by Athenaeus 12.53.

20 *probably to the little Summer Palace:*   The movements of Alexander

through Babylon in June 323, and later the location of his corpse, though reported only vaguely by Arrian and Plutarch, have been reconstructed in detail by Schachermeyr in the first four chapters of *Alexander in Babylon*.

21 *Rumors circulating at the time of Alexander's death:* The evidence for these is discussed in Chapter 7, section 5.

22 *Eumenes himself might have tampered with it:* This is the hypothesis of Bosworth in "Alexander's Death."

23 *Rauxsnaka:* The spelling used by Holt in "Alexander the Great's Little Star," p. 32. "Roshanak" is often given as the Persian version of her name.

23 *Rhoxane had become pregnant:* The first child born to Alexander by Rhoxane is known to us only from an obscure source, the *Metz Epitome,* chap. 70.

23 *no doubt fictionalized:* Already in the second century A.D., Arrian mocked the story as an invention (*Anabasis* 7.27.3).

24 *learning high classical Greek:* Diodorus 17.67.1.

24 *Craterus was not happy:* As related on p. 126, Craterus later detached himself from Amastris and married instead a daughter of Antipater's. It seems that in Macedonian society only the king was allowed the privilege of polygamy (see Ogden, *Polygamy, Prostitutes and Death*).

25 *Craterus revered his king:* At some point during the Asian campaign Craterus evidently aided Alexander during a lion hunt, and Plutarch says (*Alexander* 40) that he dedicated a sculpture at Delphi commemorating this moment of shared peril. The dedicatory inscription of the monument shows that it was in fact set up by Craterus' son after Craterus' death. The mosaic seen at Pella today of two men hunting a lion is often thought to represent Alexander and Craterus but probably does not.

25 *The stalwart Craterus:* Craterus' exclusion from the award ceremony is an extrapolation from Arrian *Anabasis* 7.5.4–6, where the recipients of crowns are carefully listed, but Craterus' name does not appear.

27 *who carried lighter gear:* The weapons and armor of the Hypaspists cannot be deduced from either literary or archaeological evidence. Most scholars infer from their movements in battle that these soldiers were more lightly armed than the phalanx troops.

27 *the Silver Shields:* It is not certain whether this name, *Argyraspides* in Greek, arose in Alexander's lifetime or only afterward, but Arrian suggests it was in use before 324 (*Anabasis* 7.11.3). It is fairly certain that it applies to what was once the corps called Shield Bearers; see Anson, "Alexander's Hypaspists and the Argyraspids," and Heckel, "Career of Antigenes."

28 *Among them were the Silver Shields:* The departure from Opis of this elite unit can be inferred from their later presence in Perdiccas' army in Egypt; see Heckel, "Career of Antigenes," and Hammond, "Alexander's Veterans After His Death."

28 *many years' pay:* Information about what Macedonian recruits were paid is scarce. It appears that Shield Bearers received thirty drachmas per month and "double-pay men" sixty. At that rate a "double-pay man" would earn a talent in about eight and a half years.

28 *had their salary increased:* At 7.23.3 of the *Anabasis*, Arrian speaks of "ten-*stater* men" in the new Macedonian phalanx, and some historians think he refers to gold staters rather than silver, putting the pay rate of such troops at two hundred drachmas per month—more than a fivefold increase over their probable starting rates. Arrian also appears to report at 7.8.1 that Alexander explicitly promised to reward the troops who stayed with him in Babylon, though most editors delete a word from the Greek text here so that the reward instead goes to those leaving.

29 *probably few of them did:* It is often asserted that Alexander's men longed to return to Europe, but there is little evidence that this was so. In the mutiny at the Hyphasis, in Arrian's account, the mutineer Coenus described the troops as yearning for families and homelands (*Anabasis* 5.26.6), but this speech is generally acknowledged to be a fabrication playing on popular rhetorical themes. At Opis, the troops rejected the plan to send many of them home, and after Alexander's death, as will be seen throughout this book, few Macedonians returned to Europe; those who did often set off again for Asia.

29 *Alternatively, he might have realized:* There seems no good grounds on which to choose between these nearly opposite interpretations (Schachermeyr, *Alexander in Babylon*, p. 70).

31 *Argaeus was warned:* The story is related by Justin (7.2), who adds that the Macedonians later believed that Alexander's burial outside Aegae had violated this injunction.

32 *Argaeus' father had been an exile:* The flight from Argos of Perdiccas I and his brothers, and their seizure of the Macedonian throne, are related by Herodotus 8.137–39.

32 *regard it as propaganda:* Gene Borza summarizes the consensus of recent opinion in "Greek and Macedonian Ethnicity," pp. 333–6 of *The Landmark Arrian* (ed. J. Romm, NY, 2010): "Like other ancient peoples, the Macedonians (or their ruling house) created a foundation mythology designed to suit contemporary needs—in this case, to forge closer political and cultural links with the Greeks."

33 *In some of his last instructions:* The burial request is reported by Quintus Curtius (10.5.4) and Diodorus (18.3.5). Their version of Alexander's death is obviously out of harmony with that of Arrian and Plutarch, who say the king had by this time lost the power of speech. There is no clear way to resolve such divergences, but Curtius' report gains in credibility when one considers that no one in the post-Alexander world had a motive to invent it. A full discussion can be found in the first section of Badian's "King's Notebooks."

Chapter 2: The Testing of Perdiccas

34 *he passed to his senior Bodyguard:* The story is related by the three so-called vulgate sources, Diodorus (17.117.3), Quintus Curtius (10.5.4), and

Justin (12.15.12), but not by Arrian or Plutarch, and hence some suspect its authenticity; see Badian's discussion in "The Ring and the Book," for example.

34 *the post of chiliarch:* I refer here to the office sometimes called the equestrian chiliarchy and not to the court chiliarchy, the Macedonian equivalent of the Persian post of vizier, a separate office (see Andrew Collins, "The Office of Chiliarch Under Alexander and the Successors," *Phoenix* 55 [2001], pp. 259–83). The overlap of the names, and the fact that Hephaestion apparently held both offices at once, has created much confusion, and I have tried to reduce this by not using the term "chiliarch" to refer to the vizier or court chiliarch, the administrative head of the empire. It is possible that by handing his ring to Perdiccas, Alexander meant to appoint his equestrian chiliarch to the court chiliarchy, again making one man the holder of both offices as Hephaestion had been.

35 *One ancient source:* The unnamed authors cited by Arrian at *Anabasis* 6.11.1, the only report we have of this version of events. Plutarch, in the second of his two essays titled "On the Fortune or Virtue of Alexander," gives a detailed account of the efforts to aid the wounded Alexander, but the essay ends abruptly, seemingly broken off, before naming the man who extracted the arrowhead.

35 *flipping it back:* Attested by Suidas' Greek lexicon, in the entry on Leonnatus (information thought to be derived from Arrian's *Events After Alexander* and therefore included in Roos' edition of that work).

36 *had kept them in a careful equipoise:* The point is made forcefully by Heckel in "Politics of Distrust." Alexander was wary throughout his campaign of challenges from within his ranks, but especially after 330, when a high-ranking officer named Philotas appeared to have conspired against his life.

36 *"They were so equal":* The passage is at 13.1.10. It is unclear whether the sentiment comes from Justin or from the author whose text he is summarizing, Pompeius Trogus.

36 *Alexander had been dragged:* The description that follows is taken principally from Plutarch's second essay titled "On the Fortune or Virtue of Alexander" (*Moralia* 345). It does not entirely cohere with other accounts, including that of Plutarch himself in the *Life of Alexander.*

37 *could be killed:* Plutarch reports that Alexander killed Glaucias, the doctor who was attending Hephaestion at the time of his death.

37 *a Roman statesman:* I assume, along with most scholars, that the Quintus Curtius who wrote *History of Alexander the Great* is the same person as the senator and consul Curtius Rufus discussed by Tacitus (*Annals* 1.20.3–21.3).

37 *to see Roman patterns:* At 10.9.1–6, Curtius explicitly contrasts the experience of the Macedonians, whose empire was wrecked by lack of leadership, with that of the Romans in the era of the principate. Paul McKechnie has documented the case against Curtius in "Manipulation

of Themes in Quintus Curtius Rufus Book 10," *Historia* 48 (1999), pp. 44–60, arguing against the position of Errington in "From Babylon to Triparadeisos." Elizabeth Baynham has also done much to reveal Curtius' shortcomings in *Alexander the Great: The Unique History of Quintus Curtius* (Ann Arbor, Mich., 1998).

38 *Alexander's top naval officer, spoke next:* The order of speakers and the content of their speeches are reported differently by Justin and Quintus Curtius. I have here followed the very convincing amalgam of the two made by Bosworth in the first chapter of *Legacy of Alexander.*

38 *accompanying the army:* There is no evidence of Arrhidaeus' activities during the Asian campaign until this moment, but presumably he had stayed in Alexander's entourage throughout. Alexander would not have left his half brother at home in Macedonia, where he might serve as a rallying point for his rivals.

39 *this seems a Roman fantasy:* Curtius had lived through the succession dramas at Rome following the deaths of Augustus and Caligula, and the memories of these seem to have influenced his account of the Babylon crisis. The urgency with which Alexander's generals would later seek a royal bride shows that the throne was off-limits to any who were not part of the Argead house.

40 *a task that by custom:* The role of the assembled army in the selection of monarchs is a matter of dispute among scholars, and unfortunately most of the evidence comes from the post-Alexander era. Most agree that even before this point the Macedonians summoned an army assembly to acclaim a new monarch, at the least; some would give the assembly greater powers.

41 *on several occasions:* As mentioned by Plutarch at *Eumenes* 6.3, though unfortunately without elaboration.

41 *Years before, in India:* The episode is described by Curtius (8.12.17–18) and also referred to obliquely by Plutarch (*Alexander* 59.5).

43 *A full-scale battle loomed:* Curtius (10.7.18) even reports that javelins were hurled within the throne room and wounds were incurred, though this is not confirmed by other sources.

44 *Meleager explained to King Philip:* This exchange, and the details of the arrest attempt and its aftermath, are described by Curtius (10.8.1–7).

44 *like a hollow sham:* The atmosphere among the mutineers is vividly described by Curtius 10.8.8–9.

45 *an impassioned speech:* The content of the address is preserved by Justin 13.3.9–10.

46 *a paralytic state:* The grim suggestion was first made, to my knowledge, by N. G. L. Hammond in *Alexander the Great: King, Commander, and Statesman,* 2nd ed. (London, 1989), p. 305 n. 174. Dr. David W. Oldach of the University of Maryland School of Medicine gave "ascending paralysis" as part of his diagnosis of Alexander's death, largely on the basis of the report of non-putrefaction ("A Mysterious Death," *New England Journal of Medicine* 338, no. 24 [June 11, 1998], p. 1766).

48 *a further stratagem:* This episode and the lustration that follows are described by Curtius 10.9.7–19.

49 *thirty staunchest supporters:* The manuscripts of Curtius actually give the number three hundred, but this is often changed to the more plausible thirty by editors of the Latin text. In the Greek texts on which Curtius was relying, the difference of a decimal place would be indicated by a single small slash, easily misread or miswritten by scribes.

50 *one, more likely both:* Plutarch says the victims were Stateira and "the sister," which if correct would mean Stateira and Drypetis, Hephaestion's widow. But he may have gotten his genealogy confused and referred to Parysatis, Stateira's cousin and close friend, as her sister. That at least is the view of Carney in *Women and Monarchy.*

51 *History knows the pair:* The custom of assigning Roman numerals to kings who bear the same name arose in medieval England. The ancient world distinguished such kings by the use of patronymics, for example, "Alexander son of Philip."

51 *It was resolved:* There is no clear information as to how the idea of the satrapal division arose. Diodorus (18.2.4) indicates it came from the general will of the army; Curtius (10.10.1) says that a meeting of the leadership, convened by Perdiccas, resolved on this step, and also notes that some of his sources claimed that the dead Alexander had called for it in his will (10.10.5). It is also unclear whether the Bodyguards wanted to leave Babylon to become satraps or were coerced into doing so; I have assumed the former, in contrast to Bosworth (*Legacy of Alexander,* pp. 57–58).

52 *Ptolemy wanted Egypt:* Again, my assumption is that the distribution of the satrapies was desired by the Bodyguards, not forced on them (see previous note), but this cannot be proved. Under this scenario, Ptolemy, as most powerful Bodyguard after Perdiccas, would have demanded the best satrapy, which was undoubtedly Egypt. Another view, however, regards Ptolemy's appointment to Egypt as a kind of banishment inflicted by Perdiccas.

55 *some modern scholars:* The debate over the authenticity of the last plans can best be followed in the discussion by Brian Bosworth, in chapter 8 of *From Arrian to Alexander: Studies in Historical Interpretation* (Oxford, 1988). Bosworth himself believes the plans are genuine.

55 *wanted these plans quashed:* The intention of Perdiccas to void the plans, and his fear of arbitrarily contravening the wishes of Alexander, are both reported by Diodorus (18.4.2–3). The plans themselves are reported by Diodorus at 18.4.4–5, our only source for them.

56 *Most were never contemplated again:* I say "most" because of the possibility that the Great Tumulus at Aegae, a vast mound of earth covering tombs that may well include that of Alexander's father, was built as a fulfillment of the king's last plan to memorialize Philip with a tomb greater than the pyramids. The excavator of the mound, Manolis Andronikos, made this suggestion in his book *Vergina* (p. 229).

Chapter 3: The Athenians' Last Stand (I)

57 *had defined themselves:* Some scholars reject the idea that Athenian politicians in the age of Alexander were defined primarily as "pro-" or "anti-Macedonian," or even the idea that political parties in the modern sense existed in Athens (see especially Hansen, *Athenian Democracy,* chap. 11). I do not mean to reduce Athenian politics to a two-party system, but I think it is beyond question that policy toward Macedon was the central issue of the day and that positions of political leaders were defined by the two poles of opposition and collaboration.

58 *would have been first:* Plutarch relates that Demosthenes came forward to speak in the Assembly when none else would, in the dreadful moment in 339 when the city first realized it faced attack by Philip (*Demosthenes* 18.1–2).

59 *green Athenian recruits:* Though Lycurgus had instituted an obligatory two-year training for military-age Athenian youths, and a whole generation had been through that training by 323 B.C., there had been no land warfare during that time in which the army could gain experience of battle. Philip seems to have played on their inexperience at Chaeronea, feigning a retreat that drew them into a disorderly advance, then suddenly reversing course and attacking.

59 *the League:* Often called the League of Corinth by modern historians (but not by ancient sources), after the place where its regular meetings were held. Macedonia in theory only enforced League decisions, but in practice controlled them, largely by the installation of pro-Macedonian regimes in the cities that made up the League.

60 *who had often agitated:* In the aftermath of Philip's victory at Chaeronea in 338, when the Macedonians were in fact showing no signs of planning to invade Attica, Hyperides embarrassed himself by proposing measures in the Assembly for full-scale siege preparations.

60 *Demosthenes regarded:* The efforts of Demosthenes to de-Hellenize the Macedonian kings are evident in many of his speeches (the quotation here is from the *Third Philippic*). Some Athenians, however, including the political essayist Isocrates, defended the claim to Greekness of the Argead royal house. The debate goes back long before Alexander: around 500 B.C., a Macedonian king tried to win entry into the Olympic Games, an exclusively Hellenic institution, based on his family's alleged origins in the Greek city of Argos; he was initially rejected by a board of Greek judges, but the decision was later overturned (Herodotus 5.22).

61 *the four letters:* There are actually six extant letters attributed to Demosthenes, and the question of their authenticity has occasioned much debate. I accept the view of Goldstein (*Letters of Demosthenes*) that they may all be genuine, but the first four of the six, dealing with the events during Demosthenes' exile, almost certainly are.

62 *"If the people ever":* The quip is reported by Plutarch, *Phocion* 9.

63 *The Assembly pulled back:* There is uncertainty on this point, and some

historians assume Athens did in fact send troops but the forces did not arrive in time. Diodorus (17.8.5–6) indicates the Athenians prepared troops for combat but then did not commit them.

63 *he let loose:*   Alexander's responsibility for the destruction of Thebes is assessed differently by the various sources. According to Arrian, Alexander only stepped back and let Thebes' Greek enemies exact vengeance on the city, whereas Diodorus and others portray him orchestrating the violence.

64 *perhaps paid off:*   Plutarch (*Demosthenes* 23) reports Demades received five talents for his services.

65 *Demosthenes stayed silent:*   To the extent he did make his views known, Demosthenes opposed Athenian support of the Spartan revolt (Aeschines 3.165), but he seems to have said as little as possible, as documented by Worthington in "Demosthenes' (In)activity."

67 *Quite possibly he colluded:*   There is no evidence that Aristotle aided Philip in his plans to invade Asia, but some scholars have assumed a collaboration. Anton-Hermann Chroust, who in many writings has stressed the political undertones of Aristotle's career, has even conjectured that Aristotle first went to Atarneus on Philip's instructions ("Aristotle and the Foreign Policy of Macedonia," *Review of Politics* 34 [1972], pp. 373–76). Though extreme, Chroust's views have recently received a partial endorsement from Peter Green in "Politics, Philosophy and Propaganda: Hermias of Atarneus and his Friendship with Aristotle" (pp. 29–46, *Crossroads of History: The Age of Alexander,* eds. Waldemar Heckel and Lawrence A. Tritle [Claremont, Calif. 2003]).

68 *an invaluable chronological resource:*   Ancient historians had no way to establish the dates of events other than by correlating them with the names of victors in the Olympic or Pythian games, or with the names of officials elected at Athens. The accuracy of lists of such names was therefore crucial to historical record keeping of all kinds.

69 *Himeraeus:*   He was later put to death by Antipater (Plutarch *Demosthenes* 28). The report of the dedicatory stone and its destruction by Himeraeus is related in the twelfth-century *Life of Aristotle* by Usaibia (17–21), an Arabic text based on lost Greek materials.

72 *a die-hard foe:*   Leosthenes' antipathy to Alexander, attested by Diodorus (17.111), is surprising in that Leosthenes had almost certainly fought under Alexander in Asia (see L. Tritle, "Alexander and the Greeks," pp. 129–30). Perhaps Leosthenes had witnessed the massacre of Greek mercenaries ordered by Alexander after the battle of the Granicus in 334.

73 *(almost certainly) Aristotle's nephew:*   He is identified by Diodorus as "Nicanor of Stagira," and we know that Aristotle's sister, a Stagirite, had a son named Nicanor. Aristotle gives directives to his "son" Nicanor in his will, assuming the document recorded by Diogenes Laertius is authentic.

73 *"King Alexander":*   Exact wording of the decree is preserved by Diodorus 18.8.4.

74 *Some sort of trade-off:*   The negotiations between Demosthenes and the

Macedonians can only be guessed at on the basis of the later actions of both parties. There is much uncertainty about Demosthenes' goals and policies during this confused period, but I have inclined toward the view of Badian and Worthington, that Demosthenes was in essence agreeing to abandon his opposition to Alexander in exchange for a chance to win back Samos. Like many politicians, he appears to have started out his career in a radical posture but grew more pragmatic with age.

75 *sore throat:* The anecdote is related by Plutarch, *Demosthenes* 25.5. Plutarch gives an amusing but exaggerated account of Demosthenes' susceptibility to bribes.

75 *had been bribed:* The motives for Demosthenes' indictment may have had little to do with his guilt or innocence; there were complex maneuverings at work, only dimly understood today. Nonetheless, the fact that Demosthenes had a reputation for venality, as Plutarch's life makes clear, made his political lynching easier to accomplish.

76 *partly recovered:* Hyperides has been the greatest beneficiary of any classical author of chance textual recoveries. His speeches were totally unknown to the modern world until the mid-nineteenth century; since then, several have been found in papyrus scrolls (most likely unearthed from tombs by plunderers), and in the last few years two more have turned up in recoverable form in the so-called Archimedes palimpsest (http://www.archimedespalimpsest.org).

76 *Alexander had rejected:* Plutarch (*Alexander* 28) preserves a snippet of a letter of Alexander's, believed by some to be genuine, explaining to the Athenians his reasons for denying their request.

77 *Those with money:* Diodorus (18.10.1) attests to the class divisions in the attitudes toward the war, and his testimony is affirmed by Green ("Occupation and Co-existence," pp. 4–5).

77 *under, or against:* Alexander took into his own employ many Greek mercenaries who had formerly fought on the Persian side and opposed him in battle.

78 *Some citizens:* Plutarch *Phocion* 23.

79 *A cruel parodist:* The text of this mock epitaph, and of the hymn to Hermias described in the following paragraph, is found in the life of Aristotle by Diogenes Laertius, chaps. 7–8.

80 *would escape calumnies:* Theophrastus was in fact indicted for impiety not long after Aristotle's departure, but made a successful defense. Some fifteen years later he was forced into a brief exile by a political faction at Athens that sought to ban all philosophers but soon returned to the city and lived out the remainder of his life there.

81 *"the Hellenic War":* It was also sometimes referred to as "the war against Antipater." It was rechristened the Lamian War later in antiquity and is so termed by Diodorus, as well as by most modern historians, after the place where much of the action was centered. Ashton has traced the history of the nomenclature in "Lamian War: *Stat magni nominis umbra.*" I have preferred to use the original name.

83 *Antipater tried a ruse:*   Described by Polyaenus, the Greek military writer, in his collection of tricks and subterfuges, *Stratagems of War* 4.4.3. The other movements in the opening phase of the war are found in Diodorus 18.12–13.

84 *with weary irony:*   The tone of the comment is hard to discern from Plutarch's account of it (*Phocion* 23.4). Read differently, the remark could be a straightforward expression of doubt as to the long-term prospects of Leosthenes' efforts.

85 *a total restoration:*   The details of Demosthenes' return to Athens are found in Plutarch, *Demosthenes* 27.6–8.

Chapter 4: Resistance, Rebellion, Reconquest

86 *communications lines:*   Hilltop criers are described by Diodorus 19.17.7; *astandai* by Herodotus 7.98 and Xenophon *Education of Cyrus* 8.6.17–18; fire signals by Aeschylus *Persians* 249–56, Herodotus 9.3, and Aristotle *De mundo* 398b30–35. Evidence also survives in Persian sources; see Briant's *From Cyrus to Alexander*, 369–71. The use of moving poles for coded fire-beacon messages is known from Judaic sources.

87 *particularly kind:*   The details that follow are from Quintus Curtius 5.2.16–22, 10.5.19–25.

87 *purges within her own family:*   Quintus Curtius (10.5.23) reports that eighty of Sisygambis' brothers were murdered in a single day by the notoriously cruel Artaxerxes III, head of a different line of the royal family, and that she had lost six of her seven sons.

88 *at some point:*   There is no evidence to indicate how or when this change of destination was decided. The sources agree that Alexander wished to be buried at the temple of Ammon (Diodorus 18.3.5; Curtius 10.5.4; Justin 12.15.7), but Pausanias says that when the cortege left Babylon, it was headed for Aegae (1.6.3). Discussion by Badian in the first segment of "King's Notebooks."

88 *no one yet imagined:*   Among the greatest mysteries to historians of the post-Alexander era is the scale of Antigonus' ambitions. He was to be the first of the generals to crown himself king, in 306, but at what point he set his sights on royalty, or on domination of the whole of Alexander's empire, is very difficult to determine. Almost certainly, though, these did not become his goals until several years after Alexander's death.

89 *Antigonus had always liked Eumenes:*   Their friendship is attested by Plutarch, *Eumenes* 10.6.

89 *giving satrapies to* Greeks: The only previous satrapal assignments given to Greeks were in the farthest regions of the empire, Aria, Bactria, and Sogdiana. These undesirable locations were meager spoils compared with the Cappadocian post given to Eumenes.

89 *while helping Philip:*   The anecdote, related by Plutarch in *Alexander* 70.4, actually refers to a man named Antigenes, but this is often regarded as an error for Antigonus.

89 *only surviving son:*   Antigonus had once had a second son, Philip, who died in youth.

89 *staggeringly handsome:*   Demetrius' good looks are attested by Plutarch (*Demetrius* 2) and by the (admittedly idealized) portraits on coins. In later life Demetrius was to build political power on his looks and his reputation for sexual charisma, something in the manner of a modern-day Kennedy.

91 *two years earlier:*   Accounts of the first Greek exodus from Bactria are given by Quintus Curtius (9.7.1–11) and Diodorus (17.99.5–6). Diodorus says the three thousand escapees were slaughtered by the Macedonians, but he seems to have confused this group with the second wave of Greek deserters; Curtius reports the three thousand made it home safe.

92 *largely as hostages:*   The ancient world had fewer qualms about hostage taking than the modern one. It was common practice for subject peoples to give hostages to their conquerors as a guarantee of compliance. The troop contributions required of the Greeks by their settlement with the Macedonians, following the battle of Chaeronea in 338, were understood to be pledges of good behavior.

93 *a rapturous pair of speeches:*   Their title is usually translated "On the Fortune or Virtue of Alexander," parts 1 and 2. The two orations ostensibly argue different sides of the question of whether Alexander's success was due to good luck or to innate talents, though in both admiration for Alexander's achievements is the dominant idea. They are presumed to have been written by Plutarch in youth, since the view of Alexander is more naively positive than in the *Life of Alexander.*

95 *several times told him so:*   As attested by Plutarch, at *Eumenes* 6.2, who unfortunately does not give examples. Few traces of these episodes can be found in the ancient Alexander histories, but the tendency to idealize Alexander must have largely effaced such a high-level challenge to his goals.

95 *out of dislike:*   The promotion of officers in Alexander's army in the king's last years largely depended on their attitudes toward his fusion plans. It has already been seen that Meleager, an opponent of those plans, was kept in the infantry ranks long after his fellow platoon leaders had been elevated to the cavalry (p. 41).

95 *the renowned Phila:*   The sketch of her character that follows is based on a tribute found in Diodorus 19.59.3–5. Phila would later show unflagging devotion in her long marriage to the scoundrel Demetrius.

96 *Phila was in Cilicia:*   Her presence there is not directly attested, but has been inferred as likely by Heckel on the basis of ingenious prosopographical arguments (see "A Grandson" and "Nicanor Son of Balacrus"). Even Badian, who disputes Heckel's findings, concedes that Phila may well have been in Cilicia for part of Balacrus' tenure as satrap there, presumably the last part ("Two Postscripts," p. 117).

97 *second Perdiccas' proposals:*   Quintus Curtius gives him a crucial role at the council session of June 12, backing Perdiccas at a moment when he

was under challenge from Meleager (10.7.8). Justin, however, does not confirm the report.

98 *the man he had just appointed:* There is much left unclear by Diodorus' account of Perdiccas' maneuvers at 18.7.3–5, not least the fact that he depicts Perdiccas appointing the very man whose power he then tried to circumscribe. However, just the same paradox can be observed in some of his other appointments: Meleager as negotiator to the rebellious infantrymen in Babylon, and Antigonus as backup to Eumenes in Cappadocia. Perdiccas seems to have had either a shortage of trustworthy subordinates or an unfortunate tendency to test those he deemed dubious by giving them crucial assignments.

98 *None of over twenty thousand:* The staggering scale of the ordered slaughter, coupled with the potential for loss of control of the upper satrapies, has caused some scholars to doubt the reliability of Diodorus' report; see Holt, *Alexander the Great and Bactria,* p. 89, and Sidky, *Greek Kingdom of Bactria,* p. 99. However, since it is the only report we have, it seems unwise to call it into question based on judgments about the strategy involved (a point made by Bosworth in his review of Holt's book, *JHS* 110 [1990], p. 257).

100 *once a Persian king:* The story of Cambyses' rash attack on the Apis is told by Herodotus 3.27–29.

100 *the epithet Soter:* The name was not bestowed on Ptolemy until 304, after he defended the island of Rhodes against an assault by Antigonus, but it no doubt arose from aspects of his character that had been talked of long before then.

100 *A record survives:* The pseudo-Aristotelian treatise titled *Economics* 1352a–b.

101 *the king bought a favor:* The story and the quotation are from Arrian *Anabasis* 7.23. Arrian makes clear that Alexander had deliberately divided rule over Egypt among several men, so as to prevent it from breaking away from the empire (3.5.7). Cleomenes had been given jurisdiction only over finance, but had quickly made himself satrap, or the closest thing to it.

102 *by killing Harpalus:* This is the account of Diodorus (18.19.2); Pausanias (2.33.4) says rather that Harpalus' own servants killed him or possibly a Macedonian named Pausanias. Heckel (*Who's Who*) reconciles the two accounts by supposing that Pausanias was an agent employed by Thibron.

104 *this ingenious icon:* I am not concerned here with the question of whether the Mir Zakah coin recently uncovered in Afghanistan, seemingly containing the forerunner of Ptolemy's elephant-scalp image, is genuine or not, a question that has yet to be resolved. Perhaps Ptolemy did not invent the image, but he certainly recognized its power and made full use of it in a way the issuers of the Mir Zakah coin never did.

105 *Justin:* The relevant text is 15.4.16, where the name "Alexandrum" found in the manuscripts has been replaced by "Nandrum" in modern

editions. The original reading, certainly erroneous, had the young Chandragupta escaping from Alexander.

106 *in fact dates from later centuries:* As established on linguistic evidence by Trautmann, *Kautilya and the Arthasastra.*

106 *the brief record Plutarch made:* Alexander 62.9.

107 *they had already:* It is generally assumed that Chandragupta's attack on the Nandas preceded his reconquest of the Indus valley from the Macedonians, though almost no hard evidence exists. The flight of Eudamus, Alexander's last remaining appointee, from the region, presumably as a result of Chandragupta's advances, occurred in 318.

107 *Some have guessed:* The suggestion was first made by the great nineteenth-century British expert on the Greek experience in India, John Watson McCrindle, in his commentary on the Justin text (*The Invasion of India by Alexander the Great* [1893; reprinted numerous times]). McCrindle noted that the Sanskrit epics use a term roughly equivalent to "outlaw" in referring to the non-monarchic Malli and Oxydracae, but as he provided no citation, I am unable to confirm this intriguing verbal overlap. Vincent A. Smith endorses the idea that the takeover of the Indus valley by Chandragupta was in essence a "rising" of subject peoples or a "revolt" (*Early History,* pp. 122–23).

107 *after killing the raja Porus:* Attested by Diodorus (19.14.8) but without elaboration. We may guess that Eudamus was motivated primarily by the desire for elephants. The confused situation in India during and after Alexander's invasion has been analyzed in great detail by Bosworth in the three works cited under "Chandragupta and India" in the bibliography.

108 *Letodorus:* His name is given as Lipodorus or Leipodorus in the manuscripts but has been changed by some modern editors.

Chapter 5: The Athenians' Last Stand (II)

110 *such pleasures:* For Hyperides' fish-shopping habits, see Athenaeus 8.27; for his assortment of courtesans, 13.58. Besides the three mentioned here, Hyperides also had the famously beautiful Phryne as a lover. When defending her on a capital charge in court, he reportedly exposed her naked to the jurors and thereby won her acquittal (the subject of a dramatic nineteenth-century painting by Jean-Léon Gérôme).

111 *when Hyperides was ill:* The anecdote is related in a brief biography of Hyperides included in the pseudo-Plutarchan *Lives of the Ten Orators* (*Moralia* 849).

112 *their confidence was shaken:* The demoralizing effect of Leosthenes' death is attested by Pausanias 1.25.5.

112 *a devious tactic:* Related by Plutarch, *Phocion* 24.1–2.

113 *He even proposed:* As attested in the pseudo-Plutarchan biography, *Moralia* 849f.

114 *(among other names):* There is some confusion in the sources as to which names Olympias held and when; Myrtale and Stratonice are also

reported. According to Carney (*Olympias*, p. 16), "It seems likely that [Olympias] had different names or epithets at different periods and that the changes came at significant moments in her life."

115 *Other rumors:* Plutarch (*Alexander* 10.8) reports the suspicions surrounding Olympias after Philip's murder, and Justin (9.7.1–2) accuses her more directly of complicity, but the other Alexander sources say nothing of her involvement. Modern scholarly opinion is divided.

115 *arranged the killing:* Plutarch *Alexander* 10.8, with lurid details filled in by Pausanias 8.7.7.

115 *Mother and daughter:* Only Cleopatra is attested by the sources as having sent the letter, but it is highly unlikely she did so without her mother's participation.

116 *Hecataeus found Leonnatus:* The details of the complex scene that follows are taken from Plutarch *Eumenes* 3.3–7. I have somewhat expanded on Plutarch's inferences about the thoughts of Leonnatus and Eumenes.

117 *fondness for wrestling:* Attested by Plutarch, *Alexander* 40.1, with the outlandish detail that Leonnatus had the sand used for his wrestling practice imported from Egypt by camel train.

118 *When Leonnatus woke:* A biography of Eumenes by the Roman Nepos, differing in some places from that of Plutarch, claims that Leonnatus sought Eumenes' life after he realized the Greek meant to betray his plans, and that Eumenes' nighttime departure was actually an escape (*Eumenes* 2.4–5).

122 *"Of the words":* I have based my translation on Worthington's text of the speech (*Greek Orators II*). Because the speech is known through only one tattered copy, many of the readings remain uncertain or rely on editorial insertions. I was not able to make use of the new edition by Judson Herrman, *Hyperides: Funeral Oration* (Oxford, 2009).

124 *King Xerxes:* The Hellespont bridge built by the Persians in 480 B.C. is described in detail by Herodotus 7.33–36. The key to its construction was the immensely strong cables, made of papyrus and white flax (7.25), that were stretched across the decks of the ships to bind them together.

124 *many shirked it:* The earliest preserved political speech of Demosthenes, "On the Naval Boards," presents a plan for reforming the system for financing the navy. Demosthenes himself had served on the boards and witnessed many abuses.

125 *were hard to come by:* Bosworth, in "Why Did Athens Lose the Lamian War?" (p. 15), cites evidence that Athens had only forty ships at sea during the two summers preceding the war. That meant only eight hundred rowers had gained precious experience of naval service.

125 *110 warships:* Attested by Diodorus 18.12.2, who explains them as a treasure convoy but without specifying what the money they carried was to be used for. The assumption of most historians is that Alexander was already anticipating war with Athens before he died.

125 *details of these battles:* Because Diodorus almost totally neglects the war at sea in his narrative of the Hellenic War, much uncertainty about it

cannot be resolved. Ashton ("*Naumachia*") and Bosworth ("Why Did Athens Lose the Lamian War?") have both made brave efforts at a reconstruction.

125 *a peculiar denouement:* The strange story is told by Plutarch, *Demetrius* 11.

126 *sat idle:* Evidence assembled by Green, "Occupation and Coexistence," and Bosworth, "Why Did Athens Lose the Lamian War?"

126 *He had brought Phila:* Not attested by the sources but conjectured by Heckel and others on the grounds that Phila was in Cilicia at the start of the war (see note on p. 96). Craterus' remarkable reassignment of his existing bride, Amastris, to Dionysius of Heracleia is recounted by Strabo (12.3.10) and Memnon (4.4).

127 *usually reckoned:* Because of the vagaries of the Athenian calendar, it is not possible to give exact Gregorian correlates for the ancient dates Plutarch and other sources supply.

129 *The negotiations:* Details of the two scenes that follow are taken from Plutarch, *Phocion* 26.3–28.

130 *a winking acknowledgment:* This is my understanding of a remark that, like many pithy replies quoted by Plutarch, is open to more than one interpretation.

131 *had largely opposed:* See p. 77 and note.

131 *for a long time:* According to the *Lives of the Ten Orators* (846), Antipater began to demand the surrender of Demosthenes after he besieged the Thessalian town of Pharsalus, soon after the battle of Crannon.

131 *could find safety there:* For example, Themistocles, the great Athenian leader and hero of the Persian Wars, forced from Athens and threatened with arrest and trial after his political enemies gained ascendancy, ended his life as a satrap in the Persian empire.

132 *Arrian:* The brief reference to Archias' downfall is in chapter 13 of Photius' summary. The wording indicates Arrian made it a major episode, but Photius gives us only this tantalizing bit of information.

132 *Hyperides apologized:* *Lives of the Ten Orators* 849.

132 *was cut out:* An alternative account holds that Hyperides bit his own tongue off to avoid giving incriminating information (*Lives of the Ten Orators* 849).

133 *Demosthenes awakened:* Details taken from Plutarch, *Demosthenes* 29. Plutarch gives no guidance as to the dream's meaning or importance.

Chapter 6: A Death on the Nile

137 *coffin of hammered gold:* Diodorus 18.26.3.

137 *usually after cremation:* The question has been raised as to whether the remains in Tomb 1 at Vergina, which may be those of Philip II and his wife (see next note), were cremated before burial or simply inhumed. Both cremation and inhumation were practiced by the Macedonians,

but in the period of Alexander they favored cremation, as attested by the written sources.

138 *Tomb 1 or Tomb 2:*   Proponents of the theory that Tomb 2 contains the remains of Philip III, a.k.a. Arrhidaeus, generally believe that Tomb 1 contained Philip II, his wife Cleopatra, and their infant child. The remains of three people, roughly corresponding in age to these three royals, were scattered on the floor of the tomb by ancient robbers.

139 *Archias the Exile-chaser:*   I have assumed that the Archias mentioned by Arrian (*Events After Alexander*) is the same person as the bounty hunter encountered in Chapter 5.

140 *Alcetas argued:*   The reasoning attributed to Alcetas here is not directly attested but inferred on the basis of Justin 13.6.5. Arrian (*Events After Alexander* 21) says only that Alcetas pushed Perdiccas toward Nicaea.

141 *impaled Ariarathes:*   Diodorus 18.16.3, but contradicted by a fragment of book 31 of the same historian, which claims Ariarathes died in battle.

141 *left there by Craterus:*   The presence of the Silver Shields in Cilicia after Craterus' departure must be inferred from their later movements; see p. 28 and note.

143 *Perdiccas married:*   The term "married" is used loosely since it is not clear whether an actual marriage ceremony took place before the later rupture.

143 *Just after the arrival:*   Arrian's *Events After Alexander* claims that only a few days separated the episode of Cleopatra from that involving Cynnane.

144 *In her teens:*   Much of what follows, including the details of the confrontation between Cynnane and Alcetas, is taken from Polyaenus 8.60.

145 *(almost certainly):*   There is little evidence for Alcetas' early life, but his brother Perdiccas grew up at court as one of Philip's page boys, and there is every reason to think Alcetas did so as well.

146 *on instructions:*   This second alternative is assumed by Bosworth (*Legacy of Alexander,* pp. 11–12), as well as several contemporary observers, but there is no evidence.

147 *a name with good Argead pedigree:*   Not only Philip II's mother bore the name Eurydice; it seems to have been adopted as well by two of Philip's wives (see Ogden, *Polygamy, Prostitutes and Death,* pp. 22–24).

147 *Somehow, Antigonus had learned:*   Perhaps his friend and ally Menander, satrap of Lydia, had observed the comings and goings at Sardis of Eumenes, Perdiccas' emissary to Cleopatra, and had asked questions about the goal of his missions (this at least was what occurred later).

149 *The hearse was built:*   The description is taken from Diodorus 18.26–27. Various points are unclear in both the Greek text of the description and its interpretation. The most consequential is at 18.27.2, where the change by a nineteenth-century editor of a single letter gives a description of a sculpted-gold olive wreath, rather than a picture of one done in gold on a purple cloth. Detailed discussion by Stewart, *Faces of Power,* pp. 215–21.

151 *no doubt coordinated:*   No evidence directly suggests a conspiracy

between Arrhidaeus and Ptolemy, but most scholars assume that one existed, if only because the body snatching would have been difficult without one. It bears noting also that Ptolemy later put forward Arrhidaeus for the vacant post of guardian of the kings (see Chapter 7, section 1). Aelian, in *Historical Miscellanies* (12.64), tells a wonderful but likely spurious story in which Ptolemy constructs a decoy body and coffin, then switches these for the real ones. Aspects of the hearse and its journey are discussed by Erskine ("Life After Death") and Badian ("A King's Notebooks").

152 *A legend was fabricated:* The legend is found in a work dating from much later, the *Alexander Romance* (3.32), but its early provenance is assured by the fact that only under Ptolemy Soter did Alexander's body reside in Memphis. Pausanias (1.7.1) informs us that Ptolemy II brought the body from Memphis to Alexandria, though many scholars believe that Ptolemy I must have moved the body himself when he changed royal residences.

153 *fiercely devoted:* An inference from the later willingness of the Shields to follow the orders of Polyperchon, guardian of the kings, even when these were contravened by four other generals (Chapter 9).

154 *Perdiccas was enraged:* Attested by information recovered from one of two pages of a manuscript of Arrian's *Events After Alexander* that was broken up and overwritten, the so-called Vatican palimpsest (F 24.1 in the Roos edition of Arrian).

154 *still residing in Sardis:* Apparently, Perdiccas had made Cleopatra satrap of Lydia, demoting the former satrap, Menander, to the post of garrison commander. The extraordinary appointment of a woman as satrap is attested only by the Vatican palimpsest containing one leaf of Arrian's *Events After Alexander* (F 25.2).

154 *Eumenes almost got caught:* The story was recovered from the Vatican palimpsest (F 25.3–8), and is otherwise unknown; even Polyaenus, a collector of such deceptions, fails to mention it in *Stratagems of War.*

156 *Alcetas refused:* Details of the diplomatic maneuvers that follow are taken primarily from Plutarch *Eumenes* 5–6.2.

159 *a curious dream:* Plutarch *Eumenes* 6.3–6. Information of this kind can only have come to Plutarch from the history written by Hieronymus of Cardia, a close companion and confidant of Eumenes' throughout the post-Alexander years.

160 *Muttering curses:* An unusually piquant detail even for Plutarch, found at *Eumenes* 7.2.

161 *an intense single combat:* Plutarch's description at *Eumenes* 7.4–7 and the closely matching one by Diodorus at 18.31 have here been accepted as authentic though doubted by some scholars as deriving from Hieronymus' efforts to heroize Eumenes.

161 *He may even have had:* Plutarch says that Eumenes found Craterus still alive and conscious and mourned him while clasping his hand, but this seems too operatic to be credible. In the version of Diodorus, Craterus

dies before Eumenes has engaged Neoptolemus. Nepos (*Eumenes* 4.4), relying on a different source from either of these, reports that Eumenes made a vain effort to save Craterus' life.

162 *Eumenes sent a Macedonian:*   The episode recounted here, described in a papyrus fragment of Arrian's *Events After Alexander* (known by its catalog number, PSI 1284), has caused much debate among scholars. The coercion of an enemy phalanx might have occurred either after the battle against Neoptolemus or after that against Craterus and Neoptolemus, and the papyrus gives no clues as to which is its proper context. Cogent reasons have been advanced on either side, and the issue is still unresolved. I have preferred to locate the episode here, based on the arguments of Thompson ("PSI 1284") against those of Bosworth ("Eumenes, Neoptolemus").

163 *The humility of the gesture:*   I am guessing that Eumenes' humility is the point of Antipater's laughter. In Plutarch's account (*Eumenes* 8.3), Antipater utters a jest that explained what was so funny, but I find the remark impenetrably obscure. Brian Bosworth, in a private communication, has offered an elaborate interpretation of the joke but has also acknowledged its obscurity. Humorous or pithy remarks recorded by ancient writers often pose some of the gravest problems for modern interpreters.

163 *Ptolemy's defense:*   Probably not delivered by Ptolemy in person, though the source, *Events After Alexander* 1.28, leaves open that possibility.

164 *to draw off water:*   The stratagem is mentioned only by Diodorus (18.33.2) in terms that are somewhat obscure. It appears Perdiccas attempted to open an old, disused canal, but a sudden incursion of water destroyed his engineering works.

164 *At first light:*   The details of Perdiccas' disastrous Egyptian campaign are taken from Diodorus (18.33–36.5), by far our most complete source for the episode.

166 *Had this victory been known:*   The hypothesis is not my own but that recorded by Diodorus (18.37.1), probably based on the original judgment of Hieronymus.

Chapter 7: The Fortunes of Eumenes

169 *Whether such contacts preceded:*   There is no evidence in the sources of collusion between Peithon and Ptolemy in Perdiccas' murder, but scholars often assume it took place, based on the political skills of Ptolemy. There were enough defectors and spies passing back and forth that it would have been easy for the two to stay in contact.

169 *before the assembled army:*   Such is the version of Diodorus (18.36.6); Arrian, by contrast, seems to have described a smaller meeting, between Ptolemy and the army leadership (*Events After Alexander* 1.28).

171 *he took the liberty of commandeering:*   An inference based on the fact that Ptolemy later had Indian war elephants in his possession, and this seems

to have been his best opportunity to get hold of them. African elephants, though freely available in Egypt, were not trained for use in war until after Ptolemy's death.

172 *Alexander had promised one:* The evidence is ambiguous because of the uncertainties over the Greek text in a crucial passage of Arrian's *Anabasis*. At 7.8.1 of that work, where Alexander is dispatching the veterans from Opis, our manuscripts also have him promising to give rewards to *those staying* (with him). However, some modern editors delete the word that translates "those staying" on the assumption that Alexander wanted to reward those leaving his service, not those remaining in Asia. The demands made by his veterans after his death, however, argue in favor of the manuscript text.

172 *(Perdiccas' brother-in-law Attalus):* Attested by Arrian, *Events After Alexander* 1.33. Some scholars believe this was a different Attalus from the officer in Perdiccas' regime, who had been condemned to death by the royal army and therefore would not be quick to show himself among them. I have followed Heckel (*Who's Who*) and others in assuming this was indeed the Attalus who had served under Perdiccas.

174 *the rescue effort:* Details of the scene that follows are taken from Polyaenus 4.6.4, supplemented by Arrian, *Events After Alexander* 1.33.

176 *ten or more Nicanors:* Heckel in *Who's Who* lists twelve but with notes in the biographies of several that indicate they may be identical with others already listed. The effort to disentangle people who share common names is one of the most challenging forms of historical research; Bosworth's "New Macedonian Prince" is a brilliant example, involving the disambiguation of two other important Nicanors.

176 *his father twitted him:* Such a delightful story can have come only from Plutarch (*Demetrius* 14).

178 *as champion of that cause:* My views of the motives of Perdiccas, and especially of Eumenes, are more generous than those of many historians. It is possible to see both men as acting solely out of self-interest and desire for power, but it is also possible that the safety and authority of Alexander's heirs, especially the king's son by Rhoxane, were their primary motive. Certainly Eumenes was portrayed by the ancient sources as gravely concerned for the young Alexander, and we cannot, I think, ascribe all such depictions to the favoritism of Hieronymus, the historian on whom these sources drew. Significant new evidence has emerged from the Göteborg palimpsest, showing that Eumenes, in his proposal to his former colleagues in the Perdiccas regime—to whom he had no reason to dissemble—sought a restoration of the Babylon accords, the only legitimate plan for the organization of the empire, rather than a more ambitious goal (see p. 189).

179 *Eumenes called them together:* As reported by Justin 14.1.

181 *Whatever its purposes:* Bosworth has made an ingenious, but to my mind unconvincing, argument ("Ptolemy and the Will of Alexander") that the *Last Days* is the work of Ptolemy and his supporters and dates to

around 308 B.C. Heckel has advanced a very different theory in his book
Last Days and Testament of Alexander.

181 *Perhaps Antipater himself:*   Bosworth has most recently suggested, to my
mind unconvincingly, that Eumenes had the *Journals* published (perhaps
in a doctored version) to clear himself of poisoning charges ("Alexander's
Death," p. 409).

181 *In all likelihood, Perdiccas was dead:*   There is no agreement among
scholars about the date at which Ptolemy wrote his memoir of the Asian
campaign, but it was almost certainly later than 321. Some would argue
that Ptolemy wrote it late in life, in the 290s or 280s, but evidence is lacking.

183 *This was an awkward development:*   The reasons for Cleopatra's discom-
fort and reluctance in dealing with Eumenes are supplied by Arrian
Events After Alexander 1.40.

185 *and now accused him:*   The summary of Arrian's *Events After Alexander*
speaks of unspecified indictments that Cleopatra leveled against Antipater (1.40); presumably, the poisoning of Alexander was principal among
these.

186 *even, perhaps, entered:*   Josephus has an account, unknown from other
sources, of Alexander's negotiations with the high priests during a visit to
Jerusalem (*Jewish Antiquities* 11.8).

186 *no Greek writer:*   Herodotus is a possible exception, since he discusses a
race of "Palestinian Syrians" who practice circumcision (2.104). But the
fact that such a well-traveled and inquisitive Greek did not know this
race by a more specific name is nonetheless significant. On Theophrastus' very limited knowledge of the Jews, see chapter 1 of Bezalel Bar-
Kochva, *The Image of the Jews in Greek Literature: The Hellenistic Period*
(Berkeley, Calif., 2009).

186 *Ptolemy, however, knew a lot:*   The story is related by Josephus *Jewish
Antiquities* 12.1. It is usually correlated with Ptolemy's first invasion of
Phoenicia and "Hollow" Syria (there were others), mentioned by
Diodorus at 18.43 and dated to 319 B.C.

186 *There is a legend:*   The most complete version is found in Augustine's
City of God (4.4), though the story was already circulating well before
Augustine's time; Cicero refers to it in his *Republic* (3.14.24).

187 *somehow their stash:*   The profligacy of the Macedonian rank and file
might be the cause of this insatiable need for pay. Arrian relates in the
Anabasis (7.5) that in 324, even after despoiling much of Asia and the
richest cities of the Persian empire, thousands of Alexander's troops were
deep in debt.

188 *One day Eumenes returned:*   The story is told most fully by Justin (14.1),
but is also mentioned by Plutarch (*Eumenes* 8.6).

188 *The erased passage:*   Details of the recovery of the palimpsest by digital
imaging, and a preliminary version of the text, can be found in Dreyer's
"Arrian Parchment" (under "Fragmentary Sources and Commentaries"
in the bibliography).

189 *Eumenes reached out:*   It is not clear whether Eumenes held a summit meeting with the other former officers of Perdiccas' regime or carried on negotiations by letter. Pisidia was a few days' travel from Celaenae.

190 *the five-way parley broke up:*   Sadly, I have been unable to deduce the meaning of a remark Plutarch assigns to Eumenes here, "It's just like the old saying, *olethrou oudeis logos.*" There is no other instance in Greek of this "old saying," nor is its sense—literally, "of destruction [there is] no account"—at all clear from this context. Plutarch evidently regarded this as a very memorable remark, but its point is lost on me and on others I have consulted.

191 *He sent out a high officer:*   The story is found in Polyaenus 4.6.6. It is significant that Antigonus' list of stratagems is far longer in Polyaenus' catalog than that of any other Macedonian general (King Alexander's of course is longer).

192 *one last indignity:*   Arrian, *Events After Alexander* 1.44–45.

192 *who chose it as the end point:*   Scholars often maintain that the portion of *Events After Alexander* summarized by Photius does not represent the entirety of the original work, but I see no grounds for this assumption. The great problem for a historian of the post-Alexander period is where to conclude, and Antipater's crossing of the Hellespont makes a reasonably good end point.

193 *a demoralizing trick:*   The source is of course Polyaenus 4.6.19.

194 *a fortress called Nora:*   The fort was atop the ten-thousand-foot Mount Hasan, near a site known today by the Turkish name of Viransehir. The ruins shown to tourists there are Roman and medieval, not those of Eumenes' times, which as far as I know are no longer in evidence.

Chapter 8: The War Comes Home

197 *Loss of the right:*   It was unclear whether the poor were stripped of their voting rights de facto or de jure; see discussion by Hughes in chapter 4 of "After the Democracy."

198 *manning the oars of its warships:*   Because the Athenians were required to supply their own gear for military service, the armed forces were highly stratified according to wealth. Those who could not afford hoplite armor—the breastplate, helmet, and spear that were standard middle-class possessions—were relegated to the navy, which paradoxically was the strongest arm of Athens' war machine. Thus the poor bore an outsize share of the glory the city had won in battle.

198 *Convicted five years earlier:*   See p. 76. It is unclear whether his penalty was imposed for conviction in the bribery scandal, for support of the measure making Alexander a god (see p. 74), or for a host of different violations (Diodorus 18.18.2 mentions three unspecified convictions and Plutarch no fewer than seven).

199 *subsidize all his pleasures:*   The story that follows comes from Plutarch, *Phocion* 30.3.

200 *to stop him from deporting:* Plutarch, *Phocion* 29.3. The Ceraunian Mountains were considered the limits of European Greece to the north; Taenaron, to the south, formed a similar limit and is also mentioned by Plutarch as the place beyond which Antipater banished his enemies.

201 *Phocus:* Anecdotes about this colorful man are related by Plutarch at *Phocion* 20, 30, and 38.2. At 38.1, Plutarch tells us that Phocus ultimately hunted down and took vengeance on those who had brought down his father.

203 *According to Plutarch:* The episode of Demades' brutal execution by Cassander was compelling enough to Plutarch that he narrated it twice, *Phocion* 30.8–9 and *Demosthenes* 31.4–6. Diodorus, by contrast, leaves Cassander out of the story and instead has Antipater handing the two Athenians over for execution in a dispassionate manner (18.48.3–4).

204 *probably not Aristotle's adopted son:* See Bosworth, "A New Macedonian Prince" (in the bibliography under "Leosthenes and the Lamian War").

205 *the countryside:* The highlands surrounding central Macedonia had always been uneasy with the authority exerted from Pella.

206 *The first warning:* As described by Polyaenus 4.6.7. It is impossible that Antigonus traveled with slow-moving elephants on his forced march from Nora, even if Diodorus' estimate of his speed (18.44.2) is exaggerated. Presumably, he had been keeping the beasts stabled somewhere near Pisidia or had sent them on ahead to await his arrival there.

206 *to a fort he controlled:* The remarkable escape attempt of these three prisoners, which succeeded in gaining Docimus his freedom, is described by Diodorus at 19.16.

208 *had arrived in Pella too late:* In fact the man Antigonus had sent to confer with Antipater in Pella was the same one who returned with news of the old man's death.

209 *one last, stern injunction:* Reported by Diodorus 19.11.9.

209 *He did not belong:* Very little is known about Polyperchon's lineage or early life, but this very lack of evidence is significant. In Alexander's army he had served only as an infantry commander and never fought with the cavalry, which again suggests an inglorious family heritage.

209 *arrogantly seizing a treasure fleet:* As described by Diodorus 18.52.7.

210 *in this letter or in a later one:* It is uncertain whether the messages described differently by Diodorus (18.58.3) and Plutarch (*Eumenes* 13.1) came from the same letter or two different ones.

211 *a proclamation:* The exact wording of the decree is given, at some length, by Diodorus (18.56).

212 *He had kept up the morale:* The remarkable details that follow, undoubtedly deriving from Hieronymus, who shared Eumenes' confinement on Nora, are preserved by Plutarch (*Eumenes* 11) and Nepos (*Eumenes* 5).

214 *According to Plutarch's account:* The story of the altered oath is found only in Plutarch (*Eumenes* 12.2) and Nepos (*Eumenes* 5.7) and has been rejected by Anson ("Siege of Nora"), whose opinion is seconded by

Bosworth ("History and Artifice," pp. 66–67). Anson regards the tale as a fiction concocted by Hieronymus to excuse Eumenes from what was, in his view, a brief alliance with Antigonus and a betrayal of the Argead house. Most other historians accept the story as valid, however. Michael Dixon has brought forward new support for this position in a chronological analysis of the movements of Hieronymus, Eumenes' envoy to Antipater, showing that Eumenes must have had knowledge of the looming civil war in Europe at the time he left Nora and may even have been recruited by Polyperchon as an ally ("Corinth," pp. 163–67).

214 *or perhaps just before departing:* The timing of the arrival of the letters is unclear in the sources. Dixon (see previous note) has proposed that Eumenes had already gotten word of Polyperchon's offer from Hieronymus before he left Nora.

215 *he still drew water:* Details from Plutarch, *Phocion* 18.2.

216 *and perhaps could not:* Much remains unclear about Phocion's collaboration with the Macedonian generals, since our principal source, Plutarch, was inclined to clear him of all misdeeds and to frame his story as a tragedy (see Lamberton, "Plutarch's *Phocion*").

219 *Teutamus was an unknown quantity:* There is no evidence at all about the history of this man prior to his appearance as co-captain of the Silver Shields in 318.

220 *"I have no need":* The indirect statement found in Diodorus (18.60.2) appears to represent the precise words used by Eumenes. It should again be stressed that Hieronymus of Cardia, Diodorus' principal source for events of this period, was an eyewitness to most of Eumenes' activities. The words quoted on the following page represent a direct quotation in Diodorus.

220 *Eumenes told his officers:* The dream and the resulting erection of the tent are described, somewhat differently, by no fewer than four sources: Diodorus 18.60–61; Plutarch *Eumenes* 13.3–4; Nepos *Eumenes* 7.2–3; and Polyaenus 4.8.2. The version given here is based most closely on Polyaenus.

221 *Alexander's diadem, scepter, and armor:* There has been debate as to how these came to be at Cyinda with Eumenes. Perhaps the Greek had kept them after somehow getting control of them in Babylon; perhaps they were stored in the Cyinda fortress as part of the imperial treasure. It seems likely that more than one set of these royal objects existed.

222 *The hearing started:* Details taken from Plutarch's *Phocion*, from here to the end of the chapter.

223 *for exhibition to the mob:* My interpretation of Plutarch's comment (*Phocion* 34.2) that Phocion's return to Athens was shameful because he was carried on a cart. Others interpret the remark to mean that Phocion had become too infirm to walk.

225 *in large part as a scapegoat:* The motives behind Socrates' indictment and conviction are of course more complex than I can deal with here.

But among them was certainly the fact that two political leaders who had, at various times, collaborated with the Spartans were former students of Socrates.

226 *one expert has proposed:*   See Palagia, "Impact of Ares Macedon," cited under "Archaeological and Material Evidence" in the bibliography.

227 *Long-standing rivals:*   In a famous analysis of an earlier war, Thucydides makes the same point about the struggle for supremacy between liberal Athens and conservative Sparta. Passions of rival political parties in every Greek city were inflamed due to the fact that each could call on a superpower for support.

Chapter 9: Duels to the Death

229 *an older man:*   There is no evidence about the early life of Aristonous, and it is not known at what point he became a Bodyguard, but Heckel (*Who's Who*) supposes he was inherited by Alexander from Philip's day.

230 *no doubt ceased to matter:*   An important dividing line among historians of the Alexander period concerns the degree of constitutionality they assign to the Macedonians. Some regard this nation as lawful and observant of strict political conventions; others see them engaging in a might-makes-right free-for-all. The debate plays out in interesting ways where the succession to Alexander is concerned. I have here adhered to a moderate constitutionalist position, which I think is supported by the evidence: the impetus to install and obey a legitimate king was paramount throughout the first six years after Alexander's death, until all hope was lost that such a king could be found. The opposing position is summed up by Carney (*Olympias*, p. 86): "Legality was never a major issue in Macedonian society generally. After the death of Alexander and certainly after that of Perdiccas, legitimacy is simply not a useful concept for historians to apply."

230 *four Bodyguards to Alexander's three:*   See Heckel, "IGii2 561," cited under "Rhoxane, Alexander IV, Barsine, and Heracles" in the bibliography.

232 *the first of their species:*   Aristotle has such detailed information about elephants in his biological treatises that it has been thought he observed them firsthand, leading to the fanciful supposition that Alexander shipped one specimen back to Athens from Asia for him to examine (the premise of L. Sprague de Camp's novel *An Elephant for Aristotle*). However, the more likely explanation is that Aristotle received written reports about the beasts through Ctesias, a Greek physician serving at the court of the Persian kings.

233 *bringing with him many tales:*   Lawrence Tritle has even claimed that Damis published a treatise about elephant handling, though I have found no evidence that confirms this. See "Alexander and the Greeks," pp. 121–40 of *Alexander the Great: A New History,* Waldemar Heckel and Lawrence A. Tritle, eds. (Malden, Mass. 2009).

233 *causing a time-delayed collapse:* This is my hypothesis for the goal of the sapping method described by Diodorus (18.70.5), in which the wooden props of the mine are set on fire.

235 *to cross over into Asia:* According to Diodorus (18.63.6), the goal of Eumenes' naval strategy was to permit Polyperchon to invade Asia, though one wonders whether Eumenes would not have considered it more urgent that he himself cross into Europe.

237 *At last Eumenes' fleet was ready:* Story related by Polyaenus 4.6.9.

237 *a crushing setback:* Described in slightly varying versions by Diodorus 18.72 and Polyaenus 4.6.8.

239 *on restoring the oligarchy:* Cassander granted the Athenians a less stringent property restriction than his father had done, limiting citizenship to those with estates of a thousand drachmas.

239 *A new leader:* This was Demetrius of Phaleron, whose story, though it falls outside the scope of this book, is as fascinating as any in the post-Alexander world.

239 *a brief, defiant visit:* This first return to Macedonia of Cassander is mentioned only briefly by Diodorus at 18.75.1 and 19.35.7, and is often overlooked, even by scholars. Cassander returned to test his political support, then set out for Greece again to further shore up his position there. Adams gives a good account of Cassander's movements in "Antipater and Cassander."

242 *foiled in an attempt:* Apparently, Eumenes learned of a disused canal in the area and reopened it, causing the water to be carried away again.

242 *no doubt sensationalized report:* The description of the battle is attributed to Duris of Samos by the writer who quotes it, Athenaeus (13.560f). Duris wrote a narrative history, now lost, of events in the Greek world from the mid-fourth to the early third century. He is not regarded as a very reliable source, though Plutarch sometimes made use of him.

243 *Perhaps she thought:* Carney (*Olympias,* p. 76) offers a different explanation for the walling up of the monarchs, that Olympias hoped to force Philip to abdicate the throne.

244 *opening his grave:* See Diodorus 19.11.8 and Plutarch *Alexander* 77.1. It is curious Olympias did not do likewise to the tomb of Antipater; evidently, she still observed some limits out of respect for Macedonian public opinion.

246 *imperious and solitary:* Attested by Plutarch *Demetrius* 28.5, where the anecdote that follows can also be found.

246 *Inside the Susa cache:* Its contents were later inventoried by Antigonus and recorded by Diodorus (19.48.6–8). Chares of Mytilene attests to the use of the "Climbing Vine" as a royal bedchamber adornment (Athenaeus 12.514f).

248 *a hard road into Media:* The story of Antigonus' difficult passage through Media is told by Diodorus at 19.19. Antigonus chose a mountainous route to escape the heat, but refused to bribe the tribesmen who

lived along it and was therefore constantly harassed and blocked as he made his way north.

250 *she might hope to be rescued:* Diodorus attributes this hope to her at 19.35.6.

251 *unprecedented grandeur:* Alexander's banquet at Opis, on which Peucestas' feast was clearly modeled, is said to have had nine thousand guests.

253 *while his men fretted:* Their anxiety increased when the gleam of the enemy's armor was sighted in the distance. According to Plutarch, some of the troops vowed not to fight until Eumenes was back in command; Eumenes had his litter brought alongside them, drew back the curtains, and feebly extended a hand, prompting a vigorous battle cry from the men (Plutarch *Eumenes* 14.3). But Bosworth ("History and Artifice") and Roisman ("Hieronymus of Cardia") are skeptical.

253 *The two armies:* For details of the battles of Paraetacene and Gabene, I am grateful for the analyses in chapter 4 of Bosworth's *Legacy of Alexander* and in the two articles by Devine listed in the bibliography under "Eumenes." The basic narrative of events comes from Diodorus; Plutarch's *Eumenes* becomes confused and abbreviated when it reaches these two battles.

254 *Gabene:* The spelling here used is that found in Diodorus and Plutarch; other sources use "Gabiene," and this is often seen in modern writings as well. Bosworth locates the region near modern Isfahan, Iran (*Legacy of Alexander,* p. 127).

256 *he made haste to cremate his dead:* Polyaenus reports the ploy (4.6.10) without specifying what battle it followed, but Paraetacene gives the most fitting context.

Chapter 10: The Closing of the Tombs

257 *after which it disappeared:* The fate of Alexander's body, or the possibility of its recovery, has been the focus of much speculation and lore. An amusing survey has been compiled by Nicholas Saunders, *Alexander's Tomb: The Two-Thousand Year Obsession to Find the Lost Conqueror* (New York, 2006).

258 *They revered no commander:* Unique information provided by Justin (14.2). The details that follow regarding Eumenes' flattery of the Shields are from the same passage.

258 *oaths of allegiance:* Justin has Eumenes make reference to these in his final speech to the Shields at 14.4.

261 *plotting against his life:* The plot is discussed by Plutarch at *Eumenes* 16. Apparently, Eudamus brought word to Eumenes that the satraps and Silver Shields were planning to have him assassinated directly after the battle had ended. But Plutarch includes in the plot Antigenes, who had no discernible reason to turn on the commander he had so faithfully followed, making the information suspect. There is also the problem dis-

cussed by Bosworth in "History and Artifice," that Plutarch goes to extraordinary lengths in *Eumenes* to make points of contact with the parallel Roman life, *Sertorius,* often using unreliable reports for this purpose. Since Sertorius was killed by a conspiracy of his officers, Plutarch may have reached far into his source materials in order to find a similar episode concerning Eumenes.

262 *an act of cowardice:*   This is the judgment of the sources (Diodorus 19.38.1; Plutarch *Eumenes* 15.8), but it has long been recognized that, as they are based on Eumenes' partisan Hieronymus, they have a negative bias toward Peucestas. The truth may be more closely connected to the murder plot reported by Plutarch, or to the various differences Eumenes and Peucestas had had over grand strategy. Heckel (*Who's Who,* p. 205) suggests Peucestas may have been seeking to detach himself from Eumenes during the winter but was forestalled by Antigonus' sudden approach.

263 *Plutarch eulogizes them:*   *Eumenes* 16.4. The age range given by Plutarch has been doubted by some but demonstrated by Hammond to be quite plausible ("Alexander's Veterans After His Death," under "Antigenes, the Silver Shields, and the Macedonian Army" in the bibliography).

263 *They shouted:*   Details and quotations provided by Justin 14.3.

264 *made his valedictory speech:*   Different versions of this speech are reported by Justin (14.4) and Plutarch (*Eumenes* 17.3), though the main point is very much the same in both. Justin gives Eumenes a bitter series of reproaches against the Shields after they refuse to grant his request. I have opted, somewhat arbitrarily, to include here a portion of the version of Plutarch.

265 *called up a column of elephants:*   Another point on which I have preferred Plutarch's version over that of Justin. Justin portrays the elephants and Asian troops as part of Eumenes' army, a kind of honor guard, not a security detail sent by Antigonus.

266 *Nearchus of Crete:*   It is curious to find Nearchus in the service of Antigonus, and none of our sources explains how he got there. He was last observed advocating for Heracles as a successor to the throne, in the council at Babylon (p. 37).

266 *sent a man to kill him:*   Nepos (*Eumenes* 12) has an alternative account in which Eumenes is strangled by his guards without Antigonus' knowledge, but concurs with the other sources that Antigonus had resolved on Eumenes' death.

267 *returning his ashes:*   Plutarch *Eumenes* 19. There is no evidence concerning to whom Eumenes was married at the time of his death. In the Susa weddings eight years earlier, Alexander had matched him with a highborn Persian named Artonis. But it is unlikely this is the woman who received his ashes.

267 *The platoon was broken up:*   Portrayed by Plutarch (*Eumenes* 19), in typically moralistic fashion, as a punishment inflicted by the gods for the impiety the Shields had committed in their betrayal of Eumenes.

269 *watching for the masts:*   Diodorus (19.49.3) tells us that Olympias, not Alexander, was still clinging to hopes of rescue, but I have assumed that the grandson took his cue from his grandmother.

269 *Polyperchon devised a plan:*   As related by Polyaenus 4.11.3.

271 *or perhaps a resumption of the first:*   There is much that is unclear about Olympias' trial and death; the two accounts in the sources, those of Diodorus and Justin, diverge. The account of Diodorus has been followed here. Carney (*Olympias*, pp. 82–85) conducts a thorough review of the evidence.

272 *He did not yet know:*   Most chronologies place the deaths of Eumenes and Olympias at about the same time. News of Antigonus' victory would have taken several weeks to reach European shores.

272 *caused him to tremble with fear:*   Plutarch *Alexander* 74.6.

274 *"dry" cremation:*   This is the opinion of the paleoanthropologist Antonis Bartsiokas, as reported in *Science* 228 (2000). See note to p. 7.

274 *and a scepter:*   The scepter, according to Borza and Palagia (see note to p. 7), has subsequently disappeared from the collection of items found in the tomb.

275 *a series of kings:*   Another possibility, advanced by the tomb's excavator, is that the diadem was meant to be adjusted to be worn with or without another piece of headgear.

276 *Cassander prepared a fine chamber tomb:*   There is no clear evidence of who built Tomb 3 at Vergina, but its apparent date indicates that Cassander was responsible. Diodorus, however, says that Cassander killed Alexander in secret and hid his body (19.105). The most likely scenario is that, after the death of the boy inevitably leaked out, Cassander felt obliged to conduct a proper royal burial. See Adams, "Cassander, Alexander IV and the Tombs at Vergina," *AncW* 22 (1991) 27–33. A different theory of the tomb's construction, unconvincing in my view, has been put forward by Franca Landucci Gattinoni ("Cassander and the Legacy of Philip and Alexander II in Diodorus' *Library*," pp. 113–21 of *Philip II and Alexander the Great: Father and Son, Lives and Afterlives*, eds. Elizabeth Carney and Daniel Ogden [Oxford and N.Y., 2010]).

Epilogue

280 *Plutarch records:*   In the essay "On Compliancy," *Moralia* 530d.

280 *was strangled to death:*   Pausanias, however, records that Heracles was killed by poison. Justin (15.2.3) does not specify the form the assassination took but supplies the unique information that Barsine, Heracles' mother, was also killed on Cassander's orders.

Bibliography

The following abbreviations are used to refer to journals in the fields of classics and history:

AC	Acta Classica
AHB	Ancient History Bulletin
AJA	American Journal of Archaeology
AJP	American Journal of Philology
AM	Ancient Macedonia
AncW	Ancient World
CQ	Classical Quarterly
G&R	Greece and Rome
GRBS	Greek, Roman, and Byzantine Studies
JHS	Journal of Hellenic Studies
TAPA	Transactions of the American Philological Association
ZPE	Zeitschrift für Papyrologie und Epigraphik

WEB ADDRESSES OF PRIMARY SOURCES IN TRANSLATION

Arrian. *Events After Alexander* (summary of Photius). http://www.isidore-of-seville.com/library-arrian/events-2.htm.

Athenaeus. *Deipnosophistae.* http://digicoll.library.wisc.edu/Literature/subcollections/DeipnoSubAbout.html.

Diodorus Siculus. *Library of History.* http://penelope.uchicago.edu/Thayer/E/Roman/Texts/Diodorus_Siculus/home.html.

Justin. *Epitome of Pompeius Trogus.* http://www.ccel.org/ccel/pearse/morefathers/files/justinus_04_books11to20.htm.

Memnon. *History of Heracleia.* http://www.attalus.org/translate/memnon1.html.

Cornelius Nepos. *Eumenes.* http://www.isidore-of-seville.com/library-nepos/eumenes-2.htm.

Plutarch. *Alexander, Demosthenes, Demetrius, Eumenes, and Phocion.* http://penelope.uchicago.edu/Thayer/E/Roman/Texts/Plutarch/Lives/home.html.

Polyaenus. *Stratagems of War.* http://www.attalus.org/translate/polyaenus4B.html.

Pseudo-Plutarch. *Lives of the Ten Orators.* http://www.attalus.org/old/orators1.html.

Quintus Curtius Rufus. *Life of Alexander the Great* (full text available only in Latin). http://penelope.uchicago.edu/Thayer/E/Roman/Texts/Curtius/home.html.

GENERAL STUDIES

Adams, Winthrop Lindsay. "The Games of Alexander the Great." In Waldemar Heckel, Lawrence Tritle, and Pat Wheatley, eds., *Alexander's Empire: Formulation to Decay,* pp. 125–38. Claremont, Calif., 2007.

———. "The Hellenistic Kingdoms." In Glenn R. Bugh, ed., *The Cambridge Companion to the Hellenistic World,* pp. 28–51. Cambridge, U.K., 2006.

Agostinetti, Anna S. *Gli eventi dopo Alessandro.* Rome, 1999.

Bengtson, Hermann. *Die Diadochen: Die Nachfolger Alexanders (323–281 v. Chr.).* Munich, 1987.

Berve, Helmut. *Das Alexanderreich auf prosopographischer Grundlage.* Munich, 1926.

Billows, Richard A. *Kings and Colonists: Aspects of Macedonian Imperialism.* New York, 1995.

Bosworth, A. B. "Alexander the Great and the Creation of the Hellenistic Age." In Glenn R. Bugh, ed., *The Cambridge Companion to the Hellenistic World,* pp. 9–27. Cambridge, U.K., 2006.

———. *The Legacy of Alexander: Politics, Warfare, and Propaganda Under the Successors.* Oxford, 2002.

Briant, Pierre. *From Cyrus to Alexander: A History of the Persian Empire.* Winona Lake, Ind., 2002.

Cloché, Paul. *La dislocation d'un empire: Les premiers successeurs d'Alexandre le Grand.* Paris, 1959.

Errington, R. M. "Diodorus Siculus and the Chronology of the Early Diadochoi, 320–311 B.C." *Hermes* 105 (1977), pp. 478–504.

———. "From Babylon to Triparadeisos, 323–320 B.C." *JHS* 90 (1970), pp. 49–77.

Fontana, Maria José. *Le lotte per la successione di Alessandro Magno dal 323 al 315.* Palermo, 1960.

Goukowsky, Paul. *Essai sur les origines du mythe d'Alexandre.* Nancy, 1978.

Green, Peter. *Alexander to Actium: The Historical Evolution of the Hellenistic Age.* Berkeley, Calif., 1990.

Hammond, N. G. L. *The Macedonian State: Origins, Institutions, and History.* Oxford, 1989.

Hammond, N. G. L., and F. W. Walbank. *The History of Macedonia.* Vol. 3, *336–167 B.C.* Oxford, 2001.

Heckel, Waldemar. *The Marshals of Alexander's Empire.* New York, 1992.

——. "The Politics of Distrust: Alexander and His Successors." In Daniel Ogden, ed., *The Hellenistic World: New Perspectives,* pp. 81–95. London, 2002.

——. "The 'Somatophylakes' of Alexander the Great: Some Thoughts." *Historia* 27 (1978), pp. 224–28.

——. *Who's Who in the Age of Alexander the Great: A Prosopography of Alexander's Empire.* Malden, Mass., 2009.

Hornblower, Jane. *Hieronymus of Cardia.* Oxford, 1981.

Meeus, Alexander. "Alexander's Image in the Age of the Successors." In Waldemar Heckel and Lawrence Tritle, eds., *Alexander the Great: A New History,* pp. 235–50. Malden, Mass., 2009.

Ogden, Daniel. *Polygamy, Prostitutes and Death: The Hellenistic Dynasties.* London, 1999.

Parke, H. W. *Greek Mercenary Soldiers, from the Earliest Times to the Battle of Ipsus.* Oxford, 1933.

Romm, James. "The Breakup and Decline of Alexander's Empire." In James Romm, ed., *The Landmark Arrian: The Campaigns of Alexander,* pp. 317–24. New York, 2010.

Rosen, Klaus. "Die Bundnisformen der Diadochen und der Zerfall des Alexanderreiches." *AC* 11 (1968), pp. 182–210.

Seibert, Jakob. *Historische Beiträge zu den dynastischen Verbindungen in hellenistischer Zeit.* Wiesbaden, 1967.

——. *Das Zeitalter der Diadochen.* Darmstadt, 1983.

Shipley, Graham. *The Greek World After Alexander, 323–30 B.C.* New York, 2000.

Stewart, Andrew. *Faces of Power: Alexander's Image and Hellenistic Politics.* Berkeley, Calif., 1993.

Waterfield, Robin. *Dividing the Spoils: The War for Alexander the Great's Empire.* New York, 2011.

Wheatley, Pat. "The Diadochi, or Successors to Alexander." In Waldemar Heckel and Lawrence Tritle, eds., *Alexander the Great: A New History,* pp. 53–68. Malden, Mass., 2009.

Will, Edouard. *Histoire politique du monde hellénistique (323–30 av. J.-C.).* Nancy, 1966.

——. "The Succession to Alexander." In *The Cambridge Ancient History.* Vol. 7, *The Hellenistic World,* chap. 2. Cambridge, U.K., 1984.

CHRONOLOGICAL PROBLEMS

Anson, Edward. "The Dating of Perdiccas' Death and the Assembly at Triparadeisus." *GRBS* 43 (2002), pp. 373–90.

——. "Dating the Deaths of Eumenes and Olympias." *AHB* 20 (2006), pp. 1–8.

Boiy, Tom. *Between High and Low: A Chronology of the Early Hellenistic Period.* Frankfurt, 2007.

———. "Cuneiform Tablets and Aramaic Ostraca: Between the Low and High Chronologies of the Early Diadoch Period." In Waldemar Heckel, Lawrence Tritle, and Pat Wheatley, eds., *Alexander's Empire: Formulation to Decay,* pp. 199–208. Claremont, Calif., 2007.

Hauben, Hans. "The First War of the Successors (321 B.C.): Chronological and Historical Problems." *Ancient Society* 8 (1977), pp. 85–120.

Smith, Leonard C. "The Chronology of Books XVIII–XX of Diodorus Siculus." *AJP* 82 (1961), pp. 283–90.

Walsh, John. "Historical Method and a Chronological Problem in Diodorus, Book 18." In Pat Wheatley and Robert Hannah, eds., *Alexander & His Successors: Essays from the Antipodes,* pp. 72–87. Claremont, Calif., 2009.

Wheatley, Pat. "The Chronology of the Third Diadoch War." *Phoenix* 52 (1998), pp. 257–81.

———. "The Date of Polyperchon's Invasion of Macedonia and Murder of Heracles." *Antichthon* 32 (1998), pp. 12–23.

———. "An Introduction to the Chronological Problems in Early Diadoch Sources and Scholarship." In Waldemar Heckel, Lawrence Tritle, and Pat Wheatley, eds., *Alexander's Empire: Formulation to Decay,* pp. 179–92. Claremont, Calif., 2007.

ARCHAEOLOGICAL AND MATERIAL EVIDENCE

Andronikos, Manolis. "Regal Treasures from a Macedonian Tomb." *National Geographic* 154 (1978), pp. 55–68.

———. *Vergina: The Royal Tombs and the Ancient City.* Athens, 1984.

Borza, Eugene, and Olga Palagia. "The Chronology of the Macedonian Royal Tombs at Vergina." *Jahrbuch des Deutschen Archäologischen Instituts* 122 (2007), pp. 81–125.

Carney, Elizabeth. "The Female Burial in the Antechamber of Tomb II at Vergina." *AncW* 22 (1991), pp. 17–26.

Fredricksmeyer, E. A. "The Origin of Alexander's Royal Insignia." *TAPA* 127 (1997), pp. 97–109.

Hammond, N. G. L. "Arms and the King: The Insignia of Alexander the Great." *Phoenix* 43 (1989), pp. 217–24.

Markle, Minor M. III. "The Macedonian Sarissa, Spear, and Related Armor." *AJA* 81 (1977), pp. 323–39.

Oikonomides, A. N. "The Epigram on the Tomb of Olympias at Pydna." *AncW* 5 (1982), pp. 9–16.

Palagia, Olga. "The Grave Relief of Adea, Daughter of Cassander and Cynnana." In Timothy Howe and Jeanne Reames, eds., *Macedonian Legacies: Studies in Ancient Macedonian History and Culture in Honor of Eugene N. Borza,* pp. 195–214. Claremont, Calif., 2008.

————. "The Impact of Ares Macedon on Athenian Sculpture." In Olga Palagia and Stephen V. Tracy, eds., *The Macedonians in Athens, 322–229 B.C.*, pp. 140–51. Oxford, 2003.

FRAGMENTARY SOURCES AND COMMENTARIES

Atkinson, John E., ed., and John C. Yardley, trans. *Curtius Rufus: Histories of Alexander the Great, Book 10*. Oxford, 2009.

Bizière, François. *Diodore de Sicile: Bibliothèque historique, livre XIX*. Paris, 1975.

Dreyer, Boris. "The Arrian Parchment in Gothenburg: New Digital Processing Methods and Initial Results." In Waldemar Heckel, Lawrence Tritle, and Pat Wheatley, eds., *Alexander's Empire: Formulation to Decay*, pp. 245–64. Claremont, Calif., 2007.

————. "Zum ersten Diadochenkrieg: Der Göteborger Arrian-Palimpsest (MS Graec 1)." *ZPE* 125 (1999), pp. 39–60.

Goralski, Walter J. "Arrian's *Events After Alexander:* Summary of Photius and Selected Fragments." *AncW* 19 (1989), pp. 81–108.

Goukowsky, Paul. *Diodore de Sicile: Bibliothèque historique, livre XVIII*. Paris, 1978.

Landucci Gattinoni, F. *Diodoro Siculo: Biblioteca Storica Libro XVIII, Commento Storico*. Milan, 2008.

Noret, Jacques. "Un fragment du dixième livre de la *Succession d'Alexandre* par Arrien retrouvé dans un palimpseste de Gothenbourg." *AC* 52 (1983), pp. 235–42.

Rathmann, Michael. *Diodoros: Griechische Weltgeschichte: Buch XVIII–XX*. Stuttgart, 2005.

Yardley, John C., and Waldemar Heckel. *Justin: Epitome of the Philippic History of Pompeius Trogus*. Vol. 1, *Books 11–12: Alexander the Great*. Oxford, 1997.

ALEXANDER'S DEATH AND BURIAL

Alonso, Victor. "Some Remarks on the Funerals of the Kings: From Philip II to the Diadochi." In Pat Wheatley and Robert Hannah, eds., *Alexander & His Successors: Essays from the Antipodes*, pp. 276–98. Claremont, Calif., 2009.

Anson, Edward. "Alexander and Siwah." *AncW* 34 (2003), pp. 117–30.

Atkinson, John, Elsie Truter, and Etienne Truter. 2009. "Alexander's Last Days: Malaria and Mind Games?" *Acta Classica* (1 January). http://www.thefreelibrary.com/Alexander's+last+days%3a+malaria+and+mind+games%3f-a0221920136.

Badian, Ernst. "A King's Notebooks." *Harvard Studies in Classical Philology* 72 (1968), pp. 183–204.

———. "The Ring and the Book." In Wolfgang Will and Johannes Hein-richs, eds., *Zu Alexander der Grosse: Festschrift G. Wirth,* pp. 605–25. Amsterdam, 1987.

Borza, Eugene N. "Alexander's Death: A Medical Analysis." In James Romm, ed., *The Landmark Arrian: The Campaigns of Alexander,* pp. 404–6. New York, 2010.

Borza, Eugene N., and Jeanne Reames. "Some New Thoughts on the Death of Alexander the Great." *AncW* 31 (2000), pp. 22–30.

Bosworth, A. B. "Alexander's Death: The Poisoning Rumors." In James Romm, ed., *The Landmark Arrian: The Campaigns of Alexander,* pp. 407–10. New York, 2010.

———. "The Death of Alexander the Great: Rumour and Propaganda." *CQ* 21 (1971), pp. 112–36.

———. "Ptolemy and the Will of Alexander." In A. B. Bosworth and Elizabeth Baynham, eds., *Alexander the Great in Fact and Fiction,* pp. 207–41. Oxford, 2002.

Depuydt, Leo. "The Time of Death of Alexander the Great: 11 June 323 B.C., ca. 4:00–5:00 p.m." *Die Welt des Orients* 28 (1997), pp. 117–35.

Erskine, Andrew. "Life After Death: Alexandria and the Body of Alexander." *G&R* 49 (2002), pp. 163–79.

Green, Peter. *Alexander of Macedon.* Berkeley and Los Angeles, 1974.

Greenwalt, William. "Argaeus, Ptolemy II, and Alexander's Corpse." *AHB* 2 (1988), pp. 39–41.

Heckel, Waldemar. "The Earliest Evidence for the Plot to Poison Alexander." In Waldemar Heckel, Lawrence Tritle, and Pat Wheatley, eds., *Alexander's Empire: Formulation to Decay,* pp. 265–76. Claremont, Calif., 2007.

———. *The Last Days and Testament of Alexander the Great: A Prosopographic Study.* Stuttgart, 1988.

Landucci Gattinoni, Franca. "La morte di Alessandro e la tradizione su Antipatro." In Marta Sordi, ed., *Alessandro Magno: Tra storia e mito,* pp. 91–111. Milan, 1984.

Mayor, Adrienne. "The Deadly River Styx and the Death of Alexander." *Princeton/Stanford Working Papers in Classics* (September 2010). http://www.princeton.edu/~pswpc/pdfs/mayor/091008.pdf

McKechnie, Paul. "Omens of the Death of Alexander the Great." In Pat Wheatley and Robert Hannah, eds., *Alexander & His Successors: Essays from the Antipodes,* pp. 206–26. Claremont, Calif., 2009.

Schachermeyr, Fritz. *Alexander in Babylon und die Reichsordnung nach seinem Tode.* Vienna, 1970.

Schep, Leo. "The Death of Alexander the Great: Reconsidering Poison." In Pat Wheatley and Robert Hannah, eds., *Alexander & His Successors: Essays from the Antipodes,* pp. 227–36. Claremont, Calif., 2009.

Tomlinson, R. A. "The Tomb of Philip and the Tomb of Alexander: Contrasts and Consequences." *AM* 8 (1999), pp. 1184–87.

ANTIGENES, THE SILVER SHIELDS, AND THE MACEDONIAN ARMY

Anson, Edward. "Hypaspists and Argyraspids After 323." *AHB* 2, no. 6 (1988), pp. 131–33.

———. "Alexander's Hypaspists and the Origin of the Argyraspids." *Historia* 30 (1981), pp. 117–20.

Epplett, Christopher. "War Elephants in the Hellenistic World." In Waldemar Heckel, Lawrence Tritle, and Pat Wheatley, eds., *Alexander's Empire: Formulation to Decay*, pp. 209–32. Claremont, Calif., 2007.

Garlan, Yvon. *Recherches de poliorcétique grecque.* Paris, 1974.

Hammond, N. G. L. "Alexander's Veterans After His Death." *GRBS* 25 (1984), pp. 51–61.

Heckel, Waldemar. "The Career of Antigenes." *Symbolae Osloenses* 57 (1982), pp. 57–67.

PERDICCAS AND THE BABYLON SETTLEMENT

McKechnie, Paul. "The Power Struggle of the Diadochoi in Babylon, 323 B.C." *Ancient Society* 38 (2008), pp. 39–82.

Meeus, Alexander. "Some Institutional Problems Concerning the Succession to Alexander the Great: *Prostasia* and Chiliarchy." *Historia* 58 (2009), pp. 287–31.

Rathmann, Michael. *Perdikkas zwischen 323 und 320.* Vienna, 2005.

Rosen, Klaus. "Die Bundnisformen der Diadochen und der Zerfall des Alexanderreiches." *AC* 11 (1968), pp. 182–210.

———. "Die Reichsordnung von Babylon (323 v. Chr.)." *AC* 10 (1967), pp. 95–110.

Wirth, Gerhard. "Zur Politik des Perdikkas 323." *Helikon* 7 (1967), pp. 281–322.

PHILIP ARRHIDAEUS

Billows, Richard A. "Philip III Arrhidaeus and the Chronology of the Successors." *Chiron* 22 (1992), pp. 55–81.

Carney, Elizabeth. "The Trouble with Philip Arrhidaeus." *AHB* 15 (2001), pp. 63–89.

Greenwalt, William. "Argead Name Changes." *AM* 8 (1999), pp. 453–62.

———. "The Search for Arrhidaeus." *AncW* 10 (1984), pp. 69–77.

HYPERIDES, DEMOSTHENES, DEMADES, AND PHOCION

Bearzot, Cinzia. *Focione tra storia e trasfigurazione ideale.* Milan, 1985.

Cooper, Craig. "(Re)making Demosthenes: Demochares and Demetrius of Phalerum on Demosthenes." In Pat Wheatley and Robert Hannah, eds.,

Alexander & His Successors: Essays from the Antipodes, pp. 310–22. Claremont, Calif., 2009.

Gehrke, Hans-Joachim. *Phokion: Studien zur Erfassung seiner historischen Gestalt.* Munich, 1976.

Goldstein, Jonathan A. *The Letters of Demosthenes.* New York, 1968.

Hansen, Mogens Herman. *The Athenian Democracy in the Age of Demosthenes: Structure, Principles, and Ideology.* Oxford, 1991.

Hughes, Steven. "After the Democracy: Athens under Phocion (322/1–319/8 B.C.)." Dissertation, University of Western Australia, 2008.

Lamberton, Robert. "Plutarch's *Phocion:* Melodrama of Mob and Elite in Classical Athens." In Olga Palagia and Stephen V. Tracy, eds., *The Macedonians in Athens, 322–229 B.C.,* pp. 8–13. Oxford, 2003.

Schaefer, Arnold. *Demosthenes und seine Zeit.* Leipzig, 1887.

Tritle, Lawrence. *Phocion the Good.* New York, 1988.

Worthington, Ian. "Alexander and Athens in 324/3 B.C.: On the Greek Attitude to the Macedonian Hegemony." *Mediterranean Archaeology* 7 (1994), pp. 45–51.

———. "The Context of (Demades) on the Twelve Years." *CQ* 41 (1991), pp. 90–95.

———. "Demosthenes' (In)activity During the Reign of Alexander the Great." In Ian Worthington, ed., *Demosthenes: Statesman and Orator,* pp. 90–114. London, 2000.

———. *Greek Orators II: Dinarchus, Hyperides.* Warminster, U.K., 1999.

———. *A Historical Commentary on Dinarchus.* Ann Arbor, Mich., 1992.

Worthington, Ian, Craig Richard Cooper, and Edward Monroe Harris, trans. *Dinarchus, Hyperides, and Lycurgus.* Austin, Tex., 2001.

ANTIPATER, CASSANDER, PHILA, AND CRATERUS

Adams, Winthrop Lindsay. "Antipater and Cassander: Generalship on Restricted Resources in the Fourth Century." *AncW* 10 (1984), pp. 79–88.

———. "The Dynamics of Internal Politics in the Time of Cassander." *AM* 3 (1982), pp. 2–30.

Ashton, Norman G. "Craterus from 324 to 321 B.C." *AM* 1 (1993), pp. 125–31.

Badian, Ernst. "Two Postscripts on the Marriage of Phila and Balacrus." *ZPE* 73 (1988), pp. 116–18.

Baynham, Elizabeth. "Antipater and Athens." In Olga Palagia and Stephen V. Tracy, eds., *The Macedonians in Athens, 322–229 B.C.,* pp. 23–29. Oxford, 2003.

———. "Antipater: Manager of Kings." In Ian Worthington, ed., *Ventures into Greek History: Essays in Honor of N. G. L. Hammond,* pp. 331–56. Oxford, 1994.

Carney, Elizabeth. "The Curious Death of the Antipatrid Dynasty." *AM* 8 (1999), pp. 209–16.

Fortina, Marcello. "Cassandro, re di Macedonia." *SEI* (1965), pp. 8–122.

Heckel, Waldemar. "A Grandson of Antipatros at Delos." *ZPE* 70 (1987), pp. 161–62.

———. "Nicanor son of Balacrus." *GRBS* 47 (2007), pp. 401–12.

Landucci Gattinoni, Franca. *L'arte del potere: Vita, e opere di Cassandro di Macedonia.* Stuttgart, 2003.

———. "Cassander's Wife and Heirs." In Pat Wheatley and Robert Hannah, eds., *Alexander & His Successors: Essays from the Antipodes,* pp. 261–75. Claremont, Calif., 2009.

Wehrli, Claude. "Phila, fille d'Antipater et épouse de Démétrios, roi des Macédoniens." *Historia* 13 (1964), pp. 140–46.

LEOSTHENES AND THE LAMIAN WAR

Ashton, Norman G. "The Lamian War: A False Start?" *Antichthon* 17 (1983), pp. 47–56.

———. "The Lamian War: *Stat magni nominis umbra.*" *JHS* 104 (1984), pp. 152–57.

———. "The *Naumachia* near Amorgos in 322 B.C." *Annual of the British School of Athens* 72 (1977), pp. 1–11.

Bosworth, A. B. "A New Macedonian Prince." *CQ* 44 (1994), pp. 57–65.

———. "Why Did Athens Lose the Lamian War?" In Olga Palagia and Stephen V. Tracy, eds., *The Macedonians in Athens, 322–229 B.C.,* pp. 14–22. Oxford, 2003.

Green, Peter. "Occupation and Co-existence: the Impact of Macedon on Athens, 323–307." In Olga Palagia and Stephen V. Tracy, eds., *The Macedonians in Athens, 322–229 B.C.,* pp. 1–6. Oxford, 2003.

Habicht, Christian. *Athens from Alexander to Antony.* Cambridge, Mass., 1997.

Mathieu, Georges. "Notes sur Athènes à la veille de la guerre lamiaque." *Revue de Philologie* 3 (1929), pp. 159–83.

Schmitt, Oliver. *Der Lamische Krieg.* Bonn, 1992.

THE GREEK BACTRIAN REVOLT

Holt, Frank L. *Alexander the Great and Bactria: The Formation of a Greek Frontier in Central Asia.* New York, 1988.

Schober, Ludwig. *Untersuchungen zur Geschichte Babyloniens und der Oberen Satrapien von 323–303 v. Chr.* Frankfurt, 1981.

Sidky, H. *The Greek Kingdom of Bactria: From Alexander to Eucratides the Great.* Lanham, Md., 2000.

Thomas, C. G. "Alexander's Garrisons: A Clue to His Administrative Plans?" *Antichthon* 8 (1974), pp. 11–20.

ANTIGONUS AND DEMETRIUS

Anson, Edward. "Antigonus, the Satrap of Phrygia." *Historia* 37 (1988), pp. 471–77.

Bayliss, Andrew J. "Antigonos the One-Eyed's Return to Asia in 322: A New Restoration for a Rasura in IG II² 682." *ZPE* 155 (2006), pp. 108–26.

Billows, Richard A. *Antigonos the One-Eyed and the Creation of the Hellenistic State.* Berkeley, Calif., 1990.

Briant, Pierre. "Antigone le Borgne." *Centre de Recherches d'Histoire Ancienne* 10 (1973), pp. 145–217.

Wehrli, Claude. *Antigone et Démétrios.* Geneva, 1968.

Wheatley, Pat. "The Young Demetrius Poliorcetes." *AHB* 13, no. 1 (1999), pp. 1–13.

CHANDRAGUPTA AND INDIA

Bosworth, A. B. *Alexander and the East: The Tragedy of Triumph.* Oxford, 1996.

————. "Calanus and the Brahman Opposition." In Wolfgang Will, ed., *Alexander der Grosse: Eine Welteroberung und ihr Hintergrund,* pp. 173–203. Bonn, 1988.

————. "The Indian Satrapies Under Alexander the Great." *Antichthon* 17 (1983), pp. 37–45.

Matelli, Elisabetta. "Alessandro Magno e Candragupta: Origine delle notizie occidentali sulle dinastie Nanda e Maurya." In Marta Sordi, ed., *Alessandro Magno: Tra storia e mito,* pp. 59–72. Milan, 1984.

Smith, Vincent A. *The Early History of India: From 600 B.C. to the Muhammadan Conquest, Including the Invasion of Alexander the Great.* Oxford, 1914.

Trautmann, Thomas R. *Kautilya and the Arthasastra: A Statistical Investigation of the Authorship and Evolution of the Text.* Leiden, 1971.

PTOLEMY AND EGYPT

Bouché-Leclerq, Auguste. *Histoire des Lagides.* Paris, 1903.

Burstein, Stanley M. "Alexander's Organization of Egypt: A Note on the Career of Cleomenes of Naucratis." In Timothy Howe and Jeanne Reames, eds., *Macedonian Legacies: Studies in Ancient Macedonian History and Culture in Honor of Eugene N. Borza,* pp. 183–94. Claremont, Calif., 2008.

Ellis, Walter M. *Ptolemy of Egypt.* New York, 2010.

Huss, Werner. *Ägypten in hellenistischer Zeit, 332–30 v. Chr.* Munich, 2001.

Rodriguez, Philippe. "L'évolution du monnayage de Ptolémée Ier au regard des événements militaires." *Cahiers Glotz* 15 (2004), pp. 17–35.

Roisman, Joseph. "Ptolemy and His Rivals in His History of Alexander." *CQ* 34 (1984), pp. 373–85.

Seibert, Jakob. *Untersuchungen zur Geschichte Ptolemaios I.* Munich, 1969.

Strasburger, Hermann. *Ptolemaios und Alexander.* Leipzig, 1934.

Turner, Eric. "Ptolemaic Egypt." In *The Cambridge Ancient History.* Vol. 7, *The Hellenistic World.* Cambridge, U.K., 1984.

Wheatley, Pat. "Ptolemy Soter's Annexation of Syria, 320 B.C." *CQ* 45 (1995), pp. 433–40.

OLYMPIAS, CYNNANE, ADEA, AND THESSALONICE

Carney, Elizabeth. "The Career of Adea-Eurydike." *Historia* 36 (1987), pp. 496–502.

———. "Olympias, Adea Eurydice, and the End of the Argead Dynasty." In Ian Worthington, ed., *Ventures into Greek History: Essays in Honor of N. G. L. Hammond,* pp. 357–80. Oxford, 1994.

———. *Olympias, Mother of Alexander the Great.* New York, 2006.

———. "The Sisters of Alexander the Great: Royal Relicts." *Historia* 37 (1988), pp. 385–404.

———. "Women and Military Leadership in Macedonia." *AncW* 35 (2004), pp. 184–95.

———. *Women and Monarchy in Macedonia.* Norman, Okla., 2000.

Heckel, Waldemar. "Kynnane the Illyrian." *Rivista Storica dell'Antichità* 13–14 (1983–84), pp. 193–200.

———. "Polyxena, the Mother of Alexander the Great." *Chiron* 11 (1981), pp. 79–86.

Macurdy, Grace H. *Hellenistic Queens: A Study of Woman Power in Macedonia, Seleucid, Syria, and Ptolemaic Egypt.* New York, 1932.

Miron, Dolores. "Transmitters and Representatives of Power: Royal Women in Ancient Macedonia." *Ancient Society* 30 (1970), pp. 35–52.

EUMENES

Anson, Edward. "Discrimination and Eumenes of Cardia." *AncW* 3 (1980), pp. 55–59.

———. *Eumenes of Cardia: A Greek Among Macedonians.* Leiden, 2004.

———. "The Siege of Nora: A Source Conflict." *GRBS* 18 (1977), pp. 251–56.

Bosworth, A. B. "Eumenes, Neoptolemus, and PSI XII. 1284." *GRBS* 19 (1978), pp. 227–37.

———. "History and Artifice in Plutarch's *Eumenes*." In Philip A. Stadter, ed., *Plutarch and the Historical Tradition,* pp. 56–89. London, 1992.

Briant, Pierre. "D'Alexandre le Grand aux diadoques: Le cas d'Eumène de Kardia." *Revue des Études Anciennes* 74 (1972), pp. 32–73.

————. "D'Alexandre le Grand aux diadoques: Le cas d'Eumène de Kardia." *Revue des Études Anciennes* 75 (1973), pp. 43–81.

Devine, A. M. "Diodorus' Account of the Battle of Gabiene." *AncW* 12 (1985), pp. 87–96.

————. "Diodorus' Accounts of the Battle of Paraitacene (317 B.C.)." *AncW* 12 (1985), pp. 75–96.

Dixon, Michael. "Corinth, Greek Freedom, and the Diadochoi." In Waldemar Heckel, Lawrence Tritle, and Pat Wheatley, eds., *Alexander's Empire: Formulation to Decay*, pp. 151–78. Claremont, Calif., 2007.

Hadley, Robert A. "A Possible Lost Source for the Career of Eumenes of Kardia." *Historia* 50 (2001), pp. 3–33.

Landucci Gattinoni, Franca. "Eumene: Epelus aner kai xenos." In Marta Sordi, ed., *Conoscenze etniche e rapporti di convivenza nell'antichità*, pp. 98–107. Milan, 1979.

Picard, Charles. "Le trône vide d'Alexandre dans la cérémonie de Cyinda et le culte du trône vide à travers le monde Gréco-Romain." *Cahiers Archeologies* 7 (1964), pp. 1–17.

Roisman, Joseph. "Hieronymus of Cardia: Causation and Bias from Alexander to His Successors." In Elizabeth Carney and Daniel Ogden, eds., *Philip II and Alexander the Great: Father and Son, Lives and Afterlives*, pp. 135–48. Oxford and N.Y., 2010.

Schäfer, Christoph. *Eumenes von Kardia und der Kampf um die Macht im Alexanderreich*. Frankfurt, 2002.

Thompson, W. E. "PSI 1284, Eumenes of Cardia vs. the Phalanx." *Chronique d'Égypte* 59 (1984), pp. 113–20.

Wirth, Gerhard. "Zur grossen Schlacht des Eumenes 322 (PSI 1284)." *Klio* 46 (1965), pp. 283–88.

RHOXANE, ALEXANDER IV, BARSINE, AND HERACLES

Brunt, P. A. "Alexander, Barsine, and Heracles." *Rivista di Filologia* 103 (1975), pp. 22–34.

Heckel, Waldemar. "IGii2 561 and the Status of Alexander IV." *ZPE* 40 (1980), pp. 249–50.

Holt, Frank L. "Alexander the Great's Little Star." *History Today* 38, no. 9 (1988), pp. 30–39.

Kosmetatou, Elizabeth. "Rhoxane's Dedications to Athena Polias." *ZPE* 146 (2004), pp. 75–80.

Tarn, William W. "Heracles Son of Barsine." *JHS* 41 (1921), pp. 18–28.

Index

Page numbers in *italics* refer to illustrations.

A NOTE ON THE TYPE

This book was set in Adobe Garamond. Designed for the Adobe Corporation by Robert Slimbach, the fonts are based on types first cut by Claude Garamond (c. 1480–1561). Garamond was a pupil of Geoffroy Tory and is believed to have followed the Venetian models, although he introduced a number of important differences, and it is to him that we owe the letter we now know as "old style." He gave to his letters a certain elegance and feeling of movement that won their creator an immediate reputation and the patronage of Francis I of France.

Composed by North Market Street Graphics
Lancaster, Pennsylvania

Printed and bound by Berryville Graphics
Berryville, Virginia

Designed by Soonyoung Kwon